To Charles.
Best wishes from t...

[signature]

CW00551061

THE
CAPE TO CAIRO
RAILWAY
& RIVER ROUTES

and the
Principal Hotels
en route
through Africa

GEORGE TABOR

GENTA PUBLICATIONS
London and Cape Town
2003

First Published in Great Britain 2003
by

GENTA
PUBLICATIONS

25F Trebovir Road
London SW5 9NF
FAX 0207 460 1249

and

P.O.Box 12663, Mill Street,
Cape Town 8010
South Africa
FAX 021 424 7756

gentauk2002@yahoo.co.uk

Copyright © by George Tabor 2003
ISBN 0-9544847-0-3

Set in 11 point Plantin
DTP: Denise Warren
Scanning: Audiolens, Centrefoto, and Orms
Cape Town, South Africa

Printed and Bound in Great Britain by
Biddles Ltd, Guildford, Surrey

ACKNOWLEDGMENTS

First and foremost I am indebteded to the late Louis Bolze of Bulawayo, who left an inspiring legacy of early Rhodesian literature in the form of facsimile reprints at down-to-earth prices. I am also grateful to his son Adrian, of Books of Zimbabwe, for his invaluable recent help. Among others of that era who were a source of inspiration were Tony Tanser of Salisbury (Harare), and Tony Baxter.

On my last visit to Bulawayo I was sadly disillusioned. An old incumbent of no relevance, who supposedly 'ran' the railway archives, refused me access to everything which I had requested beforehand. It is a sad omen that such misplaced people are still around to dash the hopes of honest researchers. I turned to other sources, and I am greatly indebted to many stalwart old-timers, particularly George Barker of missionary zeal, and Webster Gatakata of the National Archives of Zimbabwe (NAZ). I must also express my sincere thanks to Chris and Alison Faber of Harare.

Across the Victoria Falls, I was greatly helped by the Curator and staff at the enchanting Livingstone Museum, and the quaint Livingstone Railway Museum. Benjamin Mibenge, of the National Heritage Committee was also most helpful

Much of my research was done in Cape Town, in the plethora of bookshops lining Long Street. The magnificent South African Library (SAL) contains more useful work on Africa than can be found outside England. With thanks to Jackie Lewis, and to Najwa Hendrickse, Chief Librarian, and to the staff of the Photographic and Library sections. To the Cape Archives, and to Leslie Hart and others of the University of Cape Town Library, I am also most grateful. I only hope that these excellent establishements do not follow the same path as those in Bulawayo, and the Transnet Library in Johannesburg.

Many others in various fields helped me along the line; Michael Walker with early photographs; Davina Kirby with advice on Zambia; Pamela & Dieter Laumeier with introductions; Kent Durr, Nicholas Truman Baker, and Diana Wren Curtis with railway and colonial anecdotes on South Africa, Egypt and Tanganyika respectively; Basil Nott and Vaughan Johnson with wide humanistic knowledge. Margaret Rowley with superb editing help and advice. In France I am indebted to Anne Morgan, granddaughter of Sir John Norton Griffiths for the use of family photographs of the Benguela Railway. To Stephen Hornung, and his son Bernard in Spain I am grateful for leads on the Sena Sugar Estate.

I spent a memorable summer day at the lofty University of Durham, where I scanned through thousands of images for the Sudan section (SAD). I thank Mrs. Jane Hogan, Assistant Keeper of the Sudan Archives & Special Collections for her exceptional assistance. I also express my gratitude to Dr. Mohammed El Hussein and his family in the Sudan, for up-to-date images of Khartoum.

In London I was helped immensely by the staff of the British Library - Humanities and Map sections, the Newspaper Library at Colindale, and the Libraries of the Royal Borough of Kensington and Chelsea, and the London Library. I am grateful to the Thomas Cook Archives, originally run by Edwin Swinglehurst, and especially to the present archivist Paul Smith, for information on the Benguela Railway and Egypt. The venerable Royal Geographical Society (RGS) with its dusty corridors and hidden 'dungeons' is an ongoing inspiration. I appreciated the short use of their wonderful library, closed for some years. I thank Justin Hobson and Pauline Hubner of the Photographic Archives, as well as Jackie Thomsen.

With endless gratitude to Roma Ashworth Briggs, whose office I used burning the midnight oil. To William James, John Cawston and Chrissie Reed for historical anecdotes. To Veronica Lucan for organising my internet problems. To Malcolm Howe for Portuguese advice. To Martha Ford Adams for superb tips and contacts. To Tony & Virginia Murray, and family, for being book-keepers and bon-vivants

In the field of publishing I am grateful to Anthea Morton Saner of Curtis Brown, for permission to include extracts from Winston Churchill's 'From London to Ladysmith' and 'The River War'. Also, I thank Erica Leith of George Ronald, the publishers of Harold Varian's autobiography.

Finally, I am particulartly grateful to Denise Warren for the superb design of this tome.

In Memory of my Mother

and to all those who forged
the Iron Spine and Ribs of Africa

"I remember saying that Africa was a difficult place to escape from.
It was like a huge devil fish.
Once it caught you escape was impossible."
Rose Blennerhasset, Pioneer Nurse in Mashonaland.

INTRODUCTION

To anyone who has ever set foot on African soil, and has wafted the sweet scent of a grateful earth hit by the first rains, and seen the colour-riot of flowering jacarandas and bouganvilleas, and heard the chatter and laughter around the wood fires of an African village, this book will be welcome.

But to those who have never visited Africa and whose knowledge is gleamed entirely from the half-baked articles and programmes put out by people suffering from Post Colonial Guilt, with the simplistic notion that everything Black was good and everything White was wicked, then this book may be an irritation. To them I make no apology. I invite them to take a deep breath and read on.

The development of Africa by Britain a century ago was a reaction to the times. In that mad scramble, every major European power strove vigorously for a foothold on the continent. It was a race; and Britain came out on top. She won largely by robust diplomacy, enlightened example and minimum coercion; in contrast to the militaristic methods of most other nations. Yet her achievements were derided at the time by a few 'Little Englanders', and she is belittled today by many more. The most successful is often the most reviled.

Britain's supreme confidence, and sometimes arrogance, in creating a great Empire, spawned a spirit of understanding which ran right through the whole strain of society. It was the one ingredient which assured her reputation for fair play, right down to the mud huts in the remotest outposts. At its best, it ensured that scores of antagonistic races, tribes and religions lived in peace and harmony, with minimum control.

Like all Empires the British one was not blameless. She did of course make some mistakes, such as in imposing western systems of government and laws on tribal societies accustomed to summary and speedy justice; in chopping and changing local officials in quick succession; in arbitrarily creating frontiers with scant regard to ethnic boundaries, and in not timeously dragging up enough African administrators by their bootlaces. But the biggest mistake of all was in handing over power prematurely. History will vindicate small indiscretions, whilst it will condemn forever the disgraceful betrayal of so many millions to the whims of a few Despots backed by the International Dross.

The so called Organisation of African Unity, and its recent successor the African Union, was originally brought about by 'politically correct'

Europeans. It consists of about 50 pot-boiled countries, over half of which are involved in either conflict or civil unrest. In fact virtually the whole of Africa has become a bottomless pit of corruption, greed and suffering, sinking back into the dark ages.

The historian Paul Johnson has calculated that Britain, ironically with no written constitution of her own, wrote some 500 constitutions for her emerging territories between 1920 and 1975. Some lasted for a few years, some lasted a few months. NONE have survived since 1985.

The supreme example is the largest country in Africa. Throughout its terrible history the long-suffering Sudan saw the annihilation of nearly three quarters of its population. A hundred years later, left to is own devices, it is once again a nation of savage slave traders. The only time in its entire history when it was at peace was when it was part of the British Empire. Yet the world of Little Englanders lies silent - as if embarassed by its own ignorance and apathy.

That great philosopher of Africa, the late Sir Laurens Van der Post, who understood the ways of Africa more than most, concluded that parts of the British Empire were the nearest that the world has ever seen to a truly Platonic Society*- an ideal world in which all worked in complete harmony for everyone else's benefit.

*Platonic - from the Greek philosopher Plato's "Republic". Sir Laurens acknowledged to the author that it was J.B. Priestley, a man most certainly not noted for his conservative, or pro-colonial views ,who first formulated this parallel with the British Empire.

He was referring particularly to the Sudan Political Service, which in its heyday before the First World War was run by an elite corps of only 120 Officers who administered one million square miles of territory - an area half the size of Europe, and one quarter the size of the United States.

There were other parts of Africa which worked unquestionably well, with small dedicated bands of administrators, most noticeably the North Western territory of Kenya, and remoter parts of Tanganyika (Tanzania) and Northern Rhodesia (Zambia). The standards of the Colonial Service were high, and in the end Britain did perhaps more than any other nation to set an example for Africans to follow if they so wished.

A century ago colonial expansion was all the rage. Half a century later the pendulum had swung the other way. Colonialism was viewed by the trendy lefties as exploitation and greed, whilst Missionaries and Traders were accused of interfering in a Dark Continent which, left to its own devices, would have found its own way into the modern world. It is now abundantly clear they were wrong. The pendulum has swung back again.

However, this is not a political book. It is an attempt to put a balance on a small part of our colonial achievements with a little light-hearted romance of the re-discovery of old places, remembered with affection for what they stood for.

It is a celebration of the building of one of Britain's greatest achievements in Africa - the Cape to Cairo Railway and River Route. Though the rail link has not yet been completed, it is ironic that the gaps of less than

500 miles lie in two of the most troubled territories on the continent - Congo and Sudan. And one of its longest and most difficult to build spurs, the Benguela Railway through Angola, has been closed for the past 28 years. It was not built as an imperial 'dream', but as a hard-headed commercial undertaking that was expected to pay its way, rarely with the backing of the British Government. So far as it went it was largely financed and built by private capital and enterprise. My family's connections with it go back to the beginning. Indeed it would not have been possible for me to write this book without the personal insight amassed during my time in Africa.

It is not only the story of the well-known characters, most notably Cecil Rhodes, whose motives have often been questioned, but who did for England what she would not do for herself.

It is predominantly the saga of all those who forged that great metal link "The Iron Spine and Ribs of Africa" and of their triumphs & tribulations. It was built by many hundreds of Europeans, with countless thousands of Africans, Asians, and Arabs, whose spirited contribution, sometimes hard to come by, has gone down in history sadly unchronicled. For railways were built by men, not by machines. "Each bolt, each nut, each metal bar could tell a story grim but true."

It is also the story of the romance the railways brought to the outposts, and of the settlements and hotels it spawned. And it is dedicated to all those who forged it.

I was fortunate to have enjoyed the very end of Britain's rule in Africa and to have spent many of the best years of my life in a troubled country, Rhodesia, at the time of its independence.

It was indeed the warm heart of Africa. Looking back I consider it a privilege to have played my own small part in it, and to have mixed with that crowd from all walks of life which made the place such an Eden. In those turbulent times there were many disappointments. Fortune smiled on very few of us. Yet there was a freedom and friendliness for almost everyone, that cannot be described - nor believed by those who never knew it. It was a utopian mix of contrasts and camaraderie combined with a real understanding of raw Africa which galvanised a Magic Spell - remembered by all of us who clung to it in that era of understanding and tolerance; an era that is, sadly, no more.

How the Past perishes is how the Future becomes.

Ovid

G.P.T. Cape Town and London 2000 - 2003

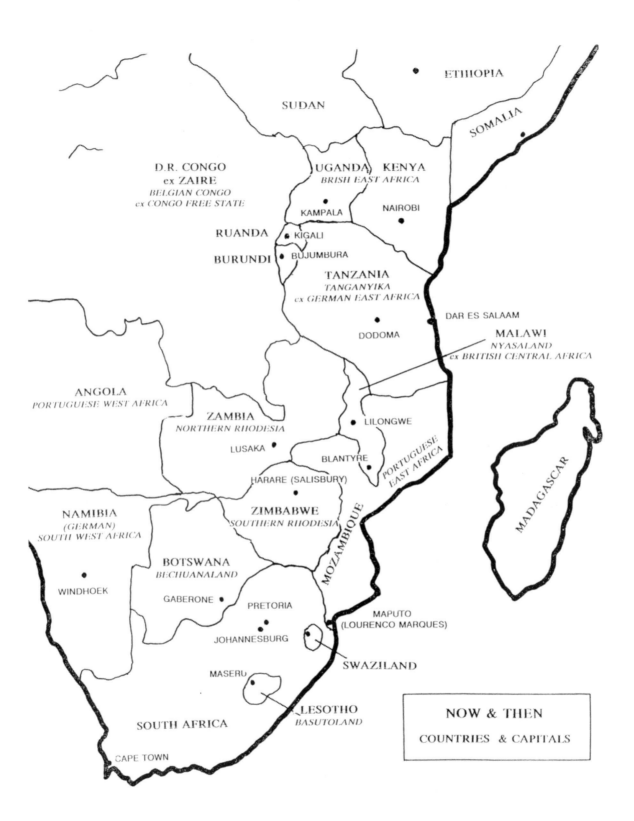

ETIIIOPIA

SUDAN

SOMALIA

D.R. CONGO
ex ZAIRE
BELGIAN CONGO
ex CONGO FREE STATE

UGANDA   KENYA
BRISH EAST AFRICA

KAMPALA   NAIROBI

RUANDA   KIGALI

BURUNDI   BUJUMBURA

TANZANIA
Tanganyika
ex GERMAN EAST AFRICA

DAR ES SALAAM

DODOMA

MALAWI
NYASALAND
ex BRITISH CENTRAL AFRICA

ANGOLA
PORTUGUESE WEST AFRICA

ZAMBIA
NORTHERN RHODESIA

LUSAKA

LILONGWE

BLANTYRE

PORTUGUESE
EAST AFRICA

HARARE (SALISBURY)

MADAGASCAR

NAMIBIA
(GERMAN)
SOUTH WEST AFRICA

ZIMBABWE
SOUTHERN RHODESIA

MOZAMBIQUE

BOTSWANA
BECHUANALAND

WINDHOEK

GABERONE

PRETORIA

JOHANNESBURG

MAPUTO
(LOURENCO MARQUES)

SWAZILAND

MASERU

LESOTHO
BASUTOLAND

SOUTH AFRICA

CAPE TOWN

NOW & THEN

COUNTRIES & CAPITALS

THE CAPE TO CAIRO RAILWAY AND RIVER ROUTES

(BOOKS OF ZIM)

"I walked on the outskirts of the Empire,
where the shouting of men, the ring of hammers on stone,
and the thud of picks in the baked earth were always in my ears."

Kingsley Fairbridge

THE IMPERIAL DREAM RAILWAY

The history of the railways is the history of the British in Africa. Everywhere that the Union Jack flew, railways appeared as the primary means of communication and imperial expansion. What roads were to the Roman Empire, railroads were to the British. Some would say bringing wicked Western ways on steel rails meandering across untamed Africa, concrete evidence of conquest. Others would say binding together all the citizens of the Mother Country by means of little strips of civilization marked on maps as railway lines.

Pre-eminent in the age of steam, the British Empire relied on technocrats for its colourful cohesion. And if one mechanism symbolised the whole imperial dream, it was unashamedly the steam locomotive. At good times chugging merrily across the savannah, over culverts and majestic bridges. At bad times struggling up mountain passes, hissing and snorting, belching forth smoke and sparks; setting fire to nearby huts and grasslands; crossing mangrove swamps, halting for wild animals on their way; constantly pulling into wayside sidings for water and wood; or picking up wanderers here and there with goods for trade. And at the most profitable times pulling into towns and cities where the bright lights beckoned or dragging endless train loads of minerals to the seaports for shipment to the factories of Britain.

No other travel on some of the most incredible journeys on earth captured the easy going romance and the sublime economy of rail travel through Africa. The railways opened up the ways for Pax Brittanica. They also changed forever the destinies and life-styles of local people. For railways made boundaries, and railways broke barriers; not only in towns and cities where 'the wrong side of the line' created artificial social buffers. In many villages up and down the line it was the only contact with the outside world.

Straddling the years of the beginning of the last century, the Cape to Cairo Railway and River Route were dominated by two unashamed Imperialists - Cecil Rhodes and Herbert Kitchener. It was primarily the dream of Rhodes to link the Cape of Good Hope with Cairo and the Mediterranean, 5000 miles up through the wilds of equatorial Africa.

It was the boldest scheme of its day, exceeding in scale and imagination the two other great trans-continental railways - the Canadian Pacific and the Trans Siberian, for it involved a large element of political manoeuvre. Yet it remained an unfinished symphony.

From Egypt down to the Sudan, engineers of Kitchener's army built a thousand miles of permanent way alongside the Nile and through the waterless desert. Its object was the military defeat of the Mahdi. At the same time it succeeded in stopping the French in their trans-African ambitions, for it thwarted their chances of a link across Africa, from the Atlantic seaboard to the Red Sea, through an Egypt which was hostile to the British and amicable to the French.

From the south to the north, Cecil Rhodes reached up from the Cape of Good Hope as far as the Congo and Tanganyika, to prevent the Germans, as well as the Portuguese, from traversing Africa between their territories.

The Railway from the coast to Rhodesia (Zimbabwe) rushed reinforcements to landlocked towns besieged during the Anglo-Boer War. The

The monumental bronze equestrian statue of 'Physical Energy' by George Frederick Watts. R.A., the pre-Raphaelite sculptor and painter. Moved from Burlington House in London, home of the Royal Academy, it stands in front of the Rhodes Memorial in Cape Town - a Corinthian temple designed by Herbert Baker, overlooking Rhodes University. Facing north up Africa, it symbolises the eclectic energy of the Empire Builder, his far vision, and his unfinished dreams. Rhodes had hoped to have a verse composed by his friend Rudyard Kipling inscribed beneath the statue, together with the names of all those who had worked on the Cape to Cairo concept.

Uganda and Nyasaland Railways hastened the defeat of the Arab slave traders. And the Benguela Railway through Angola opened out thousands of miles of unheard-of territory whilst transporting minerals on the shortest route to Europe. Even in tiny Zanzibar, a toy-town railway was built down the coast to convey the Sultan and his entourage to the seaside.

Over 80 per cent of the railways in Africa were British.

Unrivalled in excellence, British railway builders and bridge engineers scored in boldness and imagination, speed and initiative. They shared a supreme confidence, a great daring and an incredible capacity for hard work. As exponents of private enterprise in an Empire run largely by government officials, they often became the envy of the local Administrators, and leading lights in their local communities.

The British Empire in Africa was the largest of any nation; larger by a long way than that of the French - the Anglo-Egyptian Sudan saw to that. And the Railways employed more people than the Military.

Three capital cities were built entirely because of them. Nairobi, capital of Kenya was a steamy railway encampment; Lusaka, Zambia, a lion infested siding on the way north to the Congo; and Gaberone, the future capital of Botswana was a remote watering hole on the edge of the Kalahari desert, as the plate-layers passed through.

As the railways advanced and the sidings turned into townships, hotels quickly followed - welcome havens for travellers and sanctuaries for scattered communities. Lounges and club rooms became meccas for mining magnates, missionaries and remittance men, whilst bars around the corner became meeting places for the locals, castaways, scallywags and down-at-heel prospectors.

Memorable images of British-built railways in Africa endure. The most important is the width of track. The railways of Egypt were built on the wide European gauge, and those in the German territories were built on a metre wide gauge, as was the Lunatic Line - (the Uganda Railway through Kenya).

Otherwise the entire continent was linked by a gauge of 3 feet 6 inches, coined 'The Cape Gauge'. It was a happy compromise between the cumbersome 4 feet 8½ inches of Europe and the 2 feet wide early pioneer lines. Unfortunately it ensured for all time that trains would never exceed more than about 20 miles per hour, and at the most 60 miles per hour, throughout the entire network. Today speed is hardly relevant. In many parts of Africa breakdowns of rolling stock, rail-track and signalling equipment - and civil wars, have brought the system to a standstill.

Next were the records. The longest straight stretch of railway in Africa was 70 miles between Bulawayo and Victoria Falls. Across the Chifu Maji flats in Angola there was an almost straight stretch running for nearly a hundred miles. At the time of its construction the Kafue River bridge was the longest railway bridge in Africa; the Victoria Falls Bridge was the highest; whilst the second longest bridge in the world (12,000 feet) crosses the Zambezi at Sena in Mozambique. The world's longest platform was at Bulawayo Station. The world record for 'hands on' plate-laying was achieved on the way to Broken Hill in Northern Rhodesia (Zambia) in 1906 - 5³/₄ miles in 11 hours. In the normal course of plate-laying the 'mile a day' conquest of the 300 odd miles into Bulawayo was unequalled for many years.

Whenever possible, railways followed lines of least resistance; across plateau and along watersheds, avoiding river crossings, and ensuring the minimum of earthworks. In every case the most difficult parts were the rise from the coast to the central African plateau.

Lastly came the ceremony; the flashy trappings of an opulent railway empire transferred to the warm heart of Africa. Nicely apparent in brass carriage fittings, engraved glass windows and crests on carriage sides; and on china and cutlery in the restaurant cars. More usefully apparent in station benches made from hardwood sleepers, and platform names painted in black and white, boldly glaring into the dusty distance, showing the mileage from Cape Town or Cairo, and the altitudes above sea level.

The wood and corrugated iron stations were often built on stilts, to avoid termites, scorpions, and floods; and to bring in cool breezes during the summer 'suicide months' - the hot steamy weeks before the rains arrived. Squeaking sash windows, enormous swaying paraffin lamps and all manner of creepy-crawlies added to the eeriness. Outside stood fire buckets, rain gauges and sometimes neat flower boxes; but usually forlorn looking cacti guarded the doorway. Often the Stationmaster himself was a forlorn looking character ... a loner, a jack of all trades, a Ganger blown up out of all proportion to his original role; yet coping magnificently with the refuelling and watering, and the whole paraphernalia of his part of the permanent way, whilst the passengers stood around chatting, greeting old acquaintances and meeting new ones.

At wayside halts, station-masters came in all shades and shapes. Sometimes in the larger stations he was a grave grand man, a real Master of the Station, in real gilt edged apparel, reflecting the imperial importance of the railway.

Yet nothing was more impressive than watching the world go by for hours on end, with the welcome prospect of a tantalising good meal in a travelling dining car with real rattling china, starched white napkins, hand written menus and ice in the drinks. And to wake up next morning at some distant destination, without a thought or a care for the iron horse, as you wondered where in the world you had arrived from. For 'getting there was half the fun', and when it boiled down to the nitty-gritty, railway hooters were used to deter warring tribesmen and wild animals; and hot water was useful for making tea.

Behind the glamour and the romance lay hard-headed finance; for financing railways was often as difficult as constructing them. With the exception of the early Cape Colony, the Sudan Military Lines and some in East Africa, the railways were almost entirely developed by private enterprise. The half romantic, half patriotic idea of the 'Cape to Cairo dream' undoubtedly helped, but commercial decisions were made by the backers with an eye on future revenue. Whether it was a Chartered Company, a Banking House, or a Syndicate from the City of London, a respectable return was of paramount importance. Speed was linked with the lowest capital cost. When times were good, contracts overlapped, but often the rails went forward in fits and starts for lack of funds, causing endless delays and lay-offs of whole gangs of engineers and labourers. Even construction companies fell by the wayside.

Rothschilds Bank financed much of Cecil Rhodes' mining ventures as well as the Egyptian Railways. A significant investment role in the British South Africa Company was also played by the Bankers G & A de Worms.

The Anglo-French Banking House of Erlangers, which was founded by Baron Frederic d'Erlanger, originally from Frankfurt, was closely involved with the majority of the southern and central sections of the Cape to Cairo Railway. This was done largely through financial connections with Pauling & Company, the main Contractors, and the close friendship forged between George Pauling and Baron Emile d'Erlanger (1866 - 1939) the naturalized British son of Baron Frederic. Ironically, neither of the d'Erlanger's ever set foot in Africa. The Bank also bought the French Havas News Agency which was ultimately sold to Agence France Presse. Erlangers finally amalgamated with other banking interests to become Phillip Hill, Higginson & Erlangers, and ultimately part of the Hill Samuel Merchant Bank.

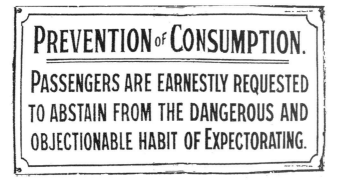

PREVENTION of CONSUMPTION.

PASSENGERS ARE EARNESTLY REQUESTED TO ABSTAIN FROM THE DANGEROUS AND OBJECTIONABLE HABIT OF EXPECTORATING.

VICTORIA
Mistress of the Empire,
cast her spell over Africa like no Monarch in History.

From **VICTORIA BAY** through **VICTORIA WEST** in the Cape
past **FORT VICTORIA** and across the **VICTORIA FALLS**
to **LAKE VICTORIA** and up the **VICTORIA NILE** to the Sudan and Egypt

"I have this evening seen Mr. Stanley who discovered Livingstone - a determined ugly little man with a strong American twang."

- Queen Victoria in a dsitinct German accent.

The CAPE TO CAIRO Concept

Cape to Cairo was not a late Victorian idea. As early as 1796, two years before Napoleon's descent on Egypt and Nelson's Battle of the Nile, a far-seeing Portuguese explorer and Governor, Francisco de Lacerda predicted a British Empire stretching from the Cape of Good Hope to Egypt. It would drive a wedge between the long held Portuguese possessions of Angola and Mozambique on the west and east coasts of Africa.

Little or nothing was heard of this scheme for another 100 years, although during that time numerous expeditions and explorations had taken place from north to south and across the greatest breadth of Africa, by explorers of many nationalities - French, German, Belgian, Italian and British.

It was the naturalised American explorer H.M.Stanley's enthralling letters home to the Daily Telegraph in 1876 that gave the first impulse to the idea of an all British link through the whole of Africa. In the same year, the leader writer of that newspaper, Edwin Arnold, expanded the idea and coined the catch phrase 'Cape to Cairo'.

Henry Morton Stanley (1841 - 1904), born John Rowland, was brought up in a workhouse in Dunbarton, Wales. Having been abandoned by his mother and all but the lunatic fringe of his family, he worked his passage as a cabin boy to New Orleans, where he assumed the name of his adopted cotton broker father, and became an American citizen. He served on both sides in the Civil War, and became a journalist. A joint expedition sponsored by the New York Times and Daily Telegraph sent him to Equatorial Africa where he 're-discovered' Livingstone at Ujiji. His offer to open up the territory for Great Britain was turned down, but was accepted by King Leopold of Belgium for his Congo Free State. He helped in the foundation of the Anglo-Egyptian Sudan, leading

"Short in stature as she is and not majestic what I admired most was the sense of power the eyes revealed."
H. M. Stanley. after meeting Queen Victoria

The Ivory trail across Africa

countless expeditions throughout the territory alongside Baker. With a ruthless reputation, more than anyone else he advanced Britain's knowledge, presence and authority in that part of Africa, which contributed to the opening out of the Cape to Cairo concept.

However it was Harry Johnston, in his various writings from Central Africa, including his book The Nile Quest of 1889, who more than anyone conveyed the concept of 'Cape to Cairo' to the powers-that-be, notably Lord Salisbury, the British Prime Minister & Foreign Secretary - a great advocate of African expansion. Although a bumptious ball-of-fire, Johnston was also a down-to-earth artist and explorer on the same wavelength as the great man, who was treading softly with a spendthrift Government. Salisbury was very impressed by the work of the English and Scottish missionaries in Nyasaland and by the achievements of the Moir brothers of the African Lakes Company. He felt strongly about the slave trade originally denounced by Livingstone, and believed that a route through Central Africa would pave the way for an end to this abomination, and promote Livingstone's doctrine of 'Christianity, Commerce and Civilisation'.

Cecil Rhodes came on to the scene, and this visionary Empire Builder hastened to build a railway through all British territory. Theoretically, trains would steam the whole way up through the centre of Africa without stopping, and in less than half the time it would take to travel by ship round the coast.

The Imperial Government, always strapped for cash from the long suffering British taxpayer, was slow in the scramble for Africa. It was Rhodes and his associates who strove to annexe as much of the unclaimed territory as possible. His Cape Colony would lead the advance north from the southern terminus of the Cape to Cairo railway and the trans-continental telegraph to link up with the British system running down from Egypt and the Nile into the Sudan. This would be the trunk line - the Iron Spine of Africa. The ribs would be the spurs of the coastal connections - through foreign territory if necessary. With preferential tariffs for British goods the economic development of Africa from end to end would be feasible. The wider Imperial federation would include America and Germany - a power bloc policing the wicked ways of the world.

"As to the commercial aspect, every one supposes that the railway is being built with the only object that a human being may be able to get in at Cairo and get out at Cape Town. This is of course, ridiculous. The object is to cut Africa through the centre, and the railway will pick up trade all the way along the route." Rhodes wrote to Ewart Grogan

Salisbury, Prime Minister and Foreign Secretary; and Joseph Chamberlain, the Colonial Secretary, were quick to realise that Rhodes would do what Her Imperial Majesty's Government could not do.

At that time, in virtually the whole of Central Africa, native porters were the only means of transport. In the north, camel caravans were constant; and in the south ox-wagons and mule carts trekked across the veldt. But in equatorial Africa the scourge of the tse-tse fly (pronounced tet-see), horse sickness and other diseases made animal transport impossible. So, across the breadth of the continent great caravans of explorers, traders and hunters marched, on trails trodden for centuries by wild animals. Over mountains and across waterless deserts, from the Atlantic to the Indian Ocean, in columns of up to 100 men they snaked, often led by a headman who carried the largest load of all. At times, over a thousand men were in one caravan, singing and chatting as they went, carrying loads of up to 80 pounds on their heads and shoulders. Day after day, covering over 20 miles a day at 3 miles an hour, they zig-zagged across Africa.

There can be no finer example of this than the mind-boggling Marchand Mission across equatorial Africa to the Upper Nile at Fashoda. For over 2 years, a total of 45,000 porters battled 2000 miles with

Transport wagon crossing Hunyani River

hundreds of tons of supplies and a demountable steel boat. In the end this valiant expedition was pipped at the post by Kitchener, and abandoned by a powerless government - destroying forever France's trans-African ambitions.

To the Great Lakes of Central Africa, other expeditions carried boats in sections. Later, larger steamer parts and boilers were dragged on wagons and pontoons, across trails and rivers, to lay claim to the interior. For apart from the Nile, no river in Africa was navigable for any great distance. The Congo and Zambezi Rivers were passable in stretches, but cataracts, gorges and sandbanks barred the way through. To travel continuously was feasible only by laborious transhipment - from water to land - and back to water... and so on.

Between 1891 and 1894, almost single-handedly, Lionel Decle accomplished the then longest walk through Africa. His epic

Lionel Decle

trip took him from the Cape to the northern extremity of Uganda, and thence to Mombasa and Zanzibar on the east coast. He subsequently followed with further punishing expeditions to report 'Progress on the African Continent' for the Daily Telegraph.

Perhaps the most remarkable, and one of the last of the great cattle treks was undertaken by Fred Cooksey, of Birmingham Butcher stock. Before the first World War, his uncle had obtained a contract to supply the British army in Egypt with meat. Cooksey drove a herd of cattle from the Cape up through the centre of Africa to the Sudan. Having crossed the Zambezi River, he traversed the one remaining natural obstacle the Kafue River - by the newly opened Kafue Railway Bridge. Skirting the Congo border, he turned north-eastwards, towards the Great Lakes, more or less following the route envisaged for the Cape to Cairo Line. Passing through Tanganyika and Uganda he reached the Sudan. Avoiding the rains as much as possible, and moving by night through the tse-tse fly belts, the trek took over two years; and as many cattle succumbed *en route*, many more were born on the hoof.

In the end the railways were inevitable, incomparable in speed and efficiency in the carrying of goods of every description, on which the progress of Africa depended. The survey parties went out into the vast uncharted territory on foot, with native carriers, mapping the routes and pegging the lines of the iron road.

Fred Cooksey's cattle trek across the Kafue River Railway bridge

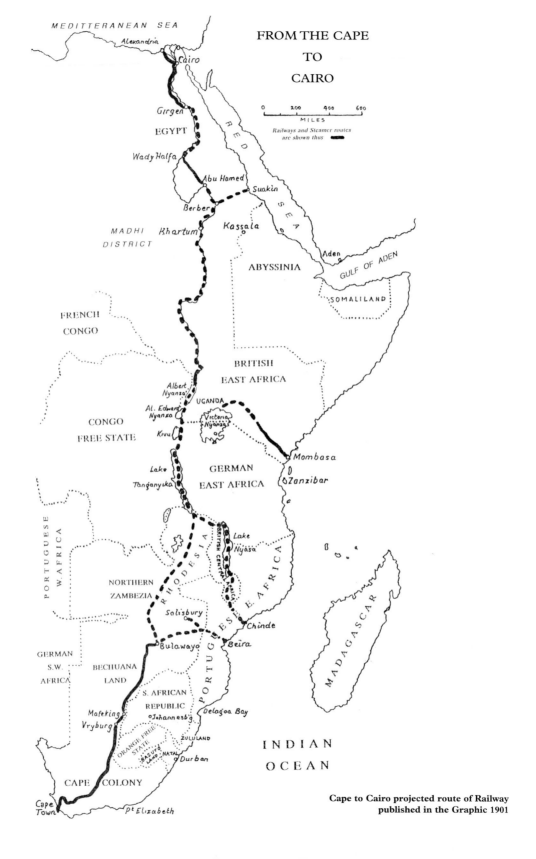

Cape to Cairo projected route of Railway
published in the Graphic 1901

RAILWAYS	OTHER EVENTS

	RAILWAYS	OTHER EVENTS
1856	First Railway in Egypt	
1863	First Railway in Cape	
1869		Suez canal opened.
1876	Worcester (Cape) reached	
1884	Brounger Jnct. (De Aar) reached	
1885	Orange River to Kimberley.	Warren Expedition.
1886		Gold struck at Johannesburg.
1888		Bechuanaland made Protectorate.
1889		British South Africa Co. formed.
1890	Kimberley to Vryburg	Fort Salisbury founded.
	Rand Steam Tram built	Rhodes made Cape Premier.
1891		Nyasaland made Protectorate.
		Shepheard's Hotel rebuilt.
1892	Beira Railway started	
	Eastern Line completed	
	Johannesburg line from O.F.S.	
1894	Vryburg to Mafeking	Roseberry Foreign Secretary.
1895		Jameson Raid.
		Salisbury re-elected PM;
		Chamberlain Colonial Secretary.
1896	Uganda Railway started	Rhodes resigns Premiership,
	Wadi Halfa started	makes peace with Matabele.
	Gaborone reached	
1897	Wadi Halfa reached	Battle of Abu Hamed.
	Mafeking to Bulawayo	
1898		Battle of Omdurman.
1899	Khartoum reached	Mount Nelson Hotel opens.
	Beira Railway widening	Anglo-Boer War starts.
	Salisbury to Umtali	
1901	Uganda Railway completed	Death of Queen Victoria.
1902		Anglo-Boer War ends.
		Death of Rhodes.
1903	Bulawayo to Wankie	
1904	Wankie to Victoria Falls	
1905	Victoria Falls to Kalomo	Victoria Falls Bridge opens.
1906	Kalomo to Broken Hill	
1908	Benguela Railway started	
1909	Broken Hill to Congo Border	Nile Bridge, Khartoum opens.
1910	Elizabethville to Star of the Congo	
	Khartoum to Kosti and to El Obeid	
	Benguela Railway Km 198 - 323	
1911 - 13	Benguela Railway Km 320 - 520	
1914	Star of Congo - Kambove - Tshilongo	World War I starts.
	Zambezi River to Port Herald	
1918	Bukama reached from Tshilongo	World War I ends.
1922	Trans Zambezi Railway	
1923	Benguela Railway Km. 520 - 627	
1925	Benguela Railway Km. 627 - 726	
1928	Benguela Railway Km. 726 - 1246	
1929	Benguela Railway Km. 1246 -1347	

The Castle of Good Hope flying the Union Jack over the newly laid 3 feet 6 inch Cape gauge lines out of Cape Town Station, whilst a train still runs on the wide 4 feet 8¹/₂ inches gauge of Europe (above)

The Mail Train leaving Cape Town Station before the turn of the century (SAL) (below)

2

TAVERN OF THE SEAS

THE CAPE OF GOOD HOPE

In the early 1800's, after the Dutch had made way for the British at the Cape of Good Hope, the first of many sailing ships, the Lady Julian, docked briefly in Table Bay on its long voyage to the penal colony of Australia. Its cargo included 240 women, aged from 11 upwards - pick-pockets, thieves and muggers, sentenced to transportation. Far from the filth of England's slums, most of these street-wise girls were destined for a better life, and to provide good breeding stock for the new colony. Having entertained the ship's company on board, the crew took to pimping for the girls in Cape Town's harbour. Eager to move them on, the colonial authorities refused them landing rights; so a brisk trade was done with boatloads of marines and sailors around the harbour. The Cape of Good Hope was truly on the map as the Tavern of the Seas, a convivial British staging post, with its attendant fleshpots, half way to India and Australia.

It became the centre of Britain's Empire at the end of Africa; and from its widening sea lanes where the Atlantic and Indian Oceans meet in a flurry of storms, many people landed from far afield. It flourished as a matrimonial fiefdom for bachelors; as well as a convenient stopover for Anglo-Indians, tea planters, forest officials, army officers, civil servants, merchants, settlers and philanderers, many of whom were on sick leave from that most favoured haven of Britain's Empire, the Indian subcontinent.

Half a century later, in 1862, an old ships bell rang the first train out of Cape Town station. Across the cobbled square the sounds echoed, mixed with the cackles and cries of the toothless Capetonians, the hoarse shouts of the barrow boys, the greetings of the farmers and fishermen, and the shunting of the solitary steam engine in the nearby station. In the harbour, the old wooden sailing vessels were making way for iron steam-ships.

The first railway line in Africa had been laid in Egypt in 1856 by Robert Stephenson, son of the inventor of the steam locomotive, George Stephenson. When the first Cape Town railway company started construction 3 years later at the other end of Africa, there were no other railways on the continent.

The Cape Town Railway and Dock Company had picked an ambitious British consulting engineer Charles Fox to pioneer this line. He was the first of the family of engineers in firms of that name (Fox & Sons, Sir Douglas Fox and Partners, and later Freeman Fox and Partners) who became stalwart consultants for the whole of the south central part of the

Cape to Cairo railway. In England he had been a partner in the building firm of Fox and Henderson which had been the main contractors for that gigantic glass and steel monument to Victorian enterprise - London's Crystal Palace. It had been designed, it was said, by Joseph Paxton on a blotter during a particularly long and boring Great Western Railway meeting.

One of Fox's star pupils, William Brounger, also sailed to the Cape of Good Hope and took charge of the fledgling Railway Company. He persuaded other engineers from Britain to follow him - for outside America, Britain laid claim to the giants of railway construction. Among them was Henry Pauling, soon to be Brounger's deputy, Wells Hood, his Field Engineer, and John Blue, later chief engineer of the Aswan Dam.

There were many capable engineers but no experienced construction companies. Local labour was almost non-existent, so navvies arrived from Ireland, Scotland, England, and other parts of the Empire. At that time the British navvy was considered the King of Labourers, described by the *Illustrated London News* as "the very elite of England as to physical power; - broad, muscular, massive fellows, who are scarcely to be matched in Europe."

William Dabbs landed from Scotland, with his young wife and his new steam locomotive. He was driver, engineer, fitter and repairer. For those were the days when operating staff turned their hands to anything. The engine he assembled was the very first of a batch of nine sent out to the Cape. And the story behind it has an ironic twist. The first railway contract *Mail Day at Cape* was awarded to Edward Pickering. New to the game, he struggled on for *Town Docks* many months, unable to make headway. His impatient employer William

Brounger eventually took over, and completed the line himself. Poor old Pickering took his revenge in the only way he could. He toppled Dabbs' engine down a steep embankment, causing extensive damage which took months to repair. Back on the rails it became Engine No 9 - overtaken numerically by its eight younger sisters. For the rest of his long life, Bill Dabbs spent hours on the footplate, accompanied always by his faithful assistant Mitchell. He lived to see his pioneer engine honourably retired as an illustrious monument in Cape Town Station - where it stands today.

The Prime Minister of the Cape Colony, John Molteno, had set the ball rolling for 'full steam north'. In his epic speech of 1874 he stirred the railway movement into action. His plan was direct. From all the coastal ports the railways would aim inwards and northwards. "Get on towards the Orange Free State and beyond it", he urged.

The obstacles were enormous. Passes through the great mountain barriers had to be found, for virtually the whole of central Africa lay on a great *highveld* plateau.

From the beginning, money was short. The Cape Colony was sorely pressed by the Imperial Government. The struggling settlers were squeezed like pips. But Molteno pursued economies of scale. After lengthy discussions, the 4 feet 8½ inches gauge - the railway gauge of the whole 'civilised' world - was reduced to 3 feet 6 inches. This 'Cape Gauge' became the standard for virtually the whole of Africa through to the Mediterranean - apart from Egypt, Kenya and the German territories.

To replace imported railway sleepers, tarring equipment was ordered to treat the local indigenous timber. Valuable Yellowood, ironwood, stinkwood and other exotic hardwoods, were about to be hewn from the forests of Knysna along the coast, when this ludicrous plan was rapidly abandoned.

The country folk of the Cape, largely Dutch speaking Afrikaners, were opposed to the railways, seeing them as a threat to their prosperous transport riders business; but John Molteno, a British politician, was also a canny countryman. He had proved his point in a field of their own, as a successful pioneer Karoo sheep farmer. He won over the Afrikaner opposition.

Natal was the first to heed his call, extending the rails from Durban to Pietermaritzburg. Here the newly arrived young Cecil Rhodes, who had joined his brother fresh from the Parsonage at Bishop's Stortford, made one of his first investments in the African sub-continent - in Natal Government railway shares.

A little later Cape Town pushed their line northwards, 45 miles to the rich agricultural town of Wellington. From that gem of glass and steel, the old Adderley Street Station, reminiscent of London's 'Liverpool Street', it

HOTELS AND BARS.

Alabama Hotel, 20, Bloem St.
Albion Hotel, 44, Buitengracht St.
All Nations Hotel, 105, Bree St.
Amsterdam Hotel, 22, Napier St.
Atlantic Hotel, 21, Mechau St.
Avenue Hotel, 11, St. John St.
Balmoral Castle Hotel, 20, Riebeek St.
Beaconsfield Hotel, corner of Roger St. and Sydney St.
Black Horse Hotel, 111, Longmarket St.
Bloemhof Inn, 15, Bloemhof St.
Bodega, The, 120, Longmarket St.
Bricklayers' Arms, corner of Hudson St. and Waterkant St.
Bristol Hotel, 96 & 98, Caledon St.
Britannia Hotel, 13, Buitenkant St.
British Hotel, 21, Riebeek St.
British India Hotel, 48, Keerom St.
Brooklyn Hotel, 14, Dorp St.
Brunswick Hotel, 13, Bree St.
Café Royal, 17, Church St.
Caledon Hotel, Mostert St.
Caledonian Hotel, corner of Loop St. and Dorp St.
Cannon Hotel, corner of Cannon St. and Longmarket St.
Carnarvon Hotel, 90, Sir Lowry Road.
Castle Hotel, corner of Constitution St. and Canterbury St.

CENTRAL HOTEL, 10, Shortmarket St.

Cheltenham Hotel, 92 & 94, Hanover St
City Arms, 50 & 52, Tennant St.
City Hall Hotel, 30, Darling Street.
City Tramway Hotel, 79, Sir Lowry Road.
Claridge's Hotel, Staal Plein.
Clyde Hotel, 5, Dorp St.
Commercial Hotel, 15, Parliament St.
Cooper's Arms Hotel, corner of Sir Lowry Road and Dorset St.
Cottage of Content Hotel, corner of Reform St. and Selkirk St.
Crescent Hotel, 6, Zieke St.
Criterion Hotel, Church Square.
Crown and Anchor Hotel, corner of Long St. and Leeuwen St.
Cumberland Hotel, 30, St. George's St.
Diamond Hotel, 13, Harrington St.
Dolphin Arms, 7, Boom St.
Dublin Castle Hotel, corner of Dixon St. and Waterkant St.
Eagle Tavern, 45, Canterbury St.
Empire Hotel, 43, Waterkant St.
Engel's, L., Private Hotel, 20, Strand St.
European Hotel, corner of Caledon St. and Vandeleur St.
Farrier's Hotel, 26, St. John St.
Fireman's Arms Hotel, 23, Mechau St.
Forester's Hotel, 51, Canterbury St.
Fountain Hotel, 1, Hout St.
Gaiety Bar, 4, Castle St.
Garrison Inn, 99, Longmarket St.
Garth Castle Hotel, corner of Long St. and Waterkant St.

Geneva Temperance Hotel, 139a, Long St.
Germania Hotel, 102, Loop St.
Gloucester Arms, 47, Boom St.
Good Hope Hotel, 75, Loop St.
Governor's Hotel, corner of Wale St. and Bree St.
GRAND HOTEL, Main Entrance, Grand Hotel Buildings, Strand St.
Grand Hotel Bar, corner of Strand St. and St. George's St.
Grand Parade Restaurant and Theatre Bar, Theatre Buildings, Parliament St.
Great Eastern Hotel, corner of Prestwich St. and Bree St.
Gresham Hotel, corner of Long St. and Wale St.
Harp Hotel, 148, Long St.
Harrington Hotel, 54, Darling St.
His Lordship's Larder, 67, Loop St.
Hope and Anchor, 18, Rose St.
Hope Hotel, 37, Hope St.
Hotel Germania, corner of Loop St. and Wale St.
Hotel Hansa, corner of Burg St. and Strand St.
Hotel Metropole, Long St. (corner of Castle St).
Imhoff Castle Hotel, corner of Mount St. and Wicht St.
Imperial Bar, 49, Long St.
INTERNATIONAL HOTEL, Mill St. The most beautifully situated hotel in Cape Town. Telephone No. 21 ; Telegraphic and Cable Address, " International."
Johannesburg Hotel, corner of Long St. and Church St.
Kimberley Hotel, corner of Buitenkant St. and Roeland St.
Kloof Temperance Hotel, Kloof Road.
Koeberg Hotel, Nelson St.
Langham Hotel, 33, Long St.
Lion's Head Hotel, 143, Bree St.
London Hotel, 142, Loop St.
Madeira Hotel, 18, Barrack St.
Mechanics' Hotel, 11, Caledon St.
Modern Hotel, 114, Long St.
Mountain View Hotel, 131, Long St.
MOUNT NELSON HOTEL, Orange St., top of Government Avenue.
Mount Pleasant Hotel, corner of Pontac St. and Reform St.
New Dock Hotel, Schiebe St.
New Hope and Anchor Hotel, 80, Rose St.
Newmarket Hotel, Newmarket St.
New Pavilion, Mostert St.
New Rose Inn, 73, Rose St.
New York Hotel, 68, Hanover St.
Nottingham Castle Hotel, 40, Barrack St.
Nova Scotia Hotel, 98, Buitengracht St.
Oddfellows' Arms, corner of Longmarket St. and Mount St.
Old House at Home, 11, Loop St.
Oriental Hotel, 5, Leeuwen St.
Original Crown Hotel, 22, Adderley St.
Palmerston Hotel, top of Plein St.
Parade Bar, Theatre Buildings.

Perseverance Hotel, 87, Buitenkant St.
Poole's Hotel, 2 to 6, Queen Victoria St.
Portsmouth Arms, 27, Bree St.
Prince of Wales Hotel, 35, Bree St.
Princess Royal Hotel, corner of Riebeek St. and Sea St.
Queen of the South Hotel, 6, Buitenkant St.
Queen's Hotel, 10, Dock Road.
Red Lion Hotel, 9, Mechau St.
Roma Hotel, 25, Waterkant St.
Rose Hotel, 15, Rose St.
Rose and Crown Hotel, corner of Tennant St. and Hanover St.
Round House Hotel, Kloof Road.
Roux's Hotel, 2, St. John St.
Royal Hotel, Plein St.
Royal Duke Hotel, corner of Loop St. and Leeuwen St.
Royal Navy Hotel, 19, Bree St.
Sarsfield Hotel, 80 & 82, Constitution St.
Shakespeare Hotel, corner of Mechau St. and Jerry St.
Sicilia Hotel, 25, Riebeek St.
Silver Cloud Hotel, 15, Constitution St.
Silver Tree Hotel, 32, Waterkant St.
Sir Garnet Hotel, 29, Hanover St.
Sir Lowry Hotel, corner of Sir Lowry Road and Stuckeris St.
South African Hope Hotel, corner of Pepper St. and Loop St.
Spes Bona Hotel, 4, Van der Meulen St.
Standard Bar, 66, Adderley Street.
Standard Hotel, 30, Napier St.
Star Hotel, 33, Waterkant St.
ST. GEORGE'S HOTEL, corner of Church St. and St. George's St.
Sun Hotel, 12, Zieke St.
Swan Hotel, 19, Loop St.
Taymouth Castle Hotel, corner of Vandeleur St. and Wicht St.
Temperance Hotel, 56, Strand St.
Theatre Bar, Theatre Buildings.
Thistle Hotel, corner of Prestwich St. and Cobern St.
Three United Kingdoms Hotel, 5, Harrington St.
Tramway Hotel, 54, Waterkant Street.
Transvaal Hotel, corner of Rutger St. and Sir Lowry Road.
True Blue Hotel, 22, Chiappini St.
Union Hotel, 84–86, Plein St.
United Kingdom Hotel, 50–52, Rose St.
United Service Hotel, 36, Harrington St.
United South African Hotel, 59, Hout St.
Victoria Hotel, corner of Parliament St. and Longmarket Sts.
Victoria Hotel, 12, Long St.
Waterford Arms, 10, Loop St.
Welcome Hotel, 26, Canterbury St.
White House Hotel, corner of Long St. and Strand St.
Ye Olde Thatched Tavern, Greenmarket Square.

HOTELS AND BARS.

Alfred Hotel, Durban Road, Wynberg.
Altona Hotel, Victoria Road, Woodstock.
Arthur's Seat (Private Hotel), Beach Road, Sea Point.
Bay View Hotel, Muizenberg.
British Oak Hotel, Maitland Road, Salt River.
Bromwell Hotel, 212 & 214, Albert Road, Woodstock.
Cambridge Hotel, Milnerton.
Camp's Bay Hotel, Camp's Bay.
Cardiff Castle Hotel, Main St., Newlands.
Clifton-on-Sea Hotel, Clifton, Sea Point.
Cogill's Hotel, Main Road, Wynberg.
Cowling's Hotel, Main Road, Claremont.
Crown Hotel, Main Road, Claremont.
Diep River Hotel, Main Road, Diep River.
Foresters' Arms, Newlands Avenue.

FORESTERS' HOTEL, Alphen Hill, Wynberg
Goodwin's Hotel, 310, Albert Road, Salt River.
Grand Hotel, Muizenberg.
Great Westerford Private Hotel, Westerford, Newlands.
Green Point Hotel, Main Road, Green Point.
Grosvenor Private Hotel, Links Road, Rondebosch.
Hermitage Private Hotel, Rosebank.
Hotel Cecil, Main Road, Newlands.
Junction Hotel, Maitland Road, Salt River.
King's Hotel, Kalk Bay.
Landsdown Hotel, Landsdown Road, Claremont.
Locomotive Hotel, 330, Albert Rd., Salt River.
Lord Milner Hotel, Roodebloem.
Marine Hotel, Beach Road, Sea Point.

Masonic Hotel, Main Road, Kalk Bay.
Milner Hall, Beach Road, Three Anchor Bay.
Montpellier Hotel, 142 & 144, Albert Road, Woodstock.
Mountain View Hotel, Palm Boom Road, Newlands.
Mowbray Hotel, 33, Main Road, Mowbray.
Muizenberg Hotel, Main Road, Muizenberg.
New Brighton Hotel, 49, Victoria Road, Woodstock.
Old Standard Hotel, Maitland.
Old Standard Hotel, Wolfe St., Wynberg.
PALACE HOTEL (J. T. Bennett, propr.), Main Road, Kenilworth.
Park Hotel, Main Road, Muizenberg.
Queen's Hotel, Queen's Road, Sea Point.
RAILWAY HOTEL, Main Road, Wynberg.
Randall's Hotel, Main Road, Rondebosch.
Royal Hotel, opposite Station, Wynberg

Royal Standard Hotel, Main Road, Mowbray.
St. James's Hotel, Main Road, St. James.
SANITARIUM, THE, Woodstock Beach.
Scowen's Hotel (Harry H. Scowen, propr. Muizenberg.
Sea Point Hotel, Regent Road, Sea Point.
Standard Hotel, Perth St., Maitland.
Station Hotel, Letterstedt Road, Newlands
Strand Hotel, Beach Road, Woodstock (see Sanitarium).
Vineyard Hotel, Protea Road, Newlands.
Waverley Hotel, Main Road, Three Anchor Bay.
Welcome Hotel, Maitland.
Westerford Arms Hotel, Main Road, Newlands.
Westerford Private Hotel, Main Road, Newlands.
Woodstock Hotel, Albert Road, Woodstock.

ran through the open Cape Flats onto the Peninsula mainland; past Bellville and Durbanville and the Stellenbosch loop line, where a sleepy little Masonic Hotel heralded the immense influence of the Brotherhood in all railway matters. The line ran on to Paarl, the wine centre of the day, and crossed the iron bridge to Huguenot

with its Lady Grey and Railway Hotels. At Wellington the arrival of the first train was greeted by a salute of guns. A far-sighted farmer P.J. Malan had donated the land free, on condition that all trains in both directions stopped at Wellington.

This prosperous farming area was cut off from the interior by the towering mountain range. The only way through was Bain's Kloof Pass, the finest wagon road in the whole of South Africa, built by William Bain with convict labour. So gentle were the gradients that horses hardly paused on their easy trot over. But for the iron horse there was no easy way; to build a railway was a formidable challenge. Wellington remained the terminus for some time to come.

Remote from the African interior, Cape Town was closer in spirit to Europe. There were numerous taverns and ale-houses, mostly with a nautical or dock flavour in the rat-runs and alley-ways of the harbour area. Hotels actually arrived with the British, and a century ago there were over 200 hostelries dotted around the Tavern of the Seas.

In the smarter part of town, St. George's Hotel, founded in the 1870's, boasted the first separate ladies bar, as well as the longest cocktail bar. Run by an Irishman, Tommy Mulvihal, it was frequented by racing men, and other gamblers and rich imbibers. For those who couldn't get in, another Irishman ran a nearby pub called the "I never say Nothing to Nobody Inn".

Parkes Hotel was the finest hotel of its day. The haunt of master mariners, it maintained a small luxuriant garden in the heart of the city. In the 1890's it made way for the sumptuous Grand Hotel, built in a style equal to 'London and Paris' by the Union Shipping Company. A 350 feet long balcony decorated with palms and shrubs, with shops beneath, became a promenade where the *jeunesse dore* could meet. There were electric lights on the tables, an Electric lift, Axminster carpets and a grand piano in its palatial lounge. The walls were lined with a vivid collection of rare animal trophies and horns - some renowned for their striking symmetry, others for their gross deformity, donated by such renowned hunters as Selous and Neumann. In the entrance hall stood appropriate statues of Bacchus, the God of Wine, and Persephone, the Goddess of Spring -

The Grand Hotel, Cape Town in the 1890's, on the corner of Strand and Adderley Street (SAL)

spouses that symbolised the youth and beauty of Cape Town

In the opinion of many, the Royal Hotel in nearby Plein Street, surpassed the Grand for stylish spaciousness, with a dining room holding 350 people. It was the haunt of Barney Barnato and other mining magnates. Pooles Hotel, near Parliament Buildings, earned a reputation for 'scheming and plotting'. It was frequented by politicians including Rhodes and Jameson.

Out of town, the more discreet Vineyard Hotel in Claremont, once the home of Lady Anne Barnard, the wife of the Colonial Governor, was run by Miss O'Sullivan. The nearby Crown was renowned for picnics and wedding breakfasts in its large orchard, and for the lively string quartet at weekend dances. Down the road at Wynberg, the Old Standard still stood with faded memories of a previous visitor, the Duke of Wellington, who lived nearby at Waterloo Place. Out towards Constantia were all the greatest wine estates and houses, including the exemplary *Buitenverwachting* - Beyond all Expectations. Rathfelders was an isolated farmhouse, owned and run by a King of Landlords in the style of the great roadside inns of Europe, when stage coaches ruled the road. Its rural location ensured in was the favourite 'Meet' of the Cape Hunt, which chased Cape foxes (silver jackals) through the Constantia Valley.

An early railway hotelier, Arthur Boffrey, arrived in 1898. He owned the Locomotive Hotel at Salt River, the Montpelier at Woodstock and the Royal Hotel near the station at Wynberg.

One of the first posh pub-restaurants was started by a Welsh Fishmonger, Charlie Beer. Brown stout and oysters were daily offerings, with plentiful supplies of Scotch Salmon, Yarmouth bloaters, Manx kippers and Finnan Haddock, brought in on the mail-boats. As for theatrical's, the Good Hope Theatre was seldom open for theatre; it was mostly used for concerts and meetings; yet the Opera House in Darling Street was seldom closed. Facing it was the famous Music Hall - the Tivoli, where the local girls flashed their charms, and the latest and greatest talent from Europe and America went on display.

The oldest tavern, with the oldest vine, was the Perseverance - the 'Persies' of today. The oldest barman around was MacDougal Sutherland who remembered the mining magnates in the early days of the Rand, and was particularly peeved by J.B.Robinson's habit of putting his large white sun helmet on the bar. One day he painted it black, and lost his job.

Rathfelder's Hotel, Wynberg, before the last century, looked out across the open Constantia Valley. Today, the building is surrounded by industrial development

FOR

HEALTH, COMFORT, AND CONVENIENCE

GO TO THE

INTERNATIONAL HOTEL, CAPE TOWN.

Vide opinions of the Press and Medical Faculty.
  „ *Aubertin's "Six Months in Cape Colony and Natal."*
  „ *Groser's "South African Experiences."*
  „ *Du Val's "With a Show through South Africa."*

From the beginning the Cafe Royal Grill Room and Bar became the mecca for gourmets and travellers. The bar ended up as the Press Club. It also had numerous railway connections. Its renowned *maitre d'hotel* Giuseppe di Paoli had started as a train steward; and had then became Chief Steward of Cape Town Station's dining rooms.

Strategically situated in the smart Gardens area, "away from the noise, heat and smells of town" was the International Hotel, owned by the celebrated Willie O'Callaghan. It comprised several houses joined together with extensive grounds and double verandahs; and it was "the only hotel in South Africa with on the premises Post and Telegraph Offices, Money Order Office, Savings Bank, Telephone, Tram Terminus and Cab-stand." Surrounded by the villas and gardens of the leading citizens, it was advertised as the perfect *'Rus in Urbe'*. With no swimming pool, refreshing sea water was pumped up to the bathrooms in summer.

International Hotel (SAL)

However, it was hard to rival the opulence that was later to appear down the road in the shape of the Mount Nelson Hotel.

The railway line to the north had been stuck for some time at Wellington. Towering ahead were the Tulbagh mountains, the main obstacles of challenge for Brounger's surveyors. Wells Hood and his deputy Maltby scoured the countryside for weeks on end. They located a route that would traverse the range with a single tunnel and a gradient no more than 1 in 40.

Instead of going over the old wagon pass, Bain's great monument to British road-making, the line veered northwards and out towards Tulbagh. Through the gap of the 'New Pass', it turned back on the other side of the mountain range, through Wolseley to Worcester, where once again the Masonic and Continental were the uninspiring hotels.

Well watered Worcester, full of street furrows, was a haven of oaks and poplars. Fruit and vines grew in profusion. There was horse breeding and ostrich farming, leather tanning and wagon building, and trout in the rivers. It became the oasis for Rhodes' Fruit Farms, organised by Harry Pickstone. From abundant orchards, early refrigerated rail trucks trundled down to Cape Town with endless supplies of exotic produce, carefully off-loaded onto ships bound for Europe. Then someone stumbled upon the idea of shunting the wagons directly onboard. A few weeks later exotic pears and peaches, packed in yellow-wood boxes, greeted the dinner tables of London's elite.

The line lunged onwards up the Hex River valley. Navvies worked furiously. The pay was good. More and more invaded the camps, day after day. They were swelled by the locals; labourers of all colours - Malays, Chinese, Hottentots and Africans.

Navvies were a rough, good-hearted mob, living on the job in rudimentary huts. They 'shot for the pot' and drank what they could lay their hands on. When the Cape liquor wagon passed by with its own brand of firewater, they stopped the driver by pelting him with stones, and helped themselves. Paying was a problem. The Ganger overseers held the navvies to ransom, docking their wages for the cost of the liquor. Nearby Boer farmers were also far from happy. They reckoned the arrival of the railway had devalued their property.

The wide open stretches of the Cape Colony were fast bringing new challenges for British imperial enterprise, and railway expansion was in its heyday.

When the two Pauling brothers pitched up from England, their great uncle Henry was second only to William Brounger in the Cape Government Railways. John Merriman, Commissioner of Public Works, and later Prime Minister, was inundated on the western side with calls from keen new-comers, eager to steam ahead with the 'forward' policy. The young George Pauling was almost the only person around with railway tunnel experience; so under Merriman's guidance he started in the Eastern Cape. In conjunction with his foreman, he obtained a contract for

CAPE COLONY

RAILWAY DEPARTMENT.

RAILWAY ENGINEER'S DEPARTMENT.

	£	s.
Railway Engineer for the Colony, W. G. Brounger	1,500	0
Acting Railway Engineer for the Colony, H. J. Pauling ...	...	
Chief Clerk, J. F. Davis	400	0
Clerk, S. O'Connor ... ... (... ...	175	0
„ J. A. Laurence ... ...: ...	120	0

a tunnel at Grahamstown. By dint of giving a monopoly to a local trading-store for the supply of victuals, he raised enough working funds to complete the contract. He then formed a syndicate, consisting of himself, a Scotsman, an Italian and an English navvy. The latter's unfortunate habit of over-spending on alcohol caused regular problems. He was once rescued, with the weeks wages for the entire labour gang, from a house of ill-repute.

Having whetted his appetite in the art of self-employment, Pauling obtained another contract at Port Alfred, where William Dabbs had re-located with his locomotive 'Blackie'.

The Kowie River Railway became the launch-pad of what was to become the hugely successful firm of Pauling & Company - Railway, Bridge and Dam Contractors all over the world.

A contemporary administrator,★ described them as "a firm of engineers mainly composed of members of one family - at whose head stood George Pauling, one of the boldest railway builders that Great Britain has produced; a man after Rhodes' heart; one who said he would 'get there' - *and got there*".

★ Hugh Marshall Hole, Commissioner of Matabeleland in his autobiograhy 'Old Rhodesian Days.

His brother Harry, and cousins, Harold, Henry, Willie and Percy all joined forces. It was said at the time that one Pauling or another was directly responsible for almost the entire permanent way between Cape Town and the Congo.

Archetypal of that exclusive breed of imperial railway builders, who became surveyors, engineers, contractors and even financiers in their own right, George Pauling was no newcomer to hard times. His father had been a railway Engineer at Delhi, when due to failing health he lost his job. His son had been destined for the Woods & Forestry Service of India; so at the age of 14 he was forced to take a more lucrative line, working at all hours for private railway contractors. He learnt his trade largely from the navvies. Thereafter this became for young Pauling a crusade - a clash of systems - private enterprise *versus* inefficient government. He set out to prove the advantage of the contract system which invariably worked out quicker and cheaper. It became, as Rhodes realised, the economic impulse, in fact the salvation, of the Cape to Cairo scheme.

Pauling was the stuff of which Empires were made. He recalled those strenuous early days in his rollicking autobiography *Chronicles of a Contractor:*

"By four o'clock in the morning I was generally out of bed and away on horseback to inspect the work... I was almost incessantly on the move, and on a conservative estimate covered an average of from two to three thousand miles a month by rail, cart and horseback. Every day I was up with the sun, and seldom went to rest before eleven o'clock at night. My sleep was generally taken in a cart or on the railway, and I do not believe that I enjoyed the comfort of a bed on more than seven days in every month."

Nevertheless, he often managed to end up with a hearty meal, a few rounds of drinks and a game of billiards. He tried his hand at various other enterprises, from ice-rinks to ostrich farming - a shipload of which took so long to reach Australia that the bottom had fallen out of the market. He lost other construction contracts in the Eastern Cape to government 'favouritism'. To get his own back he turned his hand to newspaper publishing. In order to spike the wheels of the big Contractors and Government Engineers he founded 'The Comet' -

George Pauling

so named for its uncertain appearance. It was the dodgiest and most scandalous newspaper of its day. A man was employed at £20 a month, called the Prison Editor, who was constantly serving terms for libellous articles. He usually conducted his own defence. On one occasion, a larger than usual trial by jury ended up in uproar and acquittal, when both the Judge and Prosecutor were exposed for their patronage of a Public Lottery. Under Roman-Dutch law they were 'rogues and vagabonds', and liable to be whipped through the streets behind a cart.

By the age of 24 Pauling had made enough money to get married, and buy a farm. He then lost it. Having laid into the bailiff who had come round to evict his wife and two boys during his absence from their house, he quietly returned to the Masonic Hotel in Grahamstown as 'Mine Host'.

Amongst his party tricks, for the occasional bet, he used his immense strength to carry his sturdy 450 pound Basuto pony around the billiard table. He would put his head and shoulders between the obliging pony's front legs and lift it onto his back. The last attempt to carry it up the stairs ended in a crash landing, and the pony refused to continue, although it still transported him up to sixty miles in a normal day's work.

He put up a spire for the local Masonic Lodge of which he was a member. He was never paid, and from then onwards avoided the brethren, making his own way in the railway world without them.

The Mount Nelson Hotel, Cape Town, a century ago.

THE MOUNT NELSON HOTEL

Largely as a result of publicity generated by the shipping lines, the Cape of Good Hope had become a winter watering, and bolt-hole, for well-heeled escapees from Europe. Sailing in on the rival Union and Castle ships they soon demanded something a little grander than the ordinary hotels, where they could all stay together. The shipping companies realised the potential of this all-inclusive aspect - and obliged. Whilst the Union Line rebuilt their Grand Hotel in the middle of the Mother City, the Castle Line launched the Mount Nelson, with the first private swimming pool.

Seated in pink splendour against the grey grandeur of Table Mountain, the pristine 'Nellie' - as she was fondly christened in an age of posh slang - still stands as a vivid reminder that it was very much the *Grande Dame* of British Colonialism at the end of Africa. From its lofty position in the Gardens of the former East India Company, everything else around it seems totally subservient. Through its columned Edwardian archway and down its palm-lined avenue, guarded by solar-hatted sentries, more statesmen and politicians, more royalty and aristocracy and more ladies of beauty and brains have passed than anywhere outside Cairo.

Standing at the crossroads of the Indian and Atlantic Oceans, the Mount Nelson's imperial links are no better symbolised than in the vaulted ceilings of the original dining room, where the Arms of the British South Africa Company join those of the Cape Colony, Natal, the Orange Free State and the Transvaal. This was Cecil Rhodes' dream combination of Britain's Empire in Southern Africa at the beginning of the last century.

Yet the name Mount Nelson stems not from any visit by Britain's greatest Admiral, since Nelson only called at the Cape of Good Hope as a young subaltern. The original homestead was renamed in 1806, a year after the naval victory of Trafalgar, in which Nelson was killed; a victory which reinforced Britain's supremacy around the sea lanes of the world.

"There is no exaggeration in the statement that London, the capital of the world, would not be able to produce anything superior" declared a contemporary newspaper at the opening of the Hotel in March 1899.

Donald Currie of The Castle Line, and his daughters and sons-in-law ensured that it had all the advantages and atmosphere of a home-from-home. A Swiss Manager and Swiss chefs were imported, along with a of the latest furniture and equipment, and a regular supply of London Newspapers.

Food unheard of in other establishments was served in the palm shaded Garden Room Restaurant. In true *fin de siecle* style it quickly became the watering hole and social centre for Cape Town's elite.

The Mount Nelson Hotel today.

Lady Edward Cecil, daughter-in-law of Lord Salisbury, the British Prime Minister, bumped into Alfred Beit, Rhodes' right hand man in the Hotel gardens. He took her in hand and introduced her to Rhodes at Groote Schuur, where she stayed regularly, sometimes with the Countess of Warwick, a mistress of the Prince of Wales.

Two other ladies who featured largely in Rhodes' life launched themselves from the Mount Nelson. The first was Princess Catherine Radziwell. Half-Polish and half-Russian, 'Princess Razzle-dazzle' did her best to get her claws into the Colossus. This scheming socialite stayed endlessly at the hotel - for which Rhodes paid the bill, until she was found forging his promissory notes and sent to prison.

Rhodes' only true, staunch female friend, Lady Sarah Wilson, was the youngest daughter of the Duke of Marlborough. She was also the wife of a 'Blues' Cavalry Officer who had been sent to Matabeleland. She regularly mixed with Rhodes and his circle, and once clashed with 'Princess Razzel-dazzle' in the foyer of the Hotel.

Hardly had the dust settled on the new hotel than the Anglo-Boer War broke out. The Mount

Nelson became the unofficial Officers Mess, where top-ranking officers and colonial officials were quartered with their wives. Other wives and girl-friends often stayed or were entertained. It became the home-from-home for the likes of Sir Redvers Buller and Lord Roberts.

The Anglo-Boer War spawned a spirit of misplaced patriotism. It was more curiosity than anything. Hordes of inexperienced young ladies, social butterflies, came out from England, ostensibly as nurses. They joined the *nouveau riche* refugees from the Transvaal, already clogging the hotel's corridors. Scandal was rife. Dinner parties with young ladies at the Mount Nelson were viewed as distractions for officers on duty. Queen Victoria herself totally disapproved and asked Joseph Chamberlain, the Colonial Secretary to send a telegram to Alfred Milner, the Cape Commissioner. This failed to stop the bewildering babble; and even more social butterflies sailed in by the boatload. When the authoritarian Lord Kitchener arrived and saw the giggling girls and bored wives lounging around outside the smoking rooms, he banished the officers up country, ostensibly to within earshot of the front line.

Rudyard Kipling, John Buchan and Arthur Conan Doyle all stayed there on their way to report news from the front. The Swiss Manager had unwisely declared the hotel for 'Officers Only.' An unheard of young reporter who gate-crashed an officers private party was unceremoniously tarred, feathered and thrown into the hotel fountain. The bad publicity which followed his unpaid claim for damages led Kitchener to arrange for the culprits to be brought back from India to face a court martial.

Rhodes' friend Lady Sarah Wilson became an enterprising Daily Mail correspondent, who covered the siege of Mafeking. She was the aunt of another young war correspondent, Winston Churchill, who had just arrived in Cape Town.

"We have left headquarters busy with matters that concerns yet none but themselves in the Mount Nelson Hotel in Cape Town - a most excellent and well appointed establishment," he laboriously reported to the Telegraph and Morning Post.

Abe Bailey suggested to Cecil Rhodes that young Winston should join an expedition to act as a correspondent to whip up support for Rhodes' trek northwards - a lucrative contract for a budding journalist. Churchill replied to Rhodes simplisticly : "It seems to me that this writing would help to attract possible attention to the Cape to Cairo route and stimulate the interest taken in your railway scheme." He never took the job.

The Anglo-Boer War brought dynamic prosperity to the Mount Nelson, and the Mother City generally. Every hotel was bursting at the seams, with all manner of refugee from the north, who arrived in whatever way they could. Trains from up country also brought an endless stream of all ranks on leave.

Inevitably when the war ended there was a sharp slump. But the 'Nellie' was on the map. She remained the stylish place for smart people to be seen amongst even smarter people, who were themselves discreetly hoping to escape the limelight.

With its unique location and lofty status this 'establishment worthy of Cairo' endured and prospered; remaining family owned right through to recent times when the Cayzer shipping family sold it to Orient Express Hotels.

In modern times it reached its pinnacle of perfection in the 1960's and 70's, before the demise of the Union Castle line. Louis Brunold, the Swiss Head Porter would remember from year to year the idiosyncrasies of the 30 odd Peers of the Realm who came out by ship and wintered in the 'Nellie', whilst their chauffeurs and valets would stay in the adjoining Helmsley Hotel, a fairy tale annexe of quaint balconies and spiral staircases - sadly no more.

Uncrowned princes of Europe, plutocrats and aristocrats, technocrats and politicians passed through. Even Harold MacMillan still pondered the aftermath of his 'Winds of Change' speech from a veranda chair, having arrived by banana boat, after the last Union Castle ship had abandoned Table Bay.

Bound for Europe on the Castle Line's 'Dunvegan Castle', Cecil Rhodes rides out a storm (UCT)

3

DIAMONDS AND DREAMS

THROUGH THE KAROO TO KIMBERLEY

" *This is the rock on which the future of South Africa will be built"* declared the Colonial Secretary as he laid a flawless white 86 carat diamond, the Star of South Africa, on the table of the Cape Assembly in 1869.

The line from Cape Town to the north was slowly advancing. Hundreds of miles ahead lay Kimberley, soon to become the richest diamond field in the world, where the wealth of South Africa was born.

Yet laying a road for the iron horse through the land of the ox was a precarious business. Hard pressed merchants were not easily persuaded to use the expensive new train. The cheapest fuel of all was still used by ox-wagons - grass.

Times had been tough. Drought, depression and financial troubles had taken their toll. Famine stalked the land. Then out of the blue a little boy, the son of a northern Cape farmer, Schalk Van Niekerk, made a lucky find. Whilst playing with pebbles in the dusty Karoo, he attracted the attention of a sharp eyed neighbour who liked the look of one of the stones. Convinced it was a diamond he agreed to share the proceeds. He took it to Hopetown and sold it for £500. Van Niekerk then bought a huge white stone from a local tribesman, who had found it in the Orange River. He exchanged it for hundreds of sheep, 10 oxen and a fine horse. This was the Star of South Africa, which eventually passed to the Countess of Dudley.

For one short period Kimberley was the wealth of the Empire. The town literally stood on diamonds. The early houses were built on gravel diggings around the 'Big Hole' - the greatest man made crater in the world. When the houses were demolished, along came the diamond washers, to sift through the rubble.

A racy young Englishman Fleetwood Rawstone had located the original site, spotted by his faithful Cape cook Damon. His more fortunate neighbours scored with the richest pickings of all; and Fleetwood Rawstone died almost penniless. The rush was on. Four months after the first discovery, Cecil Rhodes arrived in a cart with a pick and a Greek lexicon and pitched his tent in the burgeoning mad-house. Everyone who was anyone was into diamonds. Fortunes were made and lost overnight. Con-men and peddlers were in mass profusion; cutters and polishers were in short supply. Girls were sprouting 'carats' from the sides of their nostrils. Guys were tossing 'roughs' across the bars and poker tables. 'Diamond Lil' ran the Star of the West Bar, and the Diggers Rest was for earthy old timers. In this wild and wanton kaleidoscope of bars, ballrooms and brothels, the most sought after whores rewarded the man with the largest gemstone. Even the well frequented Synagogue boasted a diamond-tipped scroll pointer. Alfred Beit (1853 -1906) was a young diamond expert sent to Kimberley by a Hamburg firm. He was also a whizz-kid with finance. It was through Beit, that Rhodes, after having been turned down by the House of Erlangers, received the backing of Rothschilds Bank in London. "Without young Beit," Smuts declared later, "Rhodes might have been a mere visionary, bereft of power." He joined forces with Wernher and Porges in the consolidation of the diamond industry. After a duel with Barney Barnato from the opposing richer and stronger mining camp, de Beers was born. "One cannot resist Rhodes", admitted Barnato, after long withstanding his overtures. The sickly son of an English country Vicar had finally beaten 'the boys' at their own game. Cecil Rhodes *was* De Beers, and De Beers *was* Kimberley, controlling 90 per cent of the world's diamonds in an enduring and orderly fashion.

Financially secure, Rhodes canvassed for support to enter the Cape Parliament.

In Kimberley's Market Square, the centre of intrigue, amongst the oxen and mule carts, he met Matabele Thompson, and with Rochfort Maguire and Charles Rudd, he planned his advance northwards, to obtain concessions from Lobengula's kingdom of Matabeleland. It was the critical point of his advance up Africa. In this town of Billiards and Brandy, the British South Africa Company was formed and the Pioneer Column set forth for Mashonaland in 1890.

Kimberley had the air of solid comfort built on diamonds. The first town in Africa to have electric street lights, it had none of the zip of the Rand; none of the languidness of the Cape. When the Grand Hotel opened in 1871 it glamourised itself as the first 3 storey building north of the Orange River. The Kimberley Club became home to the magnates - the millionaires melting pot. The Sanatorium was built in 1897 as a recuperative hotel. In the Anglo-Boer War when Rhodes lived there it was a target for the gunners during the Siege of Kimberley. It became the Belgrave Hotel, and later a convent, and finally a museum. A direct hit on the Grand Hotel killed George Labran the American designer of the Long Cecil - the massive artillery gun built in the Be Beers workshops in only 3 weeks. It had a firing range of up to 6 miles. The Savoy Hotel was the colonial gem, whilst Rhodes' favourite bar, the Halfway House, was designed to serve restless travellers on the move. It obtained its unique licence because Rhodes could drink without dismounting from his horse.

The Egyptian Sphynx already featured in this 1890's advertisement for the Transvaal Hotel in Kimberley - in anticipation of a Cape to Cairo link

TRANSVAAL HOTEL

KIMBERLEY.

A. PETERSON, PROPRIETOR.

SUPERIOR ACCOMMODATION
for
TRAVELLERS AND BOARDERS.

PRIVATE SITTING ROOM
FOR FAMILIES.

Sample Room for Commercial Travellers.

BATH ROOM!
BILLIARDS!!

STABLING FOR OVER 100 HORSES.

The diamond diggers were clammering for machinery, ponderously brought up by ox wagon. Three months on the road from Cape Town to Kimberley was normal. When mule wagons appeared - providing a modicum of comfort and less delay, the ox-wagon was doomed. But where was the railway ?

As the iron horse puffed its way slowly northwards, distances for coach drivers shrank. The rail-head was the coaching terminus; a motley group of mobile stables which were quickly and easily shifted forward with the advancing rails. Some of the most efficient coach runners were the Gibson Brothers from England, (John, James and Fred). They wasted no time in taking over the makeshift services of their rivals. When they launched their 'Red Star Line' each coach was named after a Union Castle liner such as the 'Windsor Castle' or the 'Balmoral Castle' - an idea which brought little amusement to the long suffering passengers, who were obliged to address the coach driver as 'Captain'.

The dexterity of these drivers on the rough tracks was second to none. Apart from the passes through the mountains, no roads as such existed. Round hairpin bends and over swollen rivers they manoeuvred. Highway robbery, though not exactly rife, was none the less real; and after a while the drivers were armed. The odd parcel of Kimberley diamonds was

The Edwardian rustic Wolseley Hotel with its Sir Garnet Bar taken from the station platform, on the main line to the north from Cape Town

Snoozing away peacefully in the sunshine of the parched Karoo, the discreet and seductive Lord Milner Hotel, Matjiesfontein, was once an Officers convalescent home. At the height of the Anglo-Boer War, it became the largest remount depot in Africa, with 5000 horses and 10,000 troops camped out in the nearby veldt. Nearly 200 miles on the main line from Cape Town, trains still stop for a minute or two at the empty platforms, from where this picture was taken

hijacked, and bank takings occasionally disappeared without trace. The vehicles were built in America by the Wells Fargo Company and were described as 'leather springed cradle saloons'. They were the only vehicles which proved themselves in the deplorable conditions. If a capsize occurred, the body freed itself from the under-carriage, leaving the passengers hopefully intact whilst the team of horses or mules, generally 12 in number, bolted off into the blue. A dozen passengers were often crammed inside, with 6 or 8 more on top. Elbow room and toe space was limited, to say the least. The humour of passengers was all that kept sanity prevailing.

Lucy Sleeman recorded the discomforts:

"Every hour and a half we halted to change teams. At every halt the men got out and drank. No wonder. If I had been a man I would have done the same. But *noblesse oblige* ! We were women. We smiled amicably at heat, thirst, cramp and discomfort. We declared it wasn't bad, but privately wished we hadn't been born."

Until the coming of the railways, transport conditions did not improve.

Up through the winelands of the Cape, the iron horse was slowly advancing, with hiccups and inexplicable delays caused by ponderous government departments. From Worcester onwards the line snaked through the beautiful Hex River valley, and then began the climb to the dry dusty Karoo by curves and zig-zags, piercing the mountains by short tunnels and spanning the gullies by viaducts. Within a distance of 36 miles, it gained an altitude of over 3500 feet - slightly higher than Table Mountain. At Triangle Station snow fell. When the rails reached the

Karoo, it was a flat waterless domain that stretched towards Kimberley.

At Matjiesfontein a siding was laid in the bare Karoo dust. But the air was pure and dry and healthy. James Logan, the ex-railway porter who gained the catering concession for all the Cape Lines, created a magic environment to entice train passengers to enjoy his hospitality. He extended his whistle stop railway cafe to become the Lord Milner Hotel - destined to be the most discreet and seductive hotel on the Cape to Cairo route and a haven for celebrities and health seekers. It soon became the largest remount depot of the War in South Africa. Here Olive Schreiner, the woman whose intellect impressed Cecil Rhodes so vividly, lived and wrote.

Such was the jubilation when the line reached Beaufort West, that a firework display of detonators was laid out on the line. A nearby dynamite store went up in a flash and blew the top off an adjoining hill.

The plate-laying gangs toiled on, supplemented by teams of mixed Cape locals, Chinese, Japanese and Greeks. In the dry dusty heat of the open Karoo there were constant pauses for liquid refreshment. Wine from the Cape vineyards flowed more freely than it should have. At every completed section, celebrations ensued. Then 500 miles from Cape Town came the biggest celebration of all.

Brounger Junction was where the main lines met. The Western Cape joined the line from the Eastern Cape before continuing onwards to the Northern Cape and Kimberley. It was a tiny oasis where Bushmen and buck drank from the streams. A local farmer, sceptical of the iron horse, had sold his land in return for a wagon and a team of oxen. It had taken 8 years to conquer the 400 miles from Worcester - an average of only 50 miles a year. Not to be pipped at the post, such was the rivalry between the two companies that they both opened their lines on the same day. For the plate-laying gangs, hangers-on and followers from both camps the rivalry ended in tragedy. Sixty-eight of them lost their lives in an exuberant indulgence of drinking, quarrelling and in-fighting, only quelled by a troop of mounted infantry hastily rushed up on the new railway line.

Brounger Junction, soon to be renamed De Aar, opened out the whole of the Cape Colony, and significantly, many years later it became the graveyard of numerous fine steam locomotives, resting in rust-free oblivion in the dry central Karoo. Onwards lay Kimberley and the rich pickings of the unknown north.

Across the Karoo the line crept, linking farming communities whose only claim to fame was the astonishingly tender lamb nurtured off the harsh terrain, nibbling at the shrubs and mimosa trees loaded with all the ingredients for complete nutrition.

Working under the government contract were Harold and Harry Pauling. Whilst the line was advancing slowly and sporadically, they realised that all was not well with the departmental system, run on lines of favouritism, with payments by the hour irrespective of speed or efficiency. They set out to prove that incentives and penalties under private sub-contracts were the key to successful railway building, whereby diligent sub-contractors stood a chance to make their fame and fortune.

This was the way the great Railway Builders worked. The Engineering Consultant appointed the main Contractor, who in turn, gave sub-contracts to various individuals for parcels of work, such as an embankment, a cutting, culvert, or bridge - or even stretch of line. The sub-contractors in turn appointed the Gangers - in charge of each section, and they in turn appointed the Navvies. Progress and discipline was thus maintained, giving each individual a personal interest in achieving his goal.

From here onwards the rails raced forward across the open terrain, sometimes at an astonishing half a mile or more a day. Rails were laid on sleepers thrown on the dusty Karoo, and 'pinched in', when the ballast trucks followed. Much later, water tanks and wayside buildings were built under further contracts. The local coal was poor and scarce, so the engines ran on the imported Welsh variety, shipped out to the Cape; fuel was supplemented by fast growing gum trees from railway plantations along the line. Halts and hiccups were kept to a minimum, alcohol was banned and the recalcitrant Capetonians were replaced by gangs of Africans from the Eastern Cape who had joined the line at Brounger Junction. (De Aar).

The line ran past Three Sisters, where three upstanding koppies peaked out from the Karoo, visible from miles away. A distracted driver took his eyes off the signals, and the first major train crash occurred.

In this vicinity, there was an eerie feeling of invading foreign territory. The Afrikaners too were advancing north, for quite different reasons - to escape the British. Inevitably it happened. The big clash with the Iron Horse was beautifully described by Hedley Chilvers:

"An old Boer was one day on trek. His tented wagon, or ship of the veld, was headed along ravine and track into his Eldorado further north. At last he was well away from cursed Englishmen. From out of nowhere he came across two lines of shining rails, the purpose for which he did not know. Night was approaching and the lines made a suitable anchorage as he halted his wagon, outspanned his oxen and tied his wheels to the rails.

"Night fell. The farmer lit his pipe and gazed at the stars, and the mountains all around in the haze and the mist. Soon he heard a mysterious rumbling sound, and he saw a distant light, no doubt he thought, a Hottentot leading his ox-cart through the moonlight. All of a sudden the rumbling became violent. There was a hissing and roaring. The light shot towards him with fantastic speed. A long dark object raced ferociously at his poor wagon, smashed it to pieces and then disappeared into the night. The farmer stood up, shook a clenched fist at it and yelled: Verdomde Engelsman!"

Krankuil, an insignificant little farming dorp 20 miles from the Orange River, was the rail-head for a while. It was a summer evening, in the fading twilight, when Harry Pauling happened to be looking out of the window of his makeshift office. He saw 3 forlorn travellers tramping the dusty streets in search of a room for the night. These Afrikaners had been turned away by the unfriendly British. Even the hotel keeper had told them he was full. In a good hearted manner Pauling offered them a shake-down on the office floor and promised them an early morning call before the coach left the next day. This chance encounter was not forgotten by one of the Triumvirate, President Kruger of the Transvaal Republic, just back from Europe, where he had protested to the British Government about the annexation of the Transvaal.

The same little hotel became the favourite of steam enthusiasts. On the long straight run of over 50 miles the engine crews raced at up to 70 m.p.h out of sight in this waterless desert. Condensers were attached to the funnel exhausts, to turn the steam back to the engine many times over, whilst the firemen rhythmically fed thousands of pounds of coal into the firebox in the sweltering heat.

Eighty miles short of Kimberley the railway had reached the banks of the Orange River, an impenetrable barrier, which in full flood was over a quarter of a mile wide. No one had bridged a gap of this magnitude before. There were no funds from the Colonial Office in London and little interest from the Cape Colony, where Cecil Rhodes, now Prime Minister, was stamping his feet and brain-storming his complacent colleagues in his high pitched voice. Cut off in the Northern Cape, Kimberley was clamouring for transport. There was a bottle-neck of goods on the river banks waiting to go forward. The Chamber of Commerce was up in arms. Mining machinery, coal and grain was taking months to reach them. And the wealth of the Colony lay in Kimberleys hands.

Then things changed suddenly and dramatically. Into the cauldron of international power politics strode two more determined characters. President Kruger of the Transvaal Republic and Kaiser Wilhelm of Germany, Queen Victoria's grandson.

Germany's brush with Britain in Africa had started in 1883 on the Atlantic coast of South West Africa (Namibia). A dithering British Foreign Office had refused a very reasonable request from Germany to look after a few of their nationals. So an enterprising German trader Herr Luderitz hoisted the Imperial Eagle over his small trading settlement. Meanwhile the German Chancellor Bismarck had assured Britain that Germany had no intentions of colonial expansion in Africa. A year later, Luderitz's trading post was recognised as a German enclave; and on the other side of Africa a few months later, the German flag was hoisted over a Protectorate on the coastal strip of Tanganyika. This was where the real scramble for

*President Paul Kruger
of the South African
Republic*

Africa started.

In South West Africa, to add injury to insult, Germany had taken over the concessions granted by the local Chief to the courageous hunter Robert Lewis, who struggled on gamely without backing from Britain. Even Lord Salisbury grimly warned him: "We can't afford to go to war with Germany." Lewis was sacrificed on the altar of expediency and killed by a leopard.

President Kruger of the Transvaal Republic had parallel ideas. One of his aims was the building of a railway running right across Africa, almost along the 26 degree of latitude from Delagoa Bay (Lourenco Marques now Maputo) through Pretoria to Angua Pequena (Luderitz) on the Atlantic seaboard. Such a line would cross at right angles Rhodes' Cape to Cairo scheme.

The idea also suited the Portuguese, who had been eyeing a link across the continent between their long held territories of Mozambique and Angola. Whilst Kruger's Transvaal stood slap in the middle, a deal with Germany was on the cards. Rhodes realised that Germany would not stop at the Transvaal. A reason would be found to take it over and also annexe the adjoining Portuguese territory. "Poor little Portugal would not stand a chance. There would be a Germany from Angwa Pequena to Delagoa Bay", he told the Cape Parliament.

Spurred on by Rhodes, the sleeping British were beginning to rise like lions.

Whilst old President Kruger had been in Europe, he was seeking funds for his expansion, particularly into the Zambezi region to the north. In Germany he had been feted by the Kaiser. Suspicions were quickly aroused in London that the Boers and Germans might be planning to link their territories together across the sub-continent, cutting through Bechuanaland - immediately to the north of the Cape Colony.

The only unclaimed territory was the strategic Kalahari region of Bechuanaland (Botswana). This was now challenged.

If anyone knew its vital value, with its borders skirting the Witwatersrand only 160 miles away, it was Cecil Rhodes. He had already planned a small British settlement in a remote Kalahari desert location as a buffer zone against the borders of the new German South West African Protectorate.

And if the British Government weren't going to do anything to stop them, he was. He realised that the only way to spike the plans of Berlin and the Boers was to expand the Cape Colony up through this gap. "A wedge through the neck of the bottle" as he put it. The wedge would spear head the colonisation of the lands beyond the Limpopo, and across the Zambezi, to join up with the areas around the Great Lakes, already explored and settled by British traders and missionaries. Each area would be governed by its own Charter Company. What could be better than an East India Company, or a Hudson's Bay Company in the middle of Africa? - and all supplied through a "Suez Canal to the North" from the Cape.

Although eager to cooperate with the Boers, Rhodes' high hopes appeared to be dashed by Kruger's next action. In order to forestall British expansion, and encouraged by their President, a group of farmers had trekked with their ox-wagons over the border of Bechuanaland. They laid claim to large slices of land, forming self-styled Republics, in an area known as the *Rooi Grond* - the Red Ground - as much for the shade of the soil as for the colour of Rhodes' map.

This was all that was needed to finally spur the British Government into action.

Rhodes had already unsuccessfully tried to negotiate a withdrawal of these fillibusters. His party had arrived at Vryburg and installed themselves at a 'Government House', a stifling small tin shed, with a Union Jack. When the mattresses were moved out every morning the Governor's desk was moved back in. However, Rhodes was more at home in his wood and iron wagon parked nearby, where he ate, drank, slept and focused his attention on matters at hand. Even though he had received a classical education at Grammar School and Oxford, whilst his brothers had been to Eton and Winchester, he was a countryman at heart. He was more at ease with the pastoral Afrikaner on the veldt than the stiff brigade of the English Government. But Kruger didn't trust him; he didn't smoke and hardly slept.

So an expedition was hastily planned. The Warren Expedition, under Major General Warren, was 5000 strong, complete with artillery and observation balloons. In fact it was a kind of circus, but nevertheless a successful show of strength. Moving this cumbersome expedition was a logistical problem of some magnitude. Speed was essential, and the only way round it was to demand that the railway be extended. Every mile further forward would hasten the advance to the *Rooi Grond*.

Kaiser Wilhelm of Germany

The whole situation had fallen into Rhodes' lap like a dream come true. He even applied to join the expedition, much to the annoyance of General Warren, who mistrusted his motives, since Rhodes was acting for his own interests and Warren was acting for the Imperial Government. Besides, Warren was a staunch teetotaller, and

Rhodes liked a regular drop or two.

As for finance for the railway, the next stage across the Orange River to Kimberley would be provided partly from the Expedition's funds - for the permanent way of a hundred odd miles. Four tenders were submitted; the firm of Paulings won the contract.

"The one essential condition was rapidity in construction", George Pauling recalled. " At the outset I had to build a temporary bridge over the Orange River. The permanent structure was being built departmentally by the Government. One of the noblest bridges in South Africa, it consists of nine spans with a total length of 1230 feet, and it is one of the few bridges in that part of the country that remained intact at the end of the Anglo-Boer War. I made a deviation about a mile away and was able to throw across a bridge of heavy baulk timber, at a place where there were many rocks and rapids."

When the Boer farmers heard that an expedition had arrived at the Orange River and intended to advance to the *Rooi Grond*, most of these farmers brought their wagons and oxen down and hired themselves to the military authorities to transport troops and stores up to the *Rooi Grond*. When the Warren expedition arrived at its destination a somewhat Gilbertian situation naturally arose. There was no-one to fight because they were paying the majority of their enemies good money for transportation work. Later, some of the expeditionary forces were given farms along the border with the Transvaal. Very soon they sold these farms, for next to nothing, under British title, to the same farmers who had intended to form a Republic. "One has to be up early to get the better of a Boer farmer" quipped Pauling.

The Kimberley contract was completed in a record six months, four times faster than the previous average. In part this was achieved by banning alcohol and working flat out with reliable sub-contractors always on the move. Pauling had proved his point, but had trodden on some vulnerable toes.

There were jealous elements lurking in the background, elements of a fifth column within the creaking framework of the Cape Government Railways. Who were these Paulings? - they mumbled. With a finger in every pie, in every contract in the Cape. There was even a Pauling at the top, running the whole show.

Their noses had definitely been put out of joint. They were no longer in charge of dispensing favours in the right direction. They were intent on revenge.

When the line reached Kimberley, no plans had been drawn up or presented. Only a brief comparison with previous similar works on railways had been specified.

"In the time required for completion of the line it was impossible to make an accurate survey or estimate of the cost," recalled Pauling. " I had tendered for work I understood to be provisional, and similar to other contracts. I was aware of several places where much work could be carried out without adding to the costs of the line."

Unaware of the consistent hostility of government officials, Pauling took a gamble and lost. When it came to the crunch the nit-pickers produced some real nasties. They insisted on buildings seven times larger than all similar previous stations; with heavy masonry work unheard of anywhere in the Empire. And in order to make sure he was really down and out, they insisted that the Kimberley station approaches should be blasted out of hard rock several feet below ground level

Pauling tried in vain to salvage the situation. Backed by his workers and sub-contractors, and with a reputation as a pugilist, he took matters in hand. He went round to the house of the arch-culprit, the Chief Government Engineer, and in full view of his colleagues, threw him to the ground. Picking him up, he threw him back against his snivelling wife, grovelling in the doorway.

THE HOTEL BELGRAVE,
KIMBERLEY.

A First-Class Hotel, replete with every convenience, unsurpassed in South Africa for Comfort, Luxury and Style.
Magnificent Hall and Lounge.
Billiard Room (free to Visitors). Tennis and Croquet Courts.
All applications for accommodation to be addressed to the Manageress.
P.O. Box 292. Tel. Add. : " BELGRAVE."

THE Hotel of Kimberley, # THE SAVOY.
NEWLY RENOVATED.
Large Spacious Dining Room, with Palm Court adjoining.
First Class Accommodation. Cuisine Unrivalled.
Nearest Hotel from the Railway Station, to the G.P.O. and Market Square.
Special Terms to Commercials and Professionals.
Twelve Large SAMPLE ROOMS in the Centre of the City, fitted up in the Latest Style
Twelve Lock-up Garages.
L. DAVIS, PROPRIETOR.
Phone 293. Telegrams: " SAVOY." P.O. Box 231.
Appointed Hotel for Cook & Son's Tourists.

GRAND HOTEL, Market Square, KIMBERLEY.

THE MOST UP-TO-DATE HOTEL IN THE CITY.
CENTRALLY SITUATED. **CUISINE UNEXCELLED.**
Spacious Sample Rooms and 12 Separate Lock-up Garages.
SPECIAL TERMS TO COMMERCIALS.
Phones: { Office 17. P.O. Box 17.
{ Visitors 0013. Tel. Address : GRAND.
Under the Management and Personal Supervision of the
Proprietor. D. SIERADZKI.

QUEEN'S HOTEL
KIMBERLEY.
The most modern and comfortable Hotel.
Situated in the heart of the City.
Renovated throughout and further excellent Bedrooms, Bathrooms, etc., added.
HENRY ORKIN, Proprietor.
TELEGRAMS : " QUEENS." PHONES { OFFICE 267.
{ VISITORS 0013.

Pauling bankrupted his company. His old friend Moses Cornwall, the High Sheriff of Kimberley warned him to lie low to avoid arrest.

Great uncle Henry Pauling was indeed chief of the whole creaking apparatus, and also responsible for this huge waste of money. He was an influential Mason and Roving Magistrate for no less than 27 districts, ranging the entire distance between Kimberley and Cape Town. This appointment was virtually unparalleled and had a lot to do with his freedom of movement up and down the line. But he was also shortly due for retirement from government service; so however irksome, he was likely to side with his own department.

Railway surveyor's commissariat and sqaud

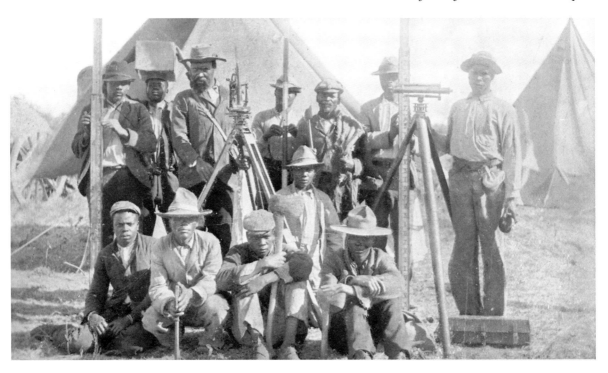

4

CAPE NORTH

KIMBERLEY TO VRYBERG 1890

"*When Rhodes stands on Table Mountain his shadow falls across the Zambezi*" is how the American visitor Mark Twain adeptly surveyed the situation.

The year 1890 saw Cecil Rhodes master of almost all that he gazed on. He was now Prime Minister of the Cape Colony and also Managing Director of the Chartered Company, an amalgamation of his own British South Africa Company and the rival Bechuanaland Companies. His pioneer column had left from Kimberley, crossed the Limpopo River and hoisted the Union Jack over Fort Salisbury (Harare) in his newly claimed land of Rhodesia (Zimbabwe).

The Bechuanaland Companies, under the direction of George Cawston and Lord Gifford, had for some time been keenly advancing where Rhodes wished to tread, with plans for a railway and mineral explorations northwards through the 'neck in the bottle'. These two entrepreneurs had impeccable connections. Gifford was an aristocrat with colonial contacts, and Cawston a stockbroker 'in' with British and French bankers. They were in a stronger position than anyone to obtain a Charter over Bechuanaland and Matabeleland. And they had been encouraged by the British Government of Lords Salisbury and Knutsford - Prime and Colonial Ministers respectively - who had originally thought Rhodes a dodgy individual.

Eventually it dawned on this sensible pair that Rhodes was, in fact, the one man who could solve all Britain's problems in Central Africa in one fell swoop... carrying the can for their own imperial ideas without recourse to the British Exchequer; taking the brunt of territorial clashes with Germany, Portugal or the Transvaal; and supporting British settlers around Lake Nyasaland. As head of the British South Africa Company - *the Chartered Company*, Rhodes took on his shoulders all these burdens, which otherwise would have landed on the plate of the spendthrift Government. In other words he was 'indispensable to the Empire'. The Pall Mall Gazette warmed to the idea of "a gigantic Amalgamated Company... to colour all that was left of unappropriated Central Africa British Red." It spoke enthusiastically of "patriotic millionaires ready to subsidise our Empire rather than allow the backbone of Africa to slip out of our hands"

Rhodes sent forth a chum from Oxford days, Charles Rudd, with a couple of colleagues to bargain with King Lo Bengula for mineral rights in his Matabeleland territory between the Limpopo and the Zambezi. This was the one natural barrier that could stop this marauding military despot, of Zulu descent, who treated his Mashona neighbours like 'dogs', and the Barotse people across the river not much better. After months of waiting outside the Royal Kraal, the Rudd Concession was signed and sealed.

The British South Africa Company also secured mineral rights through to the Great Lakes.

In the territory around Lake Nyasa (Lake Malawi), Harry Johnston, the fiery Administrator, was keen to find a transport route - without touching Portuguese territory, which would fit in nicely with an overall Cape to Cairo scheme - perhaps a spur to the Shiré Highlands. Lord Salisbury was also enthusiastic about the idea, and as convinced as Livingstone was of the potential of Central Africa, and of the need to prevent the Germans, the Belgians and the Portuguese from dividing the territory between them. However there was no money forthcoming, and Salisbury was not prepared to cause a Cabinet crisis. The Treasury, run by the blinkered George Joachim Goschen, would not provide even the modest amount necessary to maintain a British sphere of influence, or sanction any 'imperial adventure' north of the Zambezi. Goschen was the son of a German merchant, and his secretary was the German born Alfred Milner, shortly to become Commissioner for the Cape.

When Rhodes met Johnston in London in 1889, they discussed finances till three o'clock in the morning at the Westminster Palace Hotel. Rhodes parted with an offer that could hardly be refused. "You are to see Lord Salisbury at once" he told Johnston, "Give Lord Rothschild as my reference... say that if the money is the only hindrance to our striking north from the Zambezi to the headwaters of the Nile I will find the money. What was attempted by Alexander and Napoleon we practical people are going to finish." Johnston was handed a large cheque and the British Government was promised £10,000 a year to administer the district in return for granting Rhodes his coveted Charter. "Tell Lord Salisbury it shall go on as long as I live, and I'll make provision for it to go on longer, after my death."

This tidy and timely approach of having 'bought' the Government ensured that Rhodes now had concessions in nearly every corner of central Africa.

He now engineered a meeting with one of the few people to compete with Rothschilds influence in the field of finance. She was the aged Countess Burdett-Coutts, scion of the powerful banking family, who held sway from her strategic mansion at No. 1 Stratton Street, Piccadilly, London. Through missionary contacts, Rhodes was invited to dinner to obtain her patronage, as well as the Royal blessing of the Prince of Wales. Two Dukes - Fife and Abercorn, now joined the Board of the Chartered Company.

His main aim was now to extend his rail and telegraph lines to the Zambezi and beyond, through the 'neck in the bottle', or his 'Suez Canal to the north.' He wrote to Chamberlain: "I am anxious to take over the Bechuanaland Protectorate at once."

Reluctantly Rhodes had relinquished his idea of persuading Kruger to join up with a railway through the Orange Free State and the Transvaal Republic, and so create an inter-dependent Common Market, and, ultimately, political union. The intransigent Kruger would have none of it. He wanted to retain all the revenue from railway traffic through his domain. He also clung to his cherished dream of an exclusive outlet to the sea, avoiding British territory altogether - perhaps with a line to a Portuguese port such as Delagoa Bay (Lourenco Marques, now Maputo). Though Rhodes recognised to the end that nothing could be achieved in Africa without the general cooperation of the Afrikaner, and eventually the African, he abandoned his plan.

No longer would the line cross "the great, grey-green, greasy Limpopo River, all set about with fever trees" of his good friend Kipling's verse.

Sir Charles Theophilus Metcalfe (1853 - 1928), the English Baronet and Consulting Engineer with Fox and Sons had already surveyed a line from Kimberley northwards for the Bechuanaland Companies. He more than anyone, from the beginning, was looking wistfully beyond the Zambezi, and was longing for that great link with the Nile Valley via the Great Lakes. A talented and focused engineer of the old school, this itinerant aristocrat had met Rhodes at Oxford, and had caught up with him in Kimberley. He exuded an aura of 'establishment' and integrity unequalled by many of Rhodes' dubious associates. A rare born aristocrat with an Engineering degree, he also brought a certain *savoir faire* to the railway profession generally. His imperial roots were impeccable. Scion of a family linked to the Indian Colonial Service for four generations, Metcalfe's father had been a member of the Council of Madras. He was also descended, on his mother's side, from the French Huguenot Debonnaire family of the Cape Colony. His great uncle had been provisional Governor General of India, and then Governor General of Canada. The family name Theophilus carried all the overtones of classical colonial

Sir Charles Theophilus Metcalfe (1853 - 1928) the itinerant aristocrat and Consulting Engineer for the Cape to Cairo Railway was Rhodes' closest confidant

administration in the service of God and Empire. Metcalfe himself was destined to spend the best part of his down-to-earth life working with railway and bridge contractors throughout British Africa.

Together with Jameson, and shy 'Little Alfred' Beit, Metcalfe was Rhodes' closest and most constant companion, enjoying a mutual respect which brought about a certain animosity amongst the inner circle. A jovial bachelor with an impish sense of humour and a fund of good stories, Metcalfe - like the Colossus - was exclusively wedded to the Cape to Cairo concept. He never married. He was Rhodes right hand man and his "best and most intimate friend" according to his secretary Jourdan. They travelled together extensively, and Metcalfe, with Jameson, was with him at the very end.

Alongside one of the most beautifully positioned rail lines in the world, which winds down the peninsula of the Cape of Good Hope to where the Atlantic and Indian Oceans nominally meet at the end of Africa, lies Muizenberg. Squeezed between the mountains on one side, and the windswept shore on the other, "white as sands of Muizenberg spun before the gale", as Kipling put it, stands Rhode's Cottage, where Metcalfe and Jameson took their leave of him in 1902.

As a partner in the renamed Sir Douglas Fox and Partners, Charles Metcalfe was in reality the foremost protagonist of the Cape to Cairo concept as the 'Iron Spine and Ribs of Africa'. He urged Rhodes on and kept him on course. Privy to most of his schemes and dreams, he was one of the few who was able to translate 'northwards expansion' into economically viable, cast-iron reality. As early as 1888 Metcalfe had called the Bechuanaland Railway the 'Central Trunk Line of Africa.' Rhodes had thought it over-ambitious and wanted a more local title. By the time the railway had reached Bulawayo, and was aiming onwards across the Zambezi, he thought the title not a bad one.

*Not to be confused with Sir Arthur Lawley, the contemporary African Administrator

When Metcalfe's sister Kate married Alfred Leonard Lawley* (1861-1935), the Worcestershire born farmer's son who had been 'nourished on beer from the age of six months', and then became a mining engineer and a partner of Pauling & Company, the triangle was, in a way, fully complete. For it was to the Paulings that Rhodes turned to lay the rails of the Iron Snake, and much of this burden fell on the indefatigable Lawley.

**Source: S.A. Almanac 1905

In those heroic years of railway construction a century ago, the firm of Pauling and Company excelled. They built more railways on the continent of Africa than all the other construction companies put together.**

There was something almost buccaneering in the way this family had moved around the world of pioneer lines, in Greece, Syria, Borneo, India, China, South America, but especially in Africa. They had been involved in construction work of one kind or another since Elizabethan times. An early Pauling was one of the builders of St. Paul's Cathedral under Christopher

Wren. Later a Pauling had helped build Somerset House and the British Museum. Another Pauling was a partner in the firm of Brassey, Henfrey and Pauling, run by the titan Thomas Brassey, the man who more than any other symbolised Britain's expanding world-wide railway achievements. In the Crimea War a Pauling was a contractor on the British Military Railways from Balaclava to Sevastopol - that memorable contract when a few hundred navvies emerged with considerably more credit than Her Majesty's armed forces.* He ended up as Resident Railway Engineer at Delhi at the time of the Indian Mutiny. His son was George Pauling (1855 -1919).

Equal to the stiff competition between contractors was the rivalry between the cumbersome civil service and slick private enterprise. It ran right through the stream of railway building everywhere. It was George Pauling's *bete noir* - his loathing of the wasteful departmental system versus the contract system which invariably worked out quicker and cheaper:

"In all my experience whenever I have tried to obtain work from any office connected with the British Government, I have always been blocked by the same departmental system. It is my opinion simply a form of jealousy on the part of officials and the desire to have at their disposal a large amount of patronage in the shape of dispensing appointments and placing orders."

Rhodes realised the value of all this. Where the Cape Government or the Imperial Government could not, or would not, come up with the where-with-all, he turned to Paulings, who succeeded largely by their dealings with the banking house of Erlanger's, and the close association forged between George Pauling and the Barons d'Erlanger, father and son.

Rhodes admired Pauling's astonishing ability to build railways at the lowest costs per mile of any contractor. He trusted him implicitly, though this was occasionally not reciprocated. Pauling observed:

"Whilst recognising his many great qualities which history will endorse - in common with all other great personalities, he had his weaknesses. He was particularly susceptible to the plaudits of the public, which made him bumptious, and at times he seemed utterly heartless. There were also instances when he promised anything to attain his ends, and afterwards was unable to carry out his promise. But no criticism, however justified, can challenge his right to the title of Colossus." This was the only appropriate nickname for one of those Wonders of the World, like the ancient Colossus of Rhodes.

In his hasty visits to Groote Schuur, Pauling the Contractor was more than likely to meet both Rhodes and Metcalfe, the Consulting Engineer. Undoubtedly there were differences between the two parties, usually over such matters as deviations in surveys, or short cuts in alignments. The Contractor's lot was not always a happy one. Specifications were strict and

*In 1854 large British and French armies were besieging the Russians at Sevastopol. With neither clothes, food, medicine, nor ammunition, they were freezing to death and there were no roads and no organisation. The Generals had forgotten the Crimean Winter. Brassey, Peto and other British railway kings organised a well-paid volunteer force of a few hundred navvies and engineers to sail out from England. Strictly under civilian control, in the middle of winter on the most arduous terrain, they built a total of 29 miles of double track railway from the port of Balaclava up to the fortress of Sevastopol in only 2 months. Sevastopol fell a year later

detailed. For instance, no more than 2000 sleepers to the mile ensured proper earthworks. The Resident Field Engineer, under the Consulting Engineers, had complete discretion to instruct the Contractors to alter or deviate any culverts or cuttings, as the line advanced. If the Contractor did not employ enough men on the works, the Engineer had the right to take on more; he also had the right to sack any of the Contractor's men. Although a large and powerful contractor like Pauling could impose what conditions he liked on sub-contractors, he too worked for a completion date under the threat of fines and penalties from the Engineering Consultants. These rigorous conditions were bound to cause constant friction, both on the ground and in the office. But at the end of the day these competing entrepreneurs, Metcalfe and Pauling, shared an utter contempt for bureaucracy and a deep dislike of Civil Service politics. The overriding factor was to get the job done with the least possible delay and the lowest possible cost - an average of under £4000 per mile over the entire permanent way.

And for all this, George Pauling had a remarkable knack of being able to ride over a proposed route and predict with accuracy the exact cost without recourse to complicated calculations. When construction commenced he was able to deviate the route slightly to take advantage of economies in the lie of the land without increasing the gradient or distance, and so profited accordingly. And the costs per mile of Pauling's lines were consistently less than anywhere else in the whole of Africa.

Genial and gregarious, every inch a builder of the Victorian Empire, he was a railway contractor in the true sense of the word. Ready with his fists, whenever necessary, in the rough and tumble of the saloons of the frontier towns,

Alfred Lawley, George Pauling and Harold Pauling

he profited out of sheer hard grist. Unlike the diamond kings and gold speculators of the day who won and lost fortunes overnight by buying and selling claims, Pauling made his money by forging through Africa the lengthy laborious way. Not surprisingly he spoke Afrikaans and a sprinkling of Portuguese.

Of the 3 railway giants of central and southern Africa - Charles Metcalfe, George Pauling and Alfred Lawley, who symbolised the larger than life spirit of the times, Pauling easily won the rear view stakes for unreasonable girth. He lamented that he was never able to record a weight below 16 stone (102 kg). His legendary appetite ensured that wherever he went his reputation followed. "There is much virtue in a good appetite", he reflected, "so long as one is able to foot the bill."

On his visits to London he often lunched at the Cafe Royal in Regent Street, at that time the haunt of the art and literary crowd, including Oscar Wilde, and within a stone's throw of the Cork Street offices of the Charter Company. Baron d'Erlanger, the financier, records that on one occasion, wishing to get hold of him, he telephoned the restaurant and spoke to the head waiter, who, being unfamiliar with his customer, confided: "Do you mean the gentleman who has 4 grouse for his lunch every day?"

Long after Rhodes death, these three railway giants were happily working together right through Africa.

Charles Metcalfe and George Pauling survey the view from the edge of the Victoria Falls

In January 1890 Rhodes made an agreement with the Cape Government. They agreed to build the line from Kimberley northwards into Bechuanaland, and his Chartered Company would complete it. Away from Parliament in June he received word that the government was proposing to change its mind and abandon the line. He rushed back to Cape Town and made a spirited defence of the whole railway plan. The Cabinet resigned, and Rhodes was elected Prime Minister. Had he not defeated the Cape Government on this railway issue, the outcome of the line and of Rhodes' fortunes could have been altogether different.

Rhodes brought in his own Cabinet team. One of the most disreputable of all his first Ministers was James Sivewright, the clever young man who ran Railways, Telegraphs and Public Works. He was involved in unscrupulous corruption on a grand scale in gas and water contracts around Johannesburg. But his most spectacular scandal was in single-handedly awarding to a railway porter, James Logan, the exclusive contract for all the Refreshment Rooms throughout the entire Cape Railway system for a period of 18 years. When the scandal broke, Rhodes reckoned he could not do without Sivewright, and backed him. This outrage caused the resignation of the finest and most honourable members of Rhodes' first Cabinet, including John Merriman. It undoubtedly opened the way for other cronies to propel Rhodes into the disastrous Jameson Raid, which caused the awful ill-will that led to the Anglo-Boer War, and the international mistrust which sowed the seeds of World War One. Rudyard Kipling later called the Jameson Raid "the first battle of the 1914 - 18 War". Almost unbelievably, on Rhodes' recommendation, Sivewright was knighted, for ostensibly having persuaded President Kruger to link up the Cape Railway with the Netherlands Railway through the Orange Free State. This was undoubtedly Rhodes' greatest blunder, and all caused by railway refreshment rooms.

When it came to catering contracts, Rhodes never learnt his lesson. Scottie Hudson, one of his many hangers-on and riding companions, was also under the wing of James Sivewright. Both men's fathers had been arti-sans on the Duke of Fife's estate in Scotland. One morning out riding, Rhodes asked Scottie if there was anything he particularly wanted. "I will have to think about it", said Scottie diffidently. "Well don't let me do the thinking for you," replied Rhodes. Next day, after having consulted James Sivewright, Scottie advanced: "I'd like the catering contract for the new railway." "Is that all," replied Rhodes, "I thought you'd want the whole damn railway. See Metcalfe about it." Charles Metcalfe was very sceptical about Scottie's ability and highly suspicious of his connection with Sivewright. Nevertheless he gave him the catering contract for a section of the line into Mashonaland. Shortly afterwards, Scottie sold the concession, making a very handsome profit indeed.

The most able of Rhodes' associates, John Merriman, had left the Cabinet. Having started as a surveyor in the Eastern Cape, he became a Cape Town Wine Merchant and pioneered both the canning of Crayfish and the export of fruit to Europe. He was also a newspaper correspondent. He missed making a fortune in Kimberley after he opposed and lost against Rhodes' amalgamation of the diamond fields. As an MP he also struck it unlucky. Whilst Treasurer General he travelled to England to obtain a loan for the Cape Government, and in 1892 started secret nego-tiations with the Portuguese Government in Lisbon to purchase part of Delagoa Bay (Lourenco Marques now Maputo) in order to thwart Kruger's line to the coast. The aim was to ensure the Transvaal Republic would be reliant on the lines through the Cape Colony. But Portugal would neither sell nor lease either the Port or its railway.

Four days after the Royal Assent had been given to Rhodes' Charter for the British South Africa Company, railway work began northwards from Kimberley, since one of the conditions imposed an immediate start to the surveyed line.

Having carried forward the lines through the Eastern and Western Cape, and up through the Karoo as far as Kimberley, George Pauling was well placed to steam on, but was for the time being out of the equation. His recent 'punch up' with railway inspectors put paid to further immediate involvement. Fortunately his great uncle Henry Pauling (1821-1893) had just retired from the Cape Railways, having served them from the beginning. He had married the granddaughter of Alexander Biggar, that illustrious soldier-administrator from Hampshire, who had led a group of the first 1820 settlers and had become the Chief Magistrate (Landrost) of Durban.

Fortuitously too, his impatient cousin Harold was keen to join the push forward. A face saving formula was found to dilute the influence of the government railway department. The contract was split between the Cape Government Railways and Rhodes' Chartered Company, the latter providing the finance for the 125 mile extension to Vryberg. The line was then taken over by the Cape Government. Lucas and Airds who had tendered much lower for the contract, were paid compensation.

It was a happy combination of slick private enterprise and cumbersome civil service, which boded well for the future of the 'Cape to Cairo'.

Under Harold Pauling's adroit direction it was plain sailing. Fifty miles north lay Warrenton, the dorp where Rhodes and Kruger had sized each other up at the conclusion of the Warren Expedition. Within a stone's throw the line crossed a quarter-mile-long bridge over the Vaal River at Fourteen Streams. Passengers looked in vain to behold any sign of 14 streams; more often than not they saw no streams at all.

Vryberg, the Capital of Bechuanaland, remained the railway terminus for some time to come. A lonely, flyblown and unattractive little dorp, this was the erstwhile capital of the short-lived Stelleland Republic. Gateway to the north for missionaries and traders it became the 'Texas of South Africa' - a ranching and dairy centre on the edge of the Kalahari.

From the rail-head at Vryberg, and the Grand and Central Hotels, many hopeful trekkers followed on the heels of the Pioneer Column who had just raised the Union Jack over Fort Salisbury. Rhodes turned back when he foresaw the 1000 mile journey ahead of him, in a jolting wagon through torrential downpours that cut the road for months on end. The railway was even more desperately needed to feed his new settlements of Fort Salisbury and Bulawayo. Metcalfe urged the reluctant Rhodes to press on. However, he turned his attention to the construction of a line *via* the much shorter route to Mashonaland from Beira, on the east coast of Mozambique.

Long delays lay ahead on the route to Bulawayo. It was an unnerving distance even for the iron horse. The first part was waterless, and the last part menaced by the Matabele. Limited finance was eventually found. Interrupted from his gold mining activities, George Pauling recalled:

"I was summoned by telegram from Barberton to Cape Town, where Mr. Rhodes wished to see me about the extension of the line from Vryberg to Mafeking. In the early 1890's finance was hard to come by, and there was a delay of nearly two years before a deal was finally struck."

Mining shares were pledged to Rothschilds Bank for a loan. The firm of Lucas & Airds had also been competing for the job, and the price was shaved to a minimum in order to clinch the deal. Pauling commented:

"We talked over the scheme and I was not happy with some of the details. Mr. Rhodes assured me that if I was to accept on the terms proposed he would do everything in his power to obtain contracts for my firm the whole way through. This was the first instance I heard of him talk of a Cape to Cairo link, and it was the beginning of what could be truthfully termed the main impetus of the line to the north.

"I entered into a contract which was signed at midnight after a dinner at which Sir Charles Metcalfe and I were the guests of Mr. Rhodes."

The dining room at Groote Schuur was dominated by the only decent painting Rhodes ever purchased. A portrait of an aristocratic young lady by Joshua Reynolds took pride of place over the fireplace.

"Now I have my woman, I am happy." he declared.

SPORT IN BECHUANALAND AND THE KALAHARI.

DIXON'S HOTEL,

MAFEKING, BECHUANALAND,

IS ninety-six miles from the Railway Terminus at Vryburg on the Direct Road to the Bechuanaland Protectorate, Matabelelaand, Mashonaland, and the Zambesi. The Hotel is one of the finest in South Africa, and is patronised by the Administrator, Sir Sidney Shippard, Colonel Sir Frederick Carrington, the Hon. Cecil Rhodes, and all Sportsmen going into the Interior. Replete with every comfort. Smoking, Dining, Drawing, Billiard, and Reading Rooms. Three Bath Rooms (Shower Bath). Stabling for Forty Horses.

INCLUSIVE TERMS, 10s. 6d. PER DAY.

Attached to the Hotel are the large Wholesale and Retail Stores of Messrs. Dixon & Co., As excellent Big Game Shooting may be enjoyed about Six Days from Mafeking, this well-known firm will provide capable Guides for Sportsmen, Ammunition and Arms of every ... ion, Waggons and Oxen, Complete Outfits, &c., at reasonable rates.

The Royal Mail Coaches to and from Vryburg to Palapye, Macloutsie, and Mashonaland arrive and depart from Dixon's Hotel.

DIXON & CO. ⎰ MAFEKING, BECHUANALAND.
⎰ DUTOITSPAN, GRIQUALAND WEST.
⎱ BEACONSFIELD, GRIQUALAND WEST.

The 106 mile extension, at £2000 per mile, was completed in a few months under Harold Pauling's well drilled plate-layers. It steamed right through the middle of Stelleland and Goshen, previously claimed as Boer Republics. On one side lay the golden Transvaal, and on the other the shifting sands of the Kalahari Desert. The easy going on the open plateau so enthralled the gangs that after a straight stretch of nearly 30 miles they named the station Paradise.

Mafeking was a frontier settlement near the Transvaal border when the rails arrived in 1894. Hotels sprang up in this springboard for explorers, prospectors and hunters.

5

THE GLITTER AND THE GOLD

RAILS TO THE RAND

Kimberley was still the rail-head and the hub of mining operations, when hundreds of miles further north Gold was discovered. All eyes were now on an extension of the rail link to the Transvaal border. Beyond that the permanent way was blocked and was to remain so for a further 8 years. Though not part of the main Cape to Cairo Railway, the route to Johannesburg was nevertheless of paramount importance in the subcontinent's economic development, for through the fastest growing city in the world passed nearly all the protagonists in this saga.

Sitting in a land-locked backwater 6000 feet above sea level, President Paul Kruger of the Transvaal Republic was surrounded by some astonishing pastoral Afrikaners. Their only break from the wind and dust were the sparkling streams which gave the name to the region - The Witwatersrand - "The ridge of white waters". Unbeknown to them, they were sitting on the richest gold fields in the world.

Staunchly loyal to the countries of their roots, Holland and France, and open to German overtures, many of the Boers were not just, understandably, against Imperial British or Cape Government Railways. They were also opposed to almost any involvement with the 'Iron Horse'. They considered it "an invention of the devil", and a threat to their traditional livelihood of trekking ox wagons across the Old Transvaal. Besides, they looked on railway workers generally as "drunk, immoral and inclined to cohabit with native women."

Although he believed to his dying day that the Earth was flat, and that horizons were figments of the imagination, President Kruger was far-sighted and well travelled. He realised the vital necessity of a rail link to develop the riches of the Rand. He and his railway enthusiasts wanted their own independent outlet to the sea, preferably at Delagoa Bay (the bay of Lourenco Marques, now Maputo) far away from British influence. For some time, Kruger and his predecessor President Burgers had been trying to finance such a scheme. But the Transvaal Republic, in spite of its hidden wealth, was almost bankrupt. It had no revenue, no trade and was in debt to banks. It couldn't even pay the meagre salaries of its public servants. So restrictive was the mining legislation that the hordes of prospectors working feverishly away, ducked across the borders into Natal or the Cape Colony to sell their gold dust. The cost of even the shortest rail link was triple the total annual revenues of the Transvaal and Orange Free States combined. A trip to Holland had produced a paltry £94,000

A derogatory cartoon of Rhodes linking the manipulation of 'Kaffirs' - the term used for South African Mining shares, with the imagined exploitation of native labour, brought to the cities by the Cape to Cairo Railway. As the first exponent of globalisation techniques in communications, Rhodes was the greatest of all succesful 'Doers and Dreamers' with llittle Imperial backing. He founded an Empire, including De Beers, that has endured unchallenged. A hundred years after his death, he was voted Europe's greatest Businessman of the 19th and 20th centuries by Eurobusineess Magazine (Milleniun Edition).

from a sceptical Dutch Government. Most of this went on railway materials from Dutch companies, shipped out to Delagoa Bay, and then left to rust on the shore.

Whilst Rhodes' railway pushed northwards from Kimberley, the coach traffic on the main road to Johannesburg developed into undreamt of proportions. Gibson Brothers had joined forces with George Heys, and together they ran over 50 coaches with 1800 mules and horses. Nearly 100 changing stations were built of wood and galvanised iron, which were easily transported and assembled ahead of the advancing rail-head. Each building accommodated dozens of animals plus storage for fodder and stablemen. They stood 8 to 10 miles apart over the entire distance of the coach run. Such was the efficiency of the service that the fastest Mail Service covered the 300 miles from Kimberley to Johannesburg in $2\frac{1}{2}$ days, travelling day and night, virtually at the gallop. Smaller transport firms, as well as farmers far and near joined the rush. And almost every conceivable contraption on two wheels, with draught animals of every description, were pressed into service.

A small army of men were employed; grooms, blacksmiths and harness makers; wagon repairers, caterers and forage merchants. Vets were in short supply. During the height of the rindepest outbreak the stench from unburied oxen, horses, mules and donkeys, fallen by the wayside was often unbearable. Lightning storms along the ironstone ridges also took their toll. On one occasion a wagon driver with his full team of eighteen oxen was instantly struck dead.

After the first payable gold reef was discovered by George Harrison, an Australian prospector, the gold rush surged, week after week, month after month. Steamers from Europe were packed with fortune hunters, and the limited train services to the north were running at high pressure, jammed to full capacity with travellers sleeping in corridors, guards vans and trucks.

Rich men, poor men, good men, doubtful men and downright bad men; navy men and army men (some deserters), tinkers, tailors, clerks and shopkeepers, diamond and gold diggers. Ladies of fame and fortune, and ladies of the night. Tin miners from Cornwall and coal miners from Newcastle and Wales. Miners from Australia and Alaska, Canada and California; butchers, bakers, scavengers and thieves, plus the flotsam and jetsam of all nationalities and creeds.

Lucy Sleeman described their ambitions:

"Barmaids and shopgirls slipped about on the dance floors. Why not ? The wives of the "upper ten" had many of them been barmaids and shop-girls not so very long ago. Besides a lucky find might make a lowly miner a rich man in the twinkling of an eye."

Fortunes were being made and lost overnight as claims were pegged, and then sold; but no one knew for certain how deep the gold reef went, or how far it ran.

Railway engineers were on the make too.

"In those days Johannesburg was a very small place" recalled Pauling, "with a few single storey brick houses, some offices with iron roofs and a number of huts and tents. The township had been laid out by the Transvaal government, and my brother Harry bought 40 of the first central building plots at £10 each. He had relied on one of my old masons coming up from

Kimberley to erect a few brick and iron roof shanties, and thus "develop" the properties. This man failed him however and Harry accepted £50 profit on the deal.

"A few days after I arrived, Mr. Rhodes, Dr. Hans Sauer and some other Kimberley people reached Johannesburg, and I had a long conversation with Mr. Rhodes about the prospects of the Rand. Up to this time only a few rich properties had been struck. What is now the main reef was the only reef then known, and I told Mr. Rhodes I was sure it would not yield more than 8 or 10 pennyweights to the ton."

The gold was very fine and floury and difficult to catch. The other leaders which were ultimately found to be very rich and which established the success of the Rand had not by that time been discovered.

"It was years afterwards before I learned that Mr. Rhodes agreed to my view. We happened to be fellow passengers on a ship from Delagoa Bay to Beira. Walking up and down the deck one night he said to me in his characteristic abstracted way: 'You were right Pauling'. This enigmatic observation was beyond my comprehension and I asked him what he meant. He replied: 'It was right what you said about the Rand'. No one had then dreamt of the possibility of the leaders being found, of the existence of coal or of the cyanide extraction process which followed."

Like so many others, Pauling stuck his neck out, and had he been able to hold on, would have won three fortunes. "In my own business I have made few mistakes, but I have constantly been persuaded to participate in all kinds of extraneous adventures," he admitted. 'Cobbler stick to your last,' was the adage he followed thereafter.

On the look-out for new railway contracts, he befriended the State Mining Engineer for the Transvaal, Mr. Woodford. A fortuitous introduction to President Kruger was arranged. The two Englishmen met on the verandah of the President's fine Victorian dwelling in Pretoria at the unusual hour of 5.30 in the morning, whilst they conversed partly in Dutch. They sat in a haze of cigar smoke from Pauling and heavy pipe smoke from Kruger, who had already breakfasted and read a large portion of the Bible. He was dressed in his customary black suit which accentuated his rock like massiveness. Pauling recounted:

"Having ascertained my name, he stated that it was not unfamiliar to him, for a Pauling had once befriended him when he was sadly in need." It so happened that ten years previously the President, with two Dutch companions known as the Triumvirate, had just returned from England where they had protested to the British Government about the annexation of the Transvaal. They were on their way up by train from Cape Town, and the rail-head at that time was not far from Kimberley at Krankuil. Forlornly tramping the streets at dusk they were looking for a bed. Most of the British residents had given them a hostile reception and even the local hotel keeper had turned them away, saying he was full. Harry Pauling, then Engineer with the Cape Government Railways, chanced to bump into them and took pity on them. In his usual good-hearted way he offered them a shake down in his office and promised them coffee before their coach left early the next morning.

"Through Mr. Woodford I told the President that the Pauling to whom he referred was my brother," recounted George. "The old man, who whatever his faults in other directions, possessed within his breast the milk of human kindness, immediately volunteered to render me any help within his power in recognition of my brothers' service to him. He sent for Mr. Vervey, at that time the Chief Engineer of the Netherlands Company, and instructed him to give me all the railway contracts he could."

Kruger, who rarely laughed, had an uncanny sense of humour - he trusted a man who could handle a large cigar before breakfast. As a diehard Reformed Church-goer, he also thoroughly enjoyed Pauling's irreverent admission that "it is better to smoke in this world than in the next."

At that time the Dutch company Van Hattum's had been unable to complete the contract for a difficult stretch of the Eastern Line up from the coast. This was Kruger's pet 'pride and joy' which was already beginning to cause some problems. As a result, the contract for this section was given to Paulings, together with an entirely new contract for a rail network linking the mining areas around Johannesburg. This was sorely needed, for poor workers were travelling up to 3 hours every morning and evening to work, and heavy transport was required to bring in coal for the mines.

When the wily old President bullied his Volksraad Parliament for approval, he referred to this new fangled idea as a 'Steam Tramway'. 'Tram' was a euphemism for 'Train', dreamt up by the perceptive State Secretary, Dr. Leyds, to get round the Afrikaner aversion to the 'Iron Horse'. Many of the Volksraad members were unfamiliar with steam trams, but not wishing to show their ignorance, they cheerfully voted for it.

Carlton Hotel, Johannesburg

With visions of something far more modest, they soon discovered a full-blown railway. To add insult to injury, the 'Rand Tram', as it was christened, was built entirely by British companies, since Pauling had teamed up with James Butler on this 1890 project. The only deference to help from friendly countries were the German built Puffing Billies with tall chimney stacks.

Encouraged by the racy advance of the Cape line from Kimberley, the progressive and friendly Orange Free Staters, tired of being isolated, agreed to a Customs Union with the Cape, and pulled their own railway up through Bloemfontein to the banks of the Vaal River, their frontier with the Transvaal. There it languished at its rail-head, looking forlornly across at Kruger's 'wagon-head' on the opposite bank, a motley collection of old-fashioned trek vehicles, ponderous and unreliable. Eventually, having seen their own rail link from Johannesburg to Delagoa Bay finally completed, the die-hard Dutch Transvaalers relented; the gap across the Vaal River was bridged and the rails went through to the Witwatersrand and Johannesburg.

So it was that the same British construction company, Paulings, had provided both Kruger and Rhodes with whole sections of their rival rail-roads. Kruger always called the line to the south through Kimberley 'Rhodes Line', and he was determined to smash it at all costs with his own much shorter route to Delagoa Bay - his window on the world. Shorter distances would normally mean cheaper rates, but 'Rhodes Line' was run so much more efficiently, and had been built for so much less (often one third of the cost per mile) that the distance advantage was superfluous.

As a result most of the traffic came to the goldfields the longer, but far quicker and cheaper way on 'Rhodes Line'. Kruger retaliated. He imposed prohibitive tariffs; he tripled the rates over the 40 mile section of line which traversed his Republican territory. He even blocked the line with empty trucks. Undaunted, enterprising traders organised a rapid road wagon service from the border of the Transvaal to the Rand, avoiding the rail link altogether. Kruger closed the drifts to stop the wagons crossing the Vaal River. After the breakdown of a railway conference, the Imperial Government eventually declared this a breach of the London Convention. Kruger climbed down and Rhodes won through with his rails.

When the rail connection with Johannesburg to the Cape was completed, the departure of the Mail Train for Cape Town became a regular weekly social event. An ornate exhibition building was shipped out from Amsterdam for Johannesburg's new Park Station. Intricate cast iron pillars supported a domed glass roof. The walls of finely carved oak panels around the dining room and offices were surmounted by blue and white Dutch tiles. It was unsurpassed as one of the most elegant little stations anywhere in Africa, before it was pulled down in 1927.

THE EASTERN LINE

The Eastern Line from the Transvaal to the coast at Delagoa Bay in Mozambique (Lourenco Marques now Maputo) was fraught with misfortunes and behind-the-scenes manipulations on an international scale. In 1884, a year after President Kruger's inauguration, one of Britain's great Portuguese allies in Africa, Joachim Machado, (later to be Governor of Mozambique and a director of the Benguela Railway), had surveyed the line. Heavy mining machinery was urgently needed for the gold and quartz fields of the eastern Transvaal, and the Portuguese were as keen as Kruger to expand their trade. Both countries agreed to build a line to their respective borders. The Portuguese, never the most enterprising railway builders themselves, once again granted their concession to an American, Edward McMurdo. It was soon sold on to a British Company, much to the annoyance of President Kruger, whose sole aim was to avoid any contact with British interests.

In Portuguese Mozambique the 55 mile contract from the sea to the border was commenced in 1887 by Thomas Tancred's firm. It was remarkable only for the ruinous fever country it passed through from the coast, and for the inevitable ongoing results of alcohol. The Irish Brigade - a bunch of hard-drinking, but highly efficient navvies operated in full force on the construction work. When the train for the opening festivities finally passed through their railway encampment on its way to meet Thomas Tancred and the Portuguese dignitaries waiting patiently at the border, it was hijacked. Almost the entire contents of food and liquor were consumed. The driver was sent on his way with a scribbled thank-you note to Sir Thomas that read: "To be sure, we are all drinking your health, and there are no problems at our end - at all, at all... Signed the Irish Brigade."

The usual weekend haunt of the Irish Brigade in Delagoa Bay was a shack near the harbour used as the Railway Workers Club. The Portuguese, intent on teaching them a good lesson, decided to raid it one night when they were all drinking together. However the Irish got wind of this. Whilst the Police waited outside the door, one by one they quietly escaped through the back window. When the Police finally forced an entry they found only 4 Irishmen inside, loudly singing, dancing and drinking.

Spurred on by President Kruger's annoyance at British influence and involvement, the Portuguese tried almost every trick in the book to rid themselves of the "English menace". It was a real thorn in their side.

Increasing threats were made to take over the railway. Mr. Knee, the British Vice-Consul at Delagoa Bay was also the General Manager of the Line. He was 'imprisoned' in his own home, but the Portuguese, advised that this would create a grave diplomatic crisis of international proportions, soon allowed him free passage. Three British Men-of-War had arrived off the coast from Simonstown - summoned to protect the British

Residents. Meanwhile down at the railway station, the regular daily train was in readiness to depart for the border with its cargo of mining machinery. A truck load of dynamite was strategically attached to the front of the engine, and the engine-driver was raising steam when a posse of Portuguese troops arrived and endeavoured to prevent his departure by climbing on the engine and footplate. In order to forestall them, the driver opened all the steam cocks, and with an enormous blast on the whistle, sent the posse of soldiers hurtling off the footplate and scurrying in all directions to safety. Engine and dynamite truck then steadily advanced out of the station.

This confrontation between two of Europe's oldest allies continued. The Portuguese eventually found a new face-saving formula to rid themselves of the English run railway once and for all. On the pretext that the line had not been completed to the ill-defined border of the Transvaal by the prescribed contract date, they took it over. This brazen act proved to be very expensive. In the end it took 12 years for an international Swiss arbitration board to decide the outcome. The Portuguese were allowed to

Seizure of the Delagoa Bay Railway by the Portuguese 1889.

keep the railway, but were forced to pay out such huge compensation that it nearly bankrupted their economy.

Within the Transvaal Republic the railway monopoly had originally been given to a Holland-German syndicate, the NZAM, with shares of roughly one-third each to the Transvaal, Holland and German interests. The contract for the Eastern Line up from the Portuguese border had eventually gone to the firm of Van Hattum's of Holland, who brought out most of their workers from the green fields of northern Europe. They succumbed to malaria like flies. The first two Chief Engineers died, the next one beat a hasty retreat, whilst the fourth Willem Verwey, survived, thrived and succeeded in bridging the border river crossing, and bringing the line as far as Krokodile Poort.

Van Hattum's struggled on gamely, but were finally defeated by the difficult terrain of the coastal belt up to the Highveldt. The work then went out to tender. Thanks to the fortunate encounter of his brother several years previously with President Kruger, George Pauling was able to secure the 36 mile contract for the worst section:

"There were several competitors, but our price was the lowest and was accepted. Krocodile Poort enjoyed a most unenviable reputation as one of the most unhealthy parts of the country. Fever was rampant. Our first visit consisted of a fearful walk, or rather a combined scramble and climb, and it took us 8 hours to cover 8 miles. We established our main camp about two thirds of the way through the Poort from the Barberton end."

Percy Fitzpatrick, the itinerant Irishman who started as a transport rider, and later won fame as author of 'Jock of the Bushveldt', claimed to have trading rights on this section of the line from the previous contractors. However the new contract did not specify this and Pauling's essential way of earning 'cash in hand' at those early stages was to capitalise as much as possible out of selling victuals to the work gangs. He waited until Percy Fitzpatrick had set up his store at an entrance to a tunnel, and then announced that dynamite blasting would commence at the nearby rock face. The local Barberton Herald wrote scathing articles about him calling him a great Crocodile, who swallowed up smaller men in the line of business.

The immense difficulties of this section of the Eastern Line consisted notably of fever amongst the men; of tse-tse fly which prevented ox wagon transport; and of lions which found frequent, satisfying meals among the donkeys. In all, over 500 donkeys were lost.

In this poisonous territory Doc Williams set up hospital at the Crocodile River. He instituted a novel approach to prevent patients from dying through sheer funk of the fever. With a number of thermometers in hand, every afternoon he created a 'pool', into which was placed a shilling collected from each patient. If a patient was too ill to subscribe, a shilling was put in on his behalf. Then the temperatures were taken and the man registering the highest, 'scooped' the pool. Frequently patients with temperatures of 105 to 107 or 108 were off their heads, and the first indication of incipient consciousness was often an enquiry as to the result of the pool.

Barberton was the booming mining camp where Alfred Lawley was pursuing the first gold claim; he had also floated the first mining company on the local Stock exchange. He first encountered Pauling together with an old Cambridgeshire friend Bill Upsher, who was busy sinking mining shafts on a nearby claim. As a result of fever, Upsher had lost all his hair and wore a wig. One day Upsher went down the shaft to light the dynamite fuses, and had a very narrow escape. Whilst being winched back up again he took off his wig to get some relief from the heat. There were four locals on the windlass, only one of whom knew him. When the others saw Upsher's bald white head and bright red face appear out of the shaft, they were so frightened that they let go the windlass. His own worker was unequal to the task of holding his own, and Upsher started going down the shaft again. Knowing that the fuses were lit, his worker showed great presence of mind, and yelled to the others to come back - which they did just in time to pull Upsher clear of the shaft head before the dynamite exploded.

THE SCANDALOUS SELATI RAILWAY

Branching off from Kruger's Eastern Line not far from Krokodile Poort, about 40 miles from the border with Mozambique, a railway was planned, to run due north to the Selati River valley. It aimed to serve the new goldfields of Leydsdorp, and the rich agricultural and mining areas all the way up into the mist belt of the Drakensburg Mountains.

In 1890 a Volksraad member B.J.Vorster obtained a concession to build the line for the Transvaal Government. He sold the concession to a Frenchman, Baron Oppenheim, and the 192 mile long surveyed route was expected to be open in 3 years. Work commenced in 1893, but a year later stopped. The chosen route was in dispute. It was fraught with scandal, and a lengthy legal battle ensued. The contract had failed to specify the total distance of the line, and the contractors were found to have extended the railway in unnecessarily long curves and deviations in order to claim extra mileage payments for every mile tendered. The court case dragged on, and nothing happened until 1910 when the line was finally completed, passing through such exotically named places as Hazyview, Cottondale, Acorn Hoek, Mica, Banana, Rubbervale and Leydsdorp - the real gold fever country. Meandering around, up hill and down dale, the line ended up at Pietersburg, opening out the whole of the north-eastern Transvaal (Northern Province) to rail travel.

6

PIONEER GRIT AND STIFF UPPER LIP

FORT SALISBURY

The rough township of Salisbury was divided by a rippling stream which became a marshy swamp at the worst of times and a raging torrent at the best. On one side lay the pioneer business quarter, under the shadow of 'The Koppie', the hill that made a welcome haven for the weary Pioneer Column who changed their mind when they arrived in 1890. They had been aiming for the distant Mount Hampden.

On the other side of the stream the government and administrative quarter was forming up around Cecil Square, named after Lord Salisbury, where the Union Jack had recently been raised,

Frank Johnson, 23 years old, arrogant, loud-mouthed and thickset, had led the 200 strong column as transport contractor from Kimberley, bringing much ill-will with him. He had originally refused to take the 15 Apostles selected by Rhodes to form the nucleus of the first administration. Also included was the loyal Dr. Jameson who had given up the largest and most successful medical practice in Kimberley to pursue the dreams and schemes of his friend 'CJ' Rhodes. He was joined by Archibald Colquhoun, who as soon as he had installed himself as the first Administrator, sent back an order to Kimberley for large quantities of Champagne and Caviare - for 'increased entertaining'. In addition he asked for a thousand of the Best Havana Cigars, for himself, and a thousand Good Havana Cigars for his guests. This rocky first Administrator was no newcomer to turbulent times. He had been born on a ship in a violent storm, as it battled its way around the Cape of Good Hope from India.

All this was in stark contrast to the lamentable lack of supplies for the Pioneer Column which had just been disbanded. With no food they faced early starvation. The road to the south was cut off for months by heavy rains.

Hardly had the Union Jack been hoisted over 'The Fort', than Frank Johnson, Dr. Jameson and Trooper Hay hurried eastwards to Manicaland to explore a way through Portuguese territory to the coast, following the route of the hunter and road-maker Frederick Selous. Across the undefined mountain barrier near Umtali (Mutare) ancient gold claims were already being worked by prospectors from South Africa, and others like Count Penhalonga and Baron Rezende of the Mozambique Company. Rhodes considered this to be within his sphere of influence, and just as Kruger had wanted his own outlet to the sea from the land-locked Transvaal, so Rhodes had his eyes firmly set on a route to the Indian Ocean.

The Frontier Spirit. On the way north to Fort Salisbury

Throughout Manicaland, tattered Portuguese flags fluttered over a motley collection of forts, trading posts and settlements run by an even motlier collection of Goanese, Portuguese, Indians and a few African Chiefs. The main one was Chief Mutasa who ruled from an outpost on one of the highest mountains around, and dressed in an old Naval hat, some well-worn trousers and a Portuguese tunic, enhanced with the inevitable leopard skin.

Johnson had thoughtfully brought with him all the way from Kimberley a collapsible boat, which had been christened in Fort Salisbury with a bottle of champagne and named 'The Pioneer'. With a virtual monopoly of long distance transport, he had visions of opening a route to the coast. First a road and then a railway. So the party launched forth on a reconnaissance trip down the Pungwe River to the sea. They paddled through the malarial swamps and fly-ravaged wilderness to the broad open stretches nearer the coast.

Fort Salisbury was turning from Tent City into a mud heap. The first hostelries were Stewarts Hotel and Tommy's Rest, a weather worn marquee - later converted into the Salisbury Hotel. Slater's Hotel was slightly more substantial with the first burnt brick walls. The first proper hotel was The Mashonaland, with a bucksail roof, a very long bar and little else. Other mud huts collapsed in the torrential downpours of the first rainy season or were pulled down in this rat-infested camp-ground where cats were at a huge premium. Even patients in the early hospital huts were armed with sticks to ward off the rodents. The only sturdy buildings, soon to be taken over by Mother Patrick, had been built on drained ground by Father Hartmann, the Austrian ex-cobbler who had arrived with the Pioneer Column. Everyone's favourite, he knew Zambezia like the back of his hand, and conversed with the locals in their own lingo. Dressed in Norfolk tweeds, baggy breeches and felt hat, this popular little Jesuit missionary rode around on a diminutive pony specially procured for him.

Dr. Frank Rand had also arrived with the column. Very soon he ran out of quinine and his famous 'Rand Kicker' remedy came into being. It was a small dose of quinine mixed with a large dose of Epsom Salts which he doled out to the men lined up on parade.

'Curio' Brown was an American citizen sent to South Africa by the Smithsonian Institute to observe a solar eclipse and collect exotic butterflies. Along with a compatriot, Maurice Heany, he decided on a more active vocation and was accepted into the Pioneer Column. A jack of all trades and an accomplished prospector, he soon became Mayor of Salisbury, and for good measure, a British Citizen.

The first patient of the dentist-cum-chemist John Strachan to try out laughing-gas for tooth extraction was Tom Ross, an American army Captain from Atlanta, Georgia, and a nephew of Colquhoun. He surveyed the town and set it out in true American grid style.

Women were banned from the new Colony for the first year - to allow the pioneer men to settle in - by the fastidious Dr. Jameson. But the enterprising 'Wild West' spirit of the frontier girl prevailed.

The plucky cockney damsel Countess Billy was the daughter of an English Boarding House keeper. To get around the immigration regulations she dressed as a boy, and slipped into the country to join her husband, the sporty old French aristocrat Vicomte de la Panouse. He also dressed to kill, wearing his Legion of Honour whilst 'riding shotgun' bringing in convoys for the Chartered Company during the Rebellion. He dabbled in gold claims, and hid huge quantities of whiskey on his remote mining camp, which he eventually sold to the Irish for their first St. Patrick's night - on tick - since there was no money in circulation. The nearest bank was 800 miles away in Mafeking.

Dr. Leander Starr Jameson (1853-1917) painted by one of his 9 older brothers. Stocky and excitable, like 'a terrier waiting to pounce', with soft brown eyes and a magnetic warmth, he was utterly loyal to Rhodes' schemes and dreams

Another plucky pioneer girl travelled up on Selous' road from the south, avoiding police outposts by a wide berth. Mary Waterman was the wife of an Australian prospector who worked a mine called Pioneer Mary. She named her daughter Cecilia after Cecil Rhodes. After a while they all moved up to Kenya to join the Uganda Railway. Not to be outdone, Abe Bailey, the South African mining magnate insisted on calling his daughter Cecil.

The youngest son of the Marquis of Winchester, Lord Paulet, arrived with his young wife and a steam-driven circular saw. For the first time, straight timbers were available at reasonable prices for building construction.

The first 'office' was Bird and Hunter's

Attorneys. Bird was a barrister whom Rhodes had originally refused to enlist since he mistrusted lawyers. Having opened with a sail cloth over their wagon, they did a roaring trade in mining claims and property contracts.

Salisbury became a town of bicycles, rickshaws and prospectors on donkeys, usually with a saddle bag hung with a sleeping bag, a cooking pot, a pick and spade and a whisky bottle.

"Gimme a bottle of whisky a day and I'll defy the fever", was the usual cry from those who had run out of quinine, and luck.

Popular bars were strung along Pioneer Street, like the Posada with a 36 feet long counter which attracted the prospectors and old timers such as Mazoe Bill, Scorpion Jim, Garlic Pete and O'Rory of the Hills, a prospector of some luck and talent. He would go out and peg a claim, dig the prescribed depth into the ground and register the claim. More often than not he would sell it to some larger mining company for a good price. Having spent the proceeds in Pioneer Street, he would return to the hills to repeat the performance.

By the beginning of 1893 nearly a thousand men, 200 married and 100 single women had passed through Fort Tuli on their way to the hoped-for land of gold, Mashonaland.

The girls travelled up by Cape Cart, Scotch cart, ox wagon, mule cart, Zeederburg Coach and Shanks Pony, many to admire, others to settle and perpetuate the breed. Some were forerunners of the sunshine girls, some were fifth generation colonials from the Cape, others were hardy trekkers

The Queen's Hotel, Salisbury 1907

from the Transvaal. Even chancers from England arrived on foot all the way from Beira, the nearest sea port.

Fanned by the romantic novels of the times the word had gone out that the new Colony of Rhodesia was paved with heroes who were sun-bronzed, good-looking and gentlemen from English Public schools. Men smartened up, trimmed their beards, changed their socks and made their beds.

That was the good side. The down side was different. Frontier battleaxes, weather-beaten women, disillusioned and hardened with drunken husbands and sickly children, hammered to hell from every direction, still retained the virtues of patience and fortitude. Few of them were beauties yet even the scraggiest stood a chance. They possessed the saving qualities of Grit and a Sense of Humour, and were able to keep a stiff upper lip in a real crisis and to treat a minor drawback as an 'experience'.

Child birth was a gruelling experience for most women. A kindly German midwife was sometimes around, but most had to face their confinements with no-one but their husbands to help them. Many of the women had little knowledge of child-care. Poor food and bad living conditions made young children open to attacks of fever, so parents aimed to get them out of the country as soon as possible.

It was sometimes said of Rhodesia that the Flowers had no smell, the Birds had no song and the Women had no morals.

Manica Road, Salisbury's main trading street

69

Bargirls arrived, like May Jackson and 'Diamond Lil', with both bejewelled nostrils, all the way from Kimberley, because the Cape Colony had introduced a ban on women working behind bars.

Pioneer Street became truly international with its multi-cultural activities. It was a street of bars and tea rooms. Vying with the Kettledrum, a most respectable and genteel establishment, were other little 'tea rooms' lit by red lamps, with doors wide open; the women lounging in chairs in various postures - English, French, German and Colonial. Most stylish was French Marie who ran a bevy of beauties, some from as far away as San Franscisco. She handled troublesome men in true frontier style and woe betide any man who made a bee-line for her zealously protected daughter. She followed the railway line when it reached the Victoria Falls, set up shop, found it unprofitable and then moved on to Brazzaville in the French Congo.

The monarch of early Hotels was the Queens, a grand watering hole of robust gatherings and Saturday night dances which became star attractions.

Around Fort Salisbury's administration centre, the dignified Cecil Hotel appeared on the scene; it was far too gracious for those early days of diggers, gamblers and ruffians. Having struggled to survive against the pleasures of its rivals across the 'river', it became the Parliament Building, with its panelled dining room making a perfect debating chamber.

The first Club was inevitably the Civil Service Club. Only six of Rhodes' original Apostles remained to serve the community. The others had disappeared to dig for gold. There were not enough civil servants around to make the Club pay so it was thrown open to all and sundry. Dr. Jameson was asked to suggest suitable qualifications for membership.

"Anyone who has been out of gaol for 3 months", he replied.

In the smart area, the Salisbury Club began its days vying for reputation and respectability, and the patronage of the 'official' classes. Other clubs joined the throng; Sports, Athletic, Golf, Cricket. The Salisbury Hunt Club chased jackals and bat-eared foxes around the bush, pursued by a pack of hounds which had been imported from Ireland by the Chartered Company. When the 5 couple of Bitches and two Dogs landed at Beira they were brought as far as Chimoio - the then rail-head. From there they had to walk the rest of the way to Umtali. Arriving rather lame in Salisbury, they became overnight celebrities and over-fed curiosities. When hunting began they were not fussy about their quarry, chasing everything from jackals to buck. Eventually they became so overweight and out-of-condition that they were unable to keep up with the riders. Other dogs, fox terriers and local 'all-sorts' joined the chase.

As an experiment in transport, camels were brought in to defeat the tse-tse fly. They caused havoc with the oxen and panic with the horses. The very smell of them turned mules into kicking maniacs.

The Koppie Club in the old part of town retained its flavour of hardened pioneers and disillusioned merchants stirring up trouble for the administration. George Pauling took it all in his stride:

"On one occasion I was playing billiards at the Koppie when a well known prospector named McLoughlin, who was inclined for a spree, caught hold of me as I was about to make a stroke. I turned round and threw him to the floor with a backheel. He looked horrified and astonished, but when he recovered breath enough to get up, he shook hands with me and said I was the only man who had thrown him. He was renowned for his strength, and this little wrestling match did me more good with the rougher class of Prospectors and others than anything else in my official capacity."

As Minister of Transport, Commissioner of Mines, and Postmaster General, Pauling had his hands full. He became a deft manipulator at passing the buck from Ministry to Ministry. Once when the mails were weeks late in arriving from the south, he received an irate delegation of merchants in his capacity of Postmaster General. He politely pointed out that the undue delay was caused by the lamentable lack of transport, and he would refer the matter immediately to that Ministry. He then suggested retiring to the Avenue Hotel for some liquid refreshment. The next day he was confronted by the same delegation in his capacity as Transport Minister. He politely pointed out that the woeful state of the transport system was caused entirely by the slow payments received from the Ministry of Mines - the only revenue earner in the Colony. He said the matter would be referred to that department and suggested retiring to the Avenue once more for refreshment. A day later the same delegation confronted him in his capacity as Commissioner of Mines. He endorsed everything that had been said by the other Ministers and pointed out that he was sympathetic to their grievances, but that his hands were tied since the revenue was received from the British South Africa Company, the controlling body for the mining concessions. He would refer the matter to them to speed things up. Once again the entire delegation shuffled down to the nearby hotel for rounds of drinks at the Ministry's expense. A short time later the mails arrived and the hullaballoo had receded.

After arriving to take up his official appointments, Pauling moved in to a grandiose Indian style bungalow, which later became Government House, in Montagu Avenue. The real Government House was at that time still in the capital Bulawayo.

"I had selected the site shortly after my arrival in Salisbury with Mr. Rhodes from Umtali where we had planned the removal of the old town, and it was constructed according to my fancy. A huge verandah 19 feet in width ran round it on which my wife used to give a dance five or six times a year."

It became the social centre for musical evenings and dances, performed on creaking floorboards, with the BSA Police Band playing outside. Most people came on bicycles; the few ladies around arrived with their dresses pinned up. As the ratio was about 10 to 1, most men gave up the struggle and retired to the bar.

Pauling's eccentric second wife was a 28 year old raver, Kate Halliwell. She carried a colourful Congolese parrot around on her shoulder and was taken to occasional pipe-smoking - a habit she had picked up on travels with her husband. She was a deft hand at driving a six-in-hand carriage around London's Hyde Park, and whilst in Africa, a team of hard-to-harness Zebra's on the 'dirt tracks' around Salisbury. This was in deference to her late brother-in-law, who had planned to capture and tame thousands of zebra on the Beira flats for use as draught animals for coaches.

On one occasion Kate Pauling and Lady Paulet had arrived back from a hard day's hunting, chasing duiker around the burnt-out vlei. They were well known in dashing Leicestershire fox-hunting circles, and this local style of sport made an interesting challenge.

They were surprised to find slumped in a verandah chair the brooding figure of Cecil Rhodes, characteristically deep in thought and awaiting the return of Pauling, who was still entertaining another delegation of irate merchants in the bar of the Avenue Hotel. In the absence of their husbands it was a heaven sent opportunity for two sporting ladies in their late twenties to wind up the 42 year old Rhodes. Rather than being irritated as he usually was by frivolous women, Rhodes warmed to their attentions. He relaxed and showed the rare human side of himself normally hidden from reality. History does not relate what would have happened had their husbands not returned home so soon.

SALISBURY CELEBRITIES Nº1 'GEORGIE PORGIE'

'Simply Appalling'

'WHERE IS THE S.P.C.A.'

When not staying with Dr. Jameson, on his rare visits to Salisbury, Rhodes usually stayed with the Paulings. He took a fancy to the eccentric Kate and the rustic charm of this establishment which was not like any other Government House. There was no picture of Queen Victoria and only a modicum of furniture, mostly cane colonial which suited Rhodes' fastidious leanings. Here he felt at ease, sometimes playing pool with Milton, Grey and some of the younger civil servants, making prodigious flukes and chuckling with glee as he picked up their 'tickies' from the edge of the table. And those whom he once trusted he trusted absolutely. Pauling had no political axe to grind, nor any political aspirations. He found the tasks tedious and unrewarding.

Needless to say, Pauling's position as contractor, controller and operator of the railway from Beira, busily being built to the borders of land-locked Rhodesia, did not go down well.

Very soon pilferage on a large scale reared its ugly head. The early newspaper The Nugget, in an article of October 1897 wrote:

"A large amount of transport has reached Salisbury during the past few days and the merchants are jubilant once more; but their jubilation would appear to be short lived for I hear many loud and bitter complaints and invectives levelled at the heads of Mr. George Pauling and those in authority on the line between Beira and Macequece, for their gross and arrant callousness and carelessness, in knowing full well that merchants are robbed right, left and along the line, and yet winking at such robberies. Many cases that were of correct weight on leaving Beira have reached Salisbury empty - notwithstanding full freight has been paid - and many cases and bales of

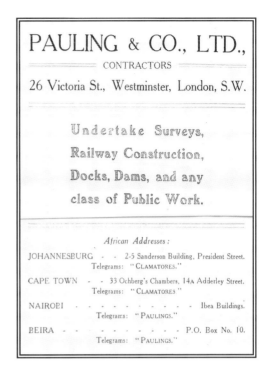

general merchandise, when opened here, are found to contain about half of their original contents. Mr. Pauling, when approached by one merchant or another airily tells them to "go to Lisbon and sue him", which is about equivalent to telling them to... . elsewhere. The consequence is, the Merchants have to increase their charges for the goods, and the Public have to pay through the nose for the ordinary necessities of life. This is a howling shame and one that will not be remedied until Mr. Pauling's control over the railway is dispensed with. Much as it is to Mr. Cecil Rhodes' benefit to 'keep in' with George Pauling, he makes himself nothing but an accessory to this robbery by his indifference to the complaints of the Salisbury merchants and residents."

Much of this criticism did not take into account the pilferage by the road transport contractors, carrying goods from the rail-head at Umtali, along the road to Salisbury, and the effects of the Rebellion which had spread from Matabeleland.

After two years in government harness Pauling decided to resign his Ministerial appointments. Even though Rhodes tried hard to persuade him to stay on with the promise of the Premiership of the Colony, he went back to his old love - Railway Building.

After a year of tribulations when lonely miners, prospectors, farmers, transport riders and friendly natives were attacked and murdered, the Rebellion subsided. It had caused much hardship when Salisbury was in siege, without food or supplies.

'Dilatory Dick' Martin, the Commandant-General had advocated appeasement. He refused to sanction crop destruction, blowing-up caves or other stern measures. This had a disastrous effect on morale, and caused even fiercer attacks by the rebels in the outlying districts. There was a shortage of men and horses, as over two-thirds of the animals brought in for the Police had died of horse sickness. When reinforcements from Beira reached the rail-head at Umtali they advanced past Chief Makoni who was still in rebellion.

Optimism vanished into the tinder-dry air of October when the rains failed. Locusts arrived *en masse* and unemployment took its toll. The opening of the line between Mafeking and Bulawayo further added to the feeling of abandonment by Salisbury citizens. There was a spate of suicides. A bridegroom took a revolver to church and shot himself in front of his bride immediately after the ceremony. Seven others did away with themselves, and the reputation of October and November as the 'suicide season' had been established.

Salisbury's skyline changed rapidly to the mood of the times. In this heyday of Empire, exporters like Hemmings of Bristol excelled in prefabricated buildings. Even complete bungalows with surrounding verandahs were instantly available from mail order catalogues, ready for shipping to all parts of the Empire. Railed up from the Cape and carted to Salisbury came wood and iron building sections, complete with *art nouveau* pressed steel ceilings, sash windows and tongued & grooved flooring. Bricks were made locally. The Chief Magistrate of Salisbury lived in a Paper House, made from *papier mache* on wooden beams.

Speke, to Stanley & Gordon about the Baker's Union was the useful *aide memoire* which recorded the order of the five main avenues through the centre of the city. Of these illustrious explorers only Stanley had ever set foot inside the country. It was typical of Rhodesia's empirical aspirations - more British than Britain herself. Whilst some called Kenya the Officers Mess, and Rhodesia the Sergeants Mess, in Kenya they were Settlers, whilst in Rhodesia they remained Pioneers first and foremost. In Rhodesia there was also a bevy of blue blood. The premier Marquis of England - Winchester, arrived in the earliest days. The premier Duke of Scotland - Montrose, settled later. At times in between came Viscounts and Baronets, German Princes and Barons, Russian and Italian Counts, and the ex King of Albania, mostly to live off the land in one of the finest climates in Africa.

When the railway reached Salisbury from Bulawayo in 1902, a continuous through link of over 2000 miles connected Cape Town with Beira on the east coast of Africa.

MEIKLES HOTEL

A successful builder from Strathaven in Scotland, John Meikle had arrived in South Africa with his wife Sarah in the 1860's to try his luck at gold prospecting and diamond digging. They bought a farm in Natal where 10 children were raised.

The family then turned their hands to transport riding in the booming Barberton Gold Rush. When the railways arrived, their business was doomed, so the three young brothers, Tom, Stewart and Jack moved up as traders in Mashonaland and Matabeleland, on the advice of John Dunlop, to join the rush of Rhodes' push to the north.

With good reserves of whiskey, purchased at judicious prices and safely stored near the undefined border, they advanced on Fort Victoria, where they cleaned out the opposition with their down-to-earth bargains. They opened stores wherever they went. Traders, cattle-ranchers, unofficial Bankers, Brewers and Hoteliers - you name it - the hardy Meikles clan prospered in many spheres, and were joined by the rest of the family.

Tempestuous times had bred an independent streak in each of them. Whilst Stewart and Jack joined up to defeat the rebellion, Tom ran the gauntlet of running supplies to the beleaguered garrisons and hard-pressed settlers. At the same time he sowed the seeds of the successful trading empire in the new townships of Salisbury and Bulawayo.

Jack set up shop in Umtali, Manicaland. When the township moved to meet the railway, he moved with it. He developed the Cecil and Royal hotels, pioneered fruit and forestry and became Town Mayor. His luck ran out when he doggedly chased the rainbow of a declining mining venture.

The easy-going Stewart soldiered on, and purchased a plot of land in the centre of Salisbury where he planned to build an enormous hotel. It

Den of scandal and haven of intrigue, the Lounge and Dining room of old Meikles, doyenne of hotels in Salisbury

covered the whole of one side of Cecil Square, where the Union Jack had been raised twenty years earlier. He died before building it.

The business-like Tom bided his time until the First World War before carrying on the enterprise. Destined to be the "finest structure north of the Limpopo" Meikles Hotel opened at the end of 1915. It was claimed by its Scottish architect to cover a larger area than any other hotel in Africa.

A side entrance was originally emblazoned with a 'Grand Hotel' sign, perhaps with visions of grander schemes to come - before the owners took stock. The graceful low lines of this Edwardian colonial edifice had an almost Indian feel about it, with lofty copper cupolas and carved stone lions looking across the Square of pink and white flowering jacarandas - diagonally planted in the shape of a Union Jack.

Meikles became the doyenne of hotels in Salisbury, and a welcome haven for new arrivals to the fledgling colony. From the beginning it boasted three bars, a card room, a reading room, self contained suites and numerous bedrooms. The famous early rival storekeeper, H.M.Barbour, described it in 1924 as "like walking into a castle in Spain... Spacious and Beautiful... with the menu as long as your arm."

The legendary dining room, according to Mullins, the Irish builder, was "the largest in Africa." It continued on as the centre of social life, of wining, dining and dancing between the wars. Around the corner, earthy old timers still frequented the Prospectors Bar, under the shady porticos.

Meikles attracted all kinds - the great and the good; the down-trodden and the dotty. Everyone, and anyone, who ever went to Salisbury met there. It was as famous a rendezvous as the Thorntree in Nairobi. "Meet you at Meikles" was the familiar cry from those who relished its colonial spaciousness and graciousness. Farmers came in and settled down in the club-like atmosphere of cane and leather, behind waving aspidistras, eyeing young ladies out on the town. Tobacco barons took permanent suites for the duration of the tobacco auctions, the largest in the world.

It was the den of scandal and haven of intrigue. For half a century, the Causerie and Colony Bars did their dusty duty for many a hopeful gold digger, both male and female, who remembered with affection the nooks and crannies, the ballustraded balconies, the bedrooms with no bathrooms, the early morning tea brought to one's bedside by the legendary English housekeeper. There were also the remarkable Seven and Sixpenny dinners, complete with marvellous Marrow Bones on Toast and carrot sauce, wonderfully served until the end by Waiter 'Number 2' who had been around since the very beginning.

Meikles swansong came in the 1960's when the legendary 40 year old was replaced by a pale new skyscraper, since added onto in various directions, and all tidied up as 'multi-star luxury.' Whilst Pepe the Italian Barman shook his last Martini in the Can Can Bar, and Norman, the Maitre d'Hotel, paraded through La Fontaine, Jack Dent's Trio played out the last waltz overlooking the fountains of Cecil Square. The hotel then moved into a drab new era.

The only reminders of Meikles former majesty are the stately stone lions, now sitting comfortably overlooking the pavement. It was always said of them that one day they would roar - when a virgin passed by.

A BALLAD OF THE B.M.R.
(THE BEIRA TO MASHONALAND RAILWAY)

Down in the land where heathens are,
   Down in the swamps where white men stew,
Amid the woods that stretch afar,
   Amid the creepers dank with dew
The Line ran out - perchance askew,
   And drunkenly designed - but, ah !
In days gone by was work to do
   Upon the lonely B.M.R.!

The Gates of Death were held ajar -
   The pegs that marked the mileage too
Have stood for tombstones - near and far
   Ghosts of a grimy, shrivelled crew,
The sun looked down from out the blue -
   Out of the night looked down the star,
And marked where men had drifted through
   The death-trap of the B.M.R.

Each bolt, each nut, each metal bar,
   Could tell a story - grim but true -
And where the gangers' houses are
   Maybe are ghosts of dead men too -
Ghosts of the men who worked and knew -
   The fever-swamp, the sickening jar
That came when life was rusted through
   Upon the lonely B.M.R.

L'ENVOI

Lo! - we may scoff - we often do -
   And jest at engine, truck and car -
But - must we then forget the few
   Who made for us the B.M.R.

HENRY CULLEN GOULDSBURY 1881 -1916

*Doctor Williams'
Hospital Camp at
Siluvu Hills 1897,
situated 34 miles from
Fontesvilla
(RGS)*

7

MAN KILLERS OF MOZAMBIQUE

LIONS AND MOSQUITOES ON THE BEIRA RAILWAY

Of all countries in the Empire, the land-locked Colony of Rhodesia was the most difficult to get into, or out of. From its capital Fort Salisbury (Harare) it was 1500 miles to the rail-head at Kimberley, and 2000 miles to the nearest workable sea port. It took 3 months to trek by ox-wagon, which often got bogged down during the rainy season. The cost of transport was simply prohibitive. The rebellion had flared up, and the long overland route from the south via Fort Tuli had become a death trap for the unwary; littered with the graves of men, dead trek oxen, and abandoned or looted wagons. Often all that got through were the mails, which sometimes took six weeks to arrive, escorted by a mounted police trooper with a pack horse moving from one relay station to another.

Dr. Jameson, the Administrator, was battling to placate the recently arrived pioneers and early settlers. A group of them, including Frank Johnson, the leader of the Pioneer Column and a transport operator, pressed the Chartered Company to open a route to the coast in Portuguese Mozambique. The new road would cross the border near Umtali (Mutare) in the eastern Highlands, drop down into the coastal plain and travel through the forests and swamps to the nearest navigable point on the Pungwe River, 50 miles inland. From there steam tugs would travel to and from the coast at Beira.

This ambitious plan was advertised as 'the fastest, shortest and cheapest route to Mashonaland' and suggested mule transport for the First class passengers, taking 2 days, and ox-wagons for all other passengers taking 10 days. A start was made, hacking away at the bush with a motley band of downhearted Africans.

Attracted by the supposed fortunes of the new Colony and the promises of gold and other mineral wealth, in a land of rich soil and unrivalled climate, scores of people ventured up from South Africa and out from England, to chance their luck. They landed at Beira. There they found that Frank Johnson's promised inland transport was non-existent. Unfortunately he had disregarded the ravages of the tse-tse fly which decimated oxen, mules and horses alike. Even 'salted' horses, having survived previous attacks, were only partially immune.

The newcomers were obliged to walk. On foot they stumbled down the native trails - having sold, if they could, most of their precious possessions, tools of trade and provisions. Three gutsy nurses, Rose Blennerhasset, Lucy Sleeman and Beryl Welby, on their way to open the first hospital in

Umtali (Mutare), trekked for 14 days through the menacing country. Where the Pungwe River narrowed and tse-tse fly country started, they were also confronted by mosquitoes. With nets draped from large hats, dressed in malaria proof vests, leggings and gloves, they successfully negotiated their way through.

When Rhodes arrived at Beira a year later, the road was still virtually non-existent. Passing dozens of derelict wagons and the bleached bones of countless oxen, he abandoned his smart new Cape cart and continued the journey on salted horses. On the way up from the coast accompanied by Frank Johnson and DC de Waal, they camped overnight in the Amatongas Forest. It was here that Rhodes was, literally, caught with his pants down. The three of them had squeezed into a tent, and Rhodes complained about the fires which had been built around the perimeter to ward off the lions. Johnson reminded him that the Times correspondent Beaumont had recently been devoured in these parts, and only his booted feet had been found. During the night, Rhodes got up and wandered off into the moonlit forest. Johnson realised all was not well when he heard the growl and grunt of a lion hunting nearby. Rhodes came running back, breathless and in a highly excitable state, with his pyjama trousers down below his knees. "A lion has been chasing me!" he exclaimed in a high pitch.

Alfred Beit, the most civilised of the Rand millionaires and Rhodes' loyal colleague, had meanwhile taken the longer and safer route from the south via Bulawayo. When they met up in Salisbury, there was a near riot on their hands. Hard pressed traders and settlers, as well as mischief-makers and firebrands were threatening to get the Imperial Government to cancel the Charter and to take over the country themselves unless something was done about the shocking transport situation.

There was only one way round it. An incident would have to be engineered to force the Portuguese Government to grant a right of way through Mozambique. Sir John Willougby was despatched forthwith to Beira to collect 230 tons of stores, two tugs and some lighters and bring them up the Pungwe River for the overland route to Rhodesia. For two days he attempted to pay the required customs dues to the Portuguese authorities - without success. On the third day he informed them that he was setting forth. As a result a Portuguese Gunboat blocked their move and forced them to retreat. Having fired a warning shot at them, it was considered by Willoughby to be the 'Insult to the British Flag' that he had been instructed to procure. As a result Lord Salisbury, to a cheering House of Commons, ordered the despatch of 3 gunboats from Simonstown.

This 'Beira Incident', and other confrontations which brought the two countries to the brink of war, hastened the signing of the Anglo-Portuguese Treaty. Under its terms Britain secured Nyasaland, and Manicaland went to Portugal, in return for which the Portuguese would build a railway from the coast through their territory along the shortest route to the border, whilst the Pungwe River would become an international waterway.

The rights for the construction of the railway were granted by the Mozambique Company to an American, Henry Theodore van Laun, who sold them a few months later to Rhodes' Charter Company.

Almost immediately, Alfred Beit summoned George Pauling, much to the annoyance of Frank Johnson, and asked him to build a two-feet gauge light railway more or less following the proposed road route down to the Pungwe River. There was some competition for this 'Empire-building' contract which had little to recommend it, but Pauling was no newcomer to challenging fever and fly country. He had just completed the most arduous section of the Eastern Line linking Pretoria with Lourenco Marques (Maputo). One of his competitors was Alfred Lawley, whom Pauling immediately engaged as Manager, such was his reputation. "He had no fear of fever and very little of anything else".

With more than a touch of 'sour grapes', Johnson, the unsuccessful tenderer, later claimed he could have built the line for half a million pounds less. He also claimed, inaccurately, that Pauling's contract was on a per mile basis, whereas in fact the total cost for the first section was set at £70,000 to be completed at a rate of one mile per day.

The average cost per mile of the early pioneer lines was very low. Pauling invariably insisted on an aggregate figue being named in his

The Agnes steaming up the Pungwe River

contract, calculated on the assumption that the exact route recommended in the Engineer's survey was followed in toto. However, he reserved the right to make any deviations calculated to shorten the line without increasing any gradients. Thus he made his contracting profit.

To soften the blow, Rhodes gave Johnson one more chance. He was awarded the contract to transport all the construction materials from Beira to Fontesvilla. He brought out an elaborate stern-wheel paddle steamer from Southampton, and assembled it at Beira. However, it ran into a submerged log on its maiden voyage. The passengers abandoned ship, and it was ignominiously sunk and never recovered. So he sold the contract to Donald Currie of the Castle Line.

Initially a 75 mile light railway would be built through the 'hairiest' stretch to the banks of the crocodile infested Pungwe River. From there, tugs would convey passengers and goods to and from the coast. The old trek route over the highlands to Umtali would complete the last part of the journey.

Fresh from the heavy toll of life on the Eastern Line, where the death rate had been 135 in every thousand from fever alone, Pauling predicted the same, if not worse to come. At the time of its construction two records

An early settler, J.M.Dunlop and his family at Macequece, on their way up from Beira to Umtali in 1897, before the railway was completed. His wife and child are carried in a Machilla by 'tenga-tengas' (NAZ)

were held by the Beira Railway. First that it was the longest narrow gauge line, and secondly that it had the highest mortality rate in the world.

In the annals of peacetime railway contracting there can be few more poignant examples of Homeric stoicism to provide an unenviable outlet for a land-locked country. Kingsley Fairbridge, who founded the homes in Australia for abandoned children, described it as "One of England's great gifts to the World".

Confronting the challenge of new uncharted territory, these reckless pioneers took the risks in their stride. The dangers were well known, none more so than by their wives and families, many of whom were sitting on the highveld around Fort Salisbury almost dying of starvation. A route from the coast would be their only salvation. The casualties were simply appalling. In each of the first two years of construction, 60% of all the white men - about 400 - died of fever. The 500 Indian employees died almost to a man, along with an estimated 30% of the entire African labour force, since Africans were only slightly more immune to the ravages of malarial mosquitoes from their experiences in infancy.★

Dysentery, cholera and sleeping sickness contributed to the mortality rate. At that time quinine was not readily available, and it wasn't for another 5 years that Manson, Ross and others really got to grips with understanding the malarial cycle.

"Almost immediately Alfred Lawley was struck down," recalled Pauling. "I found him at Beira, desperately ill with malaria, so much so that his weight had been reduced from 15 stone to under 10 stone. I sent him for a sea trip to Quelimane and Zanzibar, and he kept up and down the coast in steamers until he got well. Meanwhile I went up to Fontesvilla to take charge of construction. At one time practically every white man on the line suffered from fever, and I fervently wished that I had never heard of the Beira Railway. In one fortnight we lost six white men, including my book-keeper".

The tried and trusted remedy of alcohol came into its own, since none of the teetotallers apparently survived, records the hard-drinking Pauling.

"According to my experience, teetotallers do not stand a fever country as well as excessive drinkers. Whilst on this work I had several attacks of fever, but the Doctor pulled me through. Unhappily it was not so with my cousin who died at Beira. In those days one steamer a month or six weeks was all the communications Beira had with the outside world. Rice was the staple diet, ice was unheard of, and fresh vegetables were scarce indeed. It was the lack of these and similar luxuries that made 1892 -93 so fatal".

Yet what should have been depressing times were enlivened by the pragmatic and often hilarious approach taken by the sufferers. This was summed up by Harry Pauling: "Malaria? I'm saturated with it. We all get it. It's part of the country's resources".

★*Source: Rudland - Sunday Mail (Rhodesia) - September 1942. These figures are not exceeded by other inconclusive statistics of railway work-force casualties over unspecified periods. For example, in India during the 1859 - 60 rainy season, nearly "one third of the 30,000 to 40,000 work force died"; and on the Panama Railway "one in five workers died." (Source: Men of Steel). On the Matadi - Leopoldville Railway, in the Congo Free State, "32 Europeans and 1,800 Africans and Chinese labourers died." (Source: Railways of South Africa - Day) and "out of a work force of 2000, 150 per month died." (Source: King Leopold's Ghosts).*

From the beginning Alfred Lawley was in charge of construction and the wiry P. St. George Mansergh was Chief Surveyor. They diced with death during the height of the malarial season between December and April. It was the first 50 miles that proved so fatal. Lawley's assistant Thomas Rudland (1867 -1955) recalled : "Labour shortages, derailments and fever - always the fever - continued to dog us. At the end of the first eight months there were only four of us left of the original staff. Some had given up the job; most had died." One of the first pioneers of Rhodesia, Rudland had followed in Stanley's footsteps to Africa in 1887 at the age of 20. He turned his hand to gold prospecting, coffee growing and road making, before joining Paulings on the advice of Cecil Rhodes.

With hippos playing and crocodiles basking on the sandbanks, the romantic sounding venue of Fontesvilla (Ponte do Pungwe), 50 miles upstream from Beira, became their headquarters. There were a dozen houses and stores, a ramshackle railway station, the Railway Hotel, a hospital and a Catholic Church, all built on stilts 5 feet above the water level. There the similarity with a 'Venice of the Tropics' ended. Insufferably hot and seething with malaria, it probably had the highest death-rate of anywhere in the world. On the last bend of the Pungwe River, within sight of Fontesvilla, was the little African village called 'Champanga' - as if to celebrate the arrival of the railway at this Gateway to Delirium and Death.

Construction materials landed at Beira from England were conveyed upstream to Fontesvilla by tugs; the Agnes, the Kimberley and the Rose. They were off-loaded under contract onto the muddy banks of the Pungwe by the unenvied and popular D'Arcy Cathcart and his band of labourers. As the tugs progressed slowly through the shifting sandbanks and shallow pools a man with a measuring stick called out "Navigable", "Too shallow" or "Deep". Then, as now, this part of the Zambezi catchment area was liable to widespread flooding of devastating proportions. The first rainy season was torrential. The 200 miles between the Pungwe and the Zambezi Rivers became one vast lake, with not a tree in sight. Agnes floated off course and was marooned on a sandbank where she remained for 3 years, as the water level subsided. Eventually a channel was cut, and further heavy rains re-floated her. Navigation points were often marked by clumps of trees surrounding graves, such as

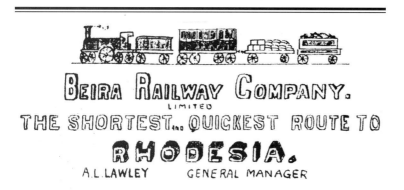

BEIRA RAILWAY COMPANY.
LIMITED
THE SHORTEST... QUICKEST ROUTE TO
RHODESIA.
A.L.LAWLEY   GENERAL MANAGER

'Smiths point', or 'Jones crossing'.

The tugs naturally carried a good supply of liquor on this 50 mile river journey, which was supposed to take 50 hours. So frequent were the groundings that it was customary for Captain Dickie to ensure that most of his stock was sold, and most of his passengers well oiled, before the trip continued. A brawny and genial north-country character, the Captain was missing two fingers, reputedly lost when he punched a poisonous African in the mouth. Cecil Rhodes, to ensure his arrival in reasonable time, bought out all the liquor stocks before setting sail.

The first few miles of railway from Fontesvilla through the Pungwe Flats were built on embankments raised high above the floodwaters. When submerged, the only indication of the railway's whereabouts was a row of telegraph poles protruding above the water level, festooned with snakes and other climbing creatures which could not swim.

Most of the workers slept out in the open. It was a monumental few months of misery in the worst fever country in the world. A good supply of ready made headstones was always in demand, but a decent burial was often impossible. Coffins were in short supply. Weighed down with stones they were hurriedly buried in the oozing mud. Some-times at night strange gurgling sounds were heard, and bubbles appeared, as gas escaped from the fast decomposing corpses. They also had a nasty habit of being washed up after heavy rains onto people's verandahs.

This was the spirit in which Doctor Williams, that goodly Welshman from Cardiff, arrived to open the first hospital at Fontesvilla. He was well

A railway embankment being constucted by labourers with hand barrows, near Chimoio, 1894 (NAZ)

prepared after his experiences at Krocodile Poort on the Eastern Line. Saturated with fever himself, he was not averse to a good night's drinking which affected his equilibrium, though not apparently his head. After a late game of billiards he would crawl back to his hut on hands and knees with a lantern round his neck, negotiating a narrow pathway through the oozing-black mud. But the

next morning he was as right as rain. During one of his serious fever bouts he appeared to be at death's door. There was a final visit from Lawley and Charlie Buchan, who tearfully suggested it was the last time they would see him. Lawley did not agree. The result was an indiscreet bet. As Lawley bent over to hear his final words, the old Doctor winked and whispered: "I heard you. Bet another £10 for me." That afternoon, though still desperately ill, there was an added impetus to his remarkable recovery.

It was seldom that a padre could be found to perform the burial rites, and this was usually done by one of the engineers or the Doctor. On one occasion the sad proceedings were relieved by a touch of humour. A platelayer had died leaving behind him a devoted chum, who, much overcome, assuaged his grief at frequent intervals by the solace of the whiskey bottle. By evening, when he joined the little group of colleagues assembled at the graveside, the poor fellow was fairly drunk, but he remained alive to his responsibilities as Chief Mourner. He took advantage of the pause when the body was being lowered to address the doctor in an alcoholic but audible whisper: "You quite understand, Doctor Williams, sir," he murmured, "on this occasion all drinksh are at my expensh."

Platelaying through wooded country (NAZ)

Drinking was the favourite pastime after a week of sweating toil; gambling followed, and entertainment of a kind was provided for the 'troops' by an itinerant team of Japanese Geisha girls from Beira. Installed for a while at Fontesvilla, there was not much demand from men who were mostly delirious - more ready for the undertaker than amorous delights.

The girls soon moved up country to more salubrious pastures and were last heard of heading for Salisbury.

Lawley and his assistants kept a tight hand on the sub-contractors and their employees, as well as the loafers and shady characters of mixed nationalities who hung around the railway camps.

As the line advanced inland it ran more or less straight to Bamboo Creek (later Vila Machado) 30 miles away on the edge of the Pungwe Flats. With immense herds of game, it was a paradise of Buffalo, Waterbuck, Wildebeeste, Eland, Zebras and even Quagga - the now extinct cross between the Zebra and Mule. And it was Lion country.

One afternoon Lawley, Moore and Pauling were creeping along at 4 miles per hour on a truck behind an engine, having derailed several times en route from the Muda River ballast hole. In the middle of a cutting they ran into a herd of 32 lions, lionesses and cubs. This awe-inspiring sight needed a knee-jerk reaction from the cool headed driver and jumpy passengers. Without risking derailment by increasing speed, they all scrambled off and advanced slowly on foot behind the engine, whilst the driver opened the steam cocks and let blast on the whistle. All the lions bolted, except one stately lioness who stood her ground and snarled as they passed.

On another occasion Pauling was whistling along the line, free wheeling downhill with the native manpower riding on the back of the trolley. They came across a lion peering at them. Screeching to a halt ... "I did my best to secrete my corpulent figure partly behind, and partly underneath the trolley. The lion however, evidently concluded that we were unworthy of his attention, for he walked across the railway into the grass."

Resuming their journey they came to a water tank for refuelling engines. Nobody was about, and after much shouting some Africans climbed down from the water tank, and two very shaky Europeans staggered out of a tent. "The noise of the trolley had driven off two lions who were sweeping their paws around in search of a repast, whilst the men inside the tent had been dodging around trying to avoid them."

At another water tank, where elephants used their long trunks to shower themselves, a very lanky fitter who was unable to complete his job, stayed overnight in a makeshift grass shed. Luckily he had unlaced his boots. During the night he felt something tugging at his feet. He let out such a yell that the Africans came running. They saw a lion trying to drag him out, so they drove it off with firebrands; but it escaped with the fitters boot and half his heel.

The man-eaters paid regular visits. "In one month lions scoffed two of our white employees - a yard foreman and a Frenchman," Pauling commented wryly, forgetting to mention the other unrecorded native casualties. Both lions were shot and given decent burials. Man-eaters were ruthlessly and rapidly despatched by professional hunters employed on the

Engineers and construction workers take a break at an earth cutting (NAZ)

Beira line, and the situation never became untenable. In contrast, on the Uganda 'Lunatic Line', the man-eaters at Tsavo were just as numerous. They became bolder and bolder, as the Indian labourers became more and more petrified. Little was done to control them until they got so out of hand that the Indians had fled to the coast and work came to a standstill.

On the Beira Line, Shangaan warriors were also used. These well known fighters from southern regions were far more aggressive than Indians. When one of their number was taken by a man-eater, the whole gang downed tools, and advanced with spears until they found the brute, which was surrounded and promptly despatched.

The railway was an amazingly successful 2 feet gauge miniature line, almost 'thrown' together like a giant Meccano set on the rough and ready earthworks. At places it ran like a fairground switch-back, with sturdy little engines hauling goods and precarious passengers at speeds up to 10 m.p.h. It also pulled specially made trucks carrying 20 ton loads of desperately needed mining machinery.

When trains came off the rails, passengers often assisted with jacking them back on again. Normally they either sat in garden seats under a tarpaulin or in open trucks at the mercy of flying sparks and cinders from the engine. Men often fired at the great herds of game from the moving trucks.

The train stopped regularly at wayside halts and sidings to pick up water and firewood, whilst the passengers enjoyed a stiff drink at a stiff price.

A French restaurant and 'hotel' was opened by Jean Menault, 'Johnnie the Frenchman', at Bamboo Creek. This rudimentary auberge was frequented mainly by the resident engine changing hands, and whatever fancy French names were conjured up for the menus, the meat was nearly always Buffalo. When special occasions demanded, such as a visit from one of the senior officials, Johnnie would present his 'Guinea Fowl flambe au Whiskey' in true flamboyant Gallic style. This was served at the table from a flaming frying pan, well saturated with the only alcohol available. Remarkably, although the flames from this magnificent creation reached straw-roof height, Johnnie's Auberge never burnt down.

From Bamboo Creek (later Vila Machado) the line struggled up the Siluvu Hills, where the train zig-zagged backwards and forwards into

52 miles from Fontesvilla (Ponte do Pungwe)
(RGS)

89

reversing spurs. Passengers would often have to help it on its way if a second engine was not available. The line meandered through the Amatongas Forest, a dense woodland of giant Mahogany, Panga Panga and Chamfuta trees with trunks 40 to 50 feet in circumference and up to 200 feet high, hung with brightly coloured orchids, creepers and a profusion of ferns.

Puffing up to Gondola, the 75 mile peg, and then to Vila Pery (Mandegos), the line reached the half-way point in October 1893, a year after construction commenced. This verdant area was opened out and became ideal for the cultivation of coffee, beans, barley and citrus orchards of the Mozambique Company. Another Savoy Hotel greeted the traveller, with Portuguese establishments such as Simoes nearby. The railway station was also inhabited by lions. Those adjusting the points required escorts of gun-bearers in case of being waylaid by man-eaters. For a time the staff barricaded themselves in their huts whilst the Lords of the Forest were prowling around outside, before they finally settled down to await the outcome, or the arrival of reinforcements from down the line.

A year later Chimoio was reached, 20 miles further inland. It remained the 'end of steel' whilst more finance was arranged. Regular trains ran the Chimoio to Fontesvilla route of 118 miles for a couple of years, taking anything from 14 to 36 hours, before the line was continued on towards the frontier and Umtali (Mutare). There had been an old Chimoio, but in true trail-blazing style the town had moved a few miles nearer the coast to meet the railway. To appease the local Portuguese it was now moving back again

Derailment of an engine on the narrow gauge line in densly wooded country, 1899.
(NAZ)

to the new terminus. As a result there was neither a hotel nor boarding house, only the inevitable shop which combined as a bar - with plenty of liquor and bags of floor space. Visitors spread their blankets, dossed down for the night and attempted to sleep. Mr. Krige from Stellenbosch arrived and opened the first proper hotel, Lawson's, a group of rondavels with beds of wire-netting, and windows of muslin to keep out insects.

On one occasion word reached Alfred Lawley by telegraph that Rhodes was coming down from Salisbury with Dr. Jameson's party on their way to Fontesvilla. Work stopped at the rail-head, and a train was held ready for them at Chimoio for the particular time requested. They waited and waited. And waited. Three days later Rhodes turned up with his party by coach, and after the usual salutations, turned on Lawley. For no apparent reason he launched into a vitriolic and abusive tirade against him in an increasingly high-pitched falsetto, in front of the whole assembly of railway workers, including a thousand Africans. Hoping to ascertain the cause of this outburst, Lawley listened to these tantrums. When no explanation was forthcoming, he turned on Rhodes in no uncertain terms, and exploded: "Who the hell are you? And who do you think you are talking to, squeaking at me like a damned rabbit. Damn your eyes! I won't allow any man on earth to talk to me like that. Are you mad?"

Washaway of an embankment and culvert during the floods of the first heavy rainy season of 1893

(NAZ)

The Station in the Amatongas Forest showing the old 2 feet gauge line alongside the newly laid 3 feet 6 inch gauge

This was followed by a flood of railway vernacular which brought the whole crowd to their senses, and left no-one in doubt as to who was in charge. Rhodes skulked away to a clump of trees, followed by Jameson. Lawley ordered the train to be loaded and informed all and sundry that it would leave as scheduled in a few minutes. Rhodes only just managed to hop on the train as it was moving off.

Later, when the train stopped for water down the line, Jameson arrived at Lawley's compartment and asked him to join Rhodes. Much to his astonishment, Rhodes had calmed down, profusely apologised with deep regret, and admitted he was entirely in the wrong. Lawley reiterated: "If I had not resented your attitude to me, my control over all my men would have gone."

This 'Chimoio Incident' became a standing joke between them ever afterwards.

Until the line was extended, a two day mule-cart drive took passengers to the frontier, stopping at the French store of Vendusi, and at Hawes Store in the hilly country of the Revue River. Mashona carriers took loads of 40 to 50 pounds all the way to Umtali.

Macequece or Massi-Kessi (later Vila Machado) was the frontier outpost and the Portuguese centre of Manicaland, where the famous skirmish had taken place, in which the local Portuguese garrison had been locked up by the British South Africa Company Police.

At last a decent climate prevailed, with a welcome sounding Human's Hotel to greet the traveller - and yet another Savoy Hotel of mud and bricks.

The last steep rise across the border over Christmas Pass was to Umtali (Mutare) nearly 4000 feet high. A motley collection of stores opened on both sides of the border, all run by pioneer 'get-rich-quick' merchants. Botley's, Fisher's, Browns's and Leslie's combined stores with bars, restaurants and refreshment rooms.

Feeding the construction gangs on the Beira Railway was no small undertaking. More than 12,000 Africans with 40 Europeans were eventually employed simply on widening the track - bringing in ballast from the Siluvu Hills 40 miles away. By any stretch of the imagination it was a monumental undertaking. There was no shortage of game, and the noted hunter Neumeyer was in charge of providing meat. Mickey Norton, one of the last of the old time elephant hunters was also employed to supply the endless quantities of meat needed to keep the labourers on the job. Later he moved on to wider fields, dodging the Belgian Congo Police, and roaming Nyasaland and Portuguese East Africa. Like a true Irishman of his day, he raised the Union Jack over an uncharted island in the Rovuma River, midway between German and Portuguese territory - poaching from both sides. No one interfered because no one knew who owned the island.

The prolific game on the Pungwe Flats and adjoining areas around the line of rail drew many other sporting characters in search of 'big bags'. Dan Mahoney, another roving Irishman, killed 34 lions in the Gorongoza district in one month. His compatriot Ewart Grogan was put on a train half dead with fever, and nursed back to health by Alfred Lawley at Beira. From there Grogan began his epic journey up Africa.

Other good shots were 'Bloody Bill' Upsher, the bald-headed maniac from Huntingdonshire, and Harry Pauling - one of the many who succumbed to malaria. One morning he felled eight buffalo before breakfast. He also envisaged a scheme to capture and tame thousands of zebra roaming the region, and much in demand for Zeederburg's coach services. The plan was to fence an area about 5 miles square, then subdivide it into smaller and smaller sections until all the animals could be captured.

One of the first train guards on the line was Larsen the Swede. He too turned to the more profitable profession of ivory poaching, roaming Central Africa when the boundaries were ill defined. Accompanied by his African woman, Maria, and a young boy, all three blasted away with their rifles, and a herd was often literally blown to pieces. He died a terrible lingering death in Angola, poisoned by a jealous coloured woman, miles from any medical attention.

By the time Harold Varian reached Mozambique and the line was being widened to 3 feet 6 inches, food had improved for the 'workers' :

"The larder at Fontesvilla was always well stocked with a wide range of meat - buck, geese, duck, guinea fowl, teal, francolin - a chef's dream, but alas with no chef. We had an African cook, and although his methods were

Temporary railway station at Macequece (or Massi-Kessi) on the Mozambique frontier 1897 (RGS)

crude in comparison with European standards of haute cuisine, they were nevertheless effective. One item consisted of a large square of bread which was toasted, or better still fried, not in the ordinary way, but first dipped quickly in water and then plunged into hot fat. This made it crisp outside and soft within. Butter was then spread on it, and then anchovy or bloater paste, then a slice of one of those almost flavourless onions, cut to the thinness of tissue paper, then the fried liver of guinea fowl, and finally a stuffed, hard boiled egg, point upwards in the middle. This was a very popular number.

"Another dish was contributed by an expert Italian, who possessed both the materials and the machine for making macaroni, which he supplied to his fellow countrymen on the works. He was an artist in cooking it as well, and always timed his efforts, watch in hand. As there was no receptacle of sufficient size to accommodate the result, we generally used an enamel wash-hand basin. Into this went first a layer of his special macaroni, then a layer of sauce of his own concoction, then another layer of macaroni, and so on until the right depth was reached. On top of the last layer of snowy macaroni he placed roast teal, one for each member of the party, which we could deal with as we liked. The combination was superb."

George Pauling's appetite for liquid refreshment was a constant source of amusement and sometimes concern to his friends and colleagues. On one 48 hour trip travelling down the line with Alfred Lawley and A.M. Moore, the company Engineer, they consumed 300 bottles of excellent German beer. Returning to Delagoa Bay at about the same time he shared a breakfast of a thousand oysters and eight bottles of champagne with two companions.

James Lawson, born in Elgin, Scotland in 1865, pitched up in the Cape Colony at the age of 16 and joined the scramble for Rhodesia. He became Catering Manager on the Beira Railway in 1893 all through the very unhealthy country between Fontesvilla and Macequece.

At some of the wayside stations it was customary to stop for the odd wee dram of fire-water, often a successful blend of Scotch Whiskey combined with the local manager's home-distilled favourite made from bamboo, maize, rice and any other ingredients to hand. In order to forestall any complaints, regulars were always offered 'the real Macoy'. At one stage of the game a whole wayside hut went up in flames, lock, stock and barrel, under suspicious circumstances.

"In April 1898 the first section to Umtali was completed," recalled Thomas Rudland; "We celebrated with a 'Railway Banquet' - and compared the spread with our former rice rations. When we drank the toast to the 400 men who had laid down their lives, we thought of the labourers from India who had died almost to a man; we knew that no other railway in the world had had such a high mortality rate. But we had built the longest narrow gauge railway in the world !"

The original rail route over the mountainous border to the little town of Umtali had been surveyed to serve the Rezende and Penhalonga Mines as a concession to the Mozambique Company. Now it was found that the gradient would be prohibitive, and the approach line would no longer be able to pass over the old wagon route of Christmas Pass.

So, if the railway couldn't get to the town, take the town to the railway, was the logical conclusion. Everything would be moved a few miles down the mountain. Charles Metcalfe and the surveyors Mansergh and Pickett selected a suitable site.

Identical plots of land were swopped in the new town, and the ramshackle buildings were transported by the railway company down through the Pass. As Commissioner of Works, Pauling reminded the residents that as no decision had been taken on where the station was to be located, none could say they had been unfairly favoured.

The railway from the south had only reached Bulawayo 4 months previously, when the first train arrived at Umtali from Beira in February 1898. The engine was decked with flowers and carried the slogan 'Now we shan't be long to Cairo'.

Umtali became a trim little town with flamboyant trees and Parks. It was a town run by that old school of landladies that took the strain whilst their husbands took the back seat, often behind the bar. Mother Brown was of that ilk. She ran the Kings Arms. Stout of body as well as stout of mind, she stood no nonsense and single-handedly threw out the odd character who made himself a nuisance. Yet her heart was not stoney and she was always a soft spot for those who genuinely fell on bad luck - they never went away hungry. Her reputation spread far and wide through-out the railway business.

In the upper part of town were the Kings Arms, the Royal, The Cecil, the Masonic and a private hotel, the Avenue. There was even a race course. The lower part of town near the Railway Station was named Paulington, at that time the seat of railway administration, with its own hotel.

No sooner had the line reached Umtali than the survey pressed on, across the highveldt nearly 200 miles to Salisbury. The native rebellion was still on, and the final surveys were carried out by the toughest of all Scotsmen, James Frame under the protection of an armed guard. With a notorious reputation for driving most of his assistants to death's door, he was described by Harold Varian, one of the few to survive, as "one of those hard, capable men whose only idea in life was work; food, recreation, even the simplest comforts, just did not matter."

From Umtali the young Kingsley Fairbridge ventured west to join his father on the survey of the new township of Rusapi.

"I walked the distance, sixty odd miles, following the survey line of the Mashonaland Railway. At the Odzi, Inyazura and Inyamapamberi rivers, bridge builders had started work. At various points on the survey line were contractor's huts, where great gangs were digging the cuttings and laying down the embankments of the permanent way.

'Chai-ire!' called the overseers; and a hundred hungry voices would respond in chorus, 'Hara-hara!'

"I camped with strange men at night, and heard strange speech and tales. Some of the men had worked on the Beira railway - you knew them by their yellow faces - but most of them came from England or the Argentine. This high-veld work was different from the struggle on the Pungwe Flats, but even here men died. I remember Robinson, a florid, jovial man who told us about his wife and three little children in a London suburb. And Dicky Marks, the mason; and his chum Angus. And Bloech of Transau and Ross of Rusapi. And the merry Irish lad at Inyazura, the bridge builder at the Odzi, and many another of whose hospitality I partook, whose names I have forgotten, but whose faces are still in my eyes.

"A lad of thirteen, dressed in knickers and shirt sleeves, I walked on the outskirts of the Empire, where the shouting of men, the ring of hammers on stone, and the thud of picks in the baked earth were always in my ears.

"And so I went ahead on the tide of progress, wondering and observing, and thinking of the thousand homesteads that would some day dot these fields."

Whilst the line was being extended near Rusapi, it traversed an area famous for its reluctant supply of labour. This was in the district of the virulent Makoni tribe, who maintain an independent streak to this day.

Chief Makoni, however, was more than happy to supply certain labourers on request. Messengers were sent by the Chief to every village and a few of the worst idlers, wasters and mischief-makers would be rounded up for such onerous tasks as wood cutting and carrying sleepers. In many cases wielding a shovel for ballast works was beyond their capabilities. Any job to do with metal work was, however, eagerly sought after. Some became excellent workers and learned a trade. In 1899 Native Commissioner Morris wrote: "I have supplied boys to the bridge contractors and have heard these men say some are equal to any of the coast boys. I have seen them using riveting machines as well as any colonial native."

Across the border in Mozambique territory, railways and roads were maintained by gangs of local labour, compulsorily recruited under the Chiboro scheme from the Chiefs and Headmen to work on the

Cecil Hotel, Umtali

sections through which the route passed. All the workers lived in the districts for which they were responsible, and were paid only a nominal amount; but were well fed. A certain stretch was apportioned to each gang, which knew exactly "when, where and how" to work it. Faithful and intelligent natives worked in gangs entirely on their own, with only occasional visits from Portuguese overseers, who didn't tolerate laziness. But the system worked, and it was hardly the sort of 'slavery' which clever little Wilberforces would have one believe.

First Train from Umtali (Mutare) to Salisbury (Harare), May 1899. The Johnson family (centre and on engine)

The railways gave whole tribes a new impetus to free enterprise, when communities began to concentrate along the line of rail. They were happy to ride to their villages either in or on the carriages, and the odd lumps of coal from the footplate came in handy for high temperature melting and-heating work.

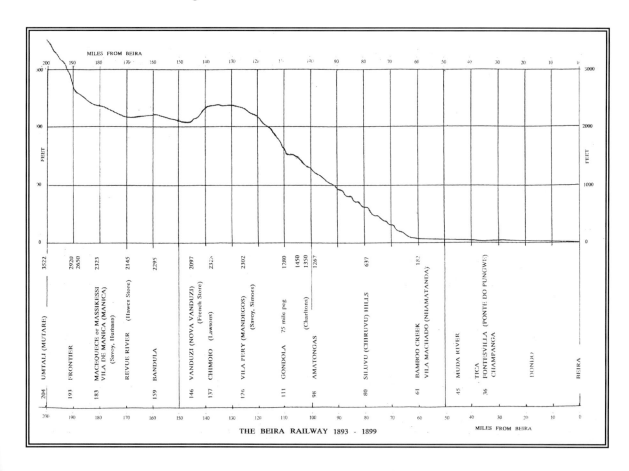

THE BEIRA RAILWAY 1893 - 1899

SATAN'S OWN SUMMER PALACE

Beira - bright and breezy;-
Beaches and Bazaars;
Red sail sunsets and warm velvet nights;
Oceans of Seafood and Exotic Charm...

...so proclaimed an early advertising message from the depths of 'despotic' Beira, which started life with a reputation as the most lawless, drunken shanty town in the whole of Africa.

The opening up of the new Colony of Rhodesia caused not only the birth, but also the overnight explosion, of Beira. Before the advent of the railway, hardly a dozen shacks existed in this steaming, evil, foul smelling, unknown Portuguese East African settlement where the Pungwe River met the sea.

When the first pioneers arrived on the coast nothing greeted them, except a flat of expanse of empty sand. As soon as the Portuguese got wind of a party unloading stores from the boats and about to open a road, a few officials garrisoned themselves in tents on the narrow strip of shifting sands. Behind them lay a swamp of black mud, breeding ground for trillions of blood-thirsty mosquitoes. Drinking water had to be carried from 5 miles away.

A more natural outlet for land-locked Rhodesia lay on the south side of the Busi Delta. Sofala was a fabled port, with origins lost in the mists of time. A thousand years ago it was a flourishing Arab settlement trading in ivory and gold to Persia, India and China. In 1505 the Portuguese landed and the fortress which arose with stone from Portugal stood intact for 400 years, only to fall to the ravages of the sea in the 20th. century. The locals still retained their distinct Arab features. Relations between London and Lisbon aimed to ensure easy access from the coast to the ill-defined border with Rhodesia, along the river which they considered to be an international waterway. But this was interpreted entirely differently by the local Portuguese - an autocratic bunch of ruffians whose view was that 'we got here first', even though they had settled not very far inland during all those centuries. They ran a campaign of constant harassment, delays, customs embargoes, fines and duty payments. This culminated in the 'Beira Incident'.

A year later in 1891, 'Port Beira', was named after a Prince of the Royal family, and was firmly established on the map. There were 400 inhabitants, mostly English. Colonial-American style chalets sprang up everywhere. The British Consul occupied a large chalet right on the edge of a magnificent mangrove swamp, which made it totally uninhabitable, so he moved to a delightful seashore cottage with waves lapping up to the verandah.

When the first section of 2 feet gauge railway had been completed between Chimoio and Fontesvilla, Beira had a population of nearly 4000. The town had spread 3 miles along the coast, with a bridge crossing the Chieve Creek, connecting the centre with the harbour.

The newly opened Beira Port was owned and operated by the British South Africa Company. It was a sort of mini British enclave; its whole existence dependant on trade with the British territories beyond, run by clearing houses such as the Manica Trading Company. For a time even the Bank of Beira dealt freely in Pounds Sterling, and golden sovereigns were in circulation for years. Even as late as 1932 a Beira hotel would not let the Portuguese Colonial Minister pay in Portuguese currency.

The Point Hotel, near the Landing Stage, run by Mr. Classerath, was the first hotel and restaurant to open its doors. It was the focal point of the infant town, surrounded by half a dozen corrugated iron shacks, providing extraordinary good nourishment considering the circumstances. The Royal Hotel followed - run by an enterprising Italian monarchist named Martini. Other establishments soon proliferated, together with scores of Bars and Clubs, and all the usual places that abound in bustling sea ports. Many of the better hotels reflected the British aspect, the paramount power on the Oceans of the day, such as the Savoy, Queens, Victoria, Central, International, and the friendly little Lisboa.

All the buildings belonged to the Portuguese Government, although the planning and surveying of the Township had been left to the British. Whilst the edifices themselves often left a lot to be desired, the hotels - leased to individuals - were excellent. They served delicious fresh fish; with vegetables and fruit from the miles of neat gardens spread along the banks of the Busi River. Bananas, lemons, mangoes, paw-paws and other exotic varieties were also grown to supply the passing ships on the fast increasing

Trollies of the Manica Trading Company - one of the pioneer shipping companies of Beira.

maritime trade of the East Coast through the Suez Canal.

Healthy sea breezes soon made Beira the 'The Sanatorium of Central Africa', complete with a large hospital for hunters and prospectors from up country, which by 1898 was run by Dr. Harry Haynes-Lovell.

The town rapidly developed into a mecca for traders from the interior. There were masses of skins, ivory and rhino horns, spices and timber displayed in large well stocked stores, together with exotic goods imported from Europe, Arabia and the Orient.

There were no horses, carriages or carts, and the only means of locomotion for 30 years were trollies, which ran on a 'tramway' of 1 foot 6 inches gauge, from the Customs Offices, close to the Landing Pier, through the wide, sandy streets of the town. Essential in hot weather, the trollies were owned by the chief hotels, trading stores and individuals. Everyone who was anyone owned a Trolley, with its garden seats and canopy, propelled by two trolley boys, and identified by racy colours and stylish lines. If a lady approached, one removed one's hat first, then descended from the Trolley, which was lifted off the rails, to allow her to

The bridge over the Chieve Creek, breeding ground for mosquitoes.
(below)

The Hub of Beira - The Savoy Hotel - later owned and operated by the genial Alfred Lawley.
(bottom)

pass. Rights of Way for men were often settled by an argument or a toss of the coin. Turntables at crossroads - at which Portuguese officials had priority - caused occasional traffic jams.

In the centre of town stood the Railway Station, prim and proper, made from a mix of mud bricks and concrete blocks, whitewashed and imperious looking - the sole and only reason for Beira's existence. From it went forth the line through 'Hell' to the Highveldt ... the line which in recent memory had taken a toll almost without parallel in railway records.

A few streets away from the Railway Station and behind the Rua Alfredo Lawley stood the Savoy Hotel, owned later by the genial and gregarious Alfred Lawley. The Savoy was Beira's grandest rendezvous, famed for its 'choice liquors and rare old

"Pre-eminent in my memory as the symbol of that dynamic half century is the figure of Alfred Lawley of the firm of Pauling. He and his hospitality, consisting of train loads of food and drink, ached as a veritable Panzer Division in forcing railways through the physical reluctance of the African veld"
Ewart Grogan

wines', which went down well with the unlimited seafood and rock lobsters of monumental proportions. It also prided itself on being "built of steel, stone and cement in the most approved style for a sub tropical climate - always cool in the hottest weather."

Known as 'The King of Beira' the famous and formidable Lawley spent much of his time here, entertaining, reminiscing and holding forth on the verandah until well into his 70's. He once described the construction of a particular bridge on the Beira line to Ronald Patterson:

"I lost seven construction engineers at that bridge - malaria and blackwater, of course".

And on enquiring what then transpired, Lawley replied laconically : "I then went out and completed the damn thing myself - with native mahogany; we had by then run out of steel - and Engineers".

Lawley also devoted his remarkable energies to the development of pioneer agricultural concessions from the Mozambique Company, which produced rubber, cotton, sugar and coconut palms.

Until the Second World War the verandah bar of the Savoy Hotel was the hub of Beira. It was the clearing house on the East Coast of Africa for the Rhodesias, Nyasaland, (Zimbabwe, Zambia and Malawi), the Congo and all the territories beyond. Vivien Meik described it in the 1930's :

"The woes and joys of planters - and their wives; tales of mighty hunting; of unbelievable safaris; of discoveries of alluvial gold beyond Lake Nyasa; of water found where water is not; rumours of tribal discontent or of brooding mischief; confidential government moves, appointments, dismissals, scandals; the frailty of wives or the duplicity of husbands - these are merely fragments of an evenings light chatter on the Savoy verandah. Weird and mysterious - and what is marvellous - the tales that were told were mostly true".

Not much had changed when in the 1960's, George Pauling's youngest daughter Jane Glass paid a 'pilgrimage' visit to Beira with her husband. In her younger days, after the death of her father, she and her sister had always referred to their endearing old god-father Lawley as "Uncle Alfred".

They travelled by train from Umtali in carriages of the same old *fin de siécle* mahogany, brass and leather variety, complete with the fans and brackish water showers that had served so well over half a century. And the train still took, with unscheduled stops, about 20 hours to cover the 200 odd miles to the coast. Unfortunately there was no refreshment or dining car attached. But as always this was not a problem. At a tiny wayside station, in the middle of the steamy Amatongas forest, the train

halted. And there they sat in solemn style, whilst a meal was whistled up from 'somewhere'. It was a meal fit for a King - the famous peri-peri chicken and prawns, with rice and fruit - all washed down with the ubiquitous Vinho Verde wine from Portugal. When the meal was finished, the yellowing, fever-stricken, scar-faced Portuguese conductor, who looked as if he had been far too long in Africa, politely advised them that 'when they were ready' the train would continue on its way down to the coast.

Banana Sellers and Water Carriers alongside narrow gauge trolley lines at Beira (UCT MACMILLAN)

Belly up on the beach at Beira, George Pauling's appetite was legendary, and his recipe to beat malaria relied largely on huge intakes of alcohol. Teetotallers, he reckoned, stood little chance. (P. & Co)

Arguably the most influential British politician of his day after Lord Salisbury, 'Radical Joe' - Joseph Chamberlain - emanated from a successful Birmingham screw manufacturing family. Much to the disgust of his puritan Unitarian relatives, he transformed into 'Pushful Joe', the aggressive imperialist and Colonial Secretary of State holding sway over one fifth of the population of this planet. He fought tooth and nail to expand Britain's Empire, aiding and abetting Cecil Rhodes in his momentous schemes, which many of Chamberlain's colleagues failed to support. His wife Mary was an eminent American beauty of the day. Their eldest son Austen became Chancellor of the Exchequer and Secretary of Foreign Affairs, whilst their youngest son Neville became the ill-fated Prime Minister in that era of appeasement leading up to World War II. Their siblings included the eccentric Pakenham (later Longford) family of literary merit, and paradoxically, left-leaning social causes.

8

TO THE PLACE OF SLAUGHTER

A MILE-A-DAY FROM MAFEKING TO BULAWAYO

"I am anxious to take over the Bechuanland Protectorate at once," Rhodes wrote to the new Colonial Secretary Joseph Chamberlain in 1895. "It will save you £80,000 a year, and if you give it to me I promise to build the railway from Mafeking to Bulawayo in four years and to begin the railway a month after transfer."

From the edge of the Kalahari desert, skirting the 'hostile' Transvaal border, the lines were poised to advance through Rhodes' 'Suez Canal' to the north. They already ran through the tiny British Bechuanaland, but Rhodes wanted more - the whole of the Bechuanaland Protectorate which was five times larger.

He planned the route up to Gaberone, some 100 miles further north where it swerved away from the Transvaal border. But Chamberlain refused to be rushed; he needed to placate the Bechuana Chiefs.

Some of them were not so happy about a railway through their territory on the edge of the Kalahari Desert; particularly Khama, the Paramount Chief. "We fear the company will take our land and sell it to others. We fear they will fill our country with liquor shops as they have in Bulawayo and some parts of Matabeleland and Mashonaland."

Emissaries hastily arranged for an unhappy trio of Indunas to parley with Queen Victoria in London. When they arrived at Southampton, suitably seasick, they took the train to Victoria Station in the heart of Her Imperial Majesty's capital. There they were left twiddling their thumbs. The man they had really come to see, Chamberlain, was away in the country. It took a combination of a hostile press, a bunch of little Englanders and a bevy of anti-Rhodes elements, as well as the meddlesome London Missionary Society on behalf of these worthy Christians, to bring Chamberlain back. After escorting them to Windsor Castle to see the Queen, Chamberlain arranged an Indaba in the Colonial Office. With a blue pencil he drew a large reserve of land which came under Queen Victoria's personal patronage. The rest of the Protectorate, including a narrow strip of land passing along the frontier, would be ceded to the Chartered Company, and for the use of the Iron Horse to Bulawayo. In return for this hundred thousand square miles of territory, the Chartered Company would forfeit the £200,000 promised by the previous government as a subsidy for the railway.

Having taken in the sights of London, and having conferred on Chamberlain the title 'Moathlodi', the Man Who Rights Things, the Chiefs duly returned home, happy in the knowledge that they were now under the protection of the all powerful Queen.

On the very same day that the narrow strip of land was ceded to Rhodes' Charter Company, President Kruger opened up his drifts across the Vaal River - thus ensuring an uninterrupted rail route to his beleaguered Johannesburg.

However, further north, in the tiny settlements of Bulawayo and Fort Salisbury, the settlers were seething. Speedy and reliable transport was non existent. Wagons spent months on the road and there was an acute shortage of almost everything. Doel Zeederburg, the road transport contractor, had already opened a service from Pietersburg in the Transvaal to Fort Tuli. From there onwards ox carts stumbled their weary way forward.

Years previously British prospectors had obtained concessions in this watershed area of the Limpopo and the Zambezi, ruled by the warrior King Lo Bengula of the Matabele. These Zulu offshoots had fled northwards from their old nation on the hinterland of Natal. One of the most disciplined tribes in all Africa, they had bloodily advanced, pillaging and subjugating their docile neighbours. Some of them had actually reached the shores of Lake Tanganyika.

Spurred by the advance of the British South Africa Company, and chasing the rainbow, settlers arrived; some great and good, others downright greedy. The wise ones moved on when they found little to exploit. The air was thick with mistrust and mischief.

In gout ridden decline, Lo Bengula was treated by Dr. Jameson with large doses of morphine. He lost control of his belligerent Indunas, his warriors scattered and he was forced to flee from his royal settlement Bulawayo, 'The Place of Slaughter'.

It was a ruined kraal when a white settlement sprang up in 1893. When gold was struck in the market square, thousands of fortune seekers arrived within weeks, including cowboys and prospectors from as far afield as California and Australia.

Fort Tuli was a strategically placed outpost near the Transvaal and Bechuanaland borders; an important telegraph station on the way north. It was garrisoned by the Charter Company's Police from a hilltop fort overlooking a wild-west style frontier township, built not of the usual mud huts, but of solid wood and corrugated iron sheds laboriously brought up by wagon. There was a Baker and Barber Shop, Hotel and restaurant and even a local newspaper - the Tuli Times. The township had all the promise of being a prosperous permanent feature on the barren landscape, until the steel rails passed it by. The narrow strip of land ceded to the Charter Company along this part of the Transvaal border, called the Pitsani Strip - today the rich farming area of the Tuli Block, proved entirely unsuitable for a railway. There were too many streams to be crossed, so in the time available it was decided to follow an easier route further to the west.

THE FAMOUS FOUR R's RESOUNDED IN QUICK SUCCESSION - RHODES, RAID, REBELLION & RINDEPEST

The rivalry between Brit and Boer continued. The Saga of the Jameson Raid was about to unfold. Stirring and muttering around Johannesburg had fanned the flames of the real, or imagined, grievances of the Uitlanders - those foreign workers of all nationalities and creeds on whom the whole wealth of the Transvaal depended.

Their complaints included absurdly high taxes, contracts for lucky Afrikaners including liquor and dynamite monopolies, and little or no say in local or State affairs. A group of the more disgruntled ones planned an invasion to annexe the Transvaal.

Rhodes was sounding out his friends and colleagues. Many of them thought the Uitlanders were too busy making money to worry about politics - including Robinson, Barnato, and Phillips. Pauling concurred: "He solicited my opinion of a prospect of an uprising in the Transvaal. I expressed the view that it would be very difficult, if not impossible, to have a successful revolution in such a country, unless the bulk of the working population were in favour of it. Rhodes replied to the effect that I knew a lot about railways and other business matters but damned little about politics."

It was later estimated that little more than about 5 per cent of the well-paid foreign workers were in a mood for revolt, even though a massive petition had been signed by several thousand of them.

With a wink from Rhodes in Cape Town and a nod from Chamberlain in London, Dr. Jameson's 500 horsemen sallied forth across the border from Mafeking, from the very strip of ground that had been ceded for railway use. Nearing Johannesburg they were ambushed by the Transvaal authorities, forewarned and fore-armed. This time it was the Brits who were the fillibusters. Traitors in the Transvaal, and Heroes at Home, it took international pressure and a lot of whitewash to ensure all the culprits were only fined and imprisoned, including the invincible Alfred Lawley, who had been drinking in the wrong bars, and was caught on his way back to Beira. He was eventually bailed out for £2000.

Kaiser Bill, or rather his Ministers, sent a belligerent telegram of congratulation to President Kruger, and earned the wrath of his grandmother Queen Victoria. It was a foretaste of the sabre rattling which led to the outbreak of the South African War three years later.

The hot-headed adventurer Frank Johnson later claimed to have been offered the job of leading the invasion force.

"Rhodes asked me if I realised the growing strength of the Transvaal Republic. They were no longer the insignificant lot of Boer farmers, but through the discovery of gold at Johannesburg, were bound to have inexhaustable wealth at their disposal, which must result in their becoming a nation of great strength. This would probably result in their joining hands with the Germans in South West Africa, who would finally cut the Cape off from Mashonaland, thus rendering Rhodes' great project of an all-British route from the Cape to Cairo an empty dream."

Rhodes unfolded his plan. The Police of the Britsh South Africa Company would be brought down to protect the survey of the railway northward of Mafeking. In due course a sudden SOS call for help would come from the Uitlanders in Johannesburg, whom the police would dash off to asssit. On arrival the Uitlanders would rise in rebellion.

Johnson claimed he turned down the idea, arguing that an internal rising by the Uitlanders was one thing, and might even catch the sympathy of the world; but an invasion by a foreign force was an act of war. The Orange Free State would very likely come to the assistance of the Transvaal, with its big guns commanded by German Officers. He suggested an alternative, which never materialised; the gradual infiltration of a Force on the railways running into Johannesburg from Delagoa Bay, Natal and the Cape. About 50 men would arrive on the six trains each day, disguised as prospectors and miners. The scheme would be coordinated from Rhodes mining office, and the men dispersed to await the order to organise the miners in revolt.

After the abortive Raid, Rhodes had no choice. He resigned, lay low, and waited for the storm to blow over. He hoped to dodge facing the music, for (in the eyes of some) having brought Britain to the brink of war. He resigned himself as best he could to the problems facing Matabeleland.

Ready for new challenges, after the first round of the Raid enquiry, he rushed back to Africa from England. The heat was still on him. Landing at Beira and ill with fever he was met by Pauling and Lawley who went on board with a dire warning. President Kruger had twisted the arms of the Portuguese Government to have him arrested on landing, and handed over for trial in the Transvaal. They also told him that the natives in Matabeleland were decidedly unfriendly and besieging Bulawayo. Rhodes stayed on board ship, in neutral territory, whilst Lawley's excellent relations with Colonel Machado, the Governor of Beira, were exploited to the full. He pleaded that if Rhodes was arrested, the whole of Beira's railway community would rise up in revolt, take the town and cause an international incident. Colonel Machado telegraphed Lisbon begging his Government to reject Kruger's scheme. Without waiting for a reply, he allowed Rhodes to land and advance through to Salisbury on his way to Bulawayo with an armed column.

Having also run the gauntlet to Government House in Bulawayo on his way to England, Pauling stayed overnight to discuss the railway and other matters:

"The next morning I was up at about 5 o'clock and had a talk with Mr.

Rhodes. As we walked up and down the verandah he said very seriously: "Now Pauling, when you reach England I would like you to go at once to see Mr. Chamberlain (the Colonial Secretary), and the Duke of Devonshire, and to tell them in your most emphatic language that if I am made to go to England now, whilst I am so absolutely necessary here I shall open my mouth and tell all I know ".

This potential threat of spilling the beans came like a bolt out of the blue. Somewhat dumbstruck, Pauling hurried down to Cape Town and took the next boat to England.

"On my arrival in London I was taken to the door of Mr. Chamberlain's office in the House of Commons. When I entered he was sitting at a small table and asked me to sit down opposite him. I gave him the message in the words that Mr. Rhodes told it to me. Mr. Chamberlain, who was playing with a pen on a piece of blank paper, looked up at me and said very quietly: "I wonder what he means." I replied: "If you do not know what he means it is not for me to suggest it to you, but I can tell you that he means what he says." Mr. Chamberlain was silent for a few moments, and then looking towards me again, he continued: "You can let Mr. Rhodes know that I will do all I can."

"Not long after my meeting, Mr. Chamberlain made a speech in the House of Commons, very much in favour of Mr. Rhodes, which practically put a stop to the clamour to send him home. What emerged at the enquiry about the Raid is public knowledge, but I consider both Mr. Rhodes and Dr. Jameson took upon their shoulders blame which others deserved; and I maintain that neither of them was responsible for the attempt to take the Transvaal in 1895."

"Mr. Chamberlain then asked me whether I thought the Boers could be supplying arms to the Matabele, since several rifles which had been captured were marked with the Transvaal Government stamp of Z.A.R. I replied that he must not believe anything of that nature, as I was absolutely certain from my knowledge of the Boers, and my long residence in South Africa, that it was contrary to their principles to arm the natives to fight against white people. Mr. Chamberlain did not appear satisfied. He banged his fist on the table and said:

"If I could only prove the Transvaal people were supplying arms to natives, I would have war with them tomorrow!"

Flora Shaw was the colourful 'Times' Colonial correspondent, and one of the most gracious women around Africa at that time. She had been a keen supporter of the Uitlanders and was also a great admirer of Rhodes, having furthered his cause of opening up Africa against much opposition. When she questioned his motives for such expensive imperial schemes Rhodes simply replied: "Some men collect butterflies. I do this. It interests me." Flora Shaw's testimony to the Raid Enquiry was crucial.

Incriminating telegrams had passed through her hands, but she insisted she was a journalist first and foremost, and not a politician. With the clearest of explanations she was the most outstanding witness in the final outcome of vindicating Rhodes.

Frank Johnson also put the blame fairly and squarely on others.

"Dr. Rutherford Harris, Secretary of the the Chartered Company is said to have falsified and delayed the transmission of telegrams from Rhodes to Jameson forbidding the Raid", he wrote. "The reason for this criminal act lay in the fact that Rutherford Harris, through his close knowledge, had been busily feathering his own nest on the London Stock Exchange, where he was acting as 'bear' on a large scale. The cancellation of the Raid would, of course, have involved him in heavy losses, so he saw to it that the raid did take place, and his own fortune ensued."

In a little known earlier rehearsal of the Raid, Rhodes had conspired with Dr. Jameson, the gullible rogue, in a mad-cap scheme to take over Matabeleland. He persuaded Frank Johnson and a wild, red-bearded American Francis Heany, to kidnap King Lo Bengula with a few Indunas, and force them to give away their territory without a fight. Heany's indiscreet drinking habits caused a spillage of the beans, which reached the ears of a missionary, who reported him to the High Commissioner. Rhodes was summoned forthwith and told to lay off this heavy-handed conspiracy. Thwarted once again, he accused the Colonial Office of being run by missionaries, philanthropists and Jews. They in turn accused Rhodes of being a self-seeking, greedy adventurer who sabotaged their efforts to maintain the balance of international peace.

After the Matabele heard that Dr. Jameson had been imprisoned for the Raid, and his forces defeated, they decided to strike back. When the Matabele struck, they struck hard. Benign storekeepers and benevolent missionaries bore the brunt. Eking out a living, doing no harm to anyone, lonely farming families were wiped out - like the entire Cunningham family who were bludgeoned to death and their homestead burnt down. In one room were the charred remains of the mother and three children. In another the bodies of four adults. A little girl escaped down to the river, where she was pounded to death by Matabele women with rocks from the river.

Bulawayo's Market Square, which 3 years earlier had almost been paved with gold, became the scene of the biggest and best laager in Africa, according to Selous. The enormous wide streets, designed to turn a span of oxen, were ringed with wagons chained together. Inside the laager, 700 men and 500 women & children waited for the cry: "Women and children to the Clubhouse." Outside, 15,000 warriors were armed with spears and assegais, and 2000 modern rifles from dubious sources. The attack never came.

Weary with war and facing defeat, the Chiefs wanted peace.

Rhodes rode into the Matopos Hills to parley with them. Unarmed, he was accompanied only by Johan Colenbrander, Vere Stent and Dr. Sauer. With armed warriors hovering in the background, seething with indignation, Rhodes stood his ground. But concessions were made. The Zulu Police would go back to their country, the bad white men who took their women would be punished, and there would be no more killings. The fierce murmurs and flashing eyes subsided. In the end the rebellion died out. It was Rhodes' greatest triumph.

Grootboon was the brave Swazi scout who had originally heard rumours that the Matabele wanted peace, and had approached the Chiefs to arrange the Indaba.

"You have done great things for me, Grootboon", Rhodes said, "what can I do for you. ?"

Turning to his Native Commissioner J.G.Macdonald he announced:

"Give Grootboon, whenever he asks for it, a hundred acres of land, a Wagon and span of Oxen, twelve cows, a decent horse and one hundred pounds."

But Grootboon replied: "I don't want it. When I leave this camp I shall go north to help the missionaries." Grootboon was never seen or heard of again.

After the Raid and rebellion, another nightmare followed. Rindepest. The

Rhodes' camp in the Matopos Hills outside Bulawayo
(BOOKS OF ZIM)

scourge of Africa started in Somaliland about 1889 and spread through the heart of the continent killing up to 90 per cent of cattle, as well as wild antelope, giraffe, eland and particularly buffalo. The disease crossed the last real line of defence, the Zambezi River in 1896. It streaked south, sometimes advancing 20 to 30 miles a day, faster than ox transport - carried by native runners and cattle drivers.

"At least 2 million head of cattle must have died in the region of Mashonaland, Matabeleland and Bechuanaland alone," estimated Pauling, "The journey from Mafeking to Bulawayo by coach took us 9 days. At every coach station and frequently along the road the stench from the unburied bodies of cattle was awful, and two or three times I was physically sick from the nauseating smell."

Transport was forbidden beyond certain points but it was too late. Many of those in authority refused to accept the inevitable. They said it was tongue fever, to be cured by doses of paraffin, salt and soot. Desperate and knowledgeable transport riders knew the difference. They tried a crude sort of inoculation. They soaked a length of string in the lung fluid of an infected victim, and threaded it through the tails of the oxen; if the tail dropped off, the animal was immune. What the rindepest did not decimate was wiped out by East Coast fever. For when rindepest killed the buffalo, it also eradicated the tse-tse fly, which bred in buffalo dung.

Rhodes in the Matopos at the meeting of the Matabele Chiefs, with Johan Colenbrander, Vere Stent and Dr. Hans Sauer (BOOKS OF ZIM)

Tse-tse fly was the one deterrent which stopped cattle from moving up from the coast. Safe from the fly, they brought East Coast fever with them. It was the end of the road for the transport riders business. Only the barest minimum of foodstuffs were getting through to Bulawayo, and transport was costing £200 per ton from Mafeking. Settlers and the local press were fuming, threatening Rhodes and everyone else to pull all the stops out and get the railway rolling. .

Rhodes gave in. He asked Pauling to rush the rails through. Taking the challenge he confidently predicted that given a free hand, the 492 miles would be completed in under 500 days.

Pauling turned to his cousin Harold, to run the lines forward. The untimely death, at the age of 39, of his brother and partner Harry, had been the hardest blow he had ever faced.

Pauling Brothers now became Pauling and Company.

Out of sight in Salisbury but not out of mind, George Pauling was also busying himself in Dr. Jameson's administration with the seemingly conflicting interests of Posts, Mines, Transport and Public Works. Operating from three different offices under the same roof, he often held forth at the Avenue Hotel bar. This was the easiest place to placate endless delegations of irate merchants, outraged by the non arrival of the mails and the railway, which had not yet reached Salisbury either from Beira or Bulawayo.

Back in Bulawayo, watching the progress of the 'ramshackle' Railway, the press and settlers were still fuming: "The rate is almost disgraceful, 45 miles in about 9 months - at that rate it will take 8 years to reach us."

Passing the buck, Rhodes told them: "By 1897 Mr. Pauling has promised to bring you the railway from the south to Bulawayo, and they are pushing on the railway from Beira as hard as they can."

Whilst Alfred Lawley was beavering away from the Mozambique coast up towards Salisbury, Harold Pauling was pressing ahead through Bechuanaland to Bulawayo. A laid back character with a hefty wit, he was under heavy pressure from all sides. At every opportunity he pressed his point to Rhodes with 'straight talking' about the pointless delays

The impetuous Colossus, inclined to tantrums, responded in kind. One day he button-holed George Pauling in an excitable state.

"Pauling, I won't be bullied by your cousin Harold", he exclaimed in a high-pitched voice. "He bullies me everytime I see him."

"All right, Mr. Rhodes, there is plenty of other work for my cousin, so you need never see him again ..."

Realising the inestimable value of the man, Rhodes interrupted:

A refuelling stop on the journey through Bechuanaland (Botswana)

"No, No, I don't want that. I was just a little excited. All I want you to do is to ask him to be a little more careful in the way he speaks to me."

Pauling replied: "I am sure that if you are civil to my cousin, he will be civil to you, as there is no-one in the world towards whom he entertains so great an admiration and respect."

After that they were always good friends.

Two thousand labourers and two hundred Europeans were toiling night and day through the dusty Kalahari. The main problem was bringing up supplies for the permanent way. The Cape Government was unable to rail through fast enough the 200 tons a day which were needed; only 60 tons were arriving. Men were standing around waiting, and the company was under heavy penalties to complete the contract in time. In the Cape Parliament questions were asked about the inability of the ports to off-load. The Press reported: "It is a pity the Cape Lines do not belong to a private company."

As the surveyors toiled on through the unglamourous Kalahari desert, marking halts as they went, they came across features which made natural breaks in the monotonous terrain. Below the granite hills of Bechuanaland (Botswana) in the domain of Chief Gaborone Matlapin, was a whistle-stop siding. It later became the prosperous capital of the country - Gaberones.

The next major problem was water. It was almost non existent, until it was found 500 feet deep at Artesia. Every water hole and culvert had been decimated by the rindepest; dead oxen were lying everywhere; the stench was unbearable and the water undrinkable; yet the surveyors working ahead of the plate-laying gangs were sometimes forced to drink from these polluted sources. All through the dry winter months before the rains started in October, water had to be hauled up from Mafeking 100 miles away. On the single track, the water train passed once daily, and hundreds of people relied on this for their survival. Earthwork subcontractors were unable to continue unless it rained soon. At Gaberones there was water famine. A correspondent on the train reported: "A crowd of natives came down to meet our train, all clamouring for water. Mr. Harold Pauling kindly allowed them to take as much as they could in 5 minutes. It was the same at every station, filling everything they could lay their hands on, and besides we stopped several time to give workmen along the line supplies of water."

Past the wagon-trail junction of Mahalapye, the line advanced. Nearby Shoshong was the centre of the old ivory trade, where in one year alone twelve thousand elephants had been sacrificed for 75 tons of ivory.

When Palapye was reached 6 months later, half way to Bulawayo, construction paused and a township sprang up almost overnight. Stores and house appeared on both sides of the steel rails. There were sheds made from old packing boxes, barrels and metal paraffin tins, which having served their purpose were flattened out to make sturdy metal sheets.

Traders and Transport agents hooked onto the telegraph line advancing alongside, with extensions to Fort Tuli and out to Serowe, the largest tribal village in Africa and the seat of Chief Khama.

Three thousand miles away, at exactly the same time, the Royal Engineers of Kitchener's Army were confronted by exactly the same problem in their epic battle across the waterless desert south to Khartoum.

Through the Kalahari the line swung northwards, avoiding the Tuli Block, a maze of streams and culverts difficult to traverse. Crossing the border of Bechuanaland into Rhodesia the long race home ran through the land of trees. Plumtree, Marula, Syringa - the handsome shade tree; and Figtree - where early emissaries had waited to see King Lo Bengula.

Edward Rosher recalled that the work went so fast that at times the survey parties were only one day ahead of the plate-laying gangs. Every man knew his task and was drilled to perfection. The sleepers were laid out in advance and positioned on the bare earth. The lengths of rail were unloaded from the construction train, carried forward and spiked to alternate sleepers to hold them in position. The construction train gingerly crept forward over the new rails, followed behind by gangs of more plate-layers, who secured the rails, and heaved the ballast between the sleepers. Bridges were sometimes temporary affairs. Sandbags and wooden trestles were laid over culverts, and where the river was dry the rails were laid down the bank, across the river bed and up the other side.

The Grand Hotel, Main Street, Bulawayo

Day after day the same procedure continued and the empty trucks brought back the exhausted gangs to the construction camp at nightfall.

At remote sidings, every ten miles or so, gangers and pumpers lived in tiny cottages or tin sheds. They were a lonely and mixed crowd of men, some married, mostly single, drawn from every class of society. Perhaps a baronet's son, or maybe an architect or solicitor down on his luck, squeezed out of Cape Town by hard times, keeping his family by an honest day's work, far from the wrath of critical contemporaries.

When Charles Metcalfe passed through these lonely sidings on the way to Bulawayo he saw twenty or thirty gangers cottages, many with children around growing up without any education. He decided to open a school for them, run by the Company, the Railway and the Church. Thus the famed Plumtree School came into being, with the steam locomotive as its emblem.

It was the largest crowd ever assembled that greeted the construction train as it chuffed into Bulawayo siding at the end of 1897. "Bulawayo is now as much a household word as London or Vienna" boasted the local Chronicle. The engine was decked with the Union Jack, the Stars and Stripes, and the Harps of Erin, with the proclamation 'Advance Rhodesia' on the front. As the railway arrived, the November rains descended; a heavenly downpour of stupendous proportions greeted the grateful earth and the shiny new ribbons of steel.

'Mile-a-day' Pauling had kept his word - to the day. He unloaded his horses and retired to the Palace Hotel, hurriedly half finished and stocked with a huge array of celebratory luxuries for the opening parties. 100 cases of whiskey and 150 cases of Champagne had been delivered, not to mention immeasurable quantities of other drinks. There were 250 beds in 130 bedrooms, and a thousand towels for only a dozen bathrooms. Queues formed in the corridors. Managed by an American Jim Patterson, the hotel bar was run by 'Greasy Kate'. Around the corner the Bodega Bar catered for earthy old timers.

The first train into Bulawayo Station at the end of 1897

Special trains brought up all the important guests for the opening ceremony. One was derailed and the passengers arrived slightly the worse for wear - the alcohol having flowed freely. The Cape Times reported the incident under the caption: "Engine derailed to Bulawayo", much to the annoyance of Harold Pauling. The driver attributed the accident to "sun-stroke" and repelled with scorn any suggestion of over indulgence.

Ten days of riotous jubilation followed. Races, polo, rifle and cricket matches; banquets and dances; outings to nearby places and a gymkhana, at which 500 men and only one woman turned up.

"I have never come across a community more free from brutality, fonder of fair play and more manly than the camp of Bulawayo", noted another lady.

The station was non existent, but the banner proclaimed: Our two roads to progress - Railroads and Cecil Rhodes. Queen Victoria sent her greetings. Rhodes sent a telegram. He was ill with malaria and suffering from a mild stroke, attended by Dr. Jameson on his farm in Inyanga (Nyanga), in the cool Eastern Highlands. Surrounded by fruit tress, experimental sheep and prize cattle from Australia, he was carving out a haven for his intended retirement, which was not to be. He was also checking on the progress of the trans-continental telegraph line which passed through Inyanga before crossing the Zambezi into Portuguese territory.

During his absence, the Administrator brazenly announced that what the French, German, Portuguese and Dutch had failed to accomplish had been achieved by one man, and his name was Cecil Rhodes: " Penetrating 1400 miles into the heart of Africa, he has introduced the most potent factor for civilization the world has ever known - he has brought the railway to Bulawayo."

One of the British Members of Parliament added equally grandly: "They have an Englishman making a railway on the Nile. They have an Englishman building a railway to Bulawayo. We would like to know what force on earth can prevent them joining hands."

James Sivewright then read the telegram from Rhodes: "We are bound, and I have made up my mind, to go on to the Zambezi without delay." The question on many peoples minds was which way?

After the speeches there were rounds of rousing cheers - for Rhodes, for the Administrator, for the Governor, and for 'mile a day' Pauling.

Henry Morton Stanley, railway enthusiast and honorary correspondent for the 'South Africa' Magazine, spoke at the Explorers banquet. This 'finder of noble Livingstone' referred to Bulawayo as the Chicago of South Africa. He put it bluntly: "The railroad is the answer to Africa's pressing problems. It is the only alternative to the wagon trails, decimated by rindepest and the tse-tse fly; and the one way to defeat slavery by opening up the continent to commerce and communication."

Electricity had arrived at the same time as the railway. Whilst many towns in England were still on gas-light, Bulawayo's streets were alive with sparking arc lamps.

At Government House there was a huge Indaba, a tribal gathering of hundreds of elders and Chiefs. The striking resemblance of Miss Edith Rhodes to her absent brother 'The Big White Chief' was a cause for much murmuring and animated discussion. For these were the same men with whom Rhodes had sat and made peace, in the nearby hills.

The average cost of the line from Mafeking to Bulawayo had been little more than £3,600 per mile, financed from debentures guaranteed by the British South Africa Company

In 1898, back in the saddle, Rhodes was invited once more to rejoin the Board of the BSA Company.

He walked into the banqueting room of the Cannon Street Hotel in London, and with a dramatic gesture unfolded his plans for opening up not just Rhodesia - but the vast known unknown heart of Africa.

"I have made up my mind to go to the Zambezi", he announced triumphantly, "I want two million pounds to extend the railway to Lake Tanganyika - about 800 miles. Look at the matter. You get the railway to Lake Tanganyika, you have Her Majesty's sanction for the railway to Uganda and then you have Kitchener coming down from Khartoum. Some would say 'another of his imaginable schemes'. It is not imaginable, it is practical. That gives you Africa, the whole of it ! The conquest of Africa by the English nation is a practical question now."

These stirring words brought the whole body of shareholders to their feet, with an ovation that rocked the walls of the staid Cannon Street Hotel.

It fell on stony ground, however, with the British Government. They were wary of the little Englanders, led by Henry 'Labby' Labouchere, a rich Etonian radical not noted for either imagination or foresight, who was against spending any money on expansion generally, and on railways in particular. He saw them only as a means of imperialism and of no benefit whatsoever to the inhabitants of Africa. The Government were also open to criticism for building the aptly named East African Lunatic Line with British taxpayers funds, as there was no apparent reason to squander such sums on imperial displays.

Rhodes was politely informed that the Government could not guarantee a loan to him. Undeterred he went to private financiers and City institutions.

So the railway up Africa was poised to continue. It would extend due north from Bulawayo to the Great Lakes, and somewhere in Uganda or the Sudan, it would meet Kitchener's line coming down from Khartoum.

Traders at a wayside halt in Bechunaland (Botswana).

Great Northern Hotel at Bulawayo Station, 1912

The Cape to Cairo Restaurant in downtown Bulawayo today

9

SINGING WIRES FROM THE SOUTH

THE AFRICAN TRANS CONTINENTAL TELEGRAPH

"The Railway is my right hand & the Telegraph is my voice."

Cecil Rhodes

The Imperial Government's cable link from London to India and Australia had only reached down as far as Aden by the time Queen Victoria's Golden Jubilee was celebrated in 1887. Her greetings were dashed half way around the globe in a matter of minutes by the miracle of Morse. But it did not escape anyone's attention that her message only reached the eyes and ears of her Citizens at the Cape of Good Hope several weeks later by mailship.

The plan of the African Transcontinental Telegraph was to link the whole continent of Africa with the Imperial Government, and with itself. From Cape Town to Alexandria, 7000 miles away, the line would pass through British territory picking up traffic en route.

This patriotic scheme was largely the brain-child of James Sivewright, one of the ablest and most corrupt of Rhodes associates, an engineering wizard from Aberdeen who became head of Telegraphs for South Africa at the age of 21. Adopted by Rhodes as his idea, as he was wont to do, it caused a certain rift between them. Sivewright's view was that it was about 10 or 20 times cheaper to build a land line than an undersea cable. Besides, submarine cables had a life span of only 15 years.

Experienced Africa hands were against the idea. Stanley thought that the unhealthy equatorial regions would decimate the telegraph staff. Baker reckoned that local tribesmen in the Sudan region would use the wire to make bracelets and arms: "I do not think any police supervision would protect a wire of gold from London to Inverness and I think it would be equally impossible to protect a wire of iron through the tribes I have named."

Another view was that until railways had opened up Africa, the best link north of Lake Nyasa would be to cross over and make contact at Aden with the undersea cable - another British invention, which linked London with Bombay, along an all British route via Gibraltar, Malta, Alexandria and Suez.

The cost of the 4000 mile land-line from Pretoria to Khartoum was estimated at nearly half a million pounds, with maintenance costs of about 10 per cent, and an annual death rate of 20 per cent of operating staff from fever, wild animals and attacks from unfriendly natives.

Sivewright's energetic activity in London for his overland scheme

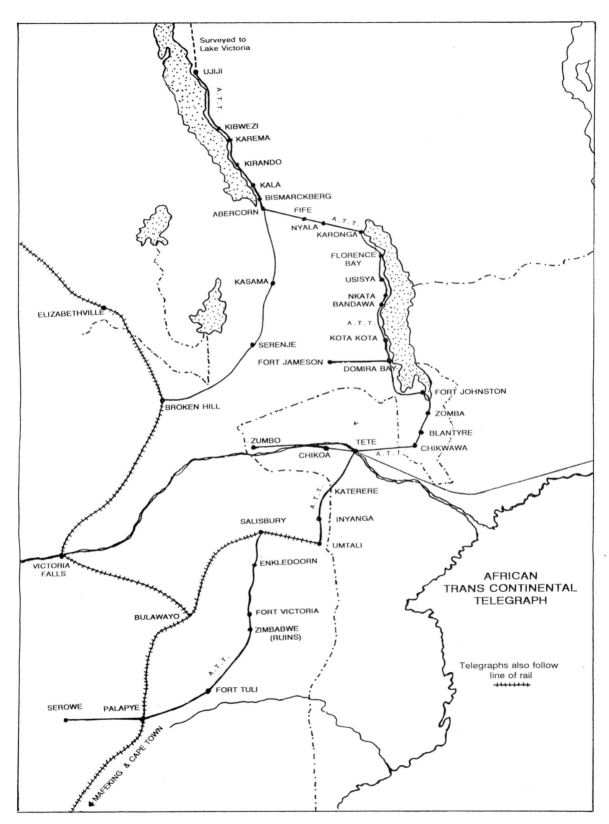

Surveyed to
Lake Victoria

UJIJI

KIBWEZI
KAREMA

KIRANDO

KALA
BISMARCKBERG
ABERCORN   FIFE
                  A.T.T.
          NYALA
          KARONGA

                  FLORENCE
                  BAY

                  USISYA

KASAMA   NKATA
                  BANDAWA
                  A.T.T.
ELIZABETHVILLE   KOTA KOTA

          SERENJE

FORT JAMESON
          DOMIRA BAY
                              FORT JOHNSTON

BROKEN HILL   ZOMBA

                              BLANTYRE
ZUMBO   TETE   CHIKWAWA
        CHIKOA   A.T.T

                        A.T.T.

                   KATERERE

SALISBURY   INYANGA

                   UMTALI
VICTORIA
FALLS   ENKLEDOORN

BULAWAYO   FORT VICTORIA
             ZIMBABWE
             (RUINS)

**AFRICAN
TRANS CONTINENTAL
TELEGRAPH**

Telegraphs also follow
line of rail
++++++++

             A.T.T.

             FORT TULI
SEROWE PALAPYE

    MAFEKING & CAPE TOWN

reached the ears of his rivals. In order to forestall any competition the Eastern Telegraph Company (renamed Cable & Wireless in 1934) extended their submarine cable down to Zanzibar and then to Durban. It was an unqualified success; the operators clattering away at their instruments round the clock, unable to cope with the demand. The longest stretch was an incredible 2000 miles, with a cable of extremely pure copper wires sheathed in gutta percha. On the western side cables were laid down the Atlantic seaboard, around the enormous bulge of Africa, as far as Port Nolloth, with a landline to Cape Town. All the way it ran through British controlled oceans, lying safe and secure with a single point of contact on foreign soil when it landed at Lisbon in Portugal - Britain's oldest ally. During the Anglo-Boer war, a further cable was laid in deeper waters to circumvent sabotage. Eventually a link was made by the same company from Durban all the way to Australia.

However Rhodes insisted that he would have both a Cape to Cairo Railway and a Telegraph right through the centre of Africa along his All Red Route. "The Railway is my right hand, and the Telegraph is my voice," he imperiously announced. He proposed that the many thousands of shareholders of the British South Africa Company, De Beers and Gold Fields should each invest £10 in the telegraph scheme, giving him £3 million to work with. In the end, most of the money came out of his own pocket. "If this telegraph is made, it will also give us the keys to the continent. We shall," he predicted, "get through to Egypt with the Telegraph, and subsequently with the Railway."

Under Sivewright's direction - now a Cape cabinet member, technical assistance and trained telegraphists were sent northwards.

From the very beginning the idea proved its worth. In the 1890's Gold Rush the Transvaal postal authorities gave strict priority to telegrams within the borders of the Transvaal. Such was the backlog, that cables from frantic speculators and brokers in Johannesburg to London, Paris and Berlin sometimes took 10 days. These ruinous delays were avoided by transmitting the messages to Malmadi, an unheard of outpost on the Transvaal frontier. Every night riders on fast horses raced across the border with the telegrams 35 miles to Mafeking, in British Bechuanaland, from where the telegraph station picked up its international links to Europe.

As new territories opened up, the telegraph line followed. Salisbury (Harare), the new capital of Rhodesia was linked with the South early in 1892, by a single strand of steel wire strung on insulators atop wooden poles. It followed the pioneer route through Bechuanaland (Botswana) and then via Fort Tuli and Fort Victoria (Masvingo). Many of the Chiefs in Bechuanaland had objected to this magic wire passing through their territory, though they were happy enough to provide workers for its progress.

Chief Khama was particularly helpful and was rewarded with a side connection to Serowe, his seat of the power on the edge of the Kalahari desert.

The line advanced at a rate of about 3 miles a day, but once the highveld had been reached white ants consumed everything in wood - including tarred telegraph poles and railway sleepers - so metal poles were substituted. Shipped out from Scotland, they were made in two parts, light enough to be carried by porters through the bush. The possibility of elephants knocking down poles was also a threat to communications.

Repeater stations were necessary at regular intervals to carry Morse signals over the single strand wire with an earth return. Problems had yet to be overcome to carry the wider frequency range of voice communication over very long distances.

The repeater stations were staffed by little groups of operators and linesmen, who worked in shifts around the clock, often from rudimentary huts. For in all weathers, and at all times, the Imperial lines had to be kept open to the Mother country. In the remote wilds, the eerie silence would suddenly be broken by the clatter of the Morse machine, miraculously and evocatively linking them with Cape Town or London, and other Outposts of Empire beyond the Seas.

In 1892 Rhodes sought further finance to extend the telegraph from its terminus at Salisbury. Onwards it would go to Zomba in Nyasaland

Carriers with wooden telegraph poles assembled at Ujiji, Tanganyika

(Malawi), and then via the Lakes and Tanganyika to Uganda. From there it would go via Gondokoro (Juba), and follow the Nile all the way to Khartoum. It would finally connect with the terminus of the Egyptian telegraph system at Wady Halfa, and thence via Alexandria through to England.

By asking the British Government to extend the line through Uganda, he would ensure the headwaters of the Nile would remain in British hands, and further his own aims over the territory. "I am prepared at once to extend the line of telegraph from Salisbury to Uganda without asking Her Majesty's Government for any contribution", he wrote to the Foreign Secretary. He reckoned the 1600 mile line could reach there in 18 months for a cost of only £150,000. Double or even treble that amount would be needed to take the line up to Wadi Halfa, the border point of Egypt. The problem of the Mahdi in the Sudan naturally barred the way, but Rhodes reckoned that he could deal with that. "I have never met anyone in my life whom it was not as easy to deal with as to fight", he boasted. Besides, he reckoned the Mahdi could never survive sandwiched between the two civilised powers of Egypt and Uganda - and would be cracked like a nut.

The most direct way in Central Africa was through German territory past Lake Tanganyika, and he urged the Government to intercede with the young Kaiser on his behalf.

But north of Salisbury there were monumental problems. Tse-Tse fly, torrential rains, and the impossibility of obtaining any labour, caused end-less delays. At one point the floods were so severe that the wire was strung out along trees for miles on end. At another point where several officials had died of fever, the wire was attached to broken gin bottles, acting as insulators on poles. Worse was in store. The Mashona Uprising. The Mazoe telegraph office was besieged; and the 19 local mine inhabitants were only saved by the courageous action of the two operators. J.L.Blakiston took the only horse left, and rode the gauntlet to the telegraph hut a mile away, with his colleague T.G.Routledge clinging to the stirrups, to get a message through to Salisbury. On their return they were cut down by the rebels.

Other brutal murders followed; the entire labour force deserted, and the whole operation came to a grinding halt. Huge quantities of materials were abandoned and for many years afterwards turned up in various African kraals all over the place.

A new route northwards from Umtali (Mutare) via Inyanga (Nyanga) through Portuguese territory to Tete was planned. This took the line into 'foreign' country for the first time at Katerere where the border mission station was situated. But the Portuguese were more than willing to join their own system to the line at Tete on the Zambezi. Thus a connection was made through to the coast at Quelimane and the outside world generally.

The sections of line through Portuguese territory were subject to regular interruptions. Line boys were often despatched from Rhodesia for repair work. Across the Zambezi, the line ran on poles cemented into the river bed. Floods, floating trees and the odd Portuguese gun-boat often broke the connection, so messages were ferried across the river between the repeater stations on both banks.

The arrival of the line at Blantyre opened up the whole of that part of Africa. Links down the Shire River and the Zambezi River to the British concessionary port of Chinde at its mouth ensured rapid communication to the territories inland. Previously messages had taken a month to travel by land, river and sea between Zomba, the British capital of Nyasaland, and Mozambique Island. This strategic coastal fortress, over which the Portuguese flag had flown uninterrupted for many hundreds of years, was an important cable station of the Eastern Telegraph Co, and also of the French Madagascar Cable Company.

Arrival of the Portuguese wire at Zumbo; the first message is sent through to Tete (NAZ)

North of Blantyre the line ran via Zomba to Fort Johnston (Mangoche) at the base of Lake Nyasa (Lake Malawi). It then hugged the western lake shore via Domira Bay (Salima) from where a spur ran westwards 120 miles to Fort Jameson (Chipata). Following the lake shore it ran all the way up to Karonga. Material was shipped by steamers of the African Lakes Corporation who had contracted for the transport as far as Uganda.

During the construction of this difficult section of the line, where rugged hills dropped steeply into the lake, the wire often stretched in very long spans across rivers and gorges. A lucky escape occurred for an Australian telegraphist named Brockman, who was dragged sleeping from his grass hut by a marauding lion. Paralysed with fear he was unable to utter a sound, but in the ensuing melee the lion was shot by a colleague whilst it was chewing his fingers off under a nearby tree. Brockman survived, and after a year in hospital returned to healthier territory, minus fingers.

From the northern extremity of Lake Nyasa the line aimed directly for the southern shores of Lake Tanganyika. It followed the line of the strategic Stevenson Road, skirting the frontiers of Northern Rhodesia with German territory. This broken, hilly land through Fife to Abercorn was in some places totally impassable for road transport. Porters were the only means of conveyance. A scarcity of food in the area was also a major deterrent to finding labour, and after an outbreak of small-pox thousands of carriers abandoned their loads and fled. In 1900 the line was eventually completed to Abercorn (Mbala) near the base of Lake Tanganyika. In some places telegrams were sent by heliograph mirrors to the nearest telegraph station for onward transmission.

Rhodes had visited King Leopold in Brussels, to obtain permission for the telegraph to pass through Belgian territory between Lakes Tanganyika and Kivu. The autocratic and cranky Monarch, who ran one of the smallest countries in Europe and one of the largest in Africa as his personal fiefdom, was far too demanding, even though he had agreed to transfer a strip of Belgian territory between the lakes for the Cape to Cairo railway. Not knowing which route to take, Rhodes asked Henry Morton Stanley to intervene. "Kindly go the King", he implored "and get me the right to come up his side of Lake Tanganyika. I prefer the Belgian territory". Stanley was also unsuccessful.

So Rhodes went straight to Berlin and had several meetings with the Kaiser. Whilst the subject of the railway was left inconclusive, it was agreed that the telegraph could pass through German territory on its way from Nyasaland to Uganda.

Appetising Oxford scholarships,*which he discussed with the Kaiser, and the contract for the Siemens telegraph wire spurred this decision.

A square mile of territory was purchased at Bismarcksburg (Kasanga) on the German shore of the lake, but once more the line was dogged down by local labour difficulties. When Ewart Grogan passed through Tanganyika on his epic walk from Mozambique, he had the greatest problem in finding any porters at all. A team from the Telegraph Company had just preceded him.

He was impressed with their efficiency: "Quiet men, rotten with fever. Above their base floated a diminutive Union Jack; no pomp, no fuss, not

* *Rhodes endowed 170 scholarships at Oxford for students from the British Colonies and the United States. He also included scholarships for Germans since the Kaiser, whom he admired, had included the English language in the German school curriculum. His final hope was the re-amalgamation of America into a British Empire allied to Germany - a kind of Teutonic alliance to rule the world.*

Misguidedly named because the original Concession included development rights for land at Abercorn near the southern shores of Lake Tanganyika on the conceptual route of the Cape to Cairo line

even a bugle, yet all worked like clockwork."

With German assistance, and a certain amount of coercion, the line made its uneasy way up the lake shore to Ujiji. Thousands of loads of materials were abandoned by the carriers at Karonga half way there.

So it was arranged by Robert Williams, of Tanganyika Concessions*, for a 60 ton twin screw vessel to be shipped out from Scotland, dismantled, and carried across Africa by porters to the lake, where it was reassembled and launched as the S.S. Cecil Rhodes. Flying the red and green Cape to Cairo flag the ship carried vast quantities of construction materials up to Ujiji.

Harry Johnston was sceptical about the route from the north of Lake Tanganyika to Lake Kivus, Edward and Albert, "because the people between the lakes are very hostile to white people, and would certainly regard the telegraph line as an embodiment of witchcraft." So Rhodes was diverted from his original planned route between the lakes, and thought that the best way forward for both the telegraph and railway would be to cross from Ujiji, two-thirds of the way up Lake Tanganyika, directly to Lake Victoria.

From there the route forward had already been surveyed around Lake Victoria to Kisumu - the terminus of the Uganda railway.

The line reached Ujiji (near Kigoma) in 1901. A few mango trees and some white buildings stood overlooking the gently sloping lake shore, with a solitary telegraph hut nearby. On the rustic doorway a simple sign read: ATT Office. Ujiji, the meeting place of Stanley and Livingstone, was the final destination of the 'magic singing wires from the south' - the forerunner of the railway.

Where the last telegraph pole stood, the line stretched almost pointlessly back to the Cape. Improved submarine cables and Marconi's epoch making wireless transmissions had already overtaken the concept. British concerns over the line passing through German East Africa made an undersea connection direct to Zanzibar all the more preferable; and the high cable rates which had originally justified the African Transcontinental Telegraph no longer applied.

The South African Puck. "I will put a girdle from the Cape to Cairo in forty seconds" (UCT MACMILLAN)

NEW TELEGRAPH COMPANY

THROUGH EGYPT AND THE SUDAN

The Telegraphs in Egypt under the Ismael Pasha had been somewhat Gilbertian. In order to 'keep his fingers on the pulse' and 'his ear to the ground' all lines had to end in the Khedive's Palace in Cairo. Rickety instruments and ant-eaten poles ensured that the messages usually arrived by chance.

As part of the military campaign, the Royal Engineers became the main instruments of maintaining and expanding this new invention along the Nile. The enterprising sappers resorted to some novel ideas. They once replaced a line through a city sewer pipe by tying a fine wire to a rat, pursued by a ferret. To measure the distance across the river at Aswan for an armoured cable, the only theodolite available had no cross hairs - so one Engineer used a hair from his sister's locket. Ever adept at improvisation in the face of Kitchener's economies, and pending the arrival of morse keys, two Sappers turned a couple of old electric buzzers into vibrating instruments.

The Sudan Military campaign and the Nile expeditions owed their success almost as much to the telegraph as to the railway. So important were instructions sent down from Cairo, that Kitchener was urged never to leave the end of the wire. He was kept in touch at all stages of the campaign and at every post along the Nile. From Cairo, through Egypt to the Sudan, 70,000 messages were sent in 7 months; hundreds were in cypher and many were transmitted in Arabic.

As the military moved up the Nile the telegraph went with it. It entered the Sudan at Wady Halfa and ran on both banks in a shaky condition. In Egypt wood was used for poles whilst in the Sudan metal was preferred - to avoid the white ants and also to prevent rampant thieving. The Bedouin, who supposedly guarded the line, thought that Allah had put the poles there for the use of the faithful for huts. Ladders were stored in cemeteries to be protected by the Spirits.

Rolls of telegraph wire were transported overland in a novel way - on donkeys. The method of loading was to stand the donkey's hind feet in the coils of wire and lift it up over the tail onto the saddle. The back view of the convoy of donkeys thus resembled a number of giant footballs. The transport problem appeared to have been solved, but very soon the decrepit donkeys, tired of carrying heavy hoops, collapsed on the ground as soon as loaded. No method had been devised to unwind the wire from the donkeys, so each coil was removed and unwound by hand. Then no attempt was made to raise it off the ground, firstly because speed was essential and also because of lack of poles. The poling party was often 150 miles in the rear of the laying party, delayed by the lack of water transport. Whilst gunboats fought their way up river and through the cataracts, the telegraph detachment plodded steadily onwards alongside them, laying bare wire through the desert all the way to Abu Hamed.

As long as it did not rain, the extraordinary dryness of the Sudan made it possible to work many miles of bare wire lying on the ground without any appreciable loss of current. In normal circumstances bare wire on damp ground would 'short' the earth return circuit.

Never before had messages flashed along such distances in this fashion. From Dongola to Wadi Halfa 250 miles away there were communications through 130 miles of bare wire. In October 1897, when the wire laying party reached Berber, direct transmission was actually established through 236 miles of bare wire lying on the ground, anchored with stones. No difficulty was experienced between 9 am and 9 pm; but at night the insulating property of the sandy desert deteriorated, and distant signalling was sometimes impossible.

Whilst Kitchener was loading his ships for the advance to Omdurman, the wire was poised to cross the Nile. Various unsuccessful attempts were made, the last being when the tight-fisted Kitchener reduced the order for the calculated length of wire, and cancelled the 5 per cent allowance for contingencies. When the cable was finally paid out from the ship, the current took it down stream and the wire reached the end of the drum before the boat reached the bank.

The underwater cable was too short to cross another river, so it had to be laid to a ship anchored in mid-stream; an overhead line on poles completed the connection. When the rains arrived, the whole lot - poles and all - were swept down the river.

Overhead cables were also hung from 80 feet high tripod towers in one long span across the Nile above the Atbara River. When the line failed in stormy weather, communication was kept going by steamers between the two banks, and for urgent matters by heliograph.

Secret messages were usually sent in code. Sometimes the recipient had no access to a code book. An important and highly secret message was once sent in a spectacular way. A Morse inker was rigged up as an automatic transmitter with a variable sending speed. An extremely talented telegraphist named Sapper John Conolly could send and receive Morse so fast as to leave the rest of his colleagues way behind. At the appointed time the message was transmitted automatically at nearly 50 words per minute, i.e. nearly one word per second. Conolly confirmed he had partially received it. The speed was reduced slightly on the second and third transmissions, and the whole message received and understood by Conolly without any one of the intermediate operators being aware of it.

Local linesmen down the Nile fared better than those near the Red Sea. In that region the enemy tribesmen sometimes tied an unfortunate linesman to a telegraph pole and burnt him. They first placed the ends of the cut wires into the victims ears to find out whether he could hear the enemy's plans, reveal British secrets and talk like the telegraph.

10

TRAINS ON THE WARPATH

THE ANGLO-BOER WAR

Faster than the fastest cavalry, armoured trains rattled across the open plains of Africa as the most formidable aid to military might. As in the Sudan where the railways defeated the Mahdi, so in South Africa they came into their own. It was the only way to outreach the Boers, the finest horsemen on the continent, who were able to ride up to 40 miles a day, often without boot leather.

The opening shots in the South African War had been on an armoured train between Vryberg and Mafeking in October 1899. A train-load of ammunition and guns, escorted by a pilot engine, reached a point where the rails ahead had been cut. Creeping forward in the darkness, on a bend in the line at Kraaipan, and surrounded on both sides by Boers, the train became a sitting target. As it retreated slowly down the line the driver lay on his back on the footplate, reaching up to the regulator. Artillery shells landed straight in the engine cab, blew it away and burst the boiler.

With insufficient troops in the field, the war had been going badly for Britain. The mother country of the Empire had one of the smallest standing armies in Europe, which, as Kitchener had found in the Sudan, relied largely on reserves.

The new Colony of Rhodesia had been cut off from the south soon after war started in 1899. Boer forces controlled the vital rail link with Bulawayo. They occupied Vryberg, besieged Kimberley and Mafeking, and overran nearly 100 miles of territory through Bechuanaland (Botswana). Ladysmith was also under siege, and it fell to Lord Roberts to take command at the beginning of 1900. He launched by rail from the Cape, and then from the north, the first major offensive.

Somewhere in the depths of the War Office it was decided that the main thrust of relief would be from the north, with an expedition under Major General Carrington. Reinforcements landed at Beira in Mozambique, and were sent down the line, which had been pushed inland to Marandellas (Marondera) 50 miles short of Salisbury (Harare). Hundreds of horses from Hungary and the Argentine, and mules from Texas and Spain were camped out in vast pens on the flats near Beira. Many succumbed to horse sickness and the fly, or disappeared into the bush to run with the herds of zebra. Australians such as 'Breaker' Morant rounded them up to prevent the frequent stampedes. It was one of the worst places in Africa anyone could have chosen.

Australian, New Zealand and Canadian troops were assembled by Alfred Lawley and his team, eager to move forward on the overstretched narrow gauge line, which was still being hastily widened.

There was a monumental pile-up of traffic at Bamboo Creek where all the narrow gauge rolling stock was concentrated, whilst the laborious business of transhipment of field artillery, horses, ammunition and stores onto the wider gauge took place.

When the troops heard that Cecil Rhodes was about to pass through, they stood around, nonchalently, to catch a glimpse of the great man. He arrived with Charles Metcalfe and stayed with Alfred Lawley on what was to be his last trip to his farm at Inyanga (Nyanga), bringing with him a collection of pedigree cattle, sheep and pigs.

From the 'end of steel' at Marandellas, about 300 miles from Beira, Carrington's forces continued their journey onwards for another 300 miles overland to Bulawayo. There, Harold Pauling and his staff entrained them down the line to the relief of Mafeking. In an unostentatious fashion, this herculean effort had contributed to the ultimate success of the war effort. Salisbury and Bulawayo were not linked by rail until 3 years later.

Lord Roberts then turned his attention to Kimberley, and the Orange Free State around Bloemfontein, before advancing northwards towards Pretoria. Natal, with its difficult communications, was meanwhile ignored. The rail was paramount. Advances followed the railway lines, and the telegraph wires that ran with them. Bridges were guarded, tracks patrolled day and night and trains were armoured. Nothing was more formidable than a troop train clanking slowly across the veldt, bristling with maxim guns, with an unknown number of assailants hidden behind its armoured flanks.

Roberts also relied heavily on mounted infantry, speedily brought up by train, with horses doubled as back ups. In the whole campaign nearly half a million horses were used. Two thirds of them died from sickness and starvation; very few from enemy action.

Remount depots were located near rail tracks, like De Aar and Matjiesfontein in the wild Karoo. Two hundred miles up country from Cape Town this Victorian gem, dominated by the Lord Milner Hotel, flourished as a convalescent home for officers. A wilderness oasis, miles from anywhere, but on the main railway line, it became the largest remount depot in Africa. Tens of thousands of troops camped out in the veld, and 5000 horses peacefully grazed on the harsh shrub, before being railed up country to the front line on the miles of single track on which all supplies ran. Foolishly, Roberts had ridiculed the idea of building an additional line on this final 300 miles to the Orange Free State. Easily open to Boer saboteurs, constant repairs ensured that this was the one stretch of single line where the train did not always keep pace with the ox-wagon.

Beyond Matjiesfontein every bridge and even every culvert was watched by a native with a flag, so that the trains ran no risk of running into unexpected hazards. At the little halt before it, called Monument, also the scene of a railway accident, many of the Highland Brigade were buried, casualties of the confusingly named Battle of Magersfontein a few miles south of Kimberley, on the open plain where trench warfare was re-invented by the Boers.

The railway line was the life-line for the soldier on the ground. It was also grim reality. Exposed and abandoned to the mercy of the enemy in the baking days and bitter nights of the open veldt, the Tommy took his last forlorn look at the troop train which had brought him there, as it slowly puffed away down the line to the safety of the horizon and the open sea.

From Orange River Station, Methuen advanced along the line with artillery and supply trains. The Battle of Belmont was fought around the station. Modder River, in 1899 was also the scene of one of the fiercest battles of the War, a hundred yards from the railway line. The bridge across the river was wrecked by the Boers and repaired by the Brits.

After the battle, the war correspondent Rudyard Kipling travelled by Red Cross hospital train to pick up the wounded. He paid tribute in his articles to the weary men who kept the trains running, who guarded the culverts against treacherous attempts to blow up the track, who sat huddled over telegraph apparatus in sweltering sheds. And the wounded, who endured jolting wagon journeys from the battlefield, until, gratefully, they came under the clean sheets of the hospital train, and tender care took them back to the coast.

Another ambitious war correspondent Winston Churchill was on the train north trying to get to the front:

"The Colesburg bridge across the Orange River has been seized by the enemy, and each train from De Aar to Stormberg is expected to be the last to pass unassailed. Stormberg is itself an important railway junction. For more than a week the troops have been working day and night to put it in a state of defence, but the only order seemed to pervade the air: The enemy are coming - Retreat, Retreat, Retreat.

The Stationmaster - one of the best types of Englishmen to be found on a long journey, was calm and cheerful.

"No more traffic north of this", he said,

"Yours was the last train through from De Aar. I shall send away all my men by the special tonight. And that's the end as far as Stormberg goes."

"And you?"

"Oh, I shall stay. I have lived here for twelve years and am well known. Perhaps I may be able to protect the company's property."

So we left Stormberg in much anger and some humiliation, and jolted away towards the open sea, where British supremacy is not yet contested by the Boer."

The skirmish at Stormberg was a disaster.

General William 'Back-acher' Gatacre, renowned for his laborious marches in the Sudan, missed his way to the strategic railway station in the darkness. A surprise attack in daylight by a group of Boers caused 700 captured, killed or wounded.

Kitchener himself brought down from Egypt his respected Chief Engineer who had dragged the desert line through to Khartoum, and had then consolidated rail transport throughout the Anglo-Egyptian Sudan. He was Pierre Percy Girouard, the French Canadian and the only man reputed to stand up to the autocratic Kitchener. Under his umbrella the vital rail links of the Orange Free State and the Transvaal Republics were linked under the guise of the Imperial Military Railways. From his homeland in Montreal came another experienced engineer, Charles Armstrong, to join the staff of the IMR.

In the Rand, so vital were the rail-links on the war front, that the capture of Germiston (then called Elandsfontein) was of paramount importance and the key to victory. Roberts realised that if rail communication to Pretoria and the north were cut, Johannesburg would be indefensible. In the end its possession ensured the British victory.

Johannesburg was virtually empty for the period of the Anglo-Boer war. It was a ghost town, as almost the whole population became refugees, many fleeing in open trucks to Natal or the Cape Colony, sleeping in corridors or dining saloons on any train they could, when war broke out. A few Dutch railway, postal and municipal officials remained. The home-sick Cornelius Van Gogh, brother of Vincent, had worked for the Netherlands Railway Company as an engine assembler. Then came the war. Captured by the British he was taken ill and sent to Brandfort in the Orange Free State. Like his brother Vincent he died by his own hand in 1900.

Dr.F.E.T.Krause, the far-sighted military commandant of Johannesburg, handled the situation brilliantly. An 8 o'clock curfew was enforced. Looting, burning and a scorched earth policy were kept to a minimum. There was a wonderful spirit of cooperation. The sad tale of a war that should never have been started, ended when he surrendered the City of Johannesburg to Lords Roberts and Kitchener. The erstwhile officials took back their old jobs. Under British administration, many die-hard Boers left; the Netherlands Railway officials returned to Holland, and the town developed a distinctly British flavour.

At the end of the war Girouard remained as Commissioner of Railways and paved the way for the amalgamation of all the systems in the Union of South Africa. Other British railwaymen had followed. One was the brilliant William Wilson Hoy who had started in Bulawayo during the Anglo-Boer War, and finally became the first General Manager of S.A. Railways when the system was unified throughout the country. During WW1 he was Director of Railways in South West Africa (Namibia).

Even the clocks were changed due to the railways. Johannesburg time was 21 minutes and 44 seconds ahead of the Cape, so the whole of British south and central Africa, linked by the steel ribbon, was brought into line at 30 degrees east of longitude, exactly two hours ahead of Greenwich Mean Time (GMT). This line of longitude passed through the Eastern Cape Province, east of Johannesburg and Pretoria, a short distance east of Bulawayo, crossing the Zambezi at the northern most point of Southern Rhodesia (Zimbabwe) through Northern Rhodesia (Zambia) and up through the centre of Lake Tanganyika, touching the northern shore of Lake Albert and Uganda, up through the Sudan west of Khartoum, and then a short distance west of Cairo. It covered all the time zones through which the Cape to Cairo railway was intended to pass.

*Supply train blown up
by Boers
(UCT MACMILLAN)*

CAPE TO CAIRO.

Mr. C-c-l Rh-d-s (the "*practical man*"). "THEN, SIR, MAY I TAKE IT FOR GRANTED THAT YOU HAVE NO OBJECTION TO OUR LINE RUNNING THROUGH YOUR PROPERTY?"

Kaiser William (*quite equal to the occasion*). "NONE WHATEVER. *FOR A CONSIDERATION.*"

11

FULL STEAM NORTH

BULAWAYO TO CONGO 1900

"Glad you beat the Khalifa. My telegraph will shortly be at the south end of Tanganyika. If you don't look sharp I will reach Uganda before you", Rhodes cabled Kitchener.

The sharp reply was: "Hurry up!"

It was the last day of the century when the railway reached Khartoum. Throwing rail and telegraph lines before him Kitchener had finally defeated the dervish devils at the Battle of Omdurman.

Rhodes had already diverted locomotives destined for the Cape to help his friend's push down the Nile. He was hoping he would move further; but they were both distracted. The South African War was in full swing; construction had halted, and there had been a long pause since the railway reached Bulawayo more than two years earlier.

The original plan had been to extend the Cape to Cairo line up from Bulawayo, to bridge the Zambezi over the boiling Kariba Gorge - where the mighty dam was built some 60 years later. In 1898 a railway survey party had reached the site under the escort of Captain Jack Cardon of the British South Africa Company Police. They observed how the banks of the Gorge were only 80 yards across, narrow enough to bowl a cricket ball from one side to the other.

Northwards the rail-route would veer in an easterly direction between the borders of the Congo pedacle and Portuguese Mozambique, through a land gap of little more than a hundred miles. The original surveyed route passed within a few miles of the point where the Luangwa River touched the extremity of Portuguese territory. Turning northwards again it would travel along the watershed (the Muchinga escarpment) and pass near Serenji, Mpika and Kasama to hit the southern shore of Lake Tanganyika at a point near Abercorn (Mbala) where a terminus would be situated. From there, steamers would transport the rail trucks across Lakes Tanganyika, Kivu, Edward and Albert. The short land gaps between the lakes would be connected by rail. It would continue on to the White Nile, the navigable river which runs from Uganda through the Sudan and on to Cairo.

This then was the plan. At the Berlin Conference in 1885 all the countries involved in Africa had agreed to the Boundary Convention, except Britain - in relation to the Congo Free State, which bordered directly onto German territory. Britain was still holding back in the hope of retaining some land between the two borders in the Rwanda area.

In the summer of 1885 most of the Foreign Office officials were on holiday. London in August was stifling hot, almost empty, and only a few junior clerks were snoozing away at their desks in Whitehall. An official from the Belgian Embassy strolled across St. James's Park with a bunch of papers to the Foreign Office. These confirmed the proposals of the German-Belgian boundaries. The papers were signed for by a junior clerk. In diplomatic circles this meant that the contents had been accepted. This slip of procedure not only cost Britain a strategic slice of Rwanda, but also cost Rhodes his right of way between the Lakes for his Cape to Cairo Line.

By 1890, when Rhodes became Premier of the Cape Colony, the railway had not yet left its borders. The final rounds of the Berlin Conference were in full swing, and Rhodes was pushing Lord Salisbury to secure some British sovereignty over a lakes connection. Salisbury, however was not entirely sold on a Cape to Cairo line, and missed the point of it. He naively described it in the House of Lords as a "Curious Idea ... It would mean a long tract of narrow occupation, hedged in by two white Protectorates - those of Germany and Belgium - placed at a distance of 3 months march from our own sea base. I cannot imagine a more inconvenient possession."

Rhodes himself was also somewhat distracted, and was looking at more immediate objectives. Rather than concentrating on the important links between Lakes Tanganyika and Kivu, he was more concerned with securing the 'Stevenson Road' which ran from the base of Lake Tanganyika to the northern extremity of Lake Nyasa (L.Malawi). He realised this would control the trade route for the whole of central Africa, and would thwart German ambitions in that area. Harry Johnston had also proposed the idea of building a railway spur, partially along this route to Nyasaland, to join with the Iron Spine of Africa up the centre. (The Trans-continental telegraph line subsequently followed the strategic route of the Stevenson Road).

By the time the Berlin Conference had been wound up in 1890 Rhodes was complaining about "the paper arrangements where Africa is marked in red, green and blue blocks, under which we always get the worst bits". In fact Salisbury had negotiated a good deal. Britain had gained Kenya, Uganda and Zanzibar, and Germany had dropped their claims over the Stevenson Road and a large slice of Bechuanaland (Botswana). In return Britain had given back to Germany the innocuous but strategic little island of Heligoland near the German coast in the North Sea, as well as granting a long finger of land - the Caprivi Strip - ostensibly to join German South West Africa with the navigable Zambezi River. Everyone else seemed to know that much of this stretch of waterway was blocked by cataracts and waterfalls.

However the one crucial link which Rhodes had yearned for - between the Lakes and Uganda, remained in the hands of Germany and the Belgian Congo. To fulfil his dream he would now have to negotiate either with the Kaiser, or the King - or both.

Not much happened in this regard for a few years. The railway had advanced through the neck in the bottle - Rhodes 'Suez Canal to the North', with a clear way up to Bulawayo. The Beira line had reached the border of Rhodesia at Umtali.

In 1899 Rhodes went to Berlin to see the Kaiser. Unfortunately the Germans were still doggedly pursuing their Mittle Afrika policy, with visions of linking their territories of South West Africa and Tanganyika right across the continent - a distance of 750 miles as the crow flies between the Caprivi strip and the shores of Lake Tanganyika.

Worse still, they were in the midst of the Samoan question, which had reached a peak. These Pacific islands were run as a condominium by America, Germany and Britain. They had been Germany's very first colonial acquisitions, and the Kaiser had dug his heels in, grimly hanging on, under threat of a huge international incident and break in diplomatic relations. He was incensed that Britain and America were ganging up against him, and that Britain had grabbed all the best bits of the Globe. When Rhodes arrived in Berlin, the Kaiser hoped that he might be persuaded to twist the arms of Salisbury and Chamberlain over this vexing Samoan question.

Rhodes buttered up the Kaiser with a promise of further help with his other pet project - the Berlin to Baghdad Railway. This was Germany's grandiose imperial dream to link Europe with Asia by a mighty bridge across the Bosphorous, giving a throughway from the North Sea to the Persian Gulf. It would drive a wedge between Berlin and St. Petersburg, ally Germany with Turkish military might, and revive the spirit of trade through the Ottoman Empire, unlocking the fabulous oil and agricultural riches along the ancient land routes of Central Asia. It would also, as both Rhodes and Chamberlain hoped, bring Germany closer to Britain through a concept which was initially a British one.

Rhodes reminded the Kaiser: Had not his prize railway contractor George Pauling personally undertaken a survey of the route through Syria, and then handed the results to the Germans on a plate ?

In fact Pauling had made a remarkable trip on a fine Arab horse with a military escort, accompanied part of the way by an ex-seaman Interpreter whose vocabulary consisted entirely of profanities and expletives. Pauling's real objective was to ensure that a vital part of the route was kept within the sphere of British influence. A concession had been obtained for a railway from Alexandretta on the Turkish coast, through Syria and on to Baghdad; then across Persia (Iran) right through to India. In order to secure the contract Pauling had set forth after much smoking of hubbly-bubbly & hookah pipes and not inconsiderable palm-greasing of Turkish officials. With a pedometer attached to the horse's leg to measure the distance covered, and carrying equipment for a "flying survey", the 16 stone Pauling had located a viable route through the tricky Anatolian mountains, and the best line to Aleppo in Syria.

After several weeks hard riding, the thoroughbred horse had eventually expired beneath him. "Its demise was as much due to my excessive weight as to the insufferable heat", he admitted. Together with the local British Consul, Mr. Henderson, they then beat a hasty retreat pursued by an angry mob of Syrian tribesmen. A few miles from Antioch they were met by a procession of notables who had heard of the proposed railway. That night they were guests at a huge banquet where once again no-one knew a word of English. Returning to Constantinople Pauling visited the Grand Vizier and gave him a lump of Hottentot gold quartz from South Africa. A visit was thereby arranged to see the ruler of all the Ottomans, the Sultan. But at the last moment Pauling neglected to bribe the one most important man, the Barber - who 'had the ear' of the Grand Vizier. The outcome of the contract was only partially successful and the results of the survey were sold to the Germans.

The Kaiser was enthralled by the interest shown by Rhodes, who knew he was on a winning streak when he mentioned the magic word Mesopotania (now Iraq), and extolled the glories and riches of Babylon. The right of way for his Africa trans-continental telegraph was on the cards.

However, it very soon transpired that whilst a telegraph line passing through German Tanganyikan territory was welcome, a railway was altogether a different matter. The ambitious Kaiser was so demanding that agreement was impossible. It was all hedged about with 'ifs and buts', Rhodes told Robert Williams; but he added that "you might use it as a lever with King Leopold."

Rhodes then went to King Leopold in Brussels where he had even less luck. The dinner party got off to a bad start when Rhodes undiplomatically suggested that his Cape peaches were far juicier and sweeter than those grown by the King in his royal hot-houses. Rhodes' other suggestion, later revealed to Robert Williams* was almost mind-boggling in scale and imagination. During the fish course, Rhodes suggested the amalgamation of his British South Africa Company with the King's Congo Free State. These two huge personal fiefdoms would presumably be run by a giant civil service for the benefit of themselves and their shareholders. How their respective governments would fit in, or who would have overall control was a moot point. Rhodes no doubt reckoned that with his powerful City of London backers, he would be in charge. This was the most audacious plan he ever envisaged. It would have created an 'Empire' larger than the whole of Europe, with the richest conglomeration of minerals in the world. By the time the dinner party had reached the

Source: Robert's People. Hutchinson and Martelli

main course, the King was non-commital, and mumbled a lot about thinking it over, whilst then turning to the real reason for Rhodes' visit - to find a way through for his Cape to Cairo railway.

He was furious that Britain, under threat from Germany and France to call a new Conference on Africa, had reneged on a Lease of Land on the Nile. This was the Lado Enclave, formerly the Bahr-el-Ghazal outposts, leased to the King to give him access to the waterways of the Nile from his land-locked Congo territory. In return the King had agreed to cede a 15 mile wide strip of land to Britain between Lakes Tanganyika and Kivu, to allow the Cape to Cairo railway to pass through. This was now in the balance.

In fact the Bahr-el-Ghazal outposts had been captured from the Belgians by the French, at the time of Marchand's Nile expedition. They had only been taken back by British troops after Kitchener had thwarted Marchand's stand at Fashoda.

Not long afterwards, an astute American mining engineer, John Hays Hammond, who later became Vice President of the United States, had convinced Rhodes that Mashonaland and Matabeleland were running out of steam, mineral wise. Another of his mining associates had also come to a similar conclusion. Robert Williams, who had sharpened his teeth in both Kimberley and Johannesburg, had obtained a concession to prospect for minerals in Charterland (Zambia) and now had his eyes firmly further north, particularly in the Katanga area of the Congo Free State, where early Portuguese and German explorers had persistently reported rich mineral finds.

Prospector par excellence, Williams had guessed, quite correctly, that the watershed, or divide, of the Congo and Zambezi Rivers would yield mineral wealth almost as abundant as the deposits found on the watershed of the Zambezi and Orange Rivers - the area of the untold wealth of the Rand.

Rhodes himself had sent an expedition to claim this land from the local chiefs for Britain, but their runners had been intercepted by a party of Belgians who hoisted their own flag in the name of their King. As luck would have it, King Leopold had for years been wrongly advised by inexperienced mineral men - convinced that no worthwhile mineral deposits existed. Williams had discovered that they had only investigated the holes and debris left behind around the old workings, and not what lay underneath.

So in 1899 Tanganyika Concessions was formed by Williams to exploit minerals in that priceless, undefined area north of the Zambezi River. It was named after the Concessions it acquired, though never developed, for a township, lake pier and intended railway terminus on the shores of Lake Tanganyika, near Abercorn.

Coincidentally, a young German prospector Alfred Giese heard of 'black stones that burn' from local Africans. He had stumbled across some of the richest open-cast coal deposits in the world at Wankie (Hwange) 150 miles north-west of Bulawayo.

The riches of the Congo were too tempting for words. That set the course of the railway. It would traverse the Wankie coal fields and cross the Zambezi River at Victoria Falls, and not Kariba. It would then aim due north towards the Kafue River, avoiding a wide river crossing if possible, then turning eastwards it would pass within 10 miles of the extremity of the Congo Pedacle on its way to Abercorn at the base of Lake Tanganyika.

Rhodes appealed for finance. Once again the British cabinet rejected him out of hand. Chamberlain, almost alone, backed this ambitious project, and had faith in the Cape to Cairo scheme. The man who held the purse strings, 'Black Michael', the Chancellor of the Exchequer Michael Hicks Beach had persuaded most of his cabinet colleagues to reject this "far-fetched and fanciful idea." He did not believe in a Cape to Cairo Route, and even doubted whether its creator thought it entirely feasible. He suspected the real reason behind Rhodes' request for Imperial backing was to send up the value of shares in the Chartered Company. In any case, he maintained, Rhodes could easily pay for the whole scheme himself, right up to the Great Lakes.

There was a blazing row which reverberated all the way between Downing Street and Cork Street in Mayfair where Rhodes had his headquarters, and the nearby Burlington Hotel where he usually stayed. The more he thought of "that Beach" the more angry he became. He considered such an ill-mannered, unimaginative man who was in charge of the funds for the whole British Empire was not fit to be the Treasurer of a Village Fete. Unfortunately the one man who could have saved the situation, Joseph Chamberlain, was indisposed with a bad attack of gout.

All Rhodes wanted was a Treasury guarantee to help him raise a loan of about 2 or 3 million Pounds at low government interest rates, at that time only about $2\frac{1}{2}$ per cent. In return Chamberlain expected him to allow the Cape Government to have a one third share in the scheme, with its advantages as well as its risks and liabilities. Rhodes would have none of this, wanting the Imperial government to guarantee the whole scheme along with his Chartered Company. Chamberlain took considerable trouble to coax the Treasury, but in the end insisted that the Cape Government's involvement was cardinal, and that Rhodes could not have the use of Imperial credit entirely on his own terms.

No conclusion was reached. In the middle of May 1899 Chamberlain and Rhodes had the last of many dynamic conversations on the subject of the Cape to Cairo Railway in the House of Commons. There was no quarrel, though there was no love lost between them, and they never met again.

Rhodes had suggested a railway to the Victoria Falls in 7 years, with another 7 years to reach the Congo border. 14 years was a hellish long time to wait.

But he had reckoned without the 'mile-a-day' Paulings.

Once more George Pauling was summoned by Alfred Beit: "Go for it George! Build it ... no matter the cost."

He took the challenge, signed the contract and promised to build a mile a day, banking on the remarkable energy of his cousin Harold, with their well-drilled teams of surveyors and plate-layers.

A 2 feet narrow gauge line was first proposed, using rails from the old Beira railway which was rapidly being widened. Then Charles Metcalfe urged Rhodes to think big: "It will cost only a couple of Million to take the line to Lake Tanganyika, a thousand miles away - and almost as economically with the wider Cape gauge".

Though Metcalfe's calculations were way out, Rhodes was persuaded. He drove a hard bargain. Even at the astonishingly low cost of £3000 to £4000 per mile, it would still cost between 3 and 4 million Pounds.

With the backing of his bankers the House of Erlangers, Pauling put his own resources to work. Alfred Beit advanced a further one million Pounds, whilst De Beers and the long-suffering shareholders of the BSA Company also coughed up. They received no dividend for years.

*Till we feel
the far track
burning*

*And we see
her headlight
plain*

*And we gather
and
wait her coming*

*The wonderful
northbound train*

Rudyard Kipling

BREAKFAST.		DINNER.	
Quaker Oats, Fresh Milk.	Saute Potatoes.	Clear Ox Tail.	Assorted Vegetables.
Fried Fillets Stockfish.	Poached and Fried Eggs.	Fried Fillet Soles Tartare Sauce.	Anchovy on Toast.
Finnon Haddock.	Savoury Ome-lette (to Order).	Poulet Saute "Marengo."	Fruit Tart, Whipped Cream, Liqueur Jelly.
Curry and Rice.	Cold Ham.	Roast Haunch Mutton & Jelly.	Cheese & Biscuits
Fried Sausage.	Ox Tongue.		Dessert.
Grilled Mutton Chops.	Dry Toast.	Roast Veal and Bacon.	Black Coffee.
Broiled Ham and Bacon.	Preserves. Tea. Coffee.		

12

THE RIVER TO DIE FOR

TO THE BANKS OF THE ZAMBEZI

Travelling to the railhead in open construction trains was a dirty and uncomfortable business. Worse still, the contractors charged an exorbitant 'Shilling a Mile' for the privilege of sitting in an open truck under the blazing sun. But the speed of travel, compared with the arduous wagon trail, left no alternative.

The route from Bulawayo to Victoria Falls crossed nearly 300 miles of open savannah. It was dull dry country with long straight stretches inundated with scrub and mopani trees, criss-crossed by the odd stream. Between Gwaai and Wankie (Hwange) the line ran for over 70 miles absolutely dead straight without the slightest deviation of any kind either vertically or horizontally. This was the longest straight stretch of railway line anywhere in Africa. At night the headlight of an approaching train could be seen in the distance, hours before its arrival over the horizon. In those days the engine driver often carried a gun, so the train's rate of progress depended almost entirely on the amount of game *en route*.

Along well used game trails surveyors like Edward Rosher crawled through the bush on hands and knees to reach a clearing from which survey work could continue. So dense was the shrub, and so steep the ravines, that this was reckoned to be Livingstone's fabled Valley of Death. Many of the construction gangs slept in trees, on platforms wedged between the branches, which they dismantled every morning and sent forward as the line progressed. Others slept in tents in the open vlei - surrounded by balustrades of poles and thorn branches known as 'Scarems'.

Animals were abundant. Small sidings were christened after the African names for leopard, giraffe and zebra - Ingwe, Inthundhla and Isilwana. When the coal rich area of Chief Hwange was reached; it was then as now, a wilderness with waterholes teeming with wildlife. And a happy hunting ground for beasts of prey, mostly lion.

For nearly two years the end of steel stood at Mambanje Siding, after a long straight stretch of line near Dett (Dete). Coal from the Wankie Colliery was taken back to Bulawayo.

The Anglo-Boer War was coming to an end. The line was poised to go forward on the last hundred miles to the Zambezi River, the natural boundary between southern and central Africa. It was the request of Cecil Rhodes that it should cross at a point where the spray could be felt from the Victoria Falls.

In March 1902 he died at Muizenburg in the Cape at the age of 49. Though he never lived to see his Cape to Cairo line reach the Zambezi,

Arrival of the first construction train to reach the site of the Victoria Falls Station.
Standing : Dr. G.E.Buncombe, Unknown, G.C.Imbault, Dr. W.J.Pauling, R.Vernet, W.Loggie,
E.W.Hicks, E.R.Mansergh, Harold Pauling, W.Tower, Dr. Combes.

Seated : Fountain, Sweetlove, G.Kay, C.Everard, E.R.Marsland, H.E.Pooley.
On Engine : Miss Veale, Miss B.Pauling, C.V.Buchan, Mr.Walker (seated)
(NAZ)

and he never visited the Victoria Falls, he had already viewed and approved the plans for the majestic Bridge structure in London, after his return from the relief of Kimberley.

His body was brought up by rail to Bulawayo, escorted part of the way by an armoured train. It travelled in one the fine new carriages which Rhodes had asked Charles Metcalfe to plan for the new Train De Luxe Service from Cape Town, delayed because of the War in South Africa. Built by the Lancaster Carriage works they were designed to compete with the most luxurious trains on the Continent of Europe and America, and had already been used in the Cape by the Prince of Wales, and Joseph Chamberlain.

When Cecil Rhodes died in 1902 his body was brought to Bulawayo by train, and laid to rest in the nearby Matopos Hills, where he had made peace a few years earlier. A guard of Matabele warriors formed up to give the Zulu Royal salute "Hayete", the only time that such an honour has ever been accorded to a white man.
(BOOKS OF ZIM)

The railway finally advanced on the last leg of its journey in southern Africa; the completed line ended at the site of Victoria Falls Station in April 1904. Blanche Pauling drove the first engine up to the small gathering of about 30 Europeans. Not more than a few dozen white women, mainly wives of missionaries and traders, had previously set eyes on the Falls. The few local Africans were flabbergasted. They expected to see bullocks emerge from the boiler. Once again greenery bedecked the engine - palms for the Cairo end, and proteas from the Cape. The slogan 'We've got a long way to go!' said it all.

There was no platform and no station, only a reversing spur for the engines on the trackless clearing of high ground overlooking the Falls, half a mile away down in the gorge. It was the perfect setting for the most romantic of all the hotels to be built on the Cape to Cairo route.

Most of the party slept on the train; others stayed in nearby huts. The riotous ride from Bulawayo had been wild and wicked, with no less than 3

doctors in the party. All geared up for the welcoming occasion was the delightful 28 year old Blanche Pauling, followed everywhere by her chaperone Miss Veale. Like other lady pioneers of Africa she not only dressed for dinner; she rode and shot, and dosed Africans and animals alike, and then threw herself into all manner of activity. She was naturally earmarked by the gang of young engineers including the ubiquitous 'Charlie' Buchan, until recently Alfred Lawley's assistant on the Beira Line. Rupert Marsland and Harold Varian, also in their twenties, completed this celebrated trio; together with Georges Imbault, the French engineer who was to construct the Victoria Falls Bridge, and later, the bridge over the Nile at Khartoum.

Harold Pauling (1864 -1904) died shortly afterwards. After his pioneering 'mile a day' miracle all the way from Mafeking, and his conquest of the Kalahari through to Bulawayo, he had seen his lines finally reach the banks of the Zambezi. He left his widow Gussie Gordon Davis, of Welsh extraction, together with a family and heritage of continuing involvement in railway construction.

Victoria Falls Station in 1905 (below), and today (bottom)

Prospectors and entrepreneurs were rushing to the Victoria Falls before the first tourists and sightseers arrived *en masse*.

The first official passenger train from the Cape to the Zambezi arrived not long afterwards. A few dozen passengers constituted the first 'package tour'. It was reassuringly hauled by two engines, and comprised a Drawing Room Car with piano, a Dining Car, several Sleepers, a refrigerated truck and a luggage van. Quinine was served with breakfast, and the renowned Victoria Falls Pudding, with a spray effect of crystalised sugar, was christened. On arrival, the worn out ladies were carried down to the Rain Forest in hammocks, and crossed to the Islands in Canadian canoes.

The Zambezi Express was soon puffing up there on a regular basis, with the passengers still sleeping on the train, before the first Victoria Falls Hotel finally opened its doors.

Superior 'Trains De Luxe' of the Cape Government Railways provided a continua-

tion of the service for the well-heeled seafarers from Europe on their way from Cape Town. The crack expresses which plied this route and ran down the branch lines to Lobito Bay, Beira and Lourenco Marques were exotically named, like The Diamond Express, The Imperial Mail and the African Express. The full complement of 24 Dining Cars were each named after a river, such as Kowie, Kafue, Zambezi, Limpopo, Orange, Vaal, Hex, Sabie and Shashi. They were finished with oak panels, teak framing and mahogany mouldings; windows were hung with crimson curtains, and tables were spread with starched white linen. More importantly, superb six-course meals with highly quaffable European and South African wines were served, as the trains rattled along. The perennial meals, together with morning and afternoon refreshments taken in the compartments, broke the comfortable rhythm of the long, slow journeys on the Cape gauge lines, then, as now, at an average speed of about 35 miles an hour. The run up to Bulawayo from Cape Town took 69 hours and went back down again in 53 hours.

It was catering of the old school, at a time when railway hotels and staff vied with each other for a world-wide reputation. The two main railway stations at Johannesburg and Cape Town served absolutely superb food. Many were staffed by ex-ship's stewards, with flair, imagination and a tradition of service which was the pride of the Empire. Famed chefs sometimes forsook the comforts of a top class hotel for the stifling confines of a kitchen on wheels, with remarkable results. They were characters indeed; men like Spiros Metaxas, and the energetic and temperamental Italian Vincenzo Franconi, who was renowned for making his own fresh pasta with his imported equipment, whilst rattling through Africa.

After dinner it was customary for the men to retire to the smoking room, a somewhat cramped compartment. This was also a Writing Room complete with notepaper and materials, and a comfortable sleeping berth for one person - such as a dozy secretary or a hard working mining magnate; or perhaps a busy newspaper correspondent working to a deadline to drop off his copy at the next telegraph office en route. Hot and cold baths were available at all hours, to order from the conductor; the scalding water from the engines boiler being adjusted beforehand by the bath steward.

In 1909 the ultimate in sumptuous travel was a private carriage which could be shunted around the whole of the system run by the Rhodesia Railways, including over the Victoria Falls and up to the Congo border, or down to the sea at Beira. Each coach comprised 3 bedrooms, a bathroom, a Lounge cum Dining Car, a Writing/Smoking Room, a Reading Room for the ladies to retire to, as well as two or three spare rooms for personal servants. kitchen staff and luggage. Food and chef were included for an all-in price of £360 per week.

BRIDGING THE FALLS

The race was on to reach the minerals, hundreds of miles to the north. But first the mighty Zambezi had to be crossed. Many experts were convinced that the Old Drift, a few miles further up would be the swiftest and most serene way of fording the Zambezi. A lively public debate followed in which even the Times newspaper added fire to the fury.

But Rhodes had been insistent that the most spectacular sight on earth should be seen from trains rushing over his Cape to Cairo dream route. He had dictated: "Build the bridge across the Zambezi where the trains as they pass will catch the spray from the Falls." He viewed it as a meeting of equal forces. The steel lines crossing the perpetual waters, both racing on their way to their eventual ocean destinations. The practicality, and the real threat of corrosion on the steel bridge was overshadowed by this display of Rhodes' romanticism. Though he never lived to see it, his dream was fulfilled, and it almost appeared as if Divine Providence had intervened in the selection of the actual crossing point. Only a few hundred yards below the Falls, at the beginning of the magnificent gorge which continues on for another 30 miles, a single span of 600 feet would bridge the entire river. And the exposed banks were all found to be of black basalt rock, strong enough to anchor the foundations on both sides.

The Blondin aerial cableway

One of the world's most majestic bridges was an aesthetic as well as a logistical and acrobatic feat. The steel arch was designed by George Hobson and Ralph Freeman of the Cleveland Bridge Company which later built the bridge over the Nile at Khartoum, as well as the Sydney Harbour Bridge and the bridge across the Zambezi at Sena.

Several leading British, American and German firms had tendered for the contracts for the steelwork and for the erection on site. Most were daunted by the unknown quantity and quality of labour and the conditions in the remote African bush thousands of miles away. In the end only two firms were in the running - Paulings of Westminster, and Clevelands of Darlington. In spite of their expertise and track record throughout the world, and the superb teams of engineers and fitters at their disposal, Paulings tendered too high and they lost the contract. Clevelands ironically tendered too low and made no money.

The bosun's chair

Construction workers of the Cleveland Bridge and Engineering Compnay on completion of the Victoria Falls Bridge, 1905
(NAZ)

It was designed to be erected without scaffolding, with more than adequate margins for the massive stresses of heat, weight and wind. Neither could any chances be taken with the accuracy of the drilled steel members, so the entire bridge was assembled in the factory yard at Darlington before being shipped out to Africa in 'kit form'.

Before work had begun the 500 feet chasm had to be bridged with a cable. A kite was first tried out, but the elusive breezes blew it continually off course. Eventually a thin line was fired over the gorge by a rocket. Thicker lines followed, including a measured line to confirm the accuracy of the gap, loaded to a spring balance to calculate the amount of 'sag'. A bosun's chair hauled men and light materials to the other side to begin construction work from both banks. Then an electric 'Blondin' winch, appropriately named after the fearless French tightrope walker Pierre Blondin, was used to haul heavy materials across. It consisted of a platform suspended below pulley wheels which ran over a steel cable, attached to a crane with weights controlling the tension. At times it stuck halfway across. Rails, sleepers and rolling stock were all moved over the gorge. Even the spirited little Jack Tarr locomotive was taken to pieces and assembled on the other side. In this way the railway was advanced by Paulings all the way to Kalomo before the bridge was finally opened to traffic.

Guests assembled for the opening of the Bridge (SAL)(above)
The train ready to cross the Bridge for the opening ceremony (SAL) (below)

CAPE GOVERNMENT RAILWAYS
ROYAL MAIL ROUTE.

| QUICKEST TO THE | and | THE DIRECT ROUTE TO |
| — TRANSVAAL — | | — VICTORIA FALLS. — |

Luxurious and Rapid Travel in South Africa. Trains de Luxe between CAPE TOWN, ORANGE RIVER COLONY, and TRANSVAAL, and between KIMBERLEY and RHODESIA, including the VICTORIA FALLS.

THE SHORTEST AND MOST EXPEDITIOUS ROUTE from Europe to the GOLD and DIAMOND FIELDS of South Africa, and through communication with all towns in CAPE COLONY, ORANGE RIVER COLONY, TRANSVAAL, RHODESIA, NATAL.

MAIL BOAT TRAIN. — A DINING and SLEEPING EXPRESS train conveying FIRST, SECOND and THIRD CLASS passengers leaves CAPE TOWN DOCKS every Tuesday for KIMBERLEY, JOHANNESBURG, PRETORIA, and other stations in the CAPE COLONY and TRANSVAAL, after arrival of the Mail Steamer from England. A THROUGH SALOON for BULAWAYO and VICTORIA FALLS goes forward by this train, and is attached to the ZAMBESI EXPRESS (Rhodesia Train de Luxe) at KIMBERLEY. There is also a through connection to NATAL by the DINING AND SLEEPING EXPRESS TRAIN.

The ZAMBESI EXPRESS (Rhodesia TRAIN DE LUXE), with DINING and SLEEPING ACCOMMODATION, leaves KIMBERLEY every Wednesday, and conveys First and Second Class passengers for MAFEKING, BULAWAYO, and VICTORIA FALLS, connecting with the DINING and SLEEPING SALOON train leaving CAPE TOWN on Tuesday morning, and also (at Bulawayo) with a service of trains to GWELO, SALISBURY and BEIRA. The TRAIN DE LUXE returns from VICTORIA FALLS on Saturdays and connects with the Mail Steamer for EUROPE, leaving CAPE TOWN on Wednesdays.

AN EXPRESS SERVICE of DINING and SLEEPING SALOON trains run every morning and evening (Sundays included) between CAPE TOWN, JOHANNESBURG, and PRETORIA.

The trains leaving CAPE TOWN for JOHANNESBURG, and JOHANNESBURG for CAPE TOWN, each morning, travel *via* KIMBERLEY, KLERKSDORP, POTCHEFSTROOM, and KRUGERSDORP; the trains leaving in the evening travel *via* the ORANGE RIVER COLONY.

There is a DAILY DINING and SLEEPING SALOON PASSENGER SERVICE in both directions between CAPE TOWN and PORT ELIZABETH, BLOEMFONTEIN, DURBAN, and other principal towns in SOUTH AFRICA; also

MAFEKING (4 times weekly). **BULAWAYO** (3 times weekly).

SALISBURY, GWELO & BEIRA (twice weekly).

VICTORIA FALLS (twice weekly).

All these trains convey First, Second and Third Class passengers, with the exception of the train leaving **Cape Town** at 11.30 a.m. on Thursdays, which is **First Class only, Cape Town** to **Kimberley**, and First and Second Class from **Kimberley to Johannesburg**, and the Zambesi Express from **Kimberley** on Wednesdays for **Victoria Falls**, which is First and Second Class only.

A Fast TRAIN DE LUXE (the "Imperial Mail") leaves PRETORIA and JOHANNESBURG for CAPE TOWN on Mondays; it runs direct to CAPE TOWN DOCKS, where it connects with the MAIL STEAMER leaving for EUROPE every Wednesday. The "Imperial Mail" conveys FIRST CLASS passengers only.

CONDUCTORS accompany all trains between the COAST PORTS and the principal INLAND STATIONS, and their SOLE duty is to attend to the convenience and comfort of passengers. All through Passenger Trains are fitted with LAVATORY ACCOMMODATION. BEDDING available for the through journey is supplied on the trains. Where DINING CARS are not provided ample time is allowed en route to enable passengers to partake of BREAKFAST, LUNCHEON and DINNER at the appointed Refreshment Stations. SLEEPING BERTHS may be reserved on application.

Messrs. THOMAS COOK & SON, Tourists Agents, are Agents for the CAPE GOVERNMENT RAILWAYS, and are authorised to issue Passenger Tickets to and from all Stations on these Railways at their London Office, and all their Provincial, Indian, American, Australian, and South African Offices. Copies of Tariff Books and all other information may be obtained from the following:— ENGLAND: AGENT-GENERAL FOR THE COLONY OF THE CAPE OF GOOD HOPE, 100, Victoria Street, London, S.W.; OFFICES OF THE UNION-CASTLE COMPANY, London and Southampton. SOUTH AFRICA: GENERAL MANAGER, CAPE GOVERNMENT RAILWAYS, Cape Town; or the various Traffic Managers, Stationmasters, &c.

Cape Town, Oct., 1909.   **T. S. McEWEN,** *General Manager.*

Supervised by Clevelands Chief Engineer, Georges Imbault, the Victoria Falls Bridge was assembled in only 19 weeks by 30 skilled workers from England and about 200 local Africans, who with little training excelled in working at these dizzy heights, making an invaluable contribution in the handling of rivets and the paintwork.

The two halves of the arch were built out simultaneously from both banks, girder by girder, pinned and then riveted, and temporarily held by cables anchored into the banks until the archway was joined in the middle. A safety net was hung below the construction, 400 feet above the boiling Zambezi, to catch any steeple-jacks, riveters, fitters, or painters who missed their footing. Fortunately it was never needed.

On April Fools Day 1905 the time had come to join the two sections. Naked natives from far-afield and a group of Batonka tribesmen arrived to view this spectacular event, for until the advent of the railway not a single African lived anywhere near the Falls, so superstitious were they of 'the smoke that thunders'. Their Chief was absolutely convinced that the bridge would crash into the water, and they watched, day by day, as the spans arched out further and further from the banks without any apparent support. At last only the centre boom remained to be bolted into position. But it was found that the boom would not fit. It was midday, and the intense heat had expanded the whole structure. Next morning, before the sun was up, the last span was successfully joined, and it was a great disappointment to the waiting tribesmen to be denied their spectacular prophecy. The Old Chief did not give up. He declared that when a train went across, an even greater catastrophe would occur. So they watched, even more incredulous, whilst a light shunting engine propelled two trucks slowly across to the other side. Shortly afterwards the first 'cat' to try to cross the bridge met an unlucky end. A leopard, caught between the banks of the railway track was hit head-on by the little Jack Tarr loco-motive as it rounded the corner to the bridge approach.

Celebrations continued well after the opening. A regatta was held on a straight stretch of water well above the Falls, over a course which was to be used years later for the World Sculling Championships. A railway spur was extended from the Maramba siding near Livingstone down to the river. Crews arrived with their boats from all over South Africa; whilst 'Fours' from Oxford were acquired by Charles Metcalfe for the three local teams: 'North Rhodesia' - mainly government officials and Barotseland Police; 'Livingstone' - mostly members of Paulings; and the winning team 'Kafue', consisting of other engineers and contractors, such as Harold Varian, Rupert Marsland, Charles Cumberpatch and Ralph Micklem, few of whom had yet seen the Kafue river itself. The heavy handed North Rhodesia boat, the 'Bleeding Heart' weighed 64 stone with the cox. It only just managed to get home before ignominiously sinking. Local Barotse teams rivalled each other in their lightweight dugouts, hewn from logs and skilfully paddled by 6 standing oarsmen. Hundreds of them had arrived from miles upstream, and their races aroused terrific support from onshore spectators. King Lewanika himself arrived and threatened his Royal crew that if they lost they would be left to the crocodiles on an island in the Zambezi.

On the last night of the regatta the camp fires burned all night, with many hundreds sleeping on the river banks. Those who were staying in the railway carriages gazed across the waters near the Victoria Falls, or crossed the bridge in a special train and were shunted down to the river. Alongside this majestic course on the northern banks of the Zambezi a dinner had been set out under the bright moonlight, with the Administrator of North Rhodesia, Robert Coryndon* in the chair. It went on nearly all night. The guests wandered down to the river with the few ladies who had dared to be escorted over for this momentous occasion. North Rhodesia had come into its own. The major obstacle had been bridged. Now all eyes, hearts and minds were on the way north, to the area on both sides of the mineral rich Congo border.

*Appointed at the age of 27, Robert Coryndon was one of Rhodes' 'Apostles', who had first served in the British South Africa Company Police and then transferred to the Pioneer Column. Exemplifying the best of British interests in Africa, he started the policy of indirect rule, and laissez faire with the Chiefs. He transferred to Swaziland, then Basutoland (Lesotho) before becoming Governor of Uganda. In 1927 he was appointed Governor of Kenya and Zanzibar.

VICTORIA FALLS HOTEL

The original Victoria Falls Hotel

Between Shepheard's in Cairo and the Mount Nelson in Cape Town, perhaps the most memorable of all hotels en route is the one at Victoria Falls. Its emblem shows the Lion of Africa and the Sphinx of Egypt separated by an adventurous hunter, symbolising the Cape to Cairo link.

Owned and run by Rhodesia Railways, the staff worked in the tradition of the great railway hotels of England - transported to the heart of the dark continent. Within earshot of the thunderous waterfall, from a verandah of rudimentary elegance, which became a celebrated rendezvous, guests watched the trains meander down to cross the bridge - their little lights twinkling in the darkness like some miniature meccano railway.

When the Zambezi Express first arrived from Cape Town in 1905 the tourists slept on the train. The original wood and iron huts of the hotel had been dumped beside the line simply as temporary accommodation for the engineers working on the bridge and permanent way.

An old corrugated iron engine shed, which had been used by Paulings in Mafeking, was brought forward. Spruced up, it originally served as a dining room, and then it became the first Victoria Falls Hotel. Another shed and huts were added on - known as 'Honeymoon Suites'. Although the rooms were either baking hot in the sweltering heat, or ice cold on winter nights, these quaint edifices heralded the start of many a happy sojourn overlooking one of the most romantic sights on earth.

No other hotel in the whole of Africa started life so purely and simply because of the railway. The thin steel ribbons penetrating into the heart of Africa encouraged more and more ladies from around the world to venture forth, with effortless ease, by luxury train. On arrival they were carried on Machillas by dusky bearers to the banks of the Zambezi, through the ever-flowering rain forest - to catch a glimpse of the elusive lunar rainbows on nights of full moon. Princess Christian of Denmark and the Duchess of Aosta came soon after the service commenced, accompanied by Lord Roberts of Kandahar. Some of the islands were named after them.

The first hotel Managers were two colourful Italians, Gaetano Estran, who had worked in Cannes under Cesar Ritz, and Pierre Gavuzzi, who had worked in London at the Savoy, and then at the Grand Hotel in Bulawayo. Gaetano was well known for livening up the evenings with Italian arias. On one occasion he was hijacked by a crowd of construction engineers in the dining room, stuck up on the mantelpiece and commanded to sing. After that he avoided all bridge and railway men like

An early trader and visitor at the original Victoria Falls Hotel

the plague. Gavuzzi was one of many locals to be attacked on the river by a bad-tempered hippo. It holed their boat and they all swam for their lives to the shore. He was credited with introducing ping-pong to Rhodesia and was a deft left-hander, with the agile streak of a champion.

An outside hotel bar was established for the construction gangs where drinking and gambling went on all night, and some-times for several days

after the men were paid. Fights broke out, much to the annoyance of the genteel guests within earshot. During the regatta for the opening of the Bridge the bar ran completely dry, and some 'nasty scenes' occurred.

Pierre Gavuzzi started the hotel farm, which provided all manner of fresh vegetables and fruit. Giant cabbages, asparagus, pineapples, melons and even strawberries were some of the delicious fare carefully nurtured and served in the original engine-shed dining room. The staff were a cosmopolitan mixture of French Chefs, Arab and Indian waiters, and an American barman. As railway employees, all the African staff came from the new centre of Livingstone, across the river.

The contractor George Pauling with his wife, and colleague Ernest Stourton, at the original Victoria Falls Hotel, and down at the Boiling Pot (P. & Co)

The wooden hotel verandah became the rendezvous of the rich and the famous, and the melting pot for missionaries, traders and hunters. Owen Letcher, one of the first of the legions of safari explorers who travelled to their hunting grounds by train, used it as a stopping-off point. The legendary Selous, inspiration for the hotel's logo, was one of the first to explore the hostile country to the north. He would nonchalently stride onto the creaking hotel veranda with his rifle and bandolier, clad only in a long shirt and belt - a tropical version of a kilt - which he swore he always hunted in. He would then recount his latest bag of trophies, already on their way to Rowland Ward's famous taxidermists in London.

A whistle would announce the arrival of the mail train; and from down the line onto the station platform behind the hotel, a mixed bag of travellers would stagger in for a taste of genteel luxury. Dust covered and dishevelled, they would sink into the wicker chairs, whilst disapproving ladies would peer across at them through their lorgnettes, and Tut-tut.

The hotel and bar were incredibly well stocked. The railway brought up from the south delicacies unheard of in other outposts of Africa. London Gin, Malvern Water, Stilton Cheese, Bath Oliver Biscuits, Oxford Marmalade, Gentleman's Relish, Ceylon Tea; even perishables like Plum Pudding and Haggis - all the things that homesick Empire Builders thrived on. At no other hotel did one have that sublime feeling of utter dependency on steel rails stretching forward, hopefully to Cairo, and reaching back reassuringly to civilization. The one and only road to Bulawayo, 300 miles away, remained a rough wagon track until half a century later.

*One of the few trans-
border rail services
in operation across
southern Africa, the
Shongololo Express
(Shona for Caterpillar
and Zulu for
Food Store) at
Victoria Falls Station*

It was not until the years of rebuilding during the First World War, that the Hotel lost its engine-shed image, and became a solid bricks and mortar establishment. It was a spacious Edwardian style edifice stretching out in four directions from a central courtyard. The railway track, from which noisy engines blew soot and sparks onto the verandah in front of the hotel, was re-laid round the back, to give an uninterrupted view down the gorge to the Falls.

In the 1920's and 30's the Hotel was in its heyday. In the warm heart of Africa, memorable meals were served in the dining room under huge revolving fans. Jackets and ties were worn in the evening, since shorts clashed with chandeliers. The bar was run by an entertaining Irishman Paddy Geary. Outside, guests were transported up and down to the bridge and the Zambezi boathouse on miniature rail trolleys, propelled by local manpower - largely by gravity on the way down, and by sweat and tears on the way up. For nearly 40 years two million people were carried on these cast-off rails from the narrow gauge Beira line, until it was finally considered too demeaning a method of locomotion, especially in the humid suicide months before the rains. A rickshaw service and donkeys were also provided.

A regular visitor was Celia Salmon - almost as crack a shot as her celebrated husband, who was reputed to hold the world record for elephant trophies. She was in the same legendary league as Annie Oakley of Wild West fame, and she glamourised the art of hunting in its African heyday. In the drawing room of her London home, few guessed that this petite lady could pack a punch of such skill and accuracy in the wilds of Africa.

In the 1950's when the Sunderland flying boats of Imperial Airways skimmed to a halt in this Wagnerian setting on the wide stretches of the Zambezi above the Falls, this fascinating far corner of Africa came into its own. Not far from where four countries meet at a point in mid-river, 40 miles up the Zambezi, the Victoria Falls Hotel became known as Jungle Junction. It was a combination of the Piccadilly Circus and Capri of the antipodes; and a mecca for the Cafe Society of the day.

Trophy hunters continued to appear. George Pauling's daughter Dolores trundled up by train from Cape Town, having arrived on a coal boat from China. Genial and portly like her celebrated father, she held court in swarthy purple saris. Having rescued an orphaned jennet, she called it Tuk-Tuk after one of Rudyard Kipling's animal characters. She secreted it in her hotel bedroom, from where it attempted several break-outs. Hidden in the folds of her ample proportions, it was smuggled onto the Imperial Airways flying-boat for her trip back to England. There it slept in the warm airing cupboard of her London flat. One miserable day in the depths of winter, the homesick little creature disappeared out of the window, never to be seen again.

On cast-off rails from the narrow gauge Beira Railway, trollies plied the route from the Hotel down to the Victoria Falls for nearly 40 years - propelled by local manpower

Right from the beginning there was a certain envy of the world-wide reputation of the 'Vic Falls' by the residents of Livingstone, cut off from the mainstream of activity across the river, 7 miles up the railway line. Especially for the ladies in the bush, life continued in the most difficult fashion imaginable. They had come out to Africa with their new husbands, mostly to stay in rudimentary huts with no furniture and few home comforts. For this was real frontier territory, with just the long railroad to civilization behind them, and uncharted territory beyond.

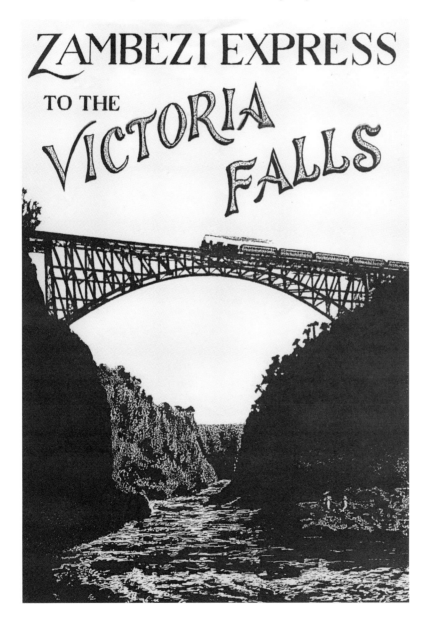

RHODES' DREAM

Up from the Cape where the wild seas thunder,
Over the Falls, where a haze of spray
Keeps the North and the South asunder,
Swings she swift on her headlong way -
Speeding tireless, night and day,
Past the Lakes in their magic chain,
Waking the Desert to wide-eyed wonder,
Racketing, rocketing, roars the Train.

"Cape to Cairo ! - Steamer to Steamer!
Rail and wire from South to North..."
Men guffawed at the Master Schemer,
Fools waxed loud in their foolish wrath...
But the project held, and the words went forth,
Sister-nations hurried to aid,
Stung by the dream of a dumb, dear Dreamer,
Men toiled on till the rails were laid.

Out of the South where the ships are plying,
Into the clutch of the parched Karoo,
Past the crags where his bones are lying
Under the slab on the World's wide View...
'Tis none so long since the world was new
And the mammoth moved in eternal snows,
But the dream he dreamed when he lay a-dying
Bids to come true. And perhaps - he knows.

Henry Cullen Gouldsbury
'The Kipling of Africa.'
(1881 - 1916)

13

LIVINGSTONE LULLABY

LIFE ON THE ZAMBEZI

Five miles above the Falls on the north bank of the Zambezi was Clarke's Drift, the main crossing point before the Zambezi was bridged a century ago. Beyond lay Barotseland with a history of despotic and feuding rulers, well known for such nasty habits as leaving unwanted babies and old wives to the crocodiles. It eventually flourished under the first King Lewanika, Paramount Chief of the Lozi (1843 - 1917), who reigned with an enlightened iron fist, and became an enthusiastic supporter of the big white Queen Victoria. His monstrous sister, also a Big Queen who lived to the ripe old age of 102, was in charge of the river section.

Early traders and prospectors were seriously deterred from crossing over; but through the influence and skilled diplomacy of the shrewd and honest hunter-trader George Westbeech, missionaries finally settled - encouraged by Chief Khama of Bechuanaland, a Christian friend of King Lewanika. All missionaries were welcome as long as they were British.

The first Jesuit Fathers of the Zambezi Mission were struck down by malaria in 1880, and their return was discouraged because they were Belgians. The Scots flourished, helped by the home comforts of their wives, that rare band of frontiers-women who battled it out alongside their husbands, often at death's door with fever.

The French Huguenot leader of the Paris Missionary Society, Francois Coillard, (1834 - 1904) inherited George Westbeech's mantle. With his Scots wife and two assistants, he assisted Lewanika's overtures to the British Government for protection, and helped him defeat slavery, establish trade settlements and negotiate mineral concessions. Lewanika feared not only the Matabele, from across the Zambezi River, but also the Portuguese. They had been established in Central Africa for even longer, and were hoping to link their territories of Angola and Mozambique across the breadth of the sub-continent.

Harry Ware, a trader from Kimberley, was quick off the mark. He had been the first to advertise the attractions of the Victoria Falls in Field Magazine of 1885. He also obtained a mining concession from Lewanika, with no strings attached. This was snapped up by Rhodes' Charter Company, and an envoy, Frank Lochner went up to confirm it with the King.

A impressive firework display on the banks of the Zambezi with plenty of roast meat constituted the first Barbecue or Braaivleis (Afrikaans for burnt meat), and clinched the deal.

Store at Livingstone (Victoria Falls)

The agreement ensured Lewanika ruled under the protection of Queen Victoria and the Chartered Company, with a share in the commercial and mining rights. Elephants would remain royal game. In return he agreed to stamp out witchcraft and slavery. It was a better deal than his arch-enemy King Lo Bengula of Matabeleland acquired.

Francois Coillard believed a charter was the only way that the more docile Barotse could avoid anhililation by the homicidal Matabele. He also wanted better transport links to aid his missionary work. He wrote to his daughter: "A break in the darkness seems to be the Chartered Company. We should at least have the advantage of regular postal communications and our transport would also become easier if not cheaper. Here they expect to push the railway through to Cairo !" This devoted ally of Britain and the Barotse died of blackwater fever two days before the railway reached Victoria Falls.

Admired and respected, King Lewanika had a relaxed sense of humour at his legendary dinner parties for honoured Europeans. A favourite delicacy was Tortoise stew, usually reserved for Chiefs, followed by succulent Hippo meat and Roast Wild Duck. This was washed down with tankards of unfermented beer, or Cape Claret - purchased from local traders.

When cruising down the Zambezi River on State occasions in his black and white Royal barge, Lewanika was followed by an armada of canoes and banana boats. Built in the boatyards of another early entrepreneur Arthur Harrington, the barge was surmounted by a huge elephant statue, and propelled by a hundred crimson-hatted oarsmen dressed in lion skins. Lewanika proudly wore an Admirals uniform, presented to him by King Edward VII on a visit to London. This had been hurriedly arranged by the Administrator Robert Coryndon, much to the embarrassment of the dilatory Colonial Office, which had repeatedly brushed aside Lewanika's early overtures. His naval regalia, with ostrich plumes, was also incongruously worn for the annual migration of his subjects and their livestock up to the safety of dry land from the flooded Zambezi plains; a pilgrimage that still takes place today from the capital Monga after heavy rains.

A small European mud and thatch village grew up around the Old Drift, with characters like 'Zambezi Browne' drifting in and out of the area. When Zeederburg's weekly coach service arrived from Bulawayo it was announced by a bugle call, and there was a mad scramble for the mails. 'Mopani' Clarke, nicknamed by Lobengula after the mopani tree, was tall straight and hard. He ran a store and a hotel with a bar, open all night, as well as a gambling joint - complete with roulette wheel - inevitably run by 'Yank' - an American croupier. Supplies were ferried across the Zambezi by canoe and barge, and 'Mopani' Clarke ran a small steamer on the river for the use of copper prospectors. Although no relation to Percy Clark, the early Livingstone photographer, both men hailed from Cambridgeshire in England.

In this atrocious climate the toll from malaria and blackwater fever was absolutely appalling. In 1903 there were 31 white residents. In the first rainy season 11 died, and by the end of the next season only 10 had survived. There was a funeral almost every week, and on more than one occasion the coffin went into the grave followed by the tipsy undertaker.

A monument at the Old Drift cemetery records some of their names: Georges Mercier (Paris Missionary 1900). John Neil Wilson (1903), Alexander W. Findlay (1904), Ernest Collins (1904), Miss E. Elliot (1904), Samuel Taylor Alexander (1904), David Smith (1905), and fourteen others whose names are unknown.

The first chemists, the first doctor and the first policeman, a Baronet, all died in the bush. Freddie Mills arrived with his wife, and whilst he opened the first restaurant shed, she started a nursing hut complete with another medico. They too were driven off by blackwater fever. Eventually Leopold Moore arrived with his wife. They survived and thrived as a happy combination of Chemist and Journalist.

The area was a paradise for game of every description. Hunters and ivory poachers had their field days. A local Greek trader made his living 'shooting for the pot'. One misty morning as he surveyed the terrain from a 12 feet high ant-heap he saw what he took to be 11 wild pigs. He fired at them, one after the other, and ended up bagging 9 Lions.

The Old Drift was doomed when the Victoria Falls bridge was opened, and the line was diverted further eastwards from the original planned route through the heart of Barotseland. The British South Africa Company decided to move to higher, healthier ground, and Livingstone became the railway centre of the region. The north-western part of the town was the administration centre and nucleus for the Traders, Entrepreneurs and Old Drifters who were 'strongly encouraged' to move there from the river bank. The south-eastern area across the line was reserved for the railway workers who kept somewhat to themselves. There was a certain animosity against these new railway people, viewed like 'express trains passing in the night' by some of the seasoned old salts who had been forced to re-settle.

Alfred Lawley lived in a cosy bungalow next to a banana grove

The original North Western Hotel built in 1906 by Pauling & Co. It was sold to the BSA Company, became Government House from 1907 - 1935, and was recently demolished.

beside the railway encampment. Not for the first time he received 'mischievous mail'. In the first edition of the Livingstone Mail (31st March 1906) he prominently advertised: 'NOTICE: If the gentleman who has addressed two or three anonymous letters to me will call at my house he will hear of something to his advantage. Signed A.L.Lawley.' No doubt a few well chosen words in railway vernacular would have followed. A nice little sweetener was added to the column: 'TENDERS WANTED: For painting three bridges of 100 feet each and one of 75 feet on the Kalomo - Broken Hill extension. Particulars at Offices: Pauling & Co.'

George Pauling put up the first North Western Hotel and supplied it with electricity from the generator which had been used to power the winches on the bridge construction site. It was an elegant Victorian brick mansion, much more luxurious than the wood and iron hotel at Victoria Falls, with better food and a milder climate - less humid and more breezy. When the British South Africa Company moved their headquarters from Kalomo, the Hotel was sold to become the seat of Government - the Boma; and Livingstone became the capital of the region. Two old timers who were unaware of the change of ownership wandered onto the veranda shortly afterwards and ordered several rounds of drinks before they discovered they had been enjoying government whiskey courtesy of Robert Coryndon the Adminisrator. Livingstone was the one place where

Freddie Mills' forlorn second North Western Hotel was the social centre of Livingstone from 1909 until recent times

the railway had no need to rival the Boma. Almost everywhere else where the Union Jack was flown, government officials considered themselves a cut above the average. "Is he Boma or Railways ?" was the often facetious question posed at official functions.

The Old Drifter, Freddie Mills had already established himself as a prosperous bar owner, catering mainly for the railway men, a cosmopolitan collection of toughs, who represented at least half the population at the time. He rebuilt his Livingstone Hotel with 10 bedrooms and a billiard room. Around the corner in 1909 he built the second North Western Hotel - a stately mansion with a long verandah which was enlarged over the years in keeping with its prominent position overlooking the railway line - racing energetically, in fits and starts as funds allowed, towards Broken Hill (Kabwe) and the Congo border.

On the banks of the Maramba River, flowing into the Zambezi, Paulings established a garden - a prolific source of fruit and vegetables of all kinds. In recognition, George Pauling named his first granddaughter, born in 1906 - Miramba.

From Livingstone ran the postal service that became the envy of the Germans, the Belgians and the Portuguese. Red coated runners took the mails up to the remote borders of Tanganyika, and even across to the west coast of Portuguese Angola at Benguela. Carrying 40 pounds of mail, most runners covered 30 miles a day; but special runners ran an astonishing 90 miles through a day and a night. They carried calico to barter for food and shelter, and were welcome everywhere. It was a prestigious job and the white man's message seldom failed to get through.

Livingstone soon became the social centre of the region. All the 'Old Drifters' had moved there. It became a town of bicycles, ice boxes, mosquito gauze and large doses of quinine. Those who survived usually prospered, and it was no place for remittance men, wasters and idlers. A local ice factory delivered huge blocks twice weekly to keep meat, milk and butter cool, rather than cold. Otherwise the tried and trusted system of a metal box with shelves covered in wet flannel cooled the contents by evaporation. Tins sent up from the Cape contained luxuries such as Butter and Lard from Holland, corned meat from New Zealand, and tinned milk from Germany, with a shelf life of 10 years.

Through the sandy streets narrow gauge trolleys were pushed by local labour down to the Zambezi Boat Club, the main weekend retreat for sports and social activities.

Nearby, another narrow gauge railway ran on wooden rails with trolleys pulled by oxen into the Barotseland forests. The line was eventually extend-ed 100 miles into the well wooded areas of the northern plateau at Mulobezi, a haven of Rhodesian 'Mukusi' Teak and other hardwoods. As well as for furniture and flooring, these same forests still supply railway sleepers,

RHODESIA & MASHONALAND RAILWAYS

To Southern and Northern Rhodesia and the Congo.

TRAINS FITTED WITH EVERY CONVENIENCE

CORRIDOR CAR SERVICES.

THE FASTEST AND QUICKEST ROUTE TO
"RHODESIA"

VICTORIA FALLS BRIDGE.

AMATONGA FOREST

VARIED FEATURES OF BEAUTY AND INTEREST.

BIG GAME SHOOTING

BULAWAYO STATION.

THE IDEAL COUNTRY FOR SETTLERS.

GOOD CLIMATE AT ANY TIME OF YEAR·

BEIRA.

MAIN FALLS—VICTORIA FALLS.

MINING, FARMING, CATTLE, GRAIN, TOBACCO.

For Full Particulars apply to :
The Secretary, Rhodesia House, 2, London Wall Buildings, E.C.2. ·

From the Zambian side of the Zambezi River, mokoro canoes ferry visitors through the crocodile and hippo infested waters, to a tranquil Island hide-away known as Jungle Junction (AUTHOR)

proving themselves more resilient and long lasting than their concrete and steel 'pea-pod' predecessors, for the rail route right through to the Congo.

The Zambezi Saw Mills developed into the longest private railway in the world, with steam engines fired on scrap wood. It was run entirely by cast-off rolling stock and locomotives, firstly from the 2 feet gauge Beira line, and later from the Cape gauge, many of which still lie in the Station yard, now the inestimable Livingstone Railway Museum.

The rails were laid on unbalasted tracks and shifted around to the new logging locations. On the single line there were no signals, so drivers

stopped at water points and telephoned ahead for clearance. Passengers perched on top of the piles of timber on the open trucks, and were exposed to firebrands from the steam engine, which caused several fatalities.

Hidden and abandoned in the depths of the forest lies an early locomotive which lost its way when the line was moved. Some say that on still nights this ghost engine can sometimes be heard, raising enough steam to find a way out.

The Pith helmet symbolised the roots of this North Western territory, and of Livingstone itself - the brave little frontier outpost which over the years fought and lost against its now unwieldy and more prosperous neighbour, the township across the Zambezi at Victoria Falls.

Livingstone still survives with all the charm and fascination of a grand little lady caught in a time capsule. This lonely little whistle-stop is a blend of colonial Edwardian and Art Deco - preserved as the old Bank, the Cinema and the Museum. Lost and forgotten in the lower part of town and occupied only by a caretaker, the North Western Hotel sprouts trees from its internal courtyard. Leading from the creaking wooden verandahs, the once beckoning bedrooms wait for better days. The painted inn sign still swings outside. There was once a thriving Jewish community here, a nucleus of early traders who trekked up from Bulawayo and beyond, settled, and virtually monopolised the merchant classes. Others, like the Susman brothers, escaped the poverty and pogroms of Europe, and established stores and cattle stations on both sides of the Zambezi. Now it is mostly Indians and Africans, and descendants of the old timers, in a cosmopolitan mix of backpacker joints, with an international conference centre 5 miles down the road. And along the banks of the Zambezi, for many miles upstream, there is every conceivable variety of hostelry.

Mokoros or dug-outs on the Kafue river 1906. Photographed by Harold Varian. (RGS)

Survey Chain - used on the stretch from Victoria Falls to the Belgian Congo. Each Chain measured 66 feet (22 yards), composed of steel links. Chains were also sub-divided into sections, identified from both ends by brass tabs with 1, 2, 3 and 4 prongs. 80 Chains measured one Mile. (10 Chains to a Furlong, 8 Furlongs to a Mile). The curvature or cornering of a section of surveyed rail line would be designated by the number of chains on end which formed the radius of that curve; e.g. a 20 chain curve would have a radius of a quarter of a mile
(PAULING ARCHIVE)

14

CANNIBAL COUNTRY

ACROSS THE GREAT CENTRAL PLATEAU.

Long before the Victoria Falls bridge had been completed the stalwart little Jack Tarr locomotive which had hauled countless loads of materials up from the coast at Beira, was painstakingly taken to pieces. Boiler, bogeys, cab and all the other elements were then perilously swung across the Zambezi gorge on the Blondin aerial cableway and re-assembled on the other side. Along with thousands of tons of materials similarly brought across, the railway advanced without waiting for the bridge to open.

The tireless George Pauling pressed on, together with Charles Metcalfe, on the survey of the route to the north. Their old friend from Kimberley days, Robert Williams was desperately anxious to open the route to the mineral deposits on both sides of the Rhodesian-Congo border which were already being exploited, and to bring up coal from the newly opened Wankie (Hwange) Colliery, the largest coalfield in Africa.

Several different routes had been proposed. The aim was to head across the great central plateau to the Congo Border 400 miles away, and to find a way over the Kafue River. This would prove almost as big a challenge as the Zambezi.

Perhaps as a kind of consolation for the loss of the Victoria Falls bridge contract to his rivals, Pauling trekked in grand style. The entourage included his secretary Henry Pooley; his valet Eduardo Delgardo, of mixed Mozambique descent, who had been with him since Beira days; the British Native Commissioner who was a superb linguist; an Irish hunter Jim Murphy, and a French chef from Cape Town. A mixed gang of 300 Porters brought up the rear, carrying the luxuries and necessities of camp life - 'chop' boxes, folding baths, chairs and beds, tents, medicine chests, and of course, surveying equipment such as theodolites for measuring distances and inclines, aneroid barometers for calculating altitude, prismatic compasses and survey chains. Also included were beads and calico for barter, and a large machilla - a hammock slung on poles - strong enough to carry the portly Pauling in case of injury or incapacity.

The well planned safari team showed astonishing stamina. Before dawn they rose. At 6 am the porters took up their 60 pound loads, to which was added their individual mats, cooking pots, calabashes for water, and leftovers of meat and maize from the night before. Then they advanced for the morning's trek, chattering and laughing, and sometimes breaking into song. In unison they shifted the loads from one well muscled shoulder to the other. At 11 o'clock they paused for an hour to allow the survey team

The portly Pauling stands beside his machilla, carried by tenga-tengas

to catch up, but the final stop was not made until the afternoon.

The headman was indeed the leader. He not only encouraged his companions, but sometimes shouldered the extra burden of a straggler or injured porter, carrying loads up to 120 pounds at the end of a days trek.

Eduardo Delgardo cuts the hair of Murphy, the hunter-manager

For speed and economy it was now decided to aim directly for the Broken Hill Mine. The original route would have taken the line through the heart of Barotseland out towards the Hook of the Kafue, following the only wagon road which was about 200 miles further west. One of the main difficulties was to find a feasible river crossing, since the Kafue in flood was over a mile wide, and a mass of islands and swamps forming a spreading lagoon.

Across the open plateau, the going was easy. Marking river crossings as they went, they arbitrarily located the sites of sidings and halts in the complete wilderness, naming them generally after the local chiefs and headmen, such as Kalomo, Choma, Pemba, Monze and Mazabuka. There was one exception - Tara - at the highest point of the plateau, exactly mid-way between Bulawayo and Broken Hill. On Murphy's instigation, this was named after the Hill of Tara, seat of the ancient Kings of Ireland, where dissident tribes had met at the crossroads of the five ancient highways.

After weeks of trekking they reached the Kafue River, from where they couldn't use horses any more because of the tse-tse fly. Having crossed it in dug-outs, they continued on foot. Travelling by compass for about 3 to 4 hours every morning and again every afternoon, they covered a robust 20 miles a day. Every evening they sent a team forward to select a camp site. Then their attention turned to food.

The magical gardens of Pauling & Company on the banks of the Maramba River, flowing into the Zambezi at Livingstone, had offered them almost every kind of vegetable. They had selected those which travelled well, such as onions, garlic, ginger, horse-radish and sweet potatoes. In the end the Irishman's ability in 'shooting for the pot', and the Frenchman's expertise in haute cuisine were the paramount ingredients for some memorable meals. Pauling observed: " Our chef, who turned out to be a regular treasure, provided magnificent dinners. How he did it none of us could conjecture. Of course we had plenty of tinned goods and a sufficiency of fresh game, but day after day he furnished us with a dinner equal to anything I have had in any of the big hotels of England or any other part of Europe. We had not neglected to include in our baggage plenty of Champagne and other liquors, and this was made cold by the method which is familiar to all travellers in tropical countries.* After dinner we occasionally played a rubber at bridge, but we were generally tired enough to lie down, indulge in a somnolent smoke and go to rest."

By the rapid evaporation of water from the surface of a damp canvas bag or porous container, which causes a heat loss from the interior contents. There is also a porous bark from a local tree which is still used for that purpose.

Here they first encountered the man-eating lions which caused so much havoc in the area. The weather was suffocating and everyone slept with the tent flaps tied open: "At the entrances to each tent," adds Pauling matter-of-factly, "we made a barricade consisting of tins, portmanteaux, bundles and other articles to make sufficient noise to awaken us. Our only

George Pauling turns his back on cannibal colleagues, waiting with empty cooking pots

casualty was one of the natives who, while sleeping with his fellows at a spot where they had allowed their fire to burn low was carried off by one of the lords of the forest."

To add insult to injury, about 30 of their carriers were cannibals. A beady eye was kept on these awful people and their disgusting habits after it was noticed that some of their meat looked suspiciously dark. It was well known that they favoured the fleshy parts of hands; and the greatest delicacy of all was a young girl's thigh. "One night," Pauling records, "Eduardo came to me and said that one of them, Jim, had a baby. At first I was unable to comprehend this alarming information, but after cross examination it appeared that he had in his possession a little piccaninny about two months old. We sent for Jim and enquired where he had got it, and why he was bringing it with him.

With charming *sang froid* he replied that he had stolen it from a kraal and that he and his brothers were looking forward to the luxury of a cooked baby that night. The culprit was severely reprimanded and the piccaninny returned to its kraal at once".

Before returning to Livingstone and the advancing railhead they picked out the route which was subsequently followed, by and large avoiding places of any great difficulty, by P. St. George Mansergh, Paulings ace surveyor.

Some weeks later, whilst the line was finally being staked out, Alfred Lawley, ill with malaria, and Harold Varian, trekked forward to find an accurate bridge site over the Kafue itself. They located it where the river narrowed to a point about a quarter of a mile wide.

This whole area was a hotbed of decidedly unfriendly tribesmen, who had announced their intention of killing anyone they could on the forthcoming construction. Unlike any others, the Mashukulungwe were 6 feet tall, and dark skinned. They wore a 3 feet high pointed headdress made of matted hair, animal horn and sticks. When sleeping they fastened it to the side of a tree or mud wall. They had no teeth and their grin was therefore unbearably menacing. As they were very proud of their manliness, they went about absolutely stark naked. Even on cold winter nights they never appeared to have a blanket. When asked why they did this their only response was: "We are not women".

Dressed to kill with a 3 feet high headress, 'Mash' warriors were not like any other tribe; they never wore clothes even on cold winter nights
(RGS)

Varian crossed the river in a dug-out canoe and set up camp overlooking the Kafue flats. He slept with his two pedigree Irish Deerhounds chained to the tent pole. Bought from a man at Victoria Falls, they had been bred from pure stock brought out from England.

That night hunting animals appeared on the plain - Lion, Leopard, Wild dog, Hyena. There was also every conceivable variety of game. Haughty Kudu; wagging tailed Oribi, sandy coloured Eland and fleet-footed Impala; Reedbuck and Duiker - all feeding together without fear. The great hunter Selous, one of the first to penetrate that region in the 1880's,

The Mashukulungwe tribe threatened to kill anyone they could on railway construction, like the surveyor P. St George Mansergh, pictured with his stalwart companion (PAULING ARCHIVE)

reckoned that there was probably no part of Africa where such a rich variety proliferated. Varian, though a keen hunter, was also a true conservationist of his day. Raised in Ceylon, his father had been a Woods and Forest Officer, and a world record elephant hunter, who had died at 34 from wounds received from a raging jumbo. Varian therefore regarded anyone who had not shot an elephant as a poor sort of person. He wrote numerous articles for 'Field' and other sporting journals.

"Next morning, when the sun rose, we saw every type of game alongside our outspanned oxen, mules and horses. As these animals had never been hunted or shot, they showed no signs of fear even at close quarter. It was an unforgettable sight, one of those memories of untouched Africa that has lived in my mind."

Later, both his deerhounds were lost to wild animals. One was taken in the night by a lion at the site of the Kafue bridge. A stone cairn was erected over her grave to prevent the hyenas digging her up. The other met a tragic death locked in deadly combat with a baboon.

Kalomo at that time was the new capital of the region; but there had been a hitch. Again the problem of finance had reared its ugly head; work halted and there were lay-offs. Finding finance took time, but eventually the rails advanced steadily more than a mile a day across the great Central Plateau under Lawley's renewed energy. The going was fast and easy. Sleepers and rails were laid on the bare earth whilst the ballast was filled in later. Near Pemba a world record in plate-laying was achieved. A visiting French Engineer had been asked by Charles Metcalfe to guess how far the lines could stretch in a good days work. "A mile or two?" "Let's see", said Metcalfe. With an eye on his pocket watch, Lawley blew the whistle. The plate-layers got busy. The quarter mile peg was passed in 20 minutes. 11 hours later they had laid an astonishing 5$\frac{1}{2}$ miles.

Advancing to Kalomo, a highly spectacular collision occurred. Rounding a bend at a steady 20 miles per hour, the construction train came across a huge bull elephant. The driver applied his brakes, threw the engine into reverse, and hooted his whistle. The stately jumbo stood his ground against the approaching iron monster. With magnificent trumpeting and bellowing the old stager smashed against the cow catcher. The bogies left the rails, and the engine tilted to a listing halt. The elephant lay there thrashing and shaking; and no rifle or other means of despatching it was available for several hours. In order to keep up the contract of a mile a day, the line had to be deviated around the wounded beast and derailed engine.

When the railhead approached the Kafue River bridge site, 3 months ahead of schedule, herds of game over a hundred strong were often seen. Shortly afterwards J Geldenhuys came up with the first ox wagons loaded with materials. The herds were ruthlessly shot by the trigger-happy transport riders out of sheer lust for slaughter.

"That part of the country was disturbed for all time, and the game vanished forever," commented Varian.

One of the first white men to arrive at the bridge site was a 'green' Greek subcontractor who, in spite of warnings, allowed his gang of workers from the south to interfere with the truculent local Mashukalungwes. One night all hell broke loose with a bloody battle, in which several were killed, and Costa all but escaped with his life. In this wild frontier district there were as yet no police or administrative posts to deal with the culprits.

CROSSING THE KAFUE

The Bridge across the Kafue River was once the longest in Africa. Tranquil waters follow a torturous course of lagoons and islands for some 200 miles upstream, and the terrain is flat as the majestic river sweeps serenely through the 1500 feet wide approaches to the bridge site. Yet the levels rise and fall dramatically with the seasons, and bridging the gap was almost as tricky as crossing the Victoria Falls.

A causeway was built from each bank, whilst concrete piers were constructed inside small coffer dams; then sunk into the rock and gravel of the river bed, protruding only a few feet above the water level.

The steel structure was designed by George Hobson of Victoria Falls bridge fame. It comprised 13 steel spans, supplied from England by a company with the intriguing title of the Patent Shaft and Axle Tree Company - better known in locomotive rolling stock circles. The sections were shipped out to Cape Town, railed up 1500 miles, and then laboriously carted from the rail-head by ox wagon. They were assembled and riveted together on the south bank. Each 100 feet span, weighing over 50 tons, was eased down a greased slipway onto a floating steel pontoon - the ends of each span protruding over the sides. The pontoon was then hauled by steam tug, and floated carefully into position between the piers, where the span was dropped into place. This rapid method of construction was devised by Alfred Lawley, in charge of the contractors Paulings. In just over a week all 13 spans were in position, with 2 more for the bridge approaches.

The Kafue Bridge took only 5½ months to complete, from March to August 1906 - the number of the year being the same as the mileage of the bridge from Cape Town.

Once again nobody waited for the bridge to be finished before pressing on. North of the river the ground was soft, and

only lightly loaded trucks could be pulled along the temporary permanent way. So for many miles the wagons were ponderously drawn by a span of oxen, affectionately known as Engine Number 32. When the first real locomotive was ferried across the river, work steamed ahead.

OPENING OF THE KAFUE RIVER BRIDGE 1906
- the same figure as the mileage from Cape Town.
In the coach:
James Butler, George Pauling, Eduardo Delgardo,
Doel Zeederburg; also Ned Clery and Dr. F. Krause.
On the bridge parapet:
Alfred Lawley, Harold Varian, S.F. Townsend.
On the open wagon of 'Pauling & Co. Contractors, London':
26 Bridge Engineers dressed to celebrate
(PAULING ARCHIVE)

As each siding or halt was reached, convoys of ox wagons were drawn up ready to transport stores and materials to the gangs working ahead.

Not far distant, at the 1938¼ mile peg, was a large group of mud huts in a wild area named after the local headman, Lusaaka's Kraal. Why anyone could have wanted to stay there was a complete mystery. When the rails reached it, the sidings were laid the same evening, and Lusaka, the future capital of Zambia, was on the map. "The most arid, desolate, windswept, cold and miserable spot in Northern Rhodesia" is how Leopold Moore described it.

OPENING OF THE KAFUE RIVER BRIDGE 1906 Left to Right: James Butler, George Pauling, Harold Varian, Alfred Lawley, G.E. Buncombe, Dr. F.E.T. Krause, Personal Staff (PAULING ARCHIVE)

As usual the ox wagons came up, but this was also one of the worst places in Africa for hungry lions. Heedless of the noise from the shunting engines, that night they came and killed some of the oxen as they lay in their traces. Unable to drag the carcasses off, they wandered elsewhere. Rupert Marsland was camped a short distance away. He had with him a large well-fed marmalade cat - the original Orlando - which had been with him all the way from the Cape. Fed on tit-bits of springbok, elephant trunk, rhino steak and other such delicacies, it always slept in a chair by the camp fire. That night the cat disappeared, and the only indication of

its sad fate was a distinct lion spoor running across the camp clearing.

When the line to Broken Hill was completed, the Kafue Bridge was also ready for hand-over to the Rhodesia Railways. Lawley had forbidden any alcohol in the camp site, so this was the first occasion many of the bridge hands had of letting off steam. A train came up from the south with guests for the opening party. Behind the contractors carriage was a truck loaded to the hilt with all manner of foods and drinks including hams, beer, whiskey and brandy. All hands were loaded onto it and at sunset it moved slowly across the bridge. In the twilight a few toasts were drunk. Then all

Platelaying into Broken Hill (Kabwe) 1906

Platelaying of the last half mile into Broken Hill. Alfred Lawley in foreground (PAULING ARCHIVE)

the bridge-hands got down to the serious business of celebrating.

Leaving the truck behind, and the riotous assembly to their devices, the train moved on to Broken Hill for further activities. When they returned two days later they met with a sorry sight. Black eyes, bruised ribs and monumental hangovers. The burley riveting squads had vied with each other in pushing the truck backwards and forwards across the Kafue bridge in individual trials of strength.

It was at the opening of the Kafue Bridge that the famous road transport contractor Doel Zeederburg announced that the American builders were closing down their coach works, and had informed him that they could no longer supply him. So passed another milestone in the saga of African transport. One of the old-time transport contractors Stanley Hyatt later reminisced:

"The railway was right up to the Victoria Falls. Our task, the task of the transport rider was finished; there was no place left for us. The Road, the Great Road, the road that always went on, had ceased to be. Today, overgrown, the drifts washed into great ruts, even the heaviest of our abandoned wagons long since rusted away.

"In these latter days I never meet anyone to whom I can talk of the Road, or any one who knew it. One or two women, women who have never even set foot in Africa, have understood, because they have understood me; but to the average man the romance of it all seems absurd, utterly impractical. Far better, infinitely better, have the Train de luxe, on which, by ringing an electric bell, you can procure much whiskey."

Feted at the bridge opening was the distinguished Afrikaans advocate Dr. F. Krause (1868 - 1956), the Saviour of Johannesburg. During the 18 months that the Golden City was besieged and abandoned during the Anglo-Boer War, he had maintained Law and Order as Military Commander. The exemplary manner of this far-sighted lawyer earned the endless thanks of the returning British community. For during their absence he had barricaded their shops and homes against looters. He had also prevented the sabotage of the Gold Mines by some of his more extremist Burghers, including Judge de Koch, whom he had personally arrested.

At the end of the War, when 'Little Bobs' Lord Roberts, whose only son had been killed in action, rode into Johannesburg along with the tall stern Kitchener, it was the dignified Dr. Krause who stood beside them whilst the Republican flag was hauled down and the Union Jack raised. The world's richest gold mines thus passed into British hands.

The contract from Kalomo to Broken Hill specified an incredible rate of one mile per day. 281 miles had been laid in 277 working days. When the line reached Broken Hill in January 1906, Paulings crack plate-layers approached the last half mile with gusto. Many of them had been on the line all the way from Vryberg in the Cape several years previously. They gave an amazing demonstration of their skill. Removing materials by hand from the construction train, they raced forward, and laid them so rapidly that the slowly moving train continued onwards without a pause over the new track.

Sweetness, Beauty and Melody joined forces with the jubilant gangs and danced in the heat and dust at the arrival of the train from the south.

The last Telegraph Pole

Before the railway arrived, the Broken Hill copper Mine was already in operation. The furnace from the top of the Koppie

Broken Hill was already a rudimentary hamlet with a working mine. Surrounded by sparks and flames from the smelting furnace the celebrations continued. A herd of fattened cattle were brought up by Lawley as a parting present for the gangs to feast on. The scene was filmed by a Pathe cameraman, though no record of this early newsreel has ever been found. Where the line halted on the open vlei, there was not even a buffer stop. On the bare earth it lay pointing northwards, ready to continue onwards to richer prizes, on its relentless route to Cairo.

Lusaka developed slowly. Many of the Afrikaans transport riders and farmers who had lost their homes and families in the War in South Africa came up from the south and settled. Yet it took several years for the future capital of Northern Rhodesia (Zambia) to advance beyond a 'dorp' of mud and thatch huts. Few and far between were brick and iron buildings, in spite of the fact that a sharp eyed Italian, Giovanni Marrapoli, working on the railway, had located abundant limestone to make cement. He opened a kiln, and like the settler J.J. Geldenhuys, farmed extensively in the lush vicinity of Lusaka. Together with the Jesuit missionary

Fr. Torrend, they were in the vanguard of European settlement.

It was not until 1913, when Lusaka officially became a township that Mr. Martin was granted the first licence for Counsell's Hotel (later the Lusaka Hotel), situated opposite the railway station on the corner of Cairo Road and Rhodes Street. On either side were the stores of Kollenberg and Glasser, pioneers in the almost entirely Jewish trading community.

At that time the whole of north-western and north-eastern Rhodesia comprised only 1500 Europeans, with an Afrikaans to English ratio of two to one.

By 1931 Lusaka's white population stood at only 600, and Counsells Hotel had been joined by the Grand and the Imperial. The famous Ridgeway Hotel followed.

Broken Hill (Kabwe)
March 20th 1909
S.F.Townsend
(Chief Engineer)
G.C.S.Pauling
F.O.Stephens
(Manager)
H.C.Carter
(Chief Surveyor)
R.Boulton (Surveyor)
(PAULING ARCHIVE)

THE COPPERBELT.

With constant cries of 'Rip off rates' there had been a crusade by the agricultural community against the railway going north of the Zambezi in pursuit of undeveloped mineral concessions.

T.G.Davey, a prospector from Australia, had stumbled across a white stone which was carbonate of lead. The rock formations of lead and zinc reminded him of the area he had worked in Australia, and so he named his new discovery Broken Hill. Copper, lead, zinc, lithium and rare quantities of radium were all magic words. Prospects were almost as great as those in the Katanga province across the Belgian border, which Robert Williams had his eyes on. Although Broken Hill did not live up to expectations, the rails served other newly discovered mines in the vicinity.

There were numerous ancient copper workings scattered throughout this territory, in which both George Grey and Frank Lewis continued to search. Whilst Grey was busy re-discovering the riches of Katanga, meaning 'Land of smelted Copper' and known for centuries by the Portuguese, he stumbled across the gigantic Star of the Congo Mine. Lewis meanwhile was searching further south, and was guided to a giant outcrop of copper sulphide, ignored by the Africans because of their inability to smelt it. This became the Nkana mine.

Another canny early prospector, Collier, had made his way from Bulawayo 700 miles away to this remote area and discovered the Copperbelt proper. He befriended the district commissioner, Jones, a tall hefty man known locally as Bwana Mkubwa - 'Great Master.' He needed to be. The area was terrorised by a nasty local chief involved in Arab slave trading - resplendent in a village complex complete with Arab Mosque. In the course of his wanderings, and after many false leads, Collier stumbled across the open cast copper workings of this hostile Chief. He named the mine Bwana Mkubwa after the friendly native commissioner.

Some time later, prospecting for more copper, Collier felled an antelope at the exact spot where a rich outcrop surfaced. This became the Roan Antelope mine. A wayside station with a Boma and a few iron shacks became Ndola, the junction for the mines in the vicinity.

Chirapula 'Beats All' Stevenson, also called Hari-Hari, was an early telegraphist from England, who started at the Cape and moved up the line. As in the Wild West of America, a Railroad Telegrapher was an important personage in the local hieracy, privvy to all sorts of secrets. Stevenson was soon appointed a Magistrate, simply because there was was no-one else around to take the job. In time he became an honoured, and honorary, local Chief - the only white man many of the locals had ever seen. He brought law and order to this frontier district with the aid of a couple of dozen askaris; eventually destroying the local slave trade.

Devoted missionaries had blazed the trail; officials then paved the way in opening up this new frontier territory, which ran for hundreds of miles in a north easterly direction to the borders of Tanganyika, and Nyasaland. The railway was their only real link with the south. New government officials would sometimes walk from the railway halt for weeks on end through the bush, with a team of porters carrying loads on their heads, to take up their new postings. And when they went on leave they would walk back again for weeks on end to the railway, which by this time had often advanced further afield.

The young Robert Codrington ran the capital of this north eastern region from Fort Jameson, whilst his near namesake and neighbour Robert Corydon, ran the north western territory from Kalomo and then Livingstone. When the trans-continental telegraph arrived at Abercorn, Fort Jameson was finally in communication; for there were no roads and no settlers in this remote unfriendly territory.

The missionaries bore the full brunt in pacifying tribal tensions. Just as Rev. Francois Coillard had woven together the fractious Barotse beyond Victoria Falls, so in this new region bordering the Congo and Tanganyika a courageous White Father, W. Van Ost, stood his ground against the Bembas. This tribe spurned all offers of protection from British emissaries, and threatened to kill any white man who dared to trespass on their territory. Father Van Ost took no notice, and brazenly marched into the Chief's village in his flowing white robes, and preached. The Chief was so astounded that instead of killing him, he promised to open up his country to missionaries and traders - a promise that was kept, and paved the way for British administration over this vast territory.

James Butler's sketch of the somnolent George Pauling about to be 'scoffed' by a lion riding on the carriage

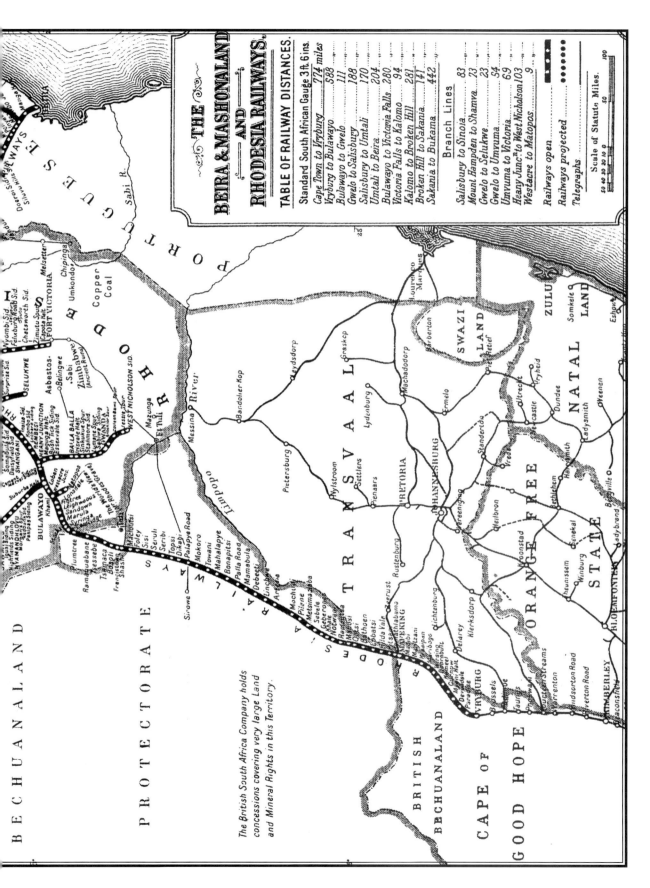

THE BEIRA & MASHONALAND AND RHODESIA RAILWAYS.

TABLE OF RAILWAY DISTANCES.

Standard South African Gauge 3 ft. 6 ins.

Cape Town to Vryburg	774 miles
Vryburg to Bulawayo	588 "
Bulawayo to Gwelo	111 "
Gwelo to Salisbury	188 "
Salisbury to Umtali	170 "
Umtali to Beira	204 "
Bulawayo to Victoria Falls	280 "
Victoria Falls to Kalomo	94 "
Kalomo to Broken Hill	281 "
Broken Hill to Sakania	141 "
Sakania to Bukama	442 "

Branch Lines

Salisbury to Sinoia	83 "
Mount Hampden to Shamva	23 "
Gwelo to Selukwe	23 "
Gwelo to Umvuma	54 "
Umvuma to Victoria	69 "
Heany Juncⁿ to West Nicholson	103 "
Westacre to Matopos	9 "

Railways open ●◆◇●◆◇
Railways projected ⋯⋯
Telegraphs ●●●●●●

Scale of Statute Miles.
50 40 30 20 10 0   50   100

The British South Africa Company holds concessions covering very large Land and Mineral Rights in this Territory.

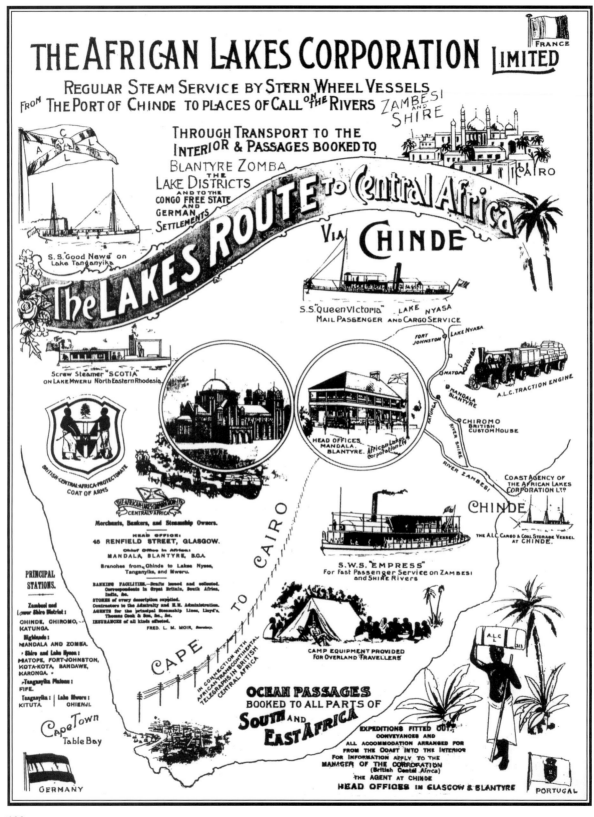

15

TWO STREAKS OF RUST...

THE SHIRÉ HIGHLANDS AND TRANS ZAMBEZI RAILWAYS

Few places in Central Africa held more fascination than the Zambezi and Shiré River routes into the heart of Nyasaland (Malawi) before the advent of the railway. The story reads like something out of Mark Twain on the Mississippi - stern-wheel paddle steamers; shifting sand banks; sugar plantations; patrolling gunboats; fetid heat, and the mangrove swamps of 'Old Man River'.

From the beginning, the Zambezi River was viewed like the Mississippi - an open sesame to the wealth of the interior of the landlocked Lake Nyasa area.

There were two threats to British sovereignty over the area; the Arabs and the Portuguese. Running battles around Lake Nyasa were fought against the Arabs, who were nominally under the control of the Sultan of Zanzibar, but were in fact 'running riot'. It was, effectively a war against the slave trade. It was largely fought in true Wild West style by stalwart British private enterprises such as the African Lakes Corporation, run by the Moir brothers from Edinburgh, and the London Missionary Society, between which there was a certain rivalry for the hearts and minds of the region's inhabitants.

John and Frederick Moir were the principal originators and constructors of the Stevenson Road - the strategic track which connected Lake Nyasa with Lake Tanganyika. More than anything else it helped to defeat the slave-raiding Arabs in this region, thus furthering British political aims for a Cape to Cairo route, whilst confronting German claims over the area.

The Portuguese too had their eyes on the area. For centuries they had sent expeditions to find ways to connect their Mozambique interior with the mouth of the Zambezi River or with the harbour of Quelimane further north. They had also attempted to claim the whole of Central Africa by controlling all the river routes into the interior.

In 1889, Daniel Rankin, an ex-British official at Mozambique was exploring the vast area around the Zambezi River mouth. He was searching for a way from the ocean across the shifting sand bar into the open stretches of this great river, navigable for 250 miles inland. For years, all but the smallest ships had refused to cross this barrier, where the water level at low tide was just a few feet deep.

One day he came across a lone Portuguese planter working a remote concession on the Zambezi delta, at a place called Chinde. The planter told him that there was a waterway nearby, devoid of sandbars, which eventually connected right through to the main Zambezi river, several miles inland. And the water depth at its mouth was not less than 20 feet deep.

Unknown to the Portuguese Government, this momentous discovery opened out the whole of Central Africa to large scale trade and development by the British. It was shorter, safer and simpler than any other outlet to the sea.

Anglo-Portuguese relations were cordial, but at times uneasy. There was a kind of unwritten alliance. Whilst Britain sent an expedition under Harry Johnston up the Shiré River, the Portuguese sent one under Major Serpa Pinto, which travelled with nearly a thousand soldiers and officials. Both sides made hasty treaties with as many chiefs as they could muster. The two rivals assisted one another to an extent, until a recalcitrant Portuguese lieutenant attempted to seize Chiromo and Blantyre. Britain threatened to break off diplomatic relations. Gunboats stood by at the mouth of the Tagus River near Lisbon, and threats were made to invade Portuguese Goa. So tiny, tottering Portugal, on the edge of bankruptcy from her far flung possessions and weak Monarchy, backed down. Serpa Pinto was called to heel. The actual boundaries of control were not finally decided until the Convention of 1891. This agreement made the Zambezi River a neutral waterway, with the 25 acre British Concession of Chinde at its mouth, railed off to avoid paying customs dues. A similar concession was granted to the Portuguese at Leopards Bay on the south-west shore of Lake Nyasa (Lake Malawi).

Ocean going ships of the Union Line called monthly on their way from Port Natal to Zanzibar. An agreement was also made with the Deutsch Ost Afrika Line. Passengers were dropped at Chinde, from where they transferred to the stern wheel paddle steamers, fired on wood and drawing only 20 inches of water. They steamed 100 miles up the Zambezi, and then a further 80 miles up the Shiré River to Chiromo. From there onwards, for a further 50 miles, passengers took a chance - either in small canoes pontooned by dusky sailors with long bamboo poles, or in flat bottomed punts dragged over the shifting sands. When the river was really dry they were carried in Machillas by 'tenga-tengas' - hammocks slung between the shoulders of bearers. Blantyre, Zomba, the Shiré Highlands and the areas around Livingstone's lake - Lake Nyasa - were their destinations.

At that time there were only about 300 Europeans and 100 Indians in the whole of the Nyasaland Protectorate. In this laborious and expensive way, cargoes of cotton, tea, sugar and tobacco were painstakingly transshipped down river to the sea. Port Herald was then the most southerly station on the Nyasaland/Mozambique frontier. For most of the year it was a veritable burning furnace with temperatures as high as 118 F (47 C) in the shade. Yet the Highlands themselves had the scenery of Scotland and the climate of the Riviera.

The efficient British transport and postal services were envied by the Germans and Portuguese for their speed and reliability. Mails were carried from the coast right up Lake Nyasa as far as the remote German territories near Lake Tanganyika, and to distant Portuguese outposts.

Two British gunboats, HMS Herald and HMS Mosquito uneasily patrolled the river stretches as far as Tete, 250 miles from the coast. There were also about 25 paddle steamers of the British Central Africa Company and the African Lakes Company, as well as boats of the Sena Sugar Company, on the river. Stern-wheelers with names like Scorpion, Hydra, Centipede, Bruce, Scott, James Stevenson, Lady Nyasa, Duchess and Empress, plus their lighters lashed at either side, steamed their way seaward. Stewards served meals, but the comforts were minimal. The steamy cabins were often only 6 feet square, with tiny bunk beds and the obligatory mosquito nets.

They cruised past the confluence of the Shiré and Zambezi Rivers, their passengers catching the breeze in deck chairs; past the Sena Sugar Factory; and past Lacerdonia to the wider reaches where they heard the songs of the Zambezi, chanted by the rivermen paddling their canoes. Some lyrics were sentimental, some a little blue, but most were of the

HMS Mosquito, with its sister ship HMS Herald, were British Gunboats patrolling the neutral waterways of the Zambezi River from its mouth at the British concessionary port of Chinde, to Tete

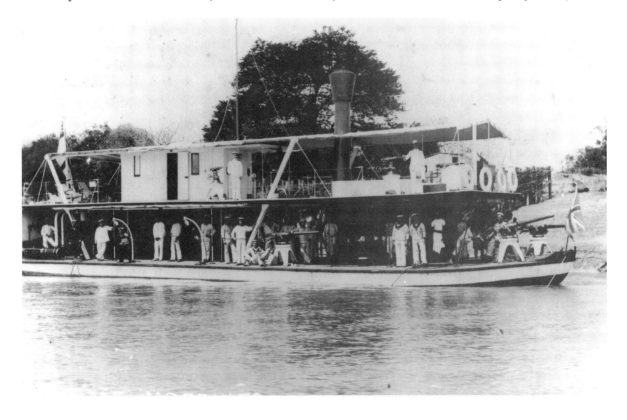

A Portuguese Stern Wheel Steamer of the Compagnia Zambezia, with barges lashed alongside,.on the lower reaches of the Zambezi River (NAZ)

mournful sea-shanty variety known by men the world over, away from their women and their homes. The broken rhythm matched the task - as they paddled, they beat the shaft on the side of the canoe, before and after it hit the water.

The rivermen were cautious of the currents and other unseen hazards such as giant crocodiles. They were also superstitious of the evil spirits that lurked on the river, and placed offerings such as utandi (flour) on the rocks to propitiate them.

> The night is long and dread the day
> Hasten father - O my home!
> The river's dark and far away!
> Hasten father - O my home!
>
> Fierce river friends they laugh and mock
> Hasten father - O my home!
> Place utandi on yonder rock
> Hasten father - O my home!

They also sang an ancient hymn, taught by the Jesuits in the 16th century from the mission station at Shupanga on the Zambezi, where the wife of David Livingstone, who caused him so much anguish with her drinking habits, lies buried under a Baobab tree.

At the Indian Ocean, passengers were landed over the side in giant wicker baskets onto a wooden wharf, built on the shifting sands of Chinde - itself situated on a great barrier reef, with its attendant burial grounds. The Club Hotel and Estrela d'Ouro were the only concessions to comfort.

The Shiré Highlands Railway was built to overcome these obstacles; firstly from Blantyre to Chiromo, and then to Port Herald (Nsanje). The original survey for the first section had been completed by the African Lakes Company. It was said that there was enough winding in it to break a snake's back. The Murchison Cataracts had to be circumnavigated. Completed in 1908 it was built by government departments from Port Herald to Blantyre. The extension from Port Herald, called the Central African Railway, passed through both British and Portuguese territory down to the Zambezi on the bank opposite the township of Sena, and then along to Chindio, with river access to the sea for exports of cotton and tobacco.

Pauling recalled this 1913 contract: "The length of the line was only

Arrival of the first train at Blantyre, March 1908, when the railway was opened by the Governor Sir Alfred Sharpe
(NAZ)

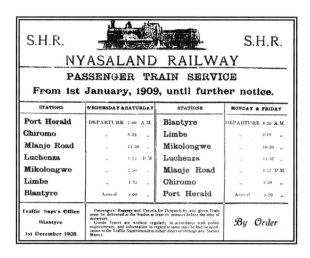

S.H.R.   **S.H.R.**

NYASALAND RAILWAY

PASSENGER TRAIN SERVICE

From 1st January, 1909, until further notice.

STATIONS	WEDNESDAY & SATURDAY	STATIONS	MONDAY & FRIDAY
Port Herald	DEPARTURE 7·00 A.M.	**Blantyre**	DEPARTURE 8·30 A.M.
Chiromo	„ 8·35 „	**Limbe**	„ 9·40 „
Mlanje Road	„ 11·30 „	**Mikolongwe**	„ 10·30 „
Luchenza	„ 1·25 P.M.	**Luchenza**	„ 11·37 „
Mikolongwe	„ 2·50 „	**Mlanje Road**	„ 1·17 P.M.
Limbe	„ 4·35 „	**Chiromo**	„ 3·50 „
Blantyre	Arrival 5·00 „	**Port Herald**	Arrival 5·20 „

Traffic Supt's Office	Passengers' Baggage and Parcels for Despatch by any given Train must be delivered at the Station at least 15 minutes before the time of departure. Goods Trains are worked regularly in accordance with public requirements, and information in regard to same may be had on application to the Traffic Superintendent either direct or through any Station Master.	*By Order*
Blantyre		
1st December 1908		

about 60 miles, but the construction took nearly two years to complete, chiefly owing to the difficulty of transport up the Zambezi River, and the need to re-handle the material when the Ziwe Ziwe River, an important tributrary of the Zambezi, was in flood. To indicate the difficulties we had in opening up new territories through the civilising influence of the 'iron horse', I might mention that in this case all the materials, rails, sleepers, bridgework, plant and the multifarious other things essential to the completion of the railway were shipped from England to Beira, where they had to be trans-shipped into sea-going barges. These were towed to Chinde, at the mouth of the Zambezi. There, everything had to be loaded onto river barges and conveyed to Chindio, about a hundred miles up the river. Discharged there, they were loaded into trucks and taken to the 'end of steel' as the construction proceeded"

Alfred Lawley of Beira Railway fame was in charge, aided by Rupert Marsland, Bill Fretton, Cooper and Southwell.

"Twenty three miles north of Chindio the line reached the Ziwe Ziwe River, which had to be negotiated by a steel screw pile bridge, consisting of 33 spans of 56 feet each. The erection of the bridge was exceptionally difficult because of the sandy nature of the river bed, and took about twelve months to complete. This was achieved by C.F.Tristram and his team. During that period Lawley was pushing on with the work on the north side of the river."

The route south of the Zambezi was linked up with Beira on the coast by the Trans-Zambezi Railway. This ran from Dondo up through the plateau to the banks of the Zambezi at Caia. Running over relatively easy terrain, between marshlands, with few gradients and only small rivers to cross, it was completed in a somewhat haphazrd manner with a shortage of efficient local labour.

Prolific game herds caused an alarming incident on the wooded Cheringoma plateau beneath the Gorongoza mountains. A train came round a bend and crashed into a herd of elephant. Five jumbos were killed and the breakdown gang had to jack up the locomotive to haul one particularly huge carcass off the line.

At the point where it met the Zambezi, ferries carried

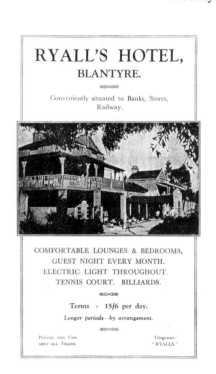

RYALL'S HOTEL,

BLANTYRE.

Conveniently situated to Banks, Stores, Railway.

COMFORTABLE LOUNGES & BEDROOMS.
GUEST NIGHT EVERY MONTH.
ELECTRIC LIGHT THROUGHOUT.
TENNIS COURT. BILLIARDS.

Terms · 15/6 per day.

Longer periods—by arrangement.

PORTER AND CAR   Telegrams :
MEET ALL TRAINS.   "RYALLS."

the traffic over the river.

When the time came to bridge the mighty Zambezi itself, the line was extended along the south bank to Sena. And likewise on the north bank, the railway was shortened to run direct to the opposing bank. There at Sena, the second longest bridge in the world of 12,000 feet, or $2^1/_4$ miles, was built by the Cleveland Bridge and Engineering Company of Darlington, the same firm which had bridged the Zambezi at Victoria Falls and the Nile at Khartoum. Thus for the second time the Zambezi was crossed by a railway, this time at one of the few convenient points 120 miles from its mouth.

The Sena Sugar Company had also built a 56 mile narrow gauge railway line along the south bank of the Zambezi from their headquarters at Marromeu.

The company was founded by John Hornung (1861 - 1940) in 1890, and became the largest and most successful of all the companies involved in the Mozambique concessions. Of Transylvanian origin and British descent, 'Pitt' Hornung, in his early twenties married his teeange Portuguese sweetheart, whose father held a concession along the Zambezi River from the Mozambique Government.

In conjunction with Jardine Matheson's of Hong Kong, Hornung explored and rejected the feasibility of growing opium poppies. Instead, he gambled on sugar cane. Battling against tse-tse fly, plagues of locusts, cyclones and drought, in the most primitive conditions imaginable, he expanded, taking over two neighbouring plantations at Caia and Marromeu from French Mauritian interests. He then persuaded the world's leading sugar broker, Caesar Czarnikow to become Chairman of his Company, in spite of the wise man's worldly misgivings that "Sugar stinks, Mozambique stinks and the Portuguese Government stinks". When Sena Rum proved a disappointment, he concentrated on cane harvesting. Eventually the Company opened a sugar refinery near Lisbon.

In spite of the shifting conditions of government controls over transport and labour, the company prospered in the boom years for sugar during the First World War.

There was some criticism of the Chiboro labour methods, a decadent relic of Portugal's early colonial empire in which all and sundry were expected to pay their way to avoid starvation. In 1931 Sena Sugar Estates was still paying most of its wages in British Sterling.

Steam-driven traction-engines and the narrow-gauge railway along the banks of the Zambezi played a significant role in both production and transport, which in the early days had been entirely down the Zambezi to the sea. A wider gauge connection was later made to the main Trans-Zambezi line.

*By the standards of colonial rule in Africa, Mozambique was a uniquely fragile creation. It was administered by a variety of different agencies and foreign concessions, which remained until the 1970's stronger and more successful than any centrifugal power

One of Pitt Hornung's daughters, and also one of his sons had married a Du Boulay brother and sister - thus cementing the enduring Anglo-Portuguese alliance of the vast estates over which the Union Jack and the Portuguese flag flew, side-by-side, for almost a century.

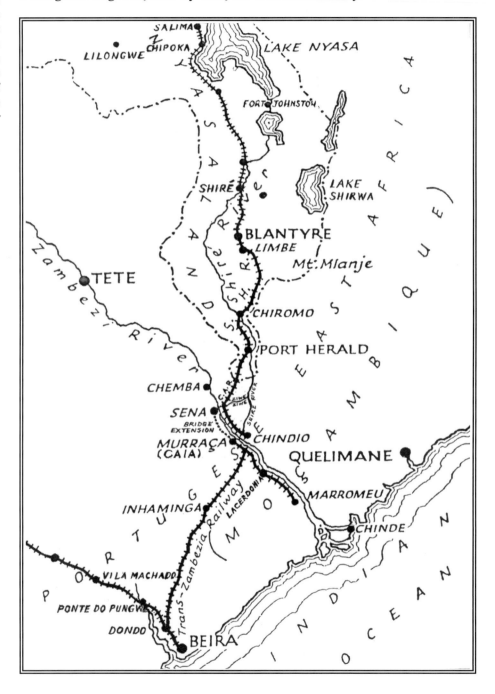

16

MILESTONES TO MINERALS

THROUGH THE BELGIAN CONGO

From the time of the building of the first railways in Africa, the Belgians had been looking at ways to link their vast Congo interior with the coast. An endless stream of Belgian railway surveyors had failed miserably to find viable land routes to the Congo River, which was the main outlet to the sea, and was in many places impassible for all but the smallest boats.

Stanley's momentous 999 day expedition from Zanzibar had also confirmed the view that railways would be the best means to join the gaps unnavigable by boats. He had traced the Congo River from its source as the Lualaba in Central Africa, along thousands of miles to its mouth on the Atlantic, traversing hundreds of rapids and waterfalls. As a result of his recommendations, the Leopold Plan was drawn up to coordinate the rail and river routes of the Congo Free State in the 1880's.

The Congo Free Sate was the personal fiefdom of King Leopold. At the Berlin Conference of 1884 under the chairmanship of Bismarck, it had been promulgated as a Trading State 'open to all', under the sovereignty of the Belgian International Association. A few months later King Leopold took over personal sovereignty in place of the Association. As one of the largest shareholders in the *Wagons-Lits Compagnie* which ran the Orient Express, he had also made a considerable fortune through shares in Railways in China.

Not surprisingly, King Leopold's fiefdom was fast approaching bankruptcy, as the trade in ivory and coconut oil declined. The Congo's economy was based on rubber, run by unspeakable rubber barons, in which the Michelin Tyre Company had a stake. Only a few Europeans had either witnessed or were prepared to speak out against the appalling atrocities then perpetrated against the locals. Among them was the Anglo-Frenchman Georges 'Bulldog' Morel, and the Anglo-Irishman Roger 'Tiger' Casement of the Elder Dempster Shipping Line who discovered that the Colony was being milked dry with exports and no money returned to it.

Only international condemnation, a timely government loan and a national lottery saved the day. Income soared ten-fold after it became Belgian Congo Territory, answerable in every way directly to the Government and Taxpayer.

On the west coast, far removed from the influence of any British scheme, the Matadi to Leopoldville railway was started in 1890 under Albert Thys. It was a 240 mile long, 2 feet gauge line, built with the most monumental difficulties and rate of casualties. The shortage of local workers caused the use of indented labour gangs by the Belgian contractors. It took 3 years to complete the first 14 miles, and 8 years in total. There were 99 bridges and millions of cubic yards of earth works with a difficult mountain range to surmount. In all 32 Europeans and 1800 African and Chinese labourers died. *So harsh were some of the methods used to keep the men on the job, that the Chinese workers rebelled and disappeared off eastwards in a desperate and futile attempt to walk across Africa to the Land of the Rising Sun.

Source: John Day 'Railways of Southern Africa'

This was nowhere near as great as the casualties on the British built Beira Railway in Mozambique, constructed at roughly the same time, in which 400 Europeans and the entire Indian labour force, together with countless numbers of Africans, perished in the first two years of construction - entirely through disease

The newly confirmed mineral wealth in the Katanga area of the Congo caused a change of direction of the Cape to Cairo railway. After it had crossed the Zambezi River the proposed aim was the south end of Lake Tanganyika, bordering German territory. Through the wide open stretches of northern Rhodesia it was poised to run tantalisingly close to the Congo border, almost touching it.

If King Leopold had not been so let down by his own mineral prospectors in the Congo Free State, and if Robert Williams, who had taken over the mantle of Cecil Rhodes had not been around, the railway might well have stayed on its original course. It would have traversed northern Rhodesia (Zambia) past Lake Bangweolo (Bangweulu), towards the southern shores of Lake Tanganyika.

Scattered around this wilderness were strategic settlements. Fort Roseberry, named from the husband of one of the Rothschild Financiers, was on the road junction at the Congo border, beside the Johnston Falls (Chutes Johnston). Not far distant on the shore of Lake Mweru, (between Nchelenge and Chiengi) was the remote little hamlet named 'Rhodesia'. It was home for the dark, fleet-footed Sitatunga antelope with curly horns and long legs, that lived among the reeds around the lakeside. Rhodesia was little more than a small fort, with a post office and a few huts, and an exceptionally unhealthy climate, where the first inhabitants all died of sleeping sickness. It was the end link in a chain of outposts built to intercept the slave traders by Harry Johnston, the Administrator. The fiery tempered Johnston often quarrelled with Rhodes and named this remote hell-hole 'Rhodesia' after the Colossus of Africa, in order to forestall the BSA Company using his name for a more congenial and important location.

Northeast of Lake Bengweulu, on the plateau, lies Kasama, strategically important in World War I. From here the men of the African Lakes Corporation battled against the Arab slave traders from their stockaded stores in true Wild West style.

Due east of Lake Bengweulu and a few miles off the Great North Road lies the remarkable Shiwa Nganda Manor House, the huge English-style colonial mansion built in the middle of 'nowhere' after World War 1 by Stuart Gore Brown. In 1911 he located this wild site whilst surveying for the Anglo-Belgian boundary commission, with visions that the Cape to Cairo dream route would still one day pass through this idyllic area on its way to Abercorn (Mbala). Ironically, the Tanzam rail route passes not far away through Mpika and Kasama on its way towards Dar es Salaam.

Standing almost at the bottom of Lake Tanganyika, a long way from anywhere, lies a town reminiscent of 'Old Africa of the Outposts'. Rhodes' original plan would have placed Abercorn (Mbala) firmly on the line of the Lake route to the north. The town that missed out was also an important outpost of the Transcontinental Telegraph line, the forerunner of the railway.

A charming place with a wonderful climate, the settlement was named after the Duke of Abercorn, and at the turn of the century it was garrisoned by Sikhs to deter any German attempt on this territory. During World War I it was shelled from across the border in Tanganyika. Its sister town further east along the Stevenson Road, Fife, was named after another ducal director of the BSA Company, and was almost totally destroyed. Rhodes had reckoned that christening these two towns after close relatives of Queen Victoria, the Kaiser's grandmother, would save them from German takeover.

The Abercorn Arms Hotel was remembered for its stuffed Sitatunga heads. It was a notorious watering hole, frequented by frontier cattle and coffee farmers, some Afrikaners, bearded White Father missionaries, and colourful characters like Mickey Norton who laid out the local Irish doctor as he attempted to extract a painful tooth.

Abercorn's lakeside station of Kituta (Mpulunga) was the headquarters of Livingstone's London Missionary Society, and also the planned berth for Rhodes' train ferries.

A century later, the grand old lady of the Lake - 'Lemba' - which was scuttled by the Germans and then restored by the British, still plies the route to the north.

When Robert Williams realised the potential of the Congo-Zambezi divide, and started negotiations with the Belgians, Rhodes had an ally in diverting the line northwards through the Congo rather than the even trickier way through German territory.

However he knew that he could get nowhere on his own with King Leopold. He had already failed in two attempts; one was when he had sent Stanley to intervene. "Go and butter-up the King and tell him I prefer the Belgian side," he told Stanley. The result was inconclusive.

So he asked Williams to intervene in a more subtle way between King Leopold and Kaiser Wilhelm of Germany. The King could share in the prosperity, and would even be allowed to choose the route northwards through Congo territory. Williams played off one side against the other by telling King Leopold that if he would give his permission to build a railway through the Congo, he, Williams would persuade Rhodes to give up his idea of going through German territory - although the decision had already been made.

Press rumours had followed Rhodes' dealings with the Kaiser, and unfounded reports inferred that a successful deal had already been struck. This only played into Williams' bargaining hand.

Williams recalled that one summer day in Cape Town, at the time of these lengthy negotiations, Rhodes had invited him to Sunday lunch at his cottage in Muizenberg to discuss the future route of the Cape to Cairo Railway. Unable to get away from an uninvited guest, they went down to the rocks on the seashore, where they sat absorbed in a map of Africa. Eventually Rhodes said "This is the way we will go", pointing through the Congo State, "but your mineral concession is only for 30 years; it is too short. Get King Leopold to extend it to 99 years; the British public love a 99 years' lease. Give the King what he wants in return, and when you have done all that, you can afford to give me a share of your minerals to assist me with my railway." By the time the pair had returned to the cottage they were up to their waists in water from the incoming tide.

Williams haggled for 3 years over the mineral concessions. Finally, a few weeks before the turn of the century, Tanganyika Concessions was formed by him to exploit that priceless territory between two of the mightiest rivers in Africa - the Congo and the Zambezi - one flowing into the Atlantic and the other into the Indian Ocean. He had correctly guessed that this Congo - Zambezi watershed would be another Eldorado.

Tanganyika Concessions was named after the concessions it acquired, though never developed, for a township, pier and railway terminus on the shores of Lake Tanganyika near Abercorn. It became one the largest conglomerated mining and transport groups in the world with a 60% Belgian and 40% British stake in a joint mining venture for copper, zinc and rare titanium. To cement the joint scheme, both parties finally agreed to build a railway to their respective borders.

"You have succeeded where I failed", Rhodes told Williams.

Once more short of finance, he asked Williams for an interest in his mining ventures in return for help with the railway.

"Alfred Beit has already advanced a million pounds for my railway to the north; he can go no further. We are looking for your copper to make a headway. Your mines need my railway. I want a stake in return", he implored.

In London the Colonial Office under Joseph Chamberlain was solidly behind Rhodes. Unfortunately the Treasury under Chancellor Michael Hicks Beach was not. Besides, Germany as well as German Jewish interests in the City of London had a stake in obstructing a rail route.

As part of the Cape to Cairo route, even Lord Cromer of Egypt agreed that the line should follow the mineral wealth, step by step, like milestones up Africa to Mahagi on Lake Albert. It could then cut across to connect with the Nile.

When Rhodes died in 1902, the line was racing towards the Zambezi, which it crossed in 1904. The message on the engine at Victoria Falls summed it up: "We've got a long way to Go!" Although the 281 mile stretch to Broken Hill was completed in 277 working days, the line was still at the Copperbelt in 1909, waiting and wondering which way to go, stalled by lack of finance.

At the end of the line, the indefatigable old Railway Builder himself, George Pauling, came to the rescue. The man who had pulled the lines up from the Cape, through the Kalahari desert and across the Zambezi, was ready to complete the job for his friend Robert Williams. But he was damned if he was going to stop at the border and let the Belgians take over. Another few hundred miles across the wilderness of the Congo-Zambezi water-shed would be plain sailing. He would show the Belgians once and for all how to open out their territory, all the way to the little

The opening ceremony under the triumphal arch at the border town of Sakania in the Belgian Congo, where the Cape to Cairo railway left British soil for the first time, in December 1909

(NAZ)

cluster of huts, newly named after their reigning Queen - Elizabethville. Nearby lay Williams' crowning glory - the fabulously rich copper mine of Etoile du Congo (Star of the Congo).

So with help from Baron d'Erlanger, Pauling put his own financial and physical resources to work. The Cape to Cairo line was poised to leave British soil for the first time. Under the circumstances, Rhodes would have approved.

At the Rhodesian-Congo border crossing of Sakania, there were the inevitable displays whilst the Union Jacks and and Belgian flags were unfurled. The opposing allies lined up under the make-shift archway of foliage at the 'Frontiere', cracked a few champagne bottles and toasted each other. But there was no display of jingoism such as 'Now we shan't be long to Cairo'. Meanwhile Paulings fellows - waiting in the wings, wasted no time. They took full advantage to down-load a lot of alcohol, in an embarassing sequel to the formal dinner party, before pressing on.

The Grand Hotel - the first hotel in Elizabethville (Lubumbashi), the town named after the Queen of Belgium

They reached Elizabethville 9 months later in September 1910, and the nearby Star of the Congo Mine subsequently.

Many of Paulings leading personnel, including Rupert Marsland, continued on this 240 kilomtere section of the Katanga Railway, in conjunction with the Societe Coloniale de Construction. The scheme was controlled on the Belgian side by Jean Jadot, who was also chairman of the Brussels bank Societe General de Belgique. Together with Albert Thys and (Baron) Edouard Empain, Jean Jadot completed the trio of the great railway builders in different parts of the Congo.

With the usual fits and starts, the Cape to Cairo line steamed on from Elizabethville northwards. To Kambove in 1913 (413 kms from the border); to Tshilongo in 1914 (524 kms from the border); and to Bukama in 1918 (727 kms from the border). At Tenke junction, near Tshilongo, the Benguela Railway later joined up with the main line.

At Bukama, on the marshy banks of the majestic tropical river where the Congo Expresses terminated, the southern section of the Cape to Cairo line finally came to an end.

It was thus possible to travel the whole way from Cape Town to Bukama in the 'Cape', 'Zambezi' and 'Congo' Expresses with sleeping-cars and restaurant-cars twice a week, on a journey of 2,600 miles which took 6 days.

From Bukama, steamers plied the Upper Congo (Lualaba now Zaire) River via Kamina to Kabalo 565 kms distant. This was the railhead off to Albertville (Kalemie) on Lake Tanganyika 273 kms away. The line was later continued back to Bukama, and on to Kindu. In this way a railway was complete from the border town of Sakania and a through service - helped for a stretch by river steamers - was available to the west shore of Lake Tanganyika.

The trains, like the boats, stopped for the night, since elephants and other animals often tore up the tracks. Simple houses along the route were provided for travellers who usually carried their own bedding.

In 1920 the American travel writer Isaac Marcosson travelled from the railhead at Bukama on steamers all the way up the Lualaba River to Stanleyville:

"Sun scorched Bukama, the southern railhead of the Cape to Cairo route was my jumping off point before plunging into the mysteries of Central Africa.

"The Louis Cousin, a 150 ton vessel, was a fair example of the type of craft providing the principle means of transport on the Congo and Lualaba. Like all her sisters she resembled the small Ohio river boats I knew as a child at Louisville."

The Congo territory had over twelve thousand miles of navigable rivers and lakes for steamers, and twice as many more for launches and canoes. All Congo craft were stern wheelers, hauling barges astride and dodging the sandbanks. At night they stopped for wood and the natives slept on the river banks. During the day they stopped anywhere to pick up the odd passenger, or for shopping expeditions, or for the Captain to visit a lonely govern-ment official for lunch. The Riverboat Captain was a jack-of-all-trades, stew-ard, doctor, postman, and dictator in general. Time counted for nil and he alone made the schedule. Many were Scandinavians like the big Norwegian Skipper who had spent 18 years in the Congo, and knew every one of the snags, turns, nooks and crannies and the sand bars of the Lualaba. Five feet was sufficient for all craft which drew only 3 feet of water. Natives took

The stern wheel paddle steamer 'Goodwill' on the slips at Bolobo in the Belgian Congo (RGS)

soundings with long sticks calling out all day.

Tiny cabins were on the upper deck with the Boiler, Freight and steerage below. The little dining rooms were filled with a mixed bag of Belgian officials. Chicken and goat was the main fare with masses of succulent wild fruit and vegetables.

Along the river banks where nature reigned supreme settlements appeared at rare intervals. Marcosson tied into one station and saw a lonely and eccentric Scotsman, a remote trader, who had been in the Congo for 15 years or more. Every night he put on his kilts and dirks and paraded with bagpipes through the native village.

"From Kabalo I went to Kongolo where navigation on the Lualaba temporarily ends. It is the southern rail-head of the Chemins de Fer des

Grands Lacs, which runs 220 miles to Kindu. At Kindu navigation on the Lualaba resumed for another 220 miles to Ponthierville (Ubundu) - a jewel in an almost unbelievable tropical setting. From Ponthierville a train journey of under 100 miles took one to Stanleyville (Kisangani), the head of navigation on the great Congo River. On one bank the town has long avenues of palm trees with well built villas and shops, whilst the other bank was almost entirely given over to railway workshops, yards and terminals".

It was the intention of the Belgians to continue the railway from Stanleyville (Kisangani) right up to the borders of the Sudan. From there it could be joined up with the line from El Obeid, which later extended right down to Wau. This would then have completed the Cape to Cairo link all bar a few hundred miles.

Rupert Marsland of Pauling & Co. paying a work gang on the construction of the Cape to Cairo line to Elizabethville in the Belgian Congo 1910 (NAZ)

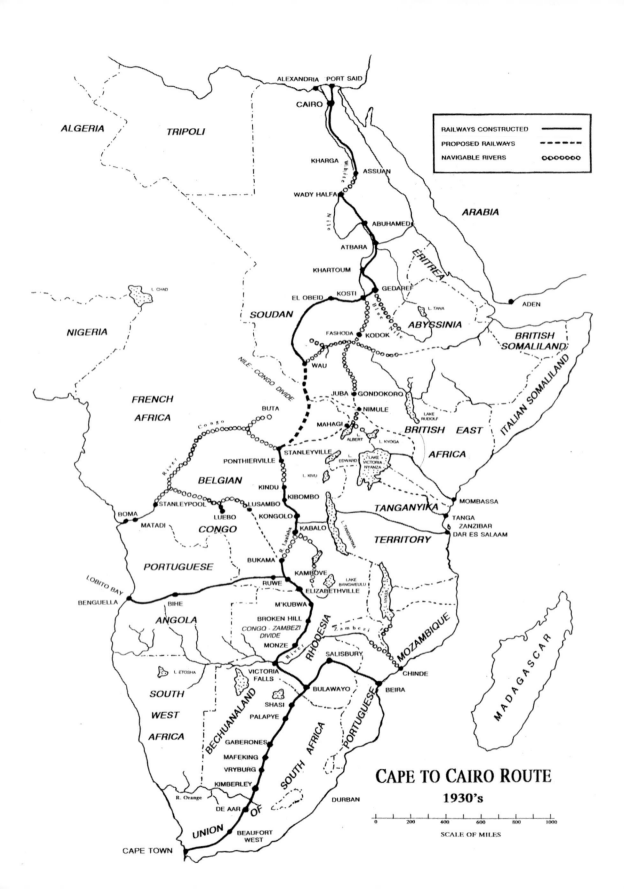

ALGERIA

TRIPOLI

ALEXANDRIA   PORT SAID

CAIRO

RAILWAYS CONSTRUCTED
PROPOSED RAILWAYS
NAVIGABLE RIVERS   ooooooooo

KHARGA

ASSUAN

WADY HALFA

ARABIA

ABUHAMED

ATBARA

ERITREA

NIGERIA

L. CHAD

KHARTOUM

GEDAREF

SOUDAN

EL OBEID   KOSTI

L. TANA

ADEN

ABYSSINIA

BRITISH
SOMALILAND

FASHODA   KODOK

WAU

FRENCH
AFRICA

NILE-CONGO DIVIDE

BUTA

JUBA   GONDOKORO

NIMULE

MAHAGI

BRITISH   EAST

ITALIAN SOMALILAND

LAKE
RUDOLF

Congo

STANLEYVILLE

PONTHIERVILLE

L. ALBERT   L. KYOGA

L. EDWARD

AFRICA

River

BELGIAN

KINDU

L. KIVU

LAKE
VICTORIA
NYANZA

MOMBASSA

STANLEYPOOL

LUSAMBO

KIBOMBO

TANGANYIKA

BOMA

CONGO

LUEBO

KONGOLO

KABALO

TANGA
ZANZIBAR
DAR ES SALAAM

MATADI

R. Lualaba

L. TANGANYIKA

TERRITORY

PORTUGUESE

BUKAMA

LOBITO BAY

RUWE

KAMBOVE

LAKE
BANGWEULU

ELIZABETHVILLE

BENGUELLA

BIHE

M'KUBWA

L. NYASA

ANGOLA

BROKEN HILL
CONGO - ZAMBEZI
DIVIDE

Zambezi

MOZAMBIQUE

MONZE

RHODESIA

River

SOUTH

L. ETOSHA

VICTORIA
FALLS

SALISBURY

CHINDE

WEST

SHASI

BULAWAYO

BEIRA

MADAGASCAR

AFRICA

PALAPYE

BECHUANALAND

GABERONES

PORTUGUESE

SOUTH AFRICA

MAFEKING

VRYBURG

KIMBERLEY

R. Orange

DE AAR

UNION   OF

DURBAN

CAPE TO CAIRO ROUTE

1930's

BEAUFORT
WEST

CAPE TOWN

0   200   400   600   800   1000

SCALE OF MILES

17

DREAMS IDLE DREAMS

BEYOND BENGUELA THROUGH PORTUGUESE WEST AFRICA

The Benguela Railway had the distinction of being the most cosmopolitan and ultimately most pointless railway in all Africa. Probably no line ever built in the world stretched so far to such a distant goal and passed through country with so little prospect of remunerative revenue on the way. It was conceived against a background of rock-solid resistance from various Governments, and was the personal triumph of Robert Williams against almost insurmountable odds, both physical and financial. It was built and financed by British private enterprise, ran two-thirds through Portuguese and one third through Belgian territory, and employed virtually every nationality in the Empire as well a good sprinkling of Americans and Continentals. On its ultimate completion in 1932 it ran for nearly 1500 miles west to east from one of the finest deep water harbours in the world at Lobito Bay to the mineral rich Katanga Province of the Belgian Congo. It indirectly connected the Portuguese territories across Africa from the Atlantic to the Indian Oceans via the Rhodesias (Zambia and Zimbabwe), yet along its entire length virtually no new mineral deposits were ever discovered.

Its purpose was to open up the shortest route to Europe from the copper fields of Katanga, saving 3000 miles of the long haul round the Cape.

Ever since Rhodes' death in 1902 much of his spirit had lived on in Robert Williams, who had taken on the mantle of pushing north the Cape to Cairo line. He had tried in vain to get agreements for railway routes to exploit his mineral concessions, both from sceptical Belgian and the British Governments. German Jewish interests in the City of London also had a stake in preventing any more British railways. So he turned to the Portuguese in a bid to obtain the concession to build a line across their Angolan territory from central Africa to the Atlantic seaboard. The ancient alliance between the two countries, and the useful connections and forceful personality of the Countess of Warwick, a girlfriend of 'Edward the Caresser', King Edward VII, helped to smooth matters further. The Portuguese were delighted with the idea of a railway to open up their hard-pressed, far flung territory. So they agreed to a 99 year lease. Yet not the faintest whisper was allowed to pass to the ears of the perfidious British Foreign Office, who had already concluded a secret deal with Germany to carve up Portugal's African Possessions between them in the possible event of their 'disposal'. (This was a protocol attached to the Anglo-German agreement of 1898). Portugal's great African dependencies had become such a drain on the finances of the mother country that Bills were prepared to sell off some of them for 25 million pounds Sterling.

So secret were the negotiations in Lisbon that the unknown young Englishman who interpreted for Robert Williams was rewarded for his discretion with the position of Secretary of the new company. The agreement was signed in November 1902 by the Queen Consort of King Dom Carlos who was away in England staying with King Edward VII at the time. It was witnessed by the Papal Nuncio, the only diplomat whose total inscrutability and neutrality could be assured,

As anticipated, Britain refused to finance the railway, and Portugal was unable to, so the endless round of fund-raising commenced. This was the single most important factor which regularly dogged the progress of the 'Cape to Cairo' line and its associated offshoots. City of London finance was eventually found through private individuals, including Lord Howard de Walden. Tanganyika Concessions was formed, with the majority of directors being Portuguese. General Joachim Machado, former Governor of Mozambique and a long standing ally of Britain, was the Managing Director. Other Portuguese, sensitive to any loss of sovereignty in their oldest overseas possession, produced a critical pamphlet entitled 'The loss of Angola - the Williams Concession' (Perda de Angola - a concessao Williams, Lisboa, Diario Illustrado 1903.) It contained the rather flattering presumption of Britain's imperial status: "Where there is one Englishman there is England."

A preliminary survey by the aptly named Livingstone Learmont had recommended that the route of the railway should rise from the old coastal slave trading port of Benguela, up the steep escarpment, and then follow the centuries old caravan and slave route across the great watershed of central Africa. This was the historic route of man's ultimate depravity to man, where only 10 per cent survived the trip to the coast. It had largely been traversed by David Livingstone himself in the 1850's. Along the escarpment on one side the rivers flow into the Congo Basin and on the other side into the Zambezi. So defined was this 'divide' of the watershed that Harold Varian, the surveyor, observed how the flow of streams in totally opposing directions was sometimes so close as to be only a few yards apart. Along this route the terrain ensured the minimum amount of bridging across rivers and drifts.

Benguela, founded by the Portuguese

'Empire Jack' John Norton Griffiths with his wife Gladwys, and their mascot Pedro, on the wooden jetty at Lobito Bay, which he built to off-load construction materials (ANNE MORGAN)

Single span Bridge over the Catumbela River between Lobito and Benguela

nearly 5 centuries ago, lies in an exposed position. Lobito Bay, 20 miles further north along the coast was therefore chosen as the port and railway terminus. Here lies one of the most majestic natural harbours in the world, sheltered from the Atlantic Ocean by a 3 mile long narrow sand break-water, enclosing a deep water bay with little or no tides or storms. Large ocean-going vessels were able to discharge their cargoes directly into railway trucks on the jetty at any state of the tide. The bay was also famous for its succulent Atlantic oysters.

The name Lobito stems from the local word upito, the passage through the hills that was used by caravans carrying goods and slaves to and from the interior. Captains who wished to avoid the taxes imposed in the legal port of Benguela anchored their ships in the dense mangroves of Lobito.

To set the ball rolling Williams turned to his old railway contacts, the Consultant Engineer Charles Metcalfe, and the Contractor George Pauling - who recalled: "Early in 1903 I was approached by my old friend from Kimberley days, Robert Williams, to commence construction of a railway from Lobito Bay, with the ultimate object of the development of Angola and the tapping of the inestimable wealth of the Belgian Congo. No finance had been provided for the work, the company had not yet been formed and only a limited contract was signed. I agreed to send out an expedition under the charge of Frank Grove who had been in Tasmania for my firm. The party carried out a certain amount of survey work and about 1200 tons of permanent way material was shipped out and the earthworks were commenced. Later on we built a very handsome bridge over the

Catumbela River. This was about half way between Lobito and Benguela and was a single span trussed girder bridge of 250 feet. At the time of building it was one the longest single spans in Africa."

After about 6 months, work stopped. Pauling's backers were unable to continue finance. Williams eventually found funds with friends in the City of London. Work was thus resumed and although for the time being Paulings had no direct involvement in it, the supervision was largely in the hands of former members of their staff. The contract continued under Norton Griffiths, the fledgling construction company run by the ambitious 'Empire Jack', who risked life and limb to complete the initial section in an ill-judged 18 months.

The adventurous, swashbuckling John Norton Griffiths (1871 - 1930) was every inch a 'Boys Own' hero. He had started life on wind-jammers to Australia, became Lord Roberts bodyguard in the Anglo-Boer War, and

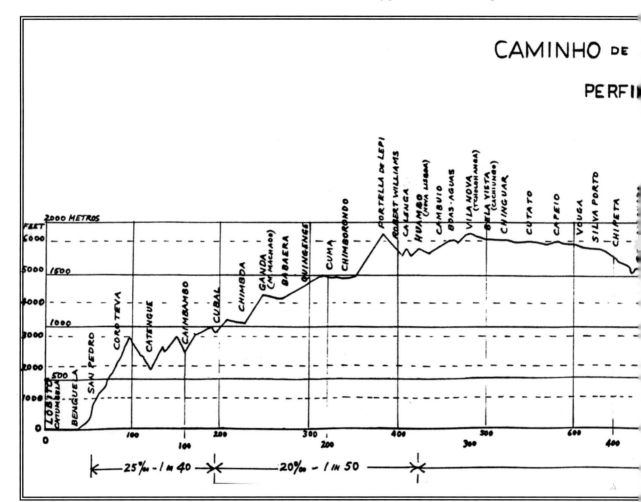

then joined the British South Africa Police in Matabeleland. With Lord Howard de Walden's help, he founded the firm which built railways in Africa, South America and Canada. As a young subaltern in Honey's Scouts, Griffiths had watched Pauling build the pioneer Beira line up from the coast to Salisbury, and been fascinated by the sight; he was convinced he could do the same. However his wife Gladwys, daughter of the Engineering Consultant Thomas Wood, pleaded with him that he was an Engineer and not a Contractor. To no avail. He was soon to realise that rail construction was more than a means to an end in an expanding Empire. It all but defeated him.

The steep climb up the Lengue Gorge from the coast was described by Charles Metcalfe, the Consulting Engineer, as "one of the most difficult feats of engineering ever undertaken in the history of railway construction anywhere in the world".

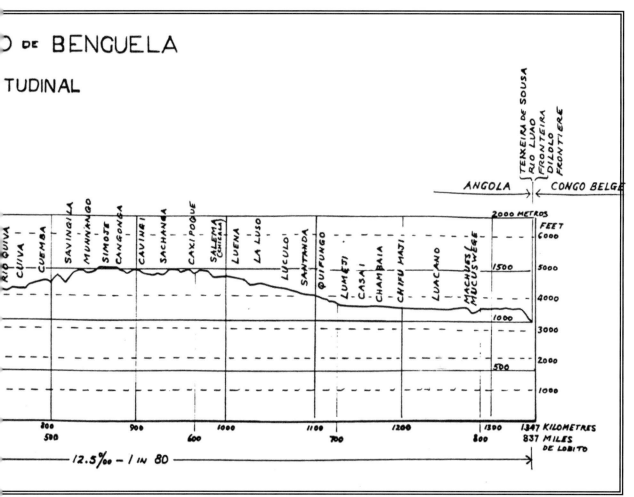

© AUTHOR

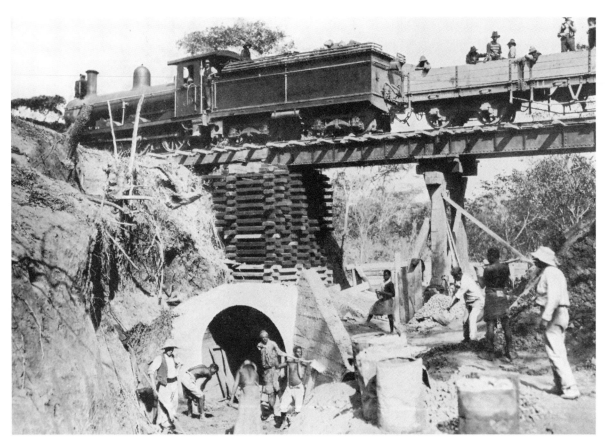

A temporary bridge over an arched culvert under construction

No sooner had work re-started than once again the old question of finance arose. The largest of the original investors, C.J.Leyland, had pulled out. The concession was in danger of cancellation by the Portuguese government unless work was re-started soon. Germany, waiting in the wings, would then have stepped in, and the whole line would have fallen into the hands of their Teutonic Railway Battalions and indented labour gangs. This was almost what the Foreign Office appeared to prefer! Williams confirmed that he had been told by the British Government that no support, cash or guarantees would be forthcoming. They added almost menacingly that to do so would bring down Germany's wrath on them. Vilified in the German press as a 'Raper of Katanga', Williams was a true thorn in their side, and the major stumbling block, after Rhodes, in their Wanderlust across Africa. They considered Angola to be part of their sphere of influence, through which they hoped to make a rail connection from their adjoining South West African territory.

In desperation, Williams went back to George Pauling. Doyen of railway constructors in Africa, he had characteristically pulled the railway up from the Cape, and was just about to launch over the border into

Belgian Congo territory. He was also busy tendering for the Uganda Railway. Perhaps with an eye for future involvement 'somewhere along the line', he was happy to help provide the finance for another 100 miles or so for Norton Griffiths to continue their laborious work. Safe in British hands once more the line progressed; the Portuguese were happy, and the German sympathisers and double-dealers in the Foreign Office were once again thwarted

Norton Griffiths had been the only contractor brave enough to attempt this monumental feat. They continued this ludicrous contract for the first gruelling 198 kilometres even though it allowed them only a matter of months before the arrival of the first train through to Katengue. Unknown to the surveyors, the line passed through totally dry country where the rainy season of the north separated from the rainy season of the south, and so caused a convergence zone with absolutely no rainfall at all. The original survey route was so distorted that several precarious mountains had to be climbed. There was no alternative, as the conditions of the original Portuguese concession had to be strictly adhered to. A correct survey would have eliminated most of the heavy gradients and steep barriers from the coast.

Practically no Angolans lived on the coastal plain. Years of hardship and the slave trade had decimated their numbers. The few locals available were, to say the least, limited in ability and enterprise. So 7000 labourers, including Senegalese from French West Africa, and 2000 Indians with their families from Natal, worked alongside a bevy of professional rock drillers hastily shipped up from Cape Town. Camels, mules, donkeys, oxen and the natives who were not much good with picks and shovels were pressed into service as carriers. The main problem was to find enough

Platelaying in hilly country near the coast

sweet water, unpolluted by minerals. At times, two men were carrying water for every man on the job.

Almost every conceivable tropical illness was encountered, such as beri-beri and sleeping sickness. Malaria was rife in the European ranks, with nursing under the direction of the formidable Sister Bessie Smythe at the Lobito Bay Hospital. Virtually all the Indians were repatriated to Natal, and it was not until the plateau was reached that local labour was available.

Having completed the first 'easy' section along the coastal perimeter, where the lines were literally thrown down on the sand, the Lengue Gorge was reached. A 3000 feet climb lay ahead, and the real race was on. It is probably one of the few railways in the world where the ocean can be seen from such a high altitude - so rapid is the rise from the coast.

The precipitous gorge had to be spanned by several bridges as well as a viaduct. Through one section a tunnel was considered, but the only solution in the time available for completion was a Rack Railway. One and a half miles of steep rack-track were laid up to San Pedro at the top, crossing the gorge three times by prefabricated steel bridges.

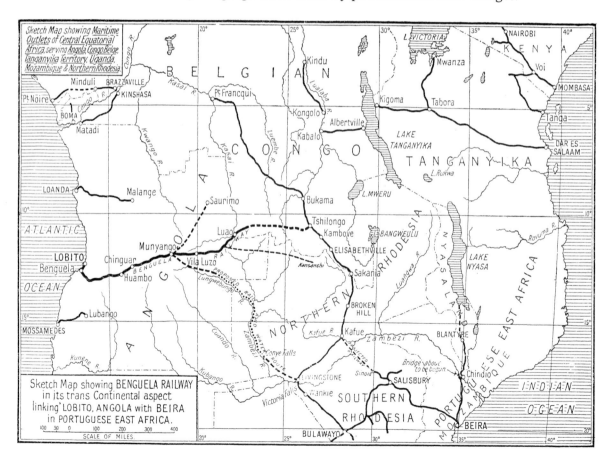

Sketch Map showing Maritime Outlets of Central Equatorial Africa, serving Angola, Congo Belge, Tanganyika Territory, Uganda, Mozambique & Northern Rhodesia.

Sketch Map showing BENGUELA RAILWAY in its trans Continental aspect linking LOBITO, ANGOLA with BEIRA in PORTUGUESE EAST AFRICA.

SCALE OF MILES.

The first locomotive, with cog wheels to engage with the teeth of the rack rail, was constructed in a record 20 days, and shipped out from England. Hundreds of trucks followed, together with permanent way material, and according to John Norton Griffiths a good slice of Britain's railway industry came to their rescue. Materials were landed onto a 'floating wharf' of Thames barges moored offshore at the entrance to Lobito Bay Harbour - since the Admiralty charts were notoriously sketchy in those African waters.

The rock drillers excelled, hewing out the granite, working day and night under arc lights, blasting and clearing as the mountain was scaled. At one point the line climbed 700 feet in 2 miles.

The first vital, herculean section was completed in time, but the cost had been prohibitive. Norton Griffiths' contract terminated. Although they completed a survey of the route for a further 400 miles inland, the work was continued by Paulings.

After the plateau was reached a small trading post with a cluster of railway buildings was named 'Robert Williams' - the first in the few stations named after personalities such as Marco de Canavezes, Mariano Machado and Texeira de Sousa.

Platelaying continued onwards. The 'thirsty' country now became the 'hungry' country. In this sparse open land, carriers and caravans who had underestimated their food supply often died of starvation. If they were lucky enough to get through, they could be waylaid by a marauding tribe - the same tribe that had molested Livingstone on his travels 50 years earlier - until the Portuguese punished them in 1910. In this area there was also a tranquil tribe of bee-keepers who lived almost entirely off honey, and carried around with them bright yellow singing birds rather like canaries, in dainty little reed cages. There was also a profusion of exotic parrots and an abundance of all kinds of flora and fauna. In these remote regions the locals were scantily clad with small pieces of bark cloth.

A team of experienced prospectors and mining engineers from California and South Africa had been recruited as part of an ongoing exercise to search for minerals up to 100 kilometres on either side of the advancing railway. Yet throughout its entire length of nearly 900 miles through Angola, only one small workable copper deposit was discovered. This was a bitter blow to Williams' colleagues and Portuguese partners.

The pressure was really on, as the Germans were still hovering in the background in Lisbon, hoping to get the concession cancelled and pick up the pieces if the conditions were not complied with. Harold Varian wrote:

"In 1912 whilst construction was proceeding about 180 miles inland a party of German engineers came up from S.W.Africa (Namibia) to visit the line. A couple of them stayed with me whilst two others stayed with Paulings.

"They seemed very well informed and asked if they could have a general plan of the Benguela Railway, but I was naturally unable to grant this request. They were extremely charming and told me, more or less in confidence, how much they regretted that I might be out of a job later, as their government was going to take over the railway for a sum of 30 million Marks - an arrangement that seemed only to be known to themselves.

"A short time later some of the key plate-laying staff applied for leave. They ended up working for the Germans in South West Africa.

"At the outbreak of WW1 two years later German prospectors, farmers, and scientists were interned by the Portuguese Government. Along the projected route of the railway from Angola into German territory were found dumps of materials and supplies ready to be used to make the connection of the line with the German railway from Tsumeb."

Varian, who had returned to work on the Benguela Railway, encountered one of those strange and uncanny phenomena of Africa which is truly inexplicable. Several years previously, when in south-central Africa, he had a faithful old servant who hailed from Portuguese East Africa (Mozambique) and who stayed on all his survey work through the territories of the Rhodesias. Having finished the contracts Varian had then departed for England, not knowing when, or if ever, he would return to Africa, since he had been offered jobs in South America and elsewhere. Eventually he changed his plans and sailed once more directly to the west coast of Africa to work on the Benguela railway. In a remote part of Angola some hundreds of miles inland, he returned to the survey camp one afternoon, to be confronted by two thin, weak Africans. They addressed him in the language of Rhodesia. At first he did not recognise them, but they were none other than his old servant accompanied by his kitchen helper. Their appearance from the other side of Africa was little short of a miracle. For 3 months they had travelled through the hungry country, and then the thirsty country, to reach their destination.

"I asked him how he knew I was in Angola, and what had brought them to my very camp," Varian confirmed, "To all my queries, then and at later dates, I received the same unvarying answer: 'My heart told me so'. He said that he had not known where I was, and could not find out, but he had a hunch - and he knew that if he started he would eventually get to me."

Such was the strength of the 'Bonds of Africa', which has been confirmed by others, and is even more inexplicable than the 'Bush Telegraph'.

On the Congo Zambezi watershed, near the point where the Zambezi River rises near the Zambian (Northern Rhodesia), Congo and Angola conflux, Varian and his party passed through the territory of Queen Nhakatola. Nearly all the tribes in this area were ruled by Chieftainesses, and Queen Nhakatola was a powerful and ambitious monarch who organised raiding parties far and wide. She also ran a very lucrative business in dried fish. She was a fine looking lady with dainty hands and feet, and features not unlike an ancient Egyptian - not at all like her subjects. This 'Cleopatra' normally travelled with her daughter, an even more fair featured maiden. It was the custom when passing through her territory to leave a tribute of food or goods at her 'Palace', a 3 roomed brick house with verandah from which she held sway. Locals who didn't pay were liable to have their ears or noses cut off. One of her royal prerogatives, which she exercised if she so fancied, was to share both board and bed with any passing stranger. Indeed the rumour was rife that her fair featured daughter was the result of a liaison with an itinerant Scottish trader. Varian, a confirmed bachelor, with no aspirations for romance with dusky Queens or their daughters, had a narrow escape. The Queen was away on one of her fishing expeditions when he passed by. So he left his tribute in the form of a roll of blue spotted calico, and beat a hasty retreat

Terrorising the border districts when the actual frontiers of the Belgian Congo and Angola were still undefined was a nasty fellow with his gang of followers. Known as the Revoltees, they had been in the Belgian service but had killed their superiors and deserted. They resorted to the most unpleasant habits. The chief considered it necessary to have a meal of a human heart every few days, and the private parts of their victims would be strung across village paths as the raiders passed through. Arriving at the remote store of a Portuguese trader one day, with 25 prisoners or slaves in tow, the chief demanded powder and shot. The Portuguese trader refused. The Chief then said he would have to destroy all the captives as he could neither feed them nor leave them behind, so before the trader's incredulous eyes, he cut all their throats at the door and departed. After several other similar deplorable incidents, the Portuguese sent up an expedition to finish them off.

Railway construction continued sporadically, as and when funds allowed. All the materials were shipped out from Britain and railed up to the railhead of this ever lengthening rib of the Cape to Cairo line.

A large slice of the work was under 'CV' Charlie Buchan, one of the most experienced tropical railway hands. As a 20 year old in the 1890's he had been Alfred Lawley's assistant on the Beira Railway, and Harold Pauling's assistant on the line to Victoria Falls.

Paulings continued to build the railway right up to the First World War,

THE BENGUELA RAILWAY

PASSENGER RAILWAY ROLLING STOCK.

PRIVATE SALOON WITH OBSERVATION BALCONY.

PRIVATE SALOON.
SLEEPING COMPARTMENT.

DINING SALOON.
1st CLASS.

BUILT BY

METROPOLITAN-CAMMELL CARRIAGE

WAGON & FINANCE COY., LTD.

Head Office: SALTLEY, BIRMINGHAM. Cables: "METRO," BIRMINGHAM.

Platelaying at Km. 1200 in 1928 across the Chifu Maji Flats, a straight stretch which runs for over 100 miles on the watershed between the Congo and Zambezi Rivers (PAULING ARCHIVE)

520 kilometres from Lobito, where the railhead languished at Chinguar.

Once more the Germans caused a native disturbance, before General Botha halted it. Lack of water played a part in heading off their advance,

After the war, construction continued onto the plateau at Silva Porto, and survey parties were sent forward under Harold Varian for Fox & Partners and Andrew Tucker for Paulings, working independently but following the same route. Beyond the Quanza River at Kohemba (Kilometre 781) the waterfalls in the river resemble a miniature Victoria Falls. This was the beginning of the hungry country on the sandy central African plateau, and the western limit of the Congo-Zambezi watershed. Here lies the highest point, and along its narrow ridge the rivers flow on one side down to the Atlantic, and on the other side to the Indian Ocean, literally a few yards apart.

150 miles further distant lay the Chifu Maji flats on the eastern side of the Hungry Country, an open treeless waste cursed by everyone. For 3 months the area was flooded, whilst for the rest of the year there was drought. Tucker, ill with malaria, returned to the coast, whilst Varian continued on, following Livingstone's route towards the Congo Railway.

Huambo (Nova Lisboa) became Paulings permanent base, and ultimately the railway headquarters for the entire system; a sizeable town with workshops and extensive marshalling yards.

Whilst the lines were being extended towards the frontier, the boundaries of Angola and the Congo actually changed. In order to obtain a route for their Matadi Railway to the mouth of the Congo River on the Atlantic seaboard, the Belgians had acquired an invaluable slice of coastal land from the Portuguese. In return, Angola secured an even larger stretch of inland Congo territory, which extended the line 60 miles further to the new border at the Luao River.

The railway spawned a strange phenomenon; the rise of the coastal Umbundu tribe to a hieracy of paramount importance. Their quick adaptability to European ways ensured that they became the clerks, telegraph operators and sometimes even station masters along the entire route of this near thousand mile stretch to the Congo border. Eventually this reached an astonishing level of influence with four and a half thousand Umbundu living near the border station of Texeira de Sousa, and eight thousand more living around Luso on the great central plateau, 700 miles from their original coastal homes.

Having trekked half-way across Africa through regions where few white man had ever been, Varian recalled:

"My 3 months survey walk across Angola to the Congo, through some of the least known and most remote parts of the continent, ended one afternoon at a solitary wood and iron telegraph hut on a lonely station of the newly laid line from Elizabethville (Lubumbashi) to Bukama. As I entered the hut the Belgian operator was at work at his instrument. Eventually he looked round to ask what I wanted. I asked if I might send a wire to which he replied that it was not possible. I then asked if he would send a message to the Director to say that Varian had arrived from Angola. His attitude changed immediately. He told me, by a curious coincidence, that when I came in he was actually dealing with a message sent through the line enquiring if there was any news of me, since I had not been heard of for many months and was long overdue. I went on by train to Elizabethville, thence to Cape Town and London, where my information was awaited."

Rupert Marsland followed Harold Varian on a 1930 survey of this route. Subject to delays caused by inevitable financial difficulties, the line was continued through to the Congo border.

It was Pauling & Company's swan-song in Africa; a series of contracts that had run from kilometre 198 to kilometre 1347 throughout the first 30 years of the twentieth century. It had cost $40 million - over 80% from British sources. The subsequent link - the Katanga connection - completed in 1932, meant that this was Africa's only true trans-continental railway; connecting Lobito Bay with Beira, 2800 miles via the Rhodesias, and linking up the Portuguese territories of Angola and Mozambique.

Dreams Idle Dreams

No longer in the years in view -
We'll book our coupe to the Cape;
No longer in the dull Karoo
Sit somnolently on the gape -
Our route should be extremely gay
from Beira to Lobito Bay.

For elephants will gambol by,
and zebras flick their gleesome tails;
And graceful hippopotami
will play the devil with the rails;
And pygmy heathen in dismay,
will book from Congo to the Bay.

Henry Cullen Gouldsbury
(1881-1916)

BENGUELA RAILWAY COMPANY
CAMINHO DE FERRO DE BENGUELA

Benguela Railway Co.'s Pier, Lobito Bay.

Capital Shares

£3,000,000

from
LOBITO BAY,
ANGOLA, PORTUGUESE WEST AFRICA

Debentures

£7,842,360

The Great Gate from the West to Central Africa
SHORTEST ROUTE TO RHODESIA

The Benguela Railway will provide an economic outlet to the sea for the copper mines of Northern Rhodesia and Katanga and is destined to play a vital part in the development of Angola, the Belgian Congo, and British Possessions in Central Africa.

A "Garratt" Locomotive used on the Benguela Railway.

Lobito Bay is destined to become the great harbour for all Central African enterprises and will entail a considerable reduction in the cost of transport both by land and sea of their produce to the world's markets.

HEAD OFFICE :

3, Largo do Quintella
Lisbon.

Comparative Distances between
SOUTHAMPTON and SOUTH
AFRICAN PORTS

BEIRA TO SOUTHAMPTON ... 7574 miles
CAPE TOWN TO SOUTHAMPTON 5978 miles
LOBITO BAY TO SOUTHAMPTON 4930 miles

HEAD OFFICE IN
AFRICA :

Lobito Bay.

The completion of the Benguela Railway to the Angola-Congo border, a distance of 830 miles from Lobito Bay, marks the dawn of a new epoch in the history of Africa which will be realised when through rail connection with Tshilongo and Elizabethville is established. By 1930 this extension will have been built, and while its construction is proceeding a motor service has been organised during the dry season of each year, April to December, for the conveyance of both passengers and their baggage between Elizabethville and railhead, the journey being undertaken in 3 days.

Apply for free Illustrated Handbook to :
PUBLICITY AGENT, Benguela Railway, Princes House, Gresham Street, London, E.C.2.

18

THE LUNATIC LINE

TO UGANDA

The bewildering piece of engineering known as the Lunatic Line, or the Uganda Railway, was built entirely through Kenya from the coast at Mombasa to the shores of Lake Victoria Nyanza, the largest lake in Africa.

It was in essence Britain's only true imperial railway in Africa. For no line on the whole continent was built so blatantly to further Pax Brittanica, with no profitable motive in sight - arriving in a new country long before the settlers. Its primary aim was to assert Britain's presence in the equatorial regions against German plans around the Great Lakes, and also to counter such adventurous Frenchmen as Colonel Marchand who had raced Kitchener to the Nile at Fashoda and had nearly brought the two countries to war. It was also one of the greatest aids in hastening the end of the slave trade in this area of the most appalling atrocities crying to heaven for vengeance. For faster, more economical rail travel would do away with the carriage of goods by caravans of men, and would speed up the opening of fortified inland outposts, with boats to patrol the Lakes.

> *What it will cost no words can express*
> *What is its object no brain can suppose*
> *Where it will start from none can guess*
> *Where it is going to nobody knows*

Whimsical words describing the almost unknown extravagance of the Lunatic Line, from the pen of the anti-imperialist Henry Labouchere, give an accurate though slightly jaundiced view of what was one of Lord Salisbury's greatest triumphs. However, this cleverly conceived idea was not followed through by the mandarins of the Foreign Office Railway Committee.

In the enterprising spirit of the times, just as Cecil Rhodes had founded the British South Africa Company, and George Goldie the Royal Niger Company, for trade purposes, so William McKinnon, a doughty Glasgow shipbuilder, had assembled together the Imperial British East Africa Company (IBEA) - a rag bag of trade ties with little or no support from the new British Liberal Government elected in 1892. The majority of the Cabinet were keen to conciliate the French and avoid overseas involvement especially around the Nile area. The Chancellor of the Exchequer Michael Hicks Beach was unable to provide funds. The Foreign Secretary, Lord Roseberry, installed by Queen Victoria, was about the only one to stand up and support Britain's role in Africa and follow Salisbury's expansionist trends. He also distrusted the 'perfidious' French and was insistent on not leaving the missionaries and their converts to the mercy of the Arabs.

It was H.M.Stanley who had set the ball rolling. In 1852 the first Arab slave traders arrived from the coast and set up shop, as well as mosques. When the impulsive Stanley turned up 20 years later he wrote about them to the Daily Telegraph. Christian missionaries were despatched forthwith. The white robed Muslin slavers fought pitched battles against both the French Catholic White Fathers and the Protestant Scottish Missionaries - all of them struggling to influence the ebbs and flows of the Court of the Kabaka of Buganda. At first he tolerated the missionaries, but then banned them, and in an evil climax, 22 African Christians were burned alive - to become the Uganda Martyrs.

When Captain Frederick Lugard arrived on behalf of the Imperial British East Africa Company (IBEA) he took over one of the seven Hills of the Impala - Kampala - fortified it agaiinst the Kabaka, and concluded trade agreements.

Meanwhile the Germans were casting longing glances over it all. It became an even more colourful region when Karl Peters of the German East Africa Company arrived dressed in crimson robes, hoping to make an impression. Then there was the gun-runner and ivory trader Charlie Stokes. Plying his trade into the frontiers of no-mans-land, this Irish ex-missionary adventurer had married a Chiefs daughter in Zanzibar and then proceeded to join his own 'Scramble for Africa.' With thousands of carriers, he ran vast caravans of ivory across the undefined borders. When the British chased him out, he latched onto the Germans, and dressed in a Officers uniform he borrowed the only steamer on Lake Victoria. Roaming around, he was nominally beholden to no one - or rather anyone who purchased his weapons and gun powder. He later made the fatal mistake of taking a stab at the untapped ivory wealth in the Congo. He was captured by the Belgians, and court martialled by a kangaroo court on unproven charges of supplying guns to rebellious natives. Whilst his only advocate, the kindly Belgian Doctor, was still asleep, he was taken out and hanged. Britain eventually washed her hands of his case, but huge compensation was paid to both the British and the Germans.

In the middle of all this *melee* stood Frederick Lugard, Administrator of the IBEA, who eventually persuaded the Kabaka of Buganda to throw in his lot with Britain.

All this was just up Rhodes' street. He proposed that Uganda, granted to Britain by the Berlin Treaty of 1890, should be run by his Chartered Company for the princely sum of just £25,000 per year. When the offer was turned down, Rhodes came back with a new sweetener. He would build his telegraph line and railway right through Uganda and onwards to the Sudan and Egypt. At the same time, a commission was set up to decide the future of the territory. Rhodes' brother Frank, twiddling his thumbs in London, was made a member of the commission. Rhodes reckoned that he would be a compliant administrator, and that he would keep in close touch with him from the Cape. Rhodes himself would be able to help with any funds over and above those voted by Parliament. Surprisingly, this astonishingly ambitious plan was also turned down.

Once more the patriotic Empire builder McKinnon was left to his own devices. But his IBEA was utterly unable to fund further administration of the territory, leave alone development, without an expensive railway. He had made a brave attempt to start, but it only reached 7 miles inland from the coast at Mombasa before being abandoned. The only option left was a hasty withdrawal from this jewel of Africa.

Pro-empire public opinion stepped in; and Queen Victoria herself would hear none of this defeatist attitude. Uganda was declared a Protectorate and in 1894 passed into the hands of a spendthrift and reluctant British government.

Immediately the Foreign Office revived the railway plan and funds were hastily whistled up by Parliament for the building of the line from the

ROWLAND WARD & CO.,
(LIMITED),

NATURALISTS,

"The Jungle," 166 Piccadilly, London, W.

Practical and Artistic Taxidermists, Designers of Trophies of Natural History, Preservers and Adapters of all Specimens of Animal Life. Natural Features of Animals adapted in Original Designs for Decorative Purposes, and every-day uses. Furriers and Plumassiers and Collectors in Natural History.

NOTICE. — ROWLAND WARD, F.Z.S., is the only member left in the profession of the Ward Family, long unrivalled for their accumulated experience and their skill in Practical Taxidermy, especially in its artistic department.

Ready this Day, the Sixth Edition, with numerous additional Illustrations, 1 vol., cr. 8vo., Bound in Crocodile Leather, Price 3s. 6d. By post, 3s. 9d.

THE SPORTSMAN'S HANDBOOK TO PRACTICAL COLLECTING, PRESERVING, AND ARTISTIC SETTING-UP OF TROPHIES AND SPECIMENS. To which is added A SYNOPTICAL GUIDE TO THE HUNTING GROUNDS OF THE WORLD. By ROWLAND WARD, F.Z.S.

coast.

It was a classic example of outrageous government extravagance which cost the British taxpayer many millions of pounds. So many culverts, bridges and sections of line were duplicated that in parts it resembled a double or triple track with a conglomeration of incomplete marshalling yards built without rhyme or reason, and with attendant expensive housing and offices. And there was no immediate hope of recouping the expenditure. A visiting German railway official from Tanganyika cast envious eyes over the progress of the line and declared: "Ach! I am ashamed of my country. The British have built two railways to the Lake and we have not even built one."

Of the choice of gauge Ewart Grogan, the Kenyan pioneer, wrote: "Presumably there is a special site reserved in the British Museum for the skull of the facetious bureaucrat, who, hearing the British railways heading north from the Cape and south from Egypt were of 3 feet 6 inches gauge, decided that the British railway heading west from Mombasa should be of metre gauge. The mind boggles at the dimension of this particular folly."

Several railway companies had shown an interest in tendering from the beginning. Among them was Paulings of Westminster. Suspicious of their association with Rhodes in railway matters, the Foreign Office turned down what would have been the 'Bargain of the Century.' George Pauling elaborated:

"At a very early period in the history of East Africa I had approached the British Government for a concession to build the railway from Mombasa to Lake Victoria. In conjunction with our Bankers Messrs. Erlangers we made an offer to construct and equip a line of 657 miles for £ 2,240,000, equal to an average of £3409 per mile, and we undertook to complete the work within 4 years. To this offer we received no official reply."

Much later, after various behind the scenes manipulations, the Uganda Railway Act was hastily rushed through Parliament with a massive and sudden unexplained increase in the cost of the line to £5 million.

"The net result was that the line cost about £10,000 per mile against the £3409 for which my firm had offered to build it, and the actual work took several more years. The only conclusion I can come to is that the engineering advisers to the Government were against us, and unfortunately for the interests of the British Empire in general, and British East Africa in particular, the advice of the engineers was taken. With little or no experience of Africa, they had acquired a reputation in India; so British East Africa was saddled with a railway of metre gauge, which cost nearly three times as much as it ought to have done."

Pauling reckoned that this was just another attempt to justify the wasteful departmental system as against the contract system.

"I do not intend to refute it specious arguments here, preferring to point out that inefficiency on the part of an employee under the contract system is generally punished with what is known in plebeian circles as 'the sack', whilst similar inefficiency under the departmental system is not infrequently rewarded with a knighthood or baronetcy. On one occasion I went to see the late Mr. Joseph Chamberlain (the Colonial Secretary) regarding some of these railways, and he promised to do what he could to get any offer I might make fair consideration, but his permanent officials were, I think, too strong for him."

There seems to have been more 'gongs' awarded out of this one debacle, from Chief Engineer downwards, than in the whole realm of African railway construction.

Kilindini Harbour 'The Deep Place', one of the finest sea-ports on the east coast of Africa was the starting point of the railway. It was later linked to Mombasa Island by a wooden bridge, then a steel structure, and eventually the Makupa Causeway.

Mombasa, the 3 by 2 mile Island of War, had a history even more blood-stained than Zanzibar or Mozambique. It held the balance of power on the east coast of Africa. The harbour entrance was guarded by Fort Jesus, built five centuries ago as the Portuguese citadel of their over-stretched African Empire. After long and courageous sieges it fell to the Arabs. With so much saga and romance this hotch-potch of Muslin and

Old Mombasa Principal Street 1900 (RGS)

THE PALACE HOTEL, MOMBASA

First class accommodation with large airy bedrooms and adjoining verandah. Electric bells and phones. Lift to each floor and to the Roof Garden, with its up-to-date Dancing Floor. Latest sanitation. The greatest comfort obtainable in Mombasa. Excellent English—French cuisine. Moderate charges. Under the personal supervision of the proprietor.

Christian communities became the seat of administration of the British - leased from the Sultan of Mombasa.

Seafarers were greeted on shore by immense mango trees and giant baobabs, their upturned primeval roots solidly silhouetted against the sea and sky. From the moorings, new arrivals were propelled on trollies by white robed Swahilis, huffing and puffing, to the heart of the island, with its strange smelling blend of dried fish, spices, cloves and roasted coffee, surrounded by coral rock houses in hues of ochre and pink. The salt saturated island stopped any grass from growing - the only ground colour was the occasional cactus flower or red flamboyant.

The first hostelries were the Africa Hotel and the Mombasa Club, set alongside the Old Port looking out across the Indian Ocean and still used by dhows that sail with the prevailing winds.

The Africa Hotel was a run down flea-pit, whilst the Mombasa Club, for members only, was a civilised establishment with excellent food, to which ladies were not permitted after 7 p.m. Early visitors were also recommended to stay at the Grand Hotel, run by Maia Anderson and her husband. This rat infested establishment was often surprisingly full; so a bed on the verandah with a torn mosquito net was the usual last resort for late arrivals. Almost next door, was the Greek run Hotel Cecil, named after the illustrious Lord Salisbury.

Then came the Manor Hotel, and the Palace. Later came the Castle Hotel - the number one central city watering hole. Beautifully positioned on the other side of the island the Tudor Hotel faced the mainland beach. The British administration was centred around Treasury Square Gardens.

The route of the railway largely followed the old caravan route inland from the coast. Surveys under Captain MacDonald of the Royal Engineers had commenced in 1891, but it was not until 5 years later that the first rails were laid by George Whitehouse, the Chief Engineer, at a grand opening ceremony. Watched by a few curious locals, the official guests included a couple of dozen Protectorate Officials and a few dozen Railway Officials with their families, a scattering of Missionaries, 10 English and 2 German businessmen, 4 Greek Contractors and 2 Greek Hotel Keepers, 2 Romanian Hoteliers, and, according to contemporary parlance, 4 Idlers - doubtless early pioneer 'remittence men.'

"It has been a long time coming and will take a long time to complete" were the prophetic words of the General Manager. A special dinner at the Mombasa Club also broke new ground. For a change, lady guests were invited, and were in for a surprise main course. It was carried in on a huge platter, and the lid removed with a flourish. Out scampered hundreds of little black crabs all over the dining table.

Crabs were not the only risks encountered. At different stages of the construction some of the more prominent members of the railway administration came unstuck. The Chief Accountant was tossed by a charging Rhino and lost his important right arm. A promising young engineer named Ogilvie died of blackwater fever. The Superintendent of Police was eaten by a lion. The principle Medical Officer succumbed to the effects of the climate, and one of the senior surveyors was killed by poisoned arrows from recalcitrant Kikuyu.

The line rose gradually from the steamy coastal strip, past palm trees laden with coconuts and bananas. Later came fruit and sugar plantations; but at the time of construction there was no labour. The locals were definitely not interested. Even a famine failed to get them off their back-sides.

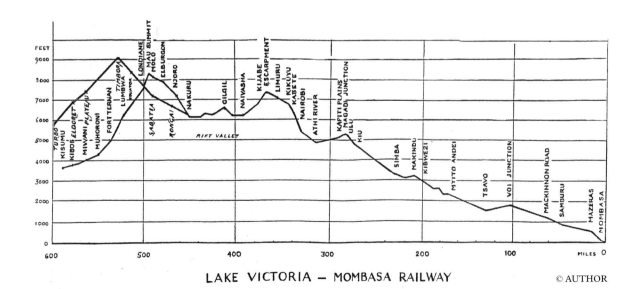

LAKE VICTORIA — MOMBASA RAILWAY

© AUTHOR

Indians on Construction work

Neither did any of the engineers in charge know how to deal with this situation, having come from India with its different working ways.

Besides, the land near the coast was almost uninhabited with only one or two men of working age per square mile; so it would have taken 25 years to complete the railway with local labour.

The Indian government was approached. Once more the cumbersome wheels of a civil service 'sped' into action and nearly shipwrecked the whole scheme. Expensive agents were employed to recruit a total of 35,000 labourers in India. To keep them from changing their mind, they stayed in specially built camps for 10 days prior to leaving India. And when they arrived in Africa all they were capable of handling was about a hundred shovelfuls of earth a day - about 16 cubic feet. This was one occasion when the government wisely climbed down, and thereafter worked to a piecemeal or contract system. Even so, the cost of labour was quadruple what it would have been in India.

Although the labourers relied almost entirely on imported Indian food for their nourishment, the Europeans also needed some home cooking. Before long a sprightly Irish-American lass arrived on the scene to follow the advancing rail-head. 'Pioneer Mary', whose husband John Walsh took a back seat, set up camp baking bread, pies, cakes and scones. She also kept order among the more robust railway hands with her hot Irish temper and a handy rhino-whip. There was one Railway Engineer called Bwana Simba - otherwise Archibald Buchan-Syderff. Only someone of that name could possibly have gone off on a days safari, leaving his labourers to their own de-vices such as pinching sheets of corrugated iron. He returned to face the wrath of Pioneer Mary in no uncertain terms. Eventually she ended up running a genteel tea shop and dairy in Nairobi.

The sudden rise from the coast caused a switch-back of reverse grades. 40 miles inland the Taru desert loomed. It was a waterless domain of scrawny thorn trees sprouting from the red earth. The little hamlet of Voi was later to become the junction of a hurriedly built branch line during World War 1. It was the strategic link across the border with the first railway built by the Germans in Tanganyika to the coastal town of Tanga. Luckily they had also chosen the metre gauge.

The Tsavo Jungle (meaning slaughter) had then to be penetrated, with a bridge over the nearby river. Here construction was completely halted by two ferocious man-eating lions, which night after night broke into the tents and carried off many of the Indian coolies. 'Scarems' and fires were of no avail. The two brutes waged a reign of terror around Christmas 1898 when the coolies threw down their tools and fled en masse to the coast - saying they had come from India to work for the Government, but not to supply food for lions, demons or poltergeists. In all, the lions devoured 28 Indians and an unknown number of Africans. When they were eventually shot, the Indians returned to work.

18 months later, when construction had progressed nearer to Nairobi, the Superintendent of Police, Mr. Ryall, was travelling in his inspection carriage with two friends. At a nearby station they were told of a man-eater on the prowl; so they decided to spend the night there and attempt to shoot it. Ryall's carriage was shunted into a siding and parked at a sloping angle. All afternoon and evening there was no sign of the man-eater so they to turned in for the night. Two of them slept on the bunk beds and one on the floor. No sooner had they dozed off than the outside door slid silently open, and the man-eater squeezed in. As the carriage was on a slope, the door slid shut, leaving the beast shut up with the three men in the compartment. What happened next was mind-boggling. The lion sprung at Ryall on the bunk bed, but in order to reach him it had to rest its feet on the man on the floor. The third man, panic stricken, attempted to open the door opposite which led to the servants quarters. He found to his horror that the door was held fast on the other side by the terrified coolies. Whilst the lion was busy grabbing Ryall, he managed to pull the door back enough to squeeze through. A moment later a great crash was heard. The whole carriage tilted violently and the lion had broken through one of the windows, carrying off poor Ryall with him.

Where the line passed Makindu the rich game country continued. On one side lay the snow capped Mount Kilimanjaro and on the other side Mount Kenya to the north, on the Equator. Simba, meaning Lion, was real Lords of the Forest country, which stretched up to Kiu at 4860 feet, where the climate changed to the more temperate highlands.

Magadi Junction is where another line branched off. In 1896 Major Burnham discovered a huge Soda lake, in almost incalculable quantities, on Lake Magadi near the border of Tanganyika, about 100 miles from the railway. The lake was so rich that as the crust was removed, new soda formed underneath, ensuring an almost unlimited supply. It lay untapped for years until the Government was approached to bring needy income to East Africa and the Lunatic Line in particular. Through British South Africa Company connections, who had a share in the enterprise, Pauling's stalwarts made various surveys for a line to the Soda lake. Harry Carter and Walter Sweetman made a trip in 1905 fraught with difficulties. Travelling down the Line which overflowed on both sides with more game than probably any other country in the world, one Station-master signalled to the next to make the train a non-stopper, since lions had taken over his platform and waiting rooms. On arrival, Carter, normally level-headed, was courting disaster. With a loaded rifle ready for a rhinoceros he advanced gingerly; then in a lapse of concentration handed it to an African porter who emptied the contents of the barrel with a blast at his rear.

The route was notorious for lack of water. Over 90 miles of water pipe was laid down the steep escarpment to the 30 mile long lake. When finished, it was the only railway in East Africa run by private enterprise.

The waterless windswept Athi plains, 40 miles short of Nairobi were saturated with animals in almost unbelievable numbers. It was so spectacular that it was sometimes unfairly suggested that those who described it were outright liars. Even the compilers of Rowland Ward's Records of Big Game had a field day, with reports of thousands of wildebeest, hartebeest, and lions. Ostriches raced around in a ridiculous fashion like wayward chorus girls. Giraffe scampered across the newly laid lines, pulling down telegraph wires with their long necks. Ronald Preston wrote of "this moving mass of animals, where the clank of rails and steel sleepers would frighten the game away in a radius of about 500 yards, so as to make the numbers greater and denser at the edges of the circle." A short-sighted rhino once stood his ground against a slowly advancing construction train, and charged the side, buckling the steel plates

For a mile on either side of the line the land was reserved for railway use. Mineral and forestry rights were considered an asset which would ultimately refund the cost of the railway

At Athi River, before Nairobi, a branch line to Thika was opened later. Passengers were able to get on or off the 'Thika Tramway' anywhere on its route by waving down the engine driver, or by telling him beforehand at which point they wanted to be dropped off. The guard acted as unofficial banker on pay days, taking cheques to Nairobi, cashing them, and then dropping off bags of coins at the various farms on his way back.

After Nairobi the line climbed the escarpment to Kikuyu, then to Limuru at an altitude of 7340 feet, with a bracing malaria-free climate of bracken covered hills. It was a touch of Ireland and Scotland rolled into one, with horse-breeding and damp, misty tea-plantations and English fruit and vegetables. The Hotel Brackenhurst and Holmes & Nairns were renowned for clandestine weekends. Limuru Railway Station turned into a sort of Club, where a day's tennis ended with an evening at the Station Stores. One member used to bring his servant with a wheelbarrow to ensure a safe return home.

At Escarpment, 7390 feet above sea level, the line peaked before dipping into the Great Rift valley below. When the rail-head reached here, people were lowered down the escarpment in steel cages.

'Rippling waters' - Naivasha overlooks the most beautiful of all the lakes. Settlers moved off from here to rich farm lands, with the Aberdare mountains and Mount Kenya in the distance. English country life continued with duck shooting and trout fishing.

Nakuru, where the Masai cows wouldn't eat the mineral deficient grass, later became the agricultural headquarters.

Summit was the coldest and highest station in the British Empire. 27 viaducts carried the line over the 8700 feet high peak to Lake Victoria below. At the next coldest and highest station, Londiani, the homesick Indian Station Master appealed for leave to visit India to bring his wife back. He sent that masterful gem of flowery Anglo-Indian prose which became a linguistic legend - signing himself off a B.A. (Bachelor of Arts failed by God's misfortune) Bombay. The request was granted.

The line reached Port Florence on the edge of Lake Victoria in December 1901. Supposedly named after Florence Preston, wife of Ronald Preston, it was actually named after

*Construction engine
climbing the Rift
Valley*

Florence Whitehouse, wife of the Chief Engineer George Whitehouse.
Everyone stood back and wondered what it was all for, and how it could
be made to pay its way.

*On the Rift Valley
incline*

NAIROBI

Nyrobe in Masai means *Place of Sweet Water*,
or more literally,
Uaso Nyarobe means *Cold River*

No other capital city developed so readily and rapidly because of the railway, as did Nairobi. When the advance survey party of Royal Engineers under Captain Macdonald paused on their way across the windswept open land where the Nyrobi River separated the territories of the warring Masai and Kikuyu, they camped for one night only, then moved on from this inhospitable, mosquito-ridden plain of red dust. A little later, James Martin endured it longer on a recruiting drive of local labour for the ballast works along the line. Other engineers followed and the site became a base camp for oxen and mule transport for the advancing rail-head.

It was to be another two years before the construction train clanked its way into Nairobi, 327 miles from Mombasa. The future capital was at last on the map. There was not a single tree anywhere in sight, yet for all its bleakness it was a level clearing where engines could turn, and trucks could be shunted around before the arduous 2000 feet climb up the Kikuyu escarpment. There was a zig-zag corkscrew for nearly 30 miles to the summit before an equally ruinous drop down the other side into the Rift Valley.

As more and more materials were off-loaded in the bush, Nairobi grew into a fully fledged railway camp. Huge piles of rails, imported wooden and pea-pod steel sleepers, telegraph poles, fishplates and bolts, lay beside the repair sheds and workshops and an unruly assortment of tents, huts, lean-to's and shaky shacks appeared in this fly-bitten, rat-infested landscape. The only decent building was the railway office which had been transported in sections on open trucks up from the coast, and which served as a Club and meeting point for all and sundry involved in railway matters.

Eventually, the railway administration moved up the line - lock, stock and barrel from Mombasa, set up camp, and stayed there ever since.

There was only one street and the town developed haphazardly. When the rains came it was a sea of mud. In the dry season the dust penetrated every nook and cranny, and there was precious little water. The outer areas were a minefield of game traps, dug by the locals to protect them from marauding wild animals. Lion, rhino, zebra and giraffe all roamed around the township.

George Whitehouse, the Chief Engineer, ran the encampment on relaxed 'military lines.' The Railways had their own administrative services, complete with police force, fire brigade and health department. Even garbage collection was handled by them. It had its own Revenue,

UGANDA RAILWAY.

THE HIGHLANDS OF
BRITISH EAST AFRICA
AS A
WINTER HOME FOR ARISTOCRATS

HAS BECOME A FASHION.

SPORTSMEN in search of BIG GAME make it a hobby.

STUDENTS of NATURAL HISTORY revel in this FIELD of NATURE'S own MAKING.

UGANDA RAILWAY Observation Cars pass through the Greatest Natural GAME PRESERVE in the WORLD.

For reliable information, etc., address:
PUBLICITY DEPT., UGANDA RAILWAY,
DEWAR HOUSE, HAYMARKET, S.W.

Accounts, Legal and Survey Departments and an efficient Telegraphic service. All land on either side of the permanent way was the exclusive property of the railway committee. They were a law unto themselves and the de facto owners of Nairobi. Not surprisingly, when the British Foreign Office instructed a Commissioner, John Ainsworth to move to Nairobi with his American wife and set up 'Boma' under the Union Jack, a certain animosity arose. It was now a question of: "Is he Railways or just boma?" rather than "Is he Boma or railways?"

Railway personnel greatly outnumbered the rest of the colonial administrators, hunters, traders, missionaries and others. Most of the early settlers were railway folk, or ex-railway folk whose contracts had expired and who stayed on in various capacities. The Chief Land Officer was an ex-surveyor; the first traders Gailey and Roberts were surveyors, and Ronald Preston, in charge of plate-laying, opened the Nairobi Exchange.

The line opened up the highlands of Kenya to a barrage of British noblemen led by Lord Delamere, Lord Francis Scott - uncle of the Duchess of Gloucester, and the Earl of Plymouth. Numerous bounders and misfits also arrived

The railway was a social lifeline for many a new immigrant. As the train chugged up country, the engines spat sparks from the green eucalyptus trees grown in special railway plantations. At wayside stations the passengers off-loaded, covered in thick red dust. They refreshed themselves and dined in small dak bungalows. The catering contract had been awarded to a Goanese, Mr. Nazareth, and the usual Bill of Fayre comprised watery Soup and tinned Salmon. The meal was rounded off with a dose of brandy to ward off mosquitoes.

Young hopefuls from England and South Africa, many escaping the depression in mining at the end of the Anglo-Boer War, arrived at the newly opened Nairobi Station. The station nameplate was about the only sign that a township even existed. A large part had been burnt to the ground by a panic-stricken Medical Officer, when bubonic plague was discovered in the Indian bazaar. All that remained were a few shacks, some of the more solid buildings like the Railway Club and a mass of hastily erected tents.

The earliest hotel was started by Tommy Wood. Sometimes called the Victoria Hotel it was bang opposite the station and, inevitably, in the one and only street - Victoria Street. For all its rudimentary worth it was a grand little double storey wood and iron affair. Wood, raised in Sheffield, had worked in South Africa, and like so many others at the end of the Anglo-Boer War, had moved north.

Richard Meinertzhagen was one of the first adventurous Englishmen to forsake life in a prosperous City of London family firm for the delights of travel and big game hunting.

He had originally come out to the country itching for action with the Kings African Rifles, and looked down on his brother officers as regimental rejects, heavily in debt, who drank a lot. They were also inclined to keep black mistresses in huts behind the Mess, which an old Harrovian like Meinertzhagen strongly objected to. His first taste of action was utterly distasteful. It was a punitive expedition against a village which had murdered a Railway Surveyor in a particularly brutal and disgusting fashion. Having pinned the poor man to the ground the whole village had defecated on him and left him to drown in their excrement under the merciless sun. Meinertzhagen arrived to see his corpse still staked to the ground and was so incensed that he left not a single villager alive. Fortunately, he commented, there were no children around.

He made full use of the railway facilities for his hunting expeditions; wining, dining and staying with Railway Engineers to obtain the best intelligence on local game. His diary is a continuous comment on the progress of the line, written in a somewhat euphoric haze:

'17th. March 1903. I marched to Mile 554 on the Uganda Railway where I camped on the line. In the evening a contractors train passed by and cut all the ropes of my tent. I had not been expecting trains.'

Hoping to impress Mrs. Maia Anderson, who had just bought the East African Standard, Meinertzhagen took her to lunch at Wood's Hotel. It turned out to be a 'miserable dirty place, serving tinned salmon, rancid butter, high meat and maggoty cheese - the whole garbage costing 8 rupees.'

Wood's Hotel also included a department store where everything and anything was sold; the only competition - apart from the Indian dukas - was George Stewart's store down the road. Wood also ran a post office with a convenient form of message service. Being near to the railway, he was in close touch with their telegraph service, often out of bounds except for official business.

The Post Office had a novel nautical system to announce the arrival of the mails. A hoisted blue flag meant the mail ship had left Aden; a red flag meant the mails had arrived at Mombasa, and a white flag announced the mail was ready for collection at Nairobi.

Wood's Hotel was the centre of Nairobi commerce. It was also the centre of intrigue, scandal, gossip and grievance as well as the focus point for D's (Lord Delamere's) first meetings for settlers.

The millinery and fashion department of this multi-faceted emporium was run by the enterprising Mayenne Bent, the common law wife of another railway official down the line at Mombasa. Having observed to a degree how to run - or how not to run - a Hotel with a virtual monopoly in a one horse town, she caused constant rows with Wood. Eventually she upped sticks and moved down the road, where she opened the Stanley

Hotel, named after the great explorer, in 1903. Unfortunately two years later it burnt down. Undeterred she rented another building and started afresh.

Meanwhile a mile from the railway station at the end of the only tarred road, Major Ringer and R. Winearls opened the Norfolk Hotel on Christmas day 1904. There had been so many delays between the Land Office and the Foreign Office over granting title deeds that as usual there were none. The building was a solid stone and brick structure with a tiled roof, and a spacious verandah. It flaunted a French chef, Louis Blanc, who after four pioneering years put the food on the map, but in a fit of Gallic temperament carved up a Somali chef so badly that he was fired.

The Norfolk became the *grande dame* of colonialism in the centre of Africa, cornering all aspects of the market, with private villa apartments for safari visitors and special terms for settler residents. So many arrived that the visitors book read like Burkes, Debretts and the Almanac of Gotha all rolled into one. 'D' - Lord Delamere, the leader of the settlers, sat on the verandah in a wicker chair surveying the scene. He led the wicked ways of his fellow revellers by taking pot shots at nearby street lamps. Constantly up against officious civil servants, he took matters into his own hands. Being a Peer of the Realm he was well able to meet Governors and Colonial Secretaries on equal terms, in the corridors of power on his few trips to London.

Elspeth Huxley recalled how on one occasion Delamere woke up on the train from Mombasa to find he was the only person in the carriage, which had been shunted into a lonely siding. Getting out he discovered that a senior Government Official plus all the other passengers and the Indian Engine Driver had gone off on safari to bag a lion. They were unlikely to be back before nightfall. Cursing and swearing at this unwarranted delay and at all things official and unofficial, Delamere procured the services of a nearby native, idly picking his nose, who said that although he had not actually done so, he had discovered how to drive an engine by watching from the footplate. Delamere demanded: "Then drive the damned train to Nairobi!", Without more ado, for in those days an order from a white man was an Order, the train shunted out of its siding, and was well on its way to Nairobi before the government official realised he was left stranded. A special train was sent down the next day to fetch him.

By 1906 the population of Nairobi had increased twenty-fold in the space of two years to 600 Europeans. The rare Englishwomen were in their element here, feted and cossetted by all men and sundry, riding about town either on rickshaws, ponies, donkeys, mules or even camel cart. Government Road became a rickshaw race track between the Norfolk and Stanley Hotels, with powerful Kikuyus competing against each other, cutting corners and running over shop-fronts for a rupee and a bonus. A

List of Principal Hotels.

MOMBASA..
  THE GRAND HOTEL.
  HOTEL CECIL.

NAIROBI.
  THE NORFOLK HOTEL.
  THE STANLEY HOTEL.
  THE MASONIC HOTEL.

Railway Dâk Bungalows are maintained at the following Stations at which passengers can stay at a moderate inclusive tariff, viz : -

VOI, MAKINDU, NAKURO, MUHORONI & PORT FLORENCE.

Passengers should provide their own bedding for night journeys on the Railway, but on the Lake Steamers all necessities are supplied.

Arrangements can be made in advance with any of the principal firms in Mombasa for the equipment of small porter caravans, for sportsmen or explorers desirous of making expeditions into the surrounding country away from the Railway.

---

farmer's daughter, Buster, was the star turn. She rode a cart with no sides at break-neck speed, standing with her legs on each shaft, cracking a whip and loudly shouting.

A penniless Lithuanian Jew, Abraham Block reached Nairobi from South Africa and stayed at the Stanley Hotel. He had worked his passage on a cargo ship from England to escape the pogroms of his native land, and finally caught up with his father in Johannesburg at the height of the Anglo-Boer War. With some Afrikaans farming friends, he moved north to Nairobi, shipping up his horses with him.

He was one of the first of a long stream of settlers to arrive from 'down south'. It was Joseph Chamberlain, the Colonial Secretary, on his first visit to East and Southern Africa with his American wife, who had set the ball rolling. The railway was losing money at an alarming rate, and its income was negligible with the expenditure on the Colony, so he encouraged a deluge of much needed immigrants.

The first pioneer Afrikaans farmers like Bon von Breda and Jansen van Rensburg proved that a meagre living could be made from the land. Arriving in 1908 at Mombasa port they chartered 5 special trains to transport 47 families. 42 wagons and 72 horses up country. Cutting a wagon road through the bush they trekked to Nakuru, their promised land on the Plateau.

In 1910 Sir Pierre Percy Girouard became Governor. More settlers arrived. His old boss from the Sudan, Lord Kitchener, also turned up and bullied Girouard into granting him a 5000 acre farm - land belonging to the Nandi tribe, which caused endless trouble later on.

The Muthaiga Country Club, 5 miles out of Nairobi, was aptly named after the bark of a local tree - a witch doctors favourite. Small doses were stimulating, large doses fatal. At its opening on New Years Eve 1913 Goanese waiters and Indian chefs served 14 exclusive settlers, with hardly an African in sight. Its reputation for bacchanalian revelry began, and it probably became the most notorious club in Africa. At one time the Committee even barred Government Officials and Jews from entry, retaining it as a safe haven and den of intrigue, not to mention amorous activities when women were finally allowed entry. The pink colonnaded building was a club for all flavours, with croquet, squash and tennis, backgammon and bridge. It heralded the height of decadence and white mischief. During twice yearly Race Weeks, every settler in the

Colony came to town. The Muthaiga Club held dances 5 nights in a row, with all manner of amorous and other goings-on; some members dabbling in a 'bit of acid and a lot of dope'.

In Nairobi's burgeoning economy Mayenne Bent, with her new husband Tate, decided to expand the Stanley into a 50 bed-roomed hotel. They scraped together to buy a central city property and once more the Stanley opened as a new stone building just in time for the boom war years. They sold the old hotel but unfortunately forgot to discuss the transfer of the Hotel name. A court contest decided against the Tates, so they were obliged to call their acquisition the New Stanley. In the centre of the new courtyard they planted a hardy thorntree which became the most celebrated meeting place in Nairobi - 'The Thorntree'.

Hoteliers and shopkeepers were about the only people who scored during wartime. Years of hard work by the weary settlers were wiped out. Drought and famine were rampant. The port of Kilindini was quiet. The railway ran at half measure, whilst new machinery, vehicles and spare parts were in short supply.

In 1929 Abraham Bloch bought the Norfolk Hotel, and years later added the Stanley to his empire. By that time D's crowd had long since moved on to the wilder pastures of the Muthaiga Club.

The grandest of Nairobi's buildings was the four storeyed Torrs Hotel, sometimes rudely known as the Tarts Rest. It was designed to resemble Stockholm Town Hall, with arched leaded windows and a first floor terrace. The plan was to rival everything around it and establish similar hotels all the way between Cape Town and Cairo. The hotel also boasted a unique storage area inside the front door, in which pets such as lion cubs could be left whilst their owners relaxed in the adjoining bar and Palm Court Lounge. Renowned for dances every night of the week, it was the brain-child of Ewart 'Grogs' Grogan,

Like many of his countrymen with a degree in Blarney, Grogan could charm the birds from the trees. Under the nose of his long-suffering wife, who stood by with far more elegance than intelligence, this generous rascal held forth among his band of admirers in an alcove of the Palm Court. Here, Nairobi Cafe Society met from mid-morning through to the early hours. He talked on any subject imaginable. Elspeth Huxley observed that words poured from his mouth like wine at some Bacchic orgy. "Intoxicating at the time, but when the orgy was over you wondered what he had actually said."

Grogan was the likeable rogue who was supposed to have walked from the Cape to Cairo and wrote a book with that title. In fact, as described by his nephew Norman Wymer in 'The Man from the Cape', he was one of the first men to take full advantage of all the rail and river connections then existing between Cape Town and Cairo:

"They jogged and swayed as far as Bulawayo by a wheezy train, and then on to Beira by road in an antiquated wagon-coach..."

Having spent some time hunting around the game-rich Gorongoza Mountains with Dan Mahoney - the Irish hunter who was employed to 'shoot for the pot' for the railway construction gangs, Grogan was rescued by Alfred Lawley. He was put on a wagon down the newly completed Beira Line to recover from a bout of fever.

His only real pedestrian achievements started half-way through Africa, after he had taken river boats and steamers to the north end of Lake Nyasa (Malawi). From here he began his actual walk along the Stevenson Road to Abercorn at the base of Lake Tanganyika. After traversing the lake by boat he ventured on foot, through the treacherous areas of Burundi and Rwanda into Uganda. Racked with malaria, he trekked as far as the British Camp at Wadelai, just north of Lake Albert Nyanza, and Fort Berkeley, from where he mostly covered the last 2000 miles though the Sudan and Egypt by canoe, gunboat, Nile steamer, and train. Sailing past the Lado Enclave, Gondokoro (Juba) he struggled through the Sudd which had only just been re-opened by the expedition of Gage and Milne. Having reached Fashoda, he finally arrived at Khartoum a year after Kitchener had brought the Railway down. He took the train to Wadi Halfa, then steamer to Aswan and finally the train again to Cairo.

Grogan's pioneer foot-slogging was in East Africa, with his companion Sharp, in exploring the remote areas around the Great Lakes, including the Rusissi River Valley between Lakes Tanganyika and Kivu, and the Mountains of the Moon, where he spent two months. They were among the first Englishmen to set eyes on Lake Kivu and confirm the lay of the land and feasibility of communications, including rail routes, between the lakes. This pioneering trek was thus of immense interest to Cecil Rhodes and Charles Metcalfe. His Intelligence was also invaluable to the British Government regarding Belgian and German presence in the area.

European and African Hospitals on the Trans Zambezi Railway 1920 (PAULING ARCHIVE)

19

HEARTS OF OAK

"At one of the little wayside ganger's houses, which serve as stations, a man crawled on a train, and gave us children in a strange land a glimpse of what some of the North-Western pioneers have to bear. He was not an old man, when you came to look at him closely, by no means old, but his form was so emaciated by fever that one would at first sight have put him down to be sixty-five or seventy. His skin was yellow, his eyes wild with malaria, three fingers on one hand had been bitten off by a wounded lion, and his arm was festered with a great scab - another evidence of the lion's mauling ability. He was going to Broken Hill Hospital with his rifle, his blankets and his water bottle, and the sight of his suffering somewhat dampened my pioneer ambitions, which had been steadily rising for days." Owen Letcher was recalling his early days in South Central Africa.

"To come out of the wilds and go into hospital was like entering the Portals of Paradise" is how another old timer described his ordeal.

The work of those countless nursing sisters, unsung throughout Africa, is perhaps exemplified best in the wonderful achievements during the short life of Mother Patrick (Mary Ann Cosgrave 1863 - 1900). With Dr. Frank Rand and a band of Dominican Sisters from Bavaria and Ireland, she pioneered both health and education in the infant colony of Rhodesia. Harold Varian, who caught malaria in 1898 described her as: "one of God's grandest women who carried her own beatification in her life of service. I shall always remember her sweet expression and gracious way during my first attack of fever."

Another contemporary from the Emerald Isle was the formidable Sister Bessie Smythe (1860 - 1931), who was closely connected with the railway construction companies. She was one of the most widely travelled ladies in Africa, working for at least 40 years in virtually every British territory.

In the early 1880's the twenty year old Bessie arrived at Kimberley Hospital and worked under Dr. Jameson. When the golden city of the Rand Reef opened, she moved up to the new Johannesburg Hospital; then on to Pretoria, nursing smallpox. In true pioneering style, she even joined a Burgher Commando. The Anglo-Boer War found her with the British troops at Vereeniging. In appalling conditions, thousands died of enteric fever and typhoid in the overcrowded, under-staffed, unhygienic military hospitals. Dedicated nurses like Bessie eventually took over from the hard-pressed doctors and ill-equipped orderlies, and turned the tide.

In 1902, at the end of the War, she went north to Kenya and was in

Mother Patrick (Mary Ann Cosgrave 1863 -1900)

*Sister Bessie Smythe
(1860 - 1931)*

charge of the new Government Hospital at Mombasa, immediately after the opening of the Uganda Railway. The next few years found her in the front line of Central Africa - at Chinde on the mouth of the Zambezi River, and then at Blantyre, north-eastern Rhodesia and the Congo. She moved on to the Great Lakes, first to Usumbura (Bujumbura) on the extremity of Lake Tanganyika. Marching with her bearers she then crossed round Lake Victoria to Port Florence (Kisumu); thence to Nairobi on the Uganda Railway, and down to Beira, Victoria Falls and Cape Town.

From 1905 to 1910 she was nursing in West Africa, first at Lobito Bay, during the first part of the construction of the Benguela Railway by Norton Griffiths, and afterwards at Lagos, Accra, Monrovia and Liberia. She went to South America, nursing on the Trans-Andean Railway also with Norton Griffiths, then journeyed through Central and South America and the West Indies.

But Africa called her back. She was soon engaged in her old haunts of the Cape to Cairo route at the then rail-head of Broken Hill. When Paulings built the railway on to Elizabethville in the Congo she moved with it. She was subsequently back in Beira; also working through the Zambezi regions. In 1915 she was in charge of the hospital at the vast Sena Sugar Estates run by the Hornungs on the banks of the Zambezi, and then at nearby Chindio, where work had commenced on the extension of the Trans Zambezi Railway by Paulings, and the great bridge which crossed the river.

By 1897 the colourful days of crimson spine pads, cholera belts, and Mediterranean style siestas as an antidote to the 'vaporous fumes' which caused tropical illness were fast being disproved by various researchers. New theories linking health with cleanliness, hygiene and diet had culminated in directives from the Colonial Office throughout the Empire. The pioneers carried Quinine, Iodine and Epsom salts with them everywhere.

Although it was a Frenchman, Alphonse Laveran (1845 - 1922) who first discovered the link with the malarial parasite, Patrick Manson (1844 - 1922) had as a young doctor in China suspected that the parasite was carried by the mosquito. Joining up with Ronald Ross (1857 - 1932) of the Indian Medical Service, they pioneered the understanding of the life cycle of malaria. Their work was completed by Grassi, Bignami and Bastianelli.

The idea was prevalent that after the sun went down, the human immune system also ran down. It had been guessed correctly that the mosquito, female of the species, was tempted to bite after dark. So was born the 'sundowner', the ritual round of drinks in the early evening taken on the verandah as a preventive measure.

George Pauling's solution was much the same. Alcohol was a remedy for everything. Whiskey and Gin were almost *de rigeur* on his construction projects in the fetid swamps and fly-belts through which his pioneer lines passed. He reckoned that no teetotaller stood a chance. The Beira Railway proved his point. His brother Harry took the jaundiced view; he treated malaria as a subject for humour and admitted: "I'm saturated with it. We all get it. It's part of the country's resources."

Blackwater fever is a complication of malaria. They used to say if you went down with blackwater, don't let them move you; get them to build a hut around you, and drink barley water, or rice water. All spirits were medicines, yet the advice was to drink nothing with meals except tea and pure water - if you could find it.

Sleeping sickness is carried by the tse-tse fly, which in contrast to the mosquito is not active at night. So travelling through the 'fly belts' during the hours of darkness was often the best precaution. For many years nothing was known of its cause. The intellectually inquisitive Mary Kingsley, regarded by some as 'the greatest white woman who ever went to West Africa', was a pioneer traveller and friend of Rhodes who died of typhoid fever at the age of 38 in Simonstown, after nursing Boer prisoners in the War. She noted in 1893 that sleeping sickness was rife near rank water. Here was the key - the perfect breeding place for tse-tse flies. After biting an infected person, the fly carried the disease to those whom it subsequently bit. The parasite was further recognised by Forde and Dutton, and then proved by the work of Bruce, Low and Castellani.

This appalling sickness started in the equatorial regions of Africa and decimated millions of people. In the ten years between 1911 and 1921, in French Equatorial Africa alone, over 6 million succumbed, more than half as many as were killed in the First World War. The disease was carried across the borders into southern Sudan, where the few doctors battled to stop an epidemic.

No finer example can be found of the dedicated work of those British and Syrian doctors who saved the lives of hundreds of thousands of men, women and children from an agonising death. Critics of 'interference' may well pause to reflect on their courage and devotion. Commenting on a Government report that much of the trouble in a remote area was due to a "continual change of medical officers", an official on the ground felt this remark should be qualified by the fact that "the first senior medical officer left the district worn out in body and mind quite unfit to return; the second died three days after reaching his base camp; the third had his health permanently impaired through an attack of blackwater fever, and the fourth left the district suffering from repeated attacks of malaria at short intervals." To those of the politically correct persuasion who say we should never have gone near Africa in the first place, and just left the inhabitants to fend for themselves, one can only address the following anecdote.

Dr. Ronald Ross, the medical pioneer who was awarded the Nobel Prize in 1902, arrived at the office of Joseph Chamberlain, the Colonial Secretary of State responsible for one quarter of the World, and one fifth of the population of this planet, with a scheme for malarial control in Africa. It was thrown out by Chamberlain on the grounds of prohibitive cost, with the comment: "I have an idea that we push sanitation and civilisation too strongly in these backward countries. If they like bad water, or insufficient water, it might be better to let them find it out for themselves."

Railways were built by men, not by machines, and only the earthworm moved more soil than the Navvy.

Navvies originated from the 'navigators' of the British canal building projects of the 1870's. They were English, Welsh, Scottish and Irish. The latter, who drank hard, prayed hard and played hard, dominated the hey-days of railway building throughout the world, and really brought the navvy to the forefront. Their immense strength and stamina, and huge appetite for meat, kept them burning energy up to 18 or 20 hours a day.

Before the turn of the century Pauling had observed the real old British navvy on some of his early contracts, "men of steam and steel" who were able to chuck between 10 and 14 cubic yards - up to 20 tons - into a wagon in one day. Not 25 years later he reckoned it would take 2 or 3 navvies to move the same colossal amount. Denigrating them below bridge builders and plate-layers was somewhat unfair, for they were not just great earth diggers, but knowledgeable and skilled in many other spheres. The more experienced men knew the compounds of soil and rock, and the ways to 'navigate' round natural obstacles

They travelled the world, yet in time, as a distinct race of men they fell by the wayside. In Africa, when the locals increased in numbers and ability, and took over their roles, the navvies became the foremen, gangers and engineers in the race of the advancing rails. But their reputation endured. Their drinking and gambling on the riotous pay nights was dreaded by the local communities through which the lines passed, for they thrived on that brand of comradeship and humour which became a legend. Ready to share their last penny with a down-at-heel colleague, and reckless alike of their lives and earnings, with no family ties, they lived, and often died, under the open skies.

Owen Letcher recorded that spirit:

"If you who travel nowadays to the Falls and beyond in a train de luxe, with a dining saloon and clean linen bed-clothes, iced drinks and shower baths, will peer closely into the eternal bush that rushes by your windows, you may here and there observe a tiny mound, a little clump of stones, perhaps a cross of wood - if it has defeated the white ants. Those are the human milestones on the Great North metalled road, the pegs that count the cost of conquest, the solitary bush-robed sarcophagus of someone who fell by the wayside. Malaria, blackwater, dysentery, lions, snake-bite - they took their toll of the men who forged the iron road to the north.

"There were the Railway men, the running staff who took the trains up to Broken Hill - at that time the spearhead of civilization - and who 'let the water go off the boil' while they spoored a wounded buck. There were too the construction gangs - Paulings fellows, who carried the line onwards from the spray of the Falls to the Congo border and beyond. They came from the four corners of the world. Englishmen, Scots, Irish, Welshmen, South African Colonials and Dutchmen, Australians and 'roughnecks' from Canada and the States. Not a few were referred to as 'Dagos'. They were a rough good-hearted mob.

"Some of them were highly educated men of obvious birth and breeding. One never enquired very closely into their antecedents or asked them if they were unable to find a healthier and more congenial job than carrying on with the dream of Rhodes, and pushing the northern extension of the Railways up towards the Equator.

"Some of course had unblemished records; others had blotted their copybooks. All were in some degree infected by the bug of adventure, that all compelling lust of primitive and cruel, but fascinating and free Africa. Cecil John Rhodes was not perhaps their idol or ideal; they were not versed in the whiles of statesmanship and trans-continental transport; but each and all had caught something of that restless spirit and rugged frame."

Edwin 'Ned' Clery, sometimes called Mike Cleary (1864 - 1926), was one of the most flamboyant Irish American entrepreneurs to hit Africa in the 1890's. Raised in Kentucky, the State of the raciest horses, this irresponsible rascal had an amazingly fertile imagination and 'the gift of the gab'. At the height of the Anglo-Boer War he collaborated with his friend George Pauling on railway sideshows on a grand scale. The celebrated 'Savage Africa' show at Earls Court in London was a contemporary sensation. It had a scene stealing conclusion - a re-enactment of a Boer attack on an armoured train as it puffed merrily around the arena on rails. This forerunner of the Royal Tournament included an African hunting drama with real lions appearing from out of the bush before being lassoed and 'slain'. There was also a Matabele attack on a mule Coach, using white men and Africans who had been involved in a real skirmish. Whilst assegais were being thrown around the arena, questions were being parried in Parliament as to why these warriors were allowed to roam London. The subsequent public outcry only hastened the removal of this popular entertainment to the much larger Olympia stadium. Anglo-Boer War

'Mad' Mike Cleary (right) with his friend and confidant George Pauling at Effingham, Surrey 1913, with one of Pauling's Great Danes

troubles eventually put paid to these profitable Shenanigans.

New modes of transport were in the offing, so 'Impresario' Clery then turned his attention, with some American friends, to promoting pioneer flying demonstrations in London, Paris and America. Unfortunately the wily Wright brothers successfully brought an action against him contending they held a master patent for 'Flying through the Air' all over the world.

Undaunted, Clery then went in search of concessions on the Ashanti Gold Mines in West Africa. In order to overcome the obstacles of the local Chief, in respect of mineral rights over his local burial grounds, Clery resorted to the dubious idea of acquiring a specially recorded phonograph. Hidden in a nearby hut, this was played at the appropriate moment to the Tribal Elders, with a convincing message from "their ancestral spirits" in praise of the white man. This overcame the obstacles of the concessions on their burial grounds.

After numerous other outrageous and entertaining incidents, Clery ended his days in the 1920's as one of London's best loved genuine Bohemians.

Having collaborated with Mike Clery on various enterprises, Henry Edward Pooley (1873 - 1934), Pauling's energetic secretary, also ran the rations department at the company's rail-heads. He had started his career in South Africa with the Union Steamship Company and completed his last contract in Africa for Paulings in 1915, on the Magadi 'Soda' Line in East Africa. He eventually became Chief Executive of the newly launched Rolls Royce aero engine branch.

Many railway stalwarts spent their last years in and out of England. Others, like Harold Varian, retired to Cape Town.

Having roamed the sub-continent of Africa for close on fifty years, the resilient 'King of Beira', Alfred Lawley forsook the warm breezes of the Indian Ocean for the gales of the English Channel. He retired to St. Leonards on Sea, Sussex. The day before he died in London in 1935, he enjoyed a splendid lunch with his old friend Ewart Grogan, whose life he had saved on the Beira railway many years previously. "Against doctor's orders I filled him up with roast grouse and the best bottle of Burgundy from the cellars of the RAC Club", recalled Grogan.

The itinerant aristocrat Charles Metcalfe retired to his imposing residence near Guildford. where he died in 1928. His Baronetcy expired with him. He left no memoirs of his paramount position as one of the prime instigators of the Cape to Cairo Railway concept, or of his close relationship with Cecil Rhodes.

Having eschewed public recognition, George Pauling returned to live quietly at Effingham, Surrey. He too had acquired a large house complete with Billiard Room and indoor Swimming Pool around which ran 'The Ultimate in Boys Toys'. Before the First World War he had obtained a miniature train set from Marklin of Germany. Running on a 5 inch wide (120 mm. gauge) line, it came complete with spirit-fired steam Locomotive and tender, 1st. and 3rd. Class Carriages, a Dining Car with verandah and a Smoking Car with luggage van. This was almost the same configuration as the Zambezi Expresses which plied the routes from Cape Town to the Congo. Whilst this model of all models whistled its way around the room, belching smoke, spitting steam and hooting to order for the benefit of his guests, his two enchanted daughters were, one by one, favoured with the occasional ride.

He had already built a church, named Our Lady of Sorrows after his Spanish wife Dolores - his third matrimonial effort. At the opening ceremony he confessed that it was partially 'fire insurance' that provoked him into such an enterprise.

Having survived the swamps and fetid heat of some of the most awful places on earth, Pauling was struck down at the age of 61 by the world-wide flu epidemic of 1919, which engulfed more than 40 million people. As always with an appetite for good living, after a generous liquid-lunch party at London's Hyde Park Hotel, he was rushed in a closed carriage to his home where he died three days later.

Alongside scores of relatives, his faithful man-servant from Mozambique, Eduardo Delgardo, was later to be buried in the same churchyard at Effingham.

In the true spirit of imperial adventure, Pauling's niece had married a nephew of Sir Francis Younghusband (1863 - 1942) the soldier-explorer who at the age of 24 was the first European since Marco Polo to cross the Gobi Desert. In 1902 he had forged a British link through Tibet and made a trade deal with the Dalai Llama - being the first Westerner to enter the forbidden city of Lhasa.

The last, and one of the most accomplished of all those Empire Builders who turned their hands to many enterprises, was 'Empire Jack' - Sir John Norton Griffiths (1871 - 1930). As a young man he had admired the way Pauling had conquered the wastes of Mozambique with his pioneer Beira Line, and was determined to emulate him as a Contractor. Ready for new challenges, like many others who came up against inept government inspectors, he was finally defeated. Having completed the torturous first section of the Benguela Railway up from the coast over the Lengue Gorge, he contracted successfully in Kenya and South America on the Trans-Andean Line. At the outbreak of WW1 he raised a Regiment of Horse, entirely at his own expense. He then joined the Royal Engineers and initiated the Tunnelling Companies, which advocated the use of coal-miners and other underground workers for military mining projects in France. His most spectacular achievements were behind enemy lines in sabotaging Romanian Oil installations and corn stocks, for which he was dubbed 'The Angel of Destruction' and was decorated by the Czar. He entered the City of London, dabbled in 'oils', stood as a Member of Parliament and was awarded a Baronetcy. His chosen Coat of Arms could hardly disguise his claim to fame as 'Empire Jack'. The supporters consisted of a figure of a Colonial Governor, resplendent in tropical regalia with feathered topee, alongside a dungaree-clad British tunneller holding a rock drill, with the motto of the age: 'For King and Empire'.

In 1929 he obtained the contract to raise the Aswan Dam on the Nile by a further 23 feet. A year later, his contracting company halted work, since they considered the resident Egyptian Engineering Inspectors incompetent, inexperienced and obstructive. An acrimonious exchange between the two parties resulted in damaging work stoppages and a withdrawal of finance by the backers. Each side blamed the other. The result was dramatically tragic. John Norton Griffiths took a small boat out to sea off Alexandria and shot himself.

20

TEUTONIC TANGANYIKA

THE LEGACY OF TWO IMPERIAL POWERS

A report arrived at the Foreign Office from the British Governor concerning an Old Chief in an area of Northern Tanganyika which was in the process of being transferred from Germany to Britain. When asked which he preferred - the Germans or the British, the old chief gave a brave and honest answer: "For my part I greatly prefer the Germans, and I hope they will come back." When asked why, he stated: "When the Germans were here I could beat my wives as often as I pleased, but since the English have come I am no longer the master in my own house." The British Governor had pencilled in the margin "Stout Fellow!"

In 1883, Herr Luderitz's trading post on the Atlantic sea-board of German South West Africa (Namibia) had been recognised as a German Enclave. A year later the Imperial Eagle was hoisted on the other side of Africa, and a Protectorate proclaimed over a coastal strip of Tanganyika. Britain had been lulled into a false sense of belief by Chancellor Bismarck's assurances that Germany had no intentions of colonial expansion in Africa.

The eastern seaboard was arguably where the scramble for Africa began. Germany made territorial claims over thousands of miles of inland territory, and had persuaded the Sultan of Zanzibar of their excellent intentions by sending 5 warships into Zanzibar harbour, with their guns protruding over the bulwarks, itching to be fired.

At the Berlin Treaty of 1890 Britain acquired control of Zanzibar, Kenya and Uganda. In return, Germany was given Tanganyika and the tiny Island of Heligoland in the North Sea, as well as a wedge of land jutting out along the Zambezi River from German South West Africa, known as the Caprivi strip. Ostensibly this was to ensure a navigable river route down to the sea, in spite of all the cataracts and waterfalls; but secretly Berlin was hoping to find a way to close the gap between their territories across Africa, only a few hundred miles apart.

Around Lake Tanganyika, Britain had been slow on the uptake. At the Conference Table, Lord Salisbury, Prime Minister and Foreign Secretary, had been badly advised. He had been unable to secure any sort of access through Central Africa for an all British route up to the Nile through Uganda. German Tanganyika bordered directly onto King Leopold's Congo Free State, creating a buffer zone for the Cape to Cairo railway. Rhodes' original aim had been to run due north, crossing the lakes with steamers and connecting the land gaps between Lakes Tanganyika, Kivu

ROVOS RAIL

Destination Dar es Salaam

One of the most luxurious trains in the world Rovos Rail's 'Pride of Africa' crosses the Victoria Falls Bridge on its way between Cape Town, Pretoria and Dar es Salaam. Beautifully rebuilt carriages and steam engines ply the routes through four countries - South Africa, Zimbabwe, Zambia and Tanzania on spectacular journeys that capture the romance of a bygone era.

and Edward with short runs of railway. Now he was thwarted.

Lord Salisbury had held a trump card, which in the normal course of events could have been played. The Conference had been inconclusive, in so far as Britain alone had refused to ratify the final details of the Belgian Congo border area. When the junior clerk signed for the papers delivered to the Foreign Office from the Belgian Embassy, the boundaries were accepted by all, and Britain lost her right of way through Africa.

Lord Salisbury then turned to King Leopold to lease him a strip of land between Lakes Tanganyika and Lake Kivu in return for a lease of the Lado Enclave on the Nile, north of Gondokoro (Juba) easily accessible as an international waterway from Belgium territory. When France and Germany protested and threatened to insist on recalling the Conference, Britain backed down.

Although a British throughway was paramount to Rhodes original scheme, he later adapted this idea, admitting it was not necessary if it paved its way through convenient foreign territory.

It was not until after the First World War that Tanganyika territory was ceded to Britain from Germany. Rwanda and Burundi were handed to Belgium for administration. The whole of southern Africa, with the exception of the Portuguese colonies, was British. British influence was also consolidated right through the Anglo-Egyptian Sudan from Cairo to the Kenya and the Uganda borders.

This made it possible - by 1928 - to travel the whole way from Cape Town to Cairo by public transport and at fixed fares without quitting territory either belonging to or administered by Great Britain.

GERMAN EAST AFRICA

In a German colony run on military lines by a Teutonic race, the construction of the Tanganyika railway lines were dogged by continual problems.

The first railway line from the coastal port of Tanga ran north-west towards Lake Victoria. At great expense the initial 30 miles took two years to build. There were endless delays due to lack of finance and labour shortages, since few if any of the locals were prepared to work. The Tanganyika plateau was not in any case densely populated. This line never reached the Lake and most of it was destroyed by the retreating Germans in their campaign against the British during WWI. A connection was made between this line and the East Africa Kenyan railway which was a vital link in the movement of British troops.

Dodoma Railway Station

From Dar es Salaam, the coastal capital, the Central railway, running due west, was built by a private German company. The original proposal had been to build a line from Dar es Salaam to the north-east corner of Lake Nyasa (Lake Malawi), but it was pointed out by the British that a line from Dar es Salaam through Tabora to Ujiji, half way up the eastern shore of Lake Tanganyika, would be far more advantageous. The intention was that this would form one of the feeders to the main trunk route, which had originally been agreed between Rhodes and the Kaiser, and that materials for the trunk route would be carried over the feeder line from the coast.

This link between the sea and the lake was started in 1906 and largely followed the old slave and caravan route inland from the coastal town of Bagamoyo, meaning 'lay down the burden of your heart', almost opposite Zanzibar. Before the construction of the railway, this settlement was the principal starting point for all inland journeys - 70 days by caravan to Ujiji on Lake Tanganyika via Tabora.

When the German Eagle flew over the shaded gardens and mango trees of Dodoma, it was a tiny township - a strategic communications junction in the middle of the central plateau. The railway arrived and handsome granite buildings with red iron roofs appeared, with one Hotel near the Station, and a Boma. The bazaars, markets and 'locations' grew up across the railway line.

Today Dodoma is the new capital of Tanzania, and Arusha 200 miles to the north lays claim to being mid-way between the Cape and Cairo.

The railway line cut across the Great Rift valley and climbed up towards Tabora, half way between the coast and the lake. This old Arab trading post was the converging point from the four corners of the compass; the centre through which half a million slaves passed in the 1860's. Speke, Stanley, Burton, Livingstone, and all the great explorers had followed this route, where ivory and humans were bartered for guns, beads and cloth. In this desolate setting the ancient trees were planted by the Arabs. The Germans later laid out an Unter den Linden from their Boma to the Railway Station. The Railway Hotel is now the resurrected Tabora Hotel, yet the only reliable route from the coast is still the railway.

When the lines reached the lake shore they aimed for Ujiji. This was the huge slave city of the Arab past, where Stanley found Livingstone in 1871, and where the transcontinental telegraph line came to its end from Cape Town. When the level of the lake fell, Ujiji was abandoned as a harbour, and the terminus was moved 5 miles north to Kigoma. Here the old lakeside hotel, once the Railway Hotel, still greets travellers sailing in from four neighbouring countries.

One of the stead-fast German Engineers who built this railway was reputed to have lived in the territory for 17 years without going on leave. With rare attacks of malaria, he survived on a diet of bananas, black coffee, cigars and Scotch Whiskey.

It was not until just before the outbreak of WWI in 1914 that the line was completed - built by labour imported from Mozambique. Once again, no local labour was forthcoming. Tribe after tribe had rebelled against the appalling conditions, in which up to 250,000 Africans had died following the Maji rebellion. As in the early Congo Free State, cruelty bred cruelty. One of the more outrageous officials, the Imperial Commissioner Karl Peters, set up a reign of terror. He hanged his native servant for stealing his cigars, and sent his black mistress to the gallows for being unfaithful. This regime of brutality caused widespread condemnation in Germany and throughout Europe. When word of his crimes reached the authorities, Peters was recalled by Berlin and dismissed from the service. As the Founder of German East Africa he had often expressed open admiration for British methods of colonising. So, in spite of his gross failings and misdemeanours, he fled to England to escape the wrath of official intrigues as well as German public opinion. Returning to Germany after the outbreak of World War I, he broke his solemn pledge to refrain from political propaganda. Having written streams of vitriolic and bitter articles, he died a sick and disillusioned man, leaving an indelible shadow across well-wishers in many countries

In Tanganyika, the overall German policy was to build railways in a military manner, with an Officer in charge of each 12 mile section. These sections often overlapped the territories of local chiefs and headmen, causing endless squabbles and lack of cooperation over labour problems. There were also ongoing disputes about surveys and other construction matters between the individual Officers in charge of each section, who refused to give ground to each other. It was a classic example of over-zealous Under Officers, which effectively killed Germany's attempts to emulate the British system of railway construction, in which sub-contractors incurred penalties for delays, and the Consulting Engineers had the final say in disputed matters. The Germans cast envious eyes on the progress of the Uganda Railway 'Lunatic Line', which for all its costly faults was advancing at the same time from Mombasa to Lake Victoria. They admitted the fact that the British had actually built 'two' railways where they had not even built one. The choice of the metre gauge by the Germans was also an ill-judged factor in the later decision to join with the other railways on the continent, since the only compatible link was with the Lunatic Line.

A century later, in Africa's darkest age, there is once again no reliable through connection to the north.

Tanganyika, under the British, had a reputation, perhaps inherited from its severe Teutonic infancy, of being more class ridden and more inclined to look askew at Africans than almost any other British colony, apart from South Africa. The Administrators and Officials of the Colonial Service, good-hearted friendlies though they might be, did not mix with lesser mortals. This also applied to almost anyone outside their government service. A settler in Tanganyika whose husband was a Geologist met some very charming railway officials one day, and said: "Of course we'll be meeting you at the club, I expect" And they replied: "Oh no, you won't. We're not allowed to join your club. We have to have our own club." The country was obsessed with social status, and it particularly affected professional people like Doctors, Forest Officers and others who had University degrees, and yet were looked down upon by underlings acting for the British Government. But as time went by, it became a shining example and role model of British administration in Africa.

DAR ES SALAAM

Dar es Salaam, the Door or Haven of Peace, was a testimonial to Arab, Teutonic and Anglo-Saxon enterprise. Laid out in military style,' Dar' grew from an Arab trading village with a Sultan's Palace, into a stately Garden City surrounding one of the finest deep-water harbours in the world. There were waving palms, acacias and flamboyants, and the ubiquitous African jacaranda, from pale mauve to deep purple and cardinal red; flame trees and yellow blossomed laburnums. And as always the strange upturned roots of the 'cream of tartar' baobab tree.

The Governor's Palace, a mock Moorish edifice, cast an autocratic eye over the whole magnificent spectacle. No other European nation put up such grand palaces for their Officials, and such enduring stations along their railway lines, as did the Germans.

After World War One, as one imperial power made way for another, the sumptuous Hotel Kaiserhof, which had been used as a Military Hospital by the Germans, was transcended by the New Africa, the Splendid, the Central, the Burger and the Sailer. Apart from the Dar Club, the Gymkhana embraced almost every sport imaginable. There was a rifle club which resounded to the ghosts of its German founders. As everywhere in East Africa the Indian Duka's sold clothes, carpets and curios, furniture and food, and tins of almost everything.

ZANZIBAR

Nowhere captured the quirks of narrow gauge lines more than the small island of Zanzibar. (Now part of Tanzania).

For some time the Sultan had enjoyed the luxuries, firstly of mule drawn transport, then of tram rides from his Palace down to his villa at the seaside. Puffing along behind a 2 feet gauge locomotive, he travelled with his entourage and the pick of his harem, who kept a discreet distance whilst His Highness alighted from his curtained carriage and wandered down to wallow in the warm waters of this magical island.

Dreaming one day of expanding the railway system in his domain, he invited tenders, through the British Commissioner, for more trams and trains. The word went out and railway contractors from all around the world, including the ubiquitous George Pauling, descended on Zanzibar in order to survey and bid for this lush contract.

An American pipped them all at the post with a real 'sweetener' - electric light and fans throughout the Sultans Palace. In 1904 Arnold Cheney & Co. were awarded the contract for a 3 feet gauge railway to run from beside the Palace (later to become the Government Offices) up the coast to Bububu 7 miles away.

From the crowded maze of Zanzibar Town, full of mosques and beggars, the rudely dubbed 'Zanzibar Express' ran past smelly open

COLONIAL STORES,
MAIN ROAD, ZANZIBAR. Cables : "SUCCESS."
P.O. Box 18   By Special Appointment Purveyors to H.H. The Sultan of Zanzibar.

Ships' Chandlers to the Union-Castle Steamship Co. and other Lines.

Wholesale and Retail Stockists of:—

Provisions, Patent Medicines, Fancy Goods, Cotton, Woollen and Silk Piece Goods, Hosiery, Haberdashery, Jewellery, Cutlery, Stationery, Perfumery, Boots & Shoes, Fancy Playing Cards, English and Indian Hats, India, Japan, China, and Maltese Curiosities, Crockery, Toilet Requisites, Leather and Steel Trunks, Spectacles and Eye-glasses, Novels, Fishing Lines, Musical Instruments, Artistic Pictures, Watches and Theatrical Sundries, and other articles too numerous to mention.

ZANZIBAR'S "UNIVERSAL PROVIDERS." No order too large and none too small.

By Special Appointment Jewellers to H.H. The Sultan of Zanzibar.

K. WILLIAM & Co.,
Gem Merchants,
MAIN ROAD, ZANZIBAR.   P.O. Box 52.

Manufacturers of Jewellery, Ivory and Ebony carved Curiosities. Tortoise-shell Wares, etc., etc. Dealers in Ceylon hand made Lace, Japanese, Chinese, Indian and African Curiosities, etc., etc. Elephant Hair Jewellery a Speciality.

MOTOR TRIPS CAN BE ARRANGED AT MODERATE PRICES.

ORDERS PROMPTLY EXECUTED.

*Branch :—*MOGADISCIO (Italian Somaliland).

BEST SHOP IN TOWN.   PRICES MODERATE.

THE MOST RELIABLE AND REPUTABLE FIRM.   ESTABLISHED 1900.

MOLOO BROTHERS & CO.
SILK, IVORY & CURIO MERCHANTS.
EVERYTHING MOST FASHIONABLE AND UP-TO-DATE.

Indian, Chinese, Japanese, African, Turkish and Arabian Curiosities in different varieties.

HIGH CLASS TAILORINGS FOR LADIES AND GENTS.

Orders Executed Promptly by Parcel Post throughout the World.

Tel. Address: "SILVERY."   P.O. Box No. 12.

Branch : DAR-ES-SALAAM.   **MAIN STREET, ZANZIBAR.**

Established 1890.   By Special Appointment to H.H. The Sultan of Zanzibar
Telegrams: "Choitram."   BRANCHES :   P.O. Box 89.

DELAGOA BAY, DAR-ES-SALAAM, MOMBASA, NAIROBI & BOMBAY.

B. CHOITRAM,
ZANZIBAR.

Direct Importers of Indian, Chinese and Japanese Silks, Ivory, Silverware and Brassware, Persian, Turkish, Indian and various Sorts of Embroideries, Extensive Stock of Asiatic and African Curiosities, Jewellery. Tailor and Outfitter.

bazaars and dark alleyways, through streets so narrow that the gap between carriage and walls was often less than 2 feet. Leaning out of windows was strictly inadvisable, even though speeds rarely exceeded 10 miles per hour. Past mesmerising colour washed walls enlivened with carved Arab doorways, little Porter tank engines pulled the quaint carriages to the coconut groves and clove plantations, the mainstay of the island. A welcome refreshment room greeted the traveller at Bububu, a sleepy settlement in a shady grove. The name bu-bu-bu stemmed not from the chuffing of the steam locomotive but from the bubbling Spring Waters which supplied most of Zanzibar town.

There were 3 classes of carriage at extremely modest fares. Hand baggage was free. The first class coaches were reserved for sightseers from passing ships. "You are not a travelled person until you have experienced one of the most thrilling journeys in the world" declared a lady traveller of the day.

Treated with amused tolerance by the Europeans, the railway was an unqualified success, paying substantial dividends. Up to 50,000 passengers a month travelled on this spectacular little line until it was closed in 1929, after smoke and flying sparks had caused much havoc, pollution and destruction. Officials of the Zanzibar Railway received free passes for rail travel throughout England and Europe. This was a reciprocal arrangement, and those unaware that the island railway was only 7 miles long were in for a short and sharp surprise.

Zanzibar was as cosmopolitan as it was colonial. Tennis, cricket, bowls and nine holes of golf could be played at the Mnazi Moja Club. There were two hotels, the Beach for languid Europeans, and the Hotel Africa which stood alongside the English Club which had been founded as early as 1888, before the island came under British patronage. Nearby lay the American Bar and the Transvaal Arms, where German and Spanish ladies greeted the wayfarer with a warm welcome. There were Italian and Belgian areas, and a Portuguese Street - a world of de Souza's, as almost everywhere else in East Africa.

THE TANZAM RAILWAY

No real story of the Cape to Cairo Railway can ignore the one important modern link, and the distasteful political overtones which brought about its eventual completion in the 1970's.

Scattered mines and abundant cattle ranches in south-west Tanzania had always been in need of transport through this vast unbroken territory. In modern times, however, the Great North Road became pot-holed and impassible for months on end in the rainy season, with breakdowns, hold-ups and the danger from bandits.

Experiments in crack-pot socialist ideas under President Julius Nyrere had driven the country to bankruptcy. Wholesale nationalisation of the country's assets and resources on the communist model, and the forced removal of peasant farmers to collectives, produced an unmitigated disaster for this once prosperous and orderly country.

To a large extent neighbouring Zambia, once the Granary of Central Africa as Northern Rhodesia, also attempted to divest itself of any connection with Southern Rhodesia's attempt to go-it-alone, and retain responsible Government for as long as possible. (The Unilateral Declaration of Independence 1965 - 1978). In order to avoid shipping monumental loads of copper by rail to the south through Rhodesia and South Africa, Zambia looked for alternatives. It was of course hypocrisy to an extreme. They relied almost entirely on engines and trucks lent to them from the struggling but self-reliant neighbouring economy of Southern Rhodesia under sanctions, and particularly the skilled European-run railway workshops of Bulawayo to keep their rolling stock and signalling equipment running. They were dependent on the electricity of the joint power authority from the Kariba dam. Nevertheless a railway linking them with their own independent outlet on the coast at Dar es Salaam was pushed for.

Driven almost to despair by being turned down by the major Western countries and the Soviet Union, on the grounds of uneconomic viability, Nyerere and Kaunda finally turned to China. A foothold in Africa, as a small stake in their first colonial venture into the lost continent, was not an offer to be turned down.

Dubbed the 'Red Railway', the Great Uhuru (or Freedom) Railway, the Tanzam Railway, or TAZARA for short, it was not always a shining example of efficiency. Surveyed by a Canadian firm, it largely followed that part of the route through Zambia (Northern Rhodesia) planned for Rhodes' original Cape to Cairo line. It then followed more or less the route that had been surveyed by the Germans in their quest for a line from the north of Lake Nyasa (Lake Malawi) to Dar es Salaam. It ran through some of the most barren regions with little hope of picking up mineral, agricultural or even large passenger loads en route. It was built by a vast army of Chinese labourers, some of them virtual slaves, as well as indented Africans of Nyerere's inept and Kaunda's bankrupt administrations. The zealous Chinese workers were away from their families for up to two years at a time. Certainly the most labour intensive railway of modern times, an astonishingly large force of nearly 100,000 people toiled for 6 years to build the 1200 mile line. As was the case with other railways in Africa virtually all the materials came from the mother country. The steel rails, sleepers, cement and timber were all shipped from China to the congested port of Dar es Salaam. The line was built from one end only, and as it advanced inland a fully serviced moving camp kept pace with the rail-head.

On the level open plains in both countries much of the route was plain sailing. Around the Southern Highlands of Tanzania the most difficult terrain was encountered. Between Mlimba (the Kingdom of Elephants) and Makambako (The Place of Bulls) the altitude rises 4000 feet through mountains, precipices and swamps in a distance of 60 miles. 4 major rivers had to be crossed and nearly 30 per cent of all the line's earthworks, viaducts, tunnels and bridges were concentrated here. In all, 300 bridges, 23 tunnels and 147 stations were built along the line.

Cave-ins and wash-aways occurred regularly, but the job was carried relentlessly to its conclusion at Kapiri Mposhi, north of Lusaka, in inscrutable style.

By nature suspicious of non English speaking foreigners, the local Africans did not readily accept the Chinese. The strange little orientals with high collars walked around in pairs as if they were spying on one another. They kept themselves to themselves and were looked upon by the Africans almost as if landed from Mars. They were alien to the relaxed open attitude of the British, and the colonial style of administration which had been inherited after independence. When they left the country, President Kaunda commented that no-one would see a half Chinese-African baby around.

There were some questionable motives of the Chinese at the time. They built all their own hospitals, houses and office centres; but they finally left an incalculable legacy, as well as a sweet and sour taste in the mouth. The TAZARA cost £350 million, or £280,000 per mile, financed by an interest free loan repayable over 30 years in hard currency.

In terms of sensible planning the 3 feet 6 inch 'Cape' gauge was chosen to join up with Southern Africa and possibly the Sudan in the north. In the rest of Tanzania, as in Kenya, the metre gauge prevails.

Running from Kapiri Mposhi, just on the edge of the Zambian Copperbelt, and crossing an area almost the same as that planned a hundred years earlier, the Tanzam Railway was thus a completion of the scheme to link the British Commonwealth territories through central Africa. It is one of the great Ironies of History that it took the Chinese Communists 6 years to complete a large slice of Cecil Rhodes' Imperial dream.

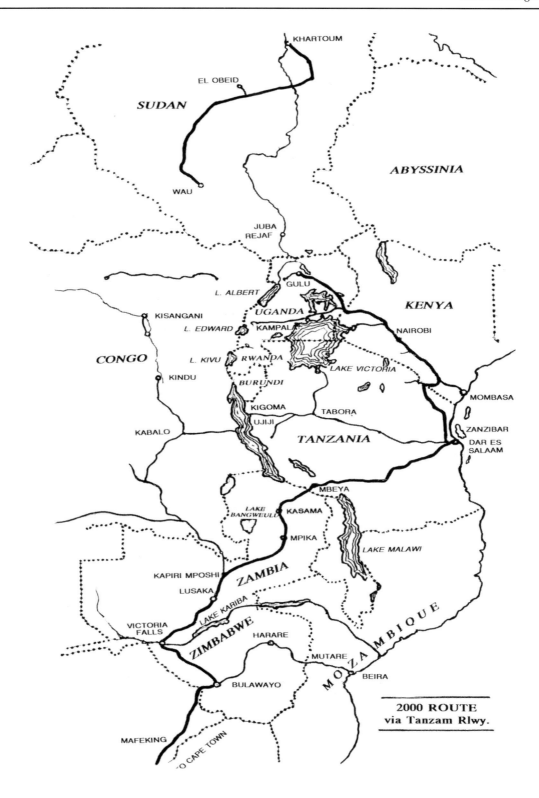

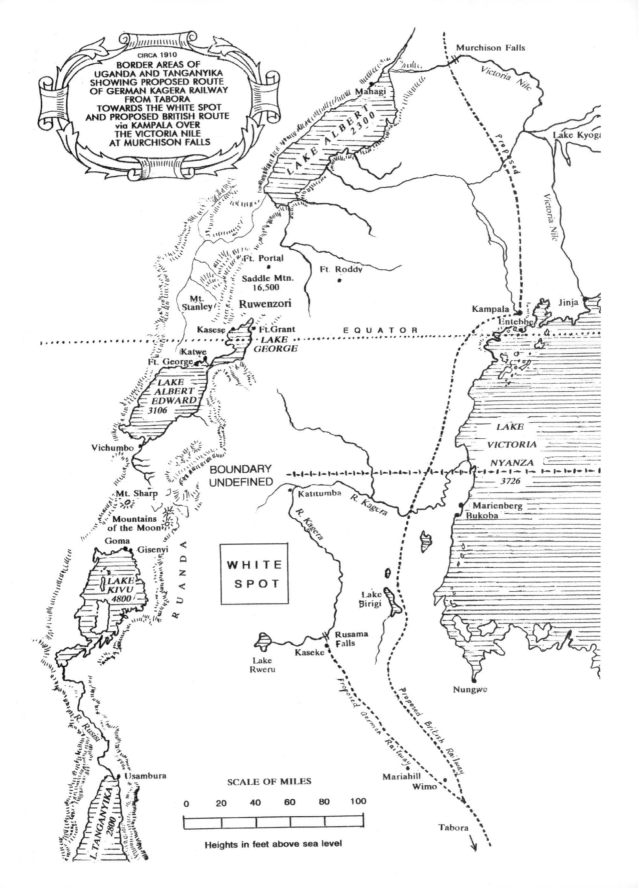

CIRCA 1910
BORDER AREAS OF
UGANDA AND TANGANYIKA
SHOWING PROPOSED ROUTE
OF GERMAN KAGERA RAILWAY
FROM TABORA
TOWARDS THE WHITE SPOT
AND PROPOSED BRITISH ROUTE
via KAMPALA OVER
THE VICTORIA NILE
AT MURCHISON FALLS

Murchison Falls

Victoria Nile

Lake Kyoga

LAKE ALBERT 2300

Mahagi

Proposed

Victoria Nile

Ft. Portal

Ft. Roddy

Saddle Mtn. 16,500

Mt. Stanley

Ruwenzori

Kampala

Jinja

Entebbe

Kasese

Ft. Grant

EQUATOR

Katwe

LAKE GEORGE

Ft. George

LAKE ALBERT EDWARD 3106

LAKE VICTORIA NYANZA 3726

Vichumbo

BOUNDARY UNDEFINED

Katitumba

R. Kagera

Mt. Sharp

R. Kagera

Marienberg
Bukoba

Mountains of the Moon

Goma

Gisenyi

R
U
A
N
D
A

WHITE SPOT

LAKE KIVU 4800

Lake Birigi

Rusama Falls

Kaseke

Lake Rweru

Nungwe

proposed German Railway

Proposed British Railway

R. Rusisi

Usambura

SCALE OF MILES

Mariahill
Wimo

0   20   40   60   80   100

L. TANGANYIKA 2800

Tabora

Heights in feet above sea level

21

THE MISSING LINK

UGANDA AND THE WHITE SPOT

The lake regions of Uganda - where the Nile rose - were of paramount strategic importance; for whoever controlled the headwaters of the longest river in the world effectively controlled the water supply for the Sudan and Egypt.

This had been known for thousands of years. The ancient Egyptian Pharaoh Ptolemey mentioned a vast lake (Lake Victoria) surrounded by the Mountains of the Moon, trespassing onto territory to the north. The Greek historian Heroditus (c 450 BC) also spoke of 3 great lakes and mountains. Yet it was only after Vasco da Gama's arrival at Mombasa in 1498 that real interest was stimulated in this heart of Africa, over which the Germans, the French, the Belgians and the Arabs cast envious eyes.

It was not until the Berlin Treaty of 1890 that the ill-defined boundary between German East Africa (Tanzania) and British East Africa (Kenya and Uganda) was partially established. A line, as straight as a die for 300 miles, was drawn from the coast through the heart of the Masai country, and with Queen Victoria's approval it bent around the base of Mount Kilimanjaro, the highest mountain in Africa. This was a birthday present to her grandson Kaiser Wilhelm.

The boundary line then continued westwards, for almost another 300 miles, through the centre of Lake Victoria and out towards the hazy area around Lake Kivu, where it petered out. At that time it was not a question of the limits of exploration. The 'Boundary Undefined' area marked on the maps bordering King Leopold's Congo Free State had not been accepted by Britain during the Berlin negotiations. It was this gap, through the border regions, that Rhodes yearned for his rail connection between north and south.

Stanley had christened Uganda the Pearl of Africa. At a high altitude with abundant rainfall, it had lakes, mountains, valleys and even bogs - and a great greenness not unlike Ireland.

"Concentrate on Uganda - that paradise on earth," urged Churchill; "Uganda is a fairy tale,... you climb up a railway instead of a bean-stalk, and at the top there is a wonderful new world."

The extension of the Lunatic Line opened out the regions around Lake Victoria. After the arrival of the original line at Port Florence (Kisumu), a later 'off-shoot' reached the lake shore at Jinja, where the Victoria Nile rises. It was finally connected up with the 60 mile long Busoga Railway, built by Norton Griffiths to connect Jinja with Namasagalla on the Nile - the first suitable place for a port for river and lake steamers.

IMPERIAL HOTEL KAMPALA

The Best Centre for Travel and Sport
Good all Weather Roads

Tours arranged through Picturesque Scenery
MURCHISON FALLS
MOUNTAINS OF THE MOON
LAKE KIVU   BELGIAN CONGO

Recently Modernised   Cool and Comfortable
Excellent Cuisine and Cellar
Coffee a Speciality

IMPERIAL   HOTEL,   KAMPALA
TELEGRAMS : IMPERIAL, KAMPALA

From Jinja the main line continued onwards to Kampala (Hill of the Impala), the capital of Uganda lying on seven hills, and once called the Athens of Africa. The Imperial Hotel reigned supreme, and the Uganda Weekly Mail then was the leisurely overnight service from the Kenyan border.

On the lake shore, in the pretty garden suburb of Entebbe, the best sort of whites and the prettiest ladies hung out in the grandest colonial settings. Here berthed the original grand old Ladies of the Lake, the steamers 'Winifred' and 'Sybil' which plied the route between the rail-head at Port Florence and Entebbe. Made in England by Deney & Sons, these sturdy 600 tonners had been taken to pieces at the coast, and railed up to the lake-shore for re-assembly

To connect Uganda by rail with the south through German territory, different ways were proposed. One route was through the rugged and little explored area of the northern stretches of Tanganyika.

From the rail junction of Tabora, the Germans had planned, and begun to construct a railway to their extreme North Western province of Ruanda. Known as the Kagera Railway its terminus would have been at Kasseke (Rusuma Falls near Ngara) where the Kagera River forms the south-western frontier of the province.

Up till 1916 no Europeans, with the exception of a few isolated German officials and missionaries, had the opportunity of staying any length of time in that area. In 1916, when the Germans were in retreat, it was occupied by Belgian troops and became a closed military district. Captain James Philipps spent 5 months there on a military mission and had a marvellous chance to study the area. He recalled:

"Early in the war, while producing a sketch map of German frontier communications, it was noticed that on every existing map of the country northwards from the proposed terminus at Kasseke of the projected rail-way, by accident or design, the area remained quite uncharted. Also from the northern edge of this area up to the Uganda frontier the map was in many instances at variance with first-hand native information.

"This uncharted area in eastern Ruanda was referred to by the Germans themselves as 'The White Spot' (Weisse Stelle). The main ancient caravan routes from Tabora passed through it. It was thus not naturally more isolated or less accessible than the adjacent mapped area. Quite the contrary. It was therefore one of the first things I went to investigate.

"In 1917 I passed through the whole length of the 'White Spot' from the north to its southern limits at Kasseke. It contained a remarkable Valley, which provides an unexpected avenue of communication, with one break, from the terminus of the German projected railway at Kasseke, to the Katitumba (Kagitumba) valley whence access is assured to the plains, to Lakes Edward and Albert and to the projected railway system of Uganda.

"This I considered to be the key to the development and junction of the Central and Northern railway systems of Africa, east of the great divide."

It subsequently transpired that Ewart Grogan who had passed through Ruanda with Belgian staff about the same time as Captain Philipps had also been struck with the possibilities of this area for an all British rail system between Tabora and Uganda via Ruanda, and had communicated his ideas to London.

The original, more difficult route, linking the land gaps between the lakes could have been approached on a line either crossing or following the valley of the Russisi River. This flows down a narrow gorge from the south shore of Lake Kivu (between Cyangugu in Ruanda and Bukama in the Congo) to the north end of Lake Tanganyika at a point near Usambura (Bujumbura) in Burundi. This route would have passed through the proposed strip of land which was to be leased to Britain by King Leopold in return for the lease of the Lado enclave on the Nile.

Lake Kivu is almost exactly half way between Lakes Tanganyika and Lake Albert. It is 2000 feet higher than both - the highest lake of any consequence in Africa. A most spectacular expanse of water with islands, it is malaria and crocodile free, with Meditteranean vistas and climate. On its northern shore, Goma lies on the Congo side of the border in the storm-studded Bay of Kisenji (Gisenyi). This was christened the Gulf of Naples in Africa, because of the palm-trees, sandy beaches and idyllic reflections in the blue waters of the peaks of distant volcanos. The neighbouring lake port of Gisenyi lies inside Ruanda. Once known as the Switzerland of Africa, Ruanda is now the most densely populated country on the continent

Out to the north-east, straddling the borders of three countries - The Congo, Ruanda and Uganda, is the land of a thousand hills, which reach up to 14,000 feet (4500 metres). The chain of six extinct volcanos are spread along a range, and form the watershed of the Nile-Congo divide. Home to the endangered mountain Gorillas, these peaks were the supposed real Mountains of the Moon of ancient Arab fame - rather than the Ruwenzori Mountains which lie much further to the north of Lake Edward.

The land link between Lake Kivu and Lake Edward would therefore lie partially within Congo territory, until it passed into Uganda. Just inside the border, nestling in the fertile hills not far from the tiny Lake Bunyonyi, is the pretty little Ugandan town of Kabale. The long established White

Horse Inn overlooks it from a magnificent hill-top setting.

From the top of Lake Edward the line would wind its way entirely through Ugandan territory northwards over the Kazinga Channel to Lake George, past the perpetually snow-capped Ruwenzori Mountains. Some, like Mount Margherita at over 5000 metres, are in the range known as the modern-day Mountains of the Moon. It would run past Kasese and the strategic Fort Portal, the Ugandan colonial capital of the region with - not surprisingly, the Mountains of the Moon Hotel.

The line would have crossed the Victoria Nile near the Murchison Falls where the river runs through a very narrow gorge. It was aired that such a magnificent project and setting would have warranted a railway bridge equally as majestic as that at the Victoria Falls. In fact the Cleveland Bridge and Engineering Company were asked to prepare surveys for just such an undertaking.

This was the key to the route through Central Africa for the Cape to Cairo line which Rhodes was cheated out of, after the Berlin Conference. It forced him to deal either with the Kaiser or King Leopold - to the east and the west of the great divide, respectively.

When it came to the crunch, the offer by King Leopold of a lease of land between the lakes was vociferously objected to by both Germany and France. They threatened to recall the Conference, so the agreement never went through.

According to Ewart Grogan who met and discussed the Cape to Cairo plan with him, Rhodes had then proposed another alternative route - through German territory, but avoiding the 3 smaller lakes in Ruanda and Uganda altogether. This way a line would be built from half-way up Lake Tanganyika at Ujiji, across to the south end of Lake Victoria. Boats would then cross the lake to Port Florence (Kisumu) - at that stage the terminus of the Uganda 'Lunatic' line.

From there northwards Rhodes intended it to pass well eastwards through the Lake Rudolph (Lake Turkama) District, along the western base of the Abyssinian Highlands to the Blue Nile. Plentiful wood supplies for the steam engines, and the easy terrain were all factors in favour of this route, well away from the impassible Sudd, and the colossal area of swampy country surrounding the White Nile north of Gondokoro (near Juba), which made railway building well nigh impossible

Other routes were proposed to join up the 'Uganda connection'. Spurring off from the Lunatic Line in Kenya, a few miles beyond Nakuru, a railway was started which it was hoped would eventually connect Nairobi with Khartoum and Cairo. It runs up to Gulu, only 50 miles from the Sudan frontier, which is only 150 miles from Juba, the first navigable point of the Nile. (See map on Page 265).

THE RIVER ROUTE

Until Kitchener's victory at Omdurman in 1898 the route from the Sudan through the upper White Nile to Uganda had been a closed book for 13 years since Gordon's death. The work of clearing the waterway, wide enough to take a gun-boat through the Sudd, was started again in 1899 by a party under Major Peake moving southwards. At the same time the Uganda government decided to open up communications with Egypt. In 1899, Captain Gage of the 7th Dragoon Guards and Dr. A.D.Milne, who were joined by the Belgian Commandant Henri, were despatched northwards in a small launch. They succeeded in fighting their way through the Sudd until they reached Major Peak's party. Gage and Milne were therefore the first Europeans to re-open the route between the Great Lakes and Egypt after the re-conquest of the Sudan. Ewart Grogan passed through shortly afterwards.

North of Lake Albert the broad open stretches of the Albert Nile were navigable up to the border of the Sudan. Wadelai, (near Mutir) was named after a local chief who was reputedly so fat that a boy could stand on his stomach while he was sitting down. It was the one time safe-haven for many explorers, after the British abandoned the Sudan, including the German born Emin Pasha. Wadelai became a remote river station, staffed by British soldiers who spent most of their time 'playing shop' and sorting mail. Nearly all the transport was used to deliver rations, belts, boots, blankets and comic uniforms to all and sundry. Being on the trade route from the Sudan the natives earned so much money that they stopped growing fruit and vegetables, and paid crazy prices for the basic necessities from elsewhere. As a result there was no fresh local produce and a continuous shortage of almost everything.

After the First World War, when German East Africa became a British mandate, a scheme to bridge the gaps on the lakes by a series of train-ferries connecting the iron spine, was revived.

In 1920, at a meeting of the Royal Geographical Society chaired by Sir Francis Younghusband, this plan was discussed and proposed by Henry Wilson Fox (1872-1921). There were widely divergent views as to which method would be the most expeditious and economic; Train Ferries on the Great Lakes or an all-rail route around them. It was pointed out that ferries would make considerable economic savings over a land route.

At about the same time, one of the last of the rail-spurs was built from Kampala due west across to the Ruwenzori Mountains and the rich copper mine of Kaseke. The route was a compromise of the earlier 'Stevenson Trace', and the 'Varian Trace', surveyed on instructions from Robert Williams of Tanganyika Concessions. It was Harold Varian's last surveyed line in Africa.

22

SUDAN CONQUEST

BY RAIL AND RIVER

When Allah made the Sudan," say the Arabs, "he laughed."

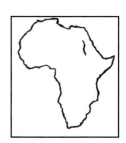

The largest country in Africa, the Sudan had been administered by the British since 1882 on behalf of the Khedive Ismael of the dynasty, sometimes dynamic, sometimes despotic, which ruled Egypt. The Nile, flowing from the highlands of Uganda for 2000 miles through the Sudan and then a further 1000 miles through Egypt to the Mediterranean, was the lifeblood of the nation; unnavigable through the cataracts; treacherous through the Sudd; but sometimes serenely passable for hundreds of miles before joining its sister waterway, the Blue Nile at Khartoum. Along its well watered hinterland all things were possible. There were rich pickings of agricultural produce; a harvest of cotton, gum, rubber, ebony, mahogany and teak.

The British had been firmly involved in finding a way through the upper reaches of the Nile ever since the days when Speke, Grant and Baker had been searching for its source in Uganda.

Samuel Baker's anti-slavery expedition was sponsored by Ismael in a rare gesture of respectability towards European ideals. Thousands of men, cavalry and artillery launched forth in a flotilla of sailing boats and steamers to defeat the Arab slavers - who at that time were taking up to 50,000 victims a year. They battled their way through the menacing Sudd, south of Khartoum, as much an obstacle as any fighting force. This strange land, the size of England, stretching to the green horizon, was a mass of papyrus swamps and rotting grass, entangled with poisonous water snakes, crocodiles, mosquitoes and large blood-sucking camel flies. Baker eventually found his way through to Gondokoro across the river from Juba, a thousand miles south, and finally, after negotiating the cataracts, over the border into Uganda. Many of the slavers were routed, others simply moved on; but it was a prelude to further punishing expeditions. His enthralling letters home to the Daily Telegraph in 1876 had extolled for the first time the virtues of the Cape to Cairo concept, and gave Harry Johnston the impetus to expand the idea.

The legendary Charles 'Chinese' Gordon (1833 - 1885) followed. He had gained fame in Shanghai by leading a group of Chinese desperadoes against local rebels. His task in Africa was to consolidate Baker's mission and establish British outposts all the way along the Nile. Having successfully cut a permanent channel through the Sudd, he sorted out the leisurely life-style of the unsupervised Egyptian troops who had run riot, and were being paid not in money, but in alcohol and nubile slave girls shipped down from Khartoum. His ultimate objective was to annexe Buganda, sandwiched between Belgian and German territory, and to open up communications as far as the Great Lakes into British East Africa. At the upper reaches of the Nile his demountable boats were taken round the rapids and floated onto Lake Albert.

Gordon secured around him the most able and dedicated group of Governors it was possible to find. Paradoxically they were of almost every nationality under the sun except British; yet they were as equal to any in the task of opening up Equatoria. One was the American Chaille-Long of Civil War fame, who brought with him a small army of colleagues. Then there was the enigmatic German doctor Eduard Schnitzer, who changed his name to Emin Pasha and pretended to be a Moslem; and the Austrian Rudolf Carl Von Slatin. Perhaps first and foremost was the heroic Italian Romolo Gessi, an almost forgotten explorer, who was Gordon's sterling lieutenant. Having mapped the regions around Lake Albert, he met his end on the way back to Egypt, after being stuck in the horrific Sudd for three months before being rescued. Most of his party of 400 men had died of starvation; many had resorted to cannibalism.

Cutt sudd floating downstream around the gunboat 'Tamai' during sudd clearance. This was achieved through constant use of cutters and dredgers, and manual labour, standing on cables dragged through the river (DURHAM UNIV)

This band of enterprising Governors were joined by others who spearheaded the drive to open up the Sudan, not just down the Nile, but east to the mountain borders of Abyssinia and west to the undefined regions of French Equatorial Africa. Under Gordon's administration the Sudan came under central control. For a while it remained at an uneasy peace, for beneath the surface simmered a hot-bed of tribal clans waiting to boil over - seething on the brink of insurrection. The prime cause was hatred of the corrupt Egyptian officials who resorted to unspeakably harsh methods to gather taxes.

Gordon's success in the Sudan and his friendly relations with the King of Buganda (Uganda) opened the way for the first real British connection from the 'Arab' north to the 'African' south. It gave impetus to the plans of Rhodes and Kitchener of combining river and rail route through the Sudan.

In the north, the appalling never-ending marches through the intense heat of the interior were monstrously unacceptable, and the only effective way to peace was by building railroads to the Upper Nile. The battle against the interminable wastes which had baffled countless explorers, not least the Belgians, the French and the Italians was about to be won by the means that the British were adept at more than anyone else - Railways.

As early as the 1870's the Khedive Ismael had planned railways connecting Egypt with the Sudan. The line eventually reached down Egypt as far as Assouan (Aswan) with a navigable river link from the First Cataract to the Second Cataract at the strategic town of Wadi Halfa on the nominal border of Sudanese territory. This unofficial line of demarcation was the 22nd. degree of latitude, about one degree below the Tropic of Cancer.

Southwards of Wadi Halfa navigation was impossible for hundreds of miles. Rough surveys were done by British engineers from Wadi Halfa all the way to Khartoum, but lack of funds ensured that Ismael's spirited plans never really got off the ground. Then a master survey was conducted with a team advancing up the Nile in great style. It included 8 English and 4 Egyptian Engineers, a Doctor, 100 drivers and guides for the 400 camels carrying supplies and equipment. The party was escorted by a large Army unit. The inauguration of the work had been impressive. Guards had stood to attention all the way along the line of survey in the blistering heat whilst the local Imman intoned the opening poems and prayers to Allah. Finally, after 35 miles of track had been laid alongside the river by Royal Engineers and Lucas & Airds, under the direction of John Fowler, the railway came to a grinding halt. Gordon, the Administrator, stopped the work due to overspending and under-estimating. In so doing he signed his own death warrant, for during the later siege of Khartoum, Wolseley's relief mission could have rescued him, had there been a rail link to speed up their advance. The short length of completed line, which had already cost £1½ million, lay wasting away in the shifting sands.

Unrest and rebellion had blown up in the Sudan, both against the Egyptian dynasty, its hated occupying forces and tax collectors, and the prospect of British rule.

The tyrant Mahdi was the centre of it all. He ruled from El Obeid, which he had taken after a long and painful siege of the Egyptian garrison. This ruthless smiling despot 'reigned' as a Prophet or Messiah, in the name of God, over a wild horde of tribesmen - with violence and cruelty unsurpassed anywhere. Flogging to death and cutting off hands were the usual penalties for the most trivial offences.

A formidable Egyptian Army army was assembled under Colonel William Hicks to bring him to heel. It consisted of a group of largely untrained and unmotivated captives and others. Cumbersome and heavy-handed, they were badly equipped for tropical duty - some wearing chain-mail armour and antique helmets. Having advanced up the Nile south from Khartoum this formidable looking force meandered across the desert out towards El Obeid. Wandering around hopelessly looking for water they ran out of supplies, and lost their way. 30 miles south of El Obeid they were attacked by a horde of 50,000 of the Mahdi's followers. The result was total annihilation. 10,000 men died; a few hundred were all that survived.

The whole country was in revolt. In every corner, in every province, Governors either retreated or surrendered. Only a few remote Egyptian garrisons stayed afloat in the vast sea of revolution. Gladstone in England washed his hands of it: "Let the Egyptian Garrisons fend for themselves", he advocated. But conservative opinion pulled him back, with the fear of the spread of Moorish influence over the whole of Egypt, and beyond.

There was one man to save the situation. Charles Gordon rushed out of semi-retirement back to Khartoum as Governor-General of the whole territory. His prescript was not to occupy, but merely to withdraw. Gordon excelled as a soldier and military engineer. Like his colleague Kitchener, and like Cecil Rhodes, he shunned feminine society and publicity, but loved power. Headstrong and somewhat erratic, he was a moody little man with piercing blue eyes, indifferent to reward, with an almost mystical courage. A keen sense of humour supported his anxious moments. He set to work with 12 Arab notables as his ruling Council. Opening the prisons and gates of Khartoum to those who wished to join the Mahdi, he prepared to evacuate the territory.

The telegraph line to Cairo buzzed repeatedly with Gordon's demands, counter-proposals and contradictions, and with Governor-General Cromer's bemused replies all the way from Cairo. When the line finally went dead, the Mahdi's forces were approaching Khartoum.

As usual the British Government prevaricated. Too late, they left Gordon to his fate. In an unusual display of interference in political affairs, Queen Victoria herself voiced her concern with the lack of any concrete action.

As the months dragged on, Khartoum was steadily surrounded and cut off. The soldiers and inhabitants were reduced to eating donkeys, cats, dogs, rats, gum and pith from palms. Many died from dysentery and starvation. Extraordinarily brave and deeply religious, Gordon visited them daily under heavy fire, which few others dared face. The Austrian priest Fr. Joseph Ohrwalder, for over seven years a prisoner of the Mahdi, observed: "Many a time each day he looked towards the north from the roof of the Palace, for the relief which never arrived."

In fact the relief force under Wolseley arrived up the Nile only 3 days after Gordon was killed on the steps of the Palace. Khartoum had finally fallen after 317 days of siege. The relief force withdrew almost immediately.

For ten painful years after Gordon's death the Sudan degenerated into a bloodstained savage wilderness. Out of a total population of some 8½ million, 3½ million died of disease and starvation, and about 3 million more were massacred by the marauding dervishes or killed fighting each other. Between 1 and 2 million were all that survived. It was one of the greatest pogroms in modern times.

This long suffering country was to experience continuing bloodshed. For in almost its entire history the only time it was at peace was when it was part of the British Empire. There was a short recent respite when a government in the south ruled with the agreement of the Arab north. As the fighting continues, the Railways ferry troops of the ruling army of the north to the southern most point of the line at Wau. When the troop trains return once a year, they stop for a while in the remote desert. The soldiers raid the nearby villages, taking young women back with them to the north, to be enslaved - with their progeny raised in an alien Moorish culture.

THE DESERT RAILWAY

The conquest of the Sudan by Kitchener between 1895 and 1898 was not simply the necessity for a military raid to avenge the death of Gordon. Nor was it just an imperial takeover of this vast territory, the size of England, France, Germany, Spain, Italy and Greece combined, and one quarter the size of the United States of America. It was a stand against the great Moorish crusade to drive Christianity from the whole of North Africa, and from Egypt in particular.

The Egyptian army, under the British, eventually became one of the finest in the world. It was the pick of the most able 20,000 men. One third of them were former Sudanese enemy; the best of the prisoners and deserters were recruited by the War Office after every victory. The cavalry was all Egyptian. Only 1 in 500 of the population were enlisted, as compared with Germany at the time which was 1 in 90, and France about 1 in

Labourers sawing mahogany logs into sleepers, at Khor Kokweee. Some trees had boles of 40 feet.
(DURHAM UNIV)

66. In contrast, Britain, which had one of the smallest standing armies of any major country in the world, had to rely heavily on officer reserves and volunteers for the Sudan campaign.

It was Kitchener above all who pushed for the railway as a rapid means of transport and relief from the Mahdi. And so it was, in effect, military ambition that spurred the advance of the Iron Horse.

Whilst Wadi Halfa remained the frontier, Kitchener's original plan was to take a line to the 3rd Cataract, along the route of the original 33 mile line laid 15 years earlier; but the dervishes had torn up the track, and a completely new line would have to be laid. The only alternative was to run hundreds of miles across the hostile desert from Wadi Halfa to Abu Hamed. Could it be done?

Kitchener asked many experts in railway engineering and military logistics. Almost all said it was utterly impossible - in view of the war, lack of water, and feeding thousands of plate-layers in the barren wastes.

Kitchener persisted, and the building of the Wadi Halfa to Abu Hamed railway turned out to be an excellent example of precision military planning combined with a large amount of luck.

In terms of engineering it was no great feat. Level ground with few natural obstacles ensured a rapid advance by the railway battalions of the Royal Engineers led by 'Gerry' Girouard.

Pierre Percy Girouard was a French Canadian with experience in rugged railway construction on the Canadian Pacific pioneer lines. His French audacity, American ingenuity and British doggedness stood him well. Out of 3 subalterns chosen to run the Railway Battalions of Egypt, he was the only one to beat the rigours of the Sudan. It was to Kitchener's credit that he accepted this brazen colonial, one of the few who dared to confront him. At Girouard's first interview in London he offered his left hand to the Commanding Officer, whilst he stood, nonchalently, with a cigar burning behind his back. Yet such was his charisma, and Kitchener's supreme confidence in him that he was allowed complete *carte blanche*. He rapidly estimated all that was needed to push a railway through the sandy wilderness from the Nile back to the Nile at Abu Hamed, cutting 250 miles across the great wide bulge and avoiding the numerous cataracts, as opposed to a 600 mile route slavishly following the river. This short-cut alone reduced the time of the advancing troops from 18 days to 24 hours.

With youth, courage and endurance on their side, there were eight subalterns including the 29 year old Gerry Girouard heading the railway contingent. They were Lieutenants Gorringe, Stevenson, Pritchard, Polwehle, Blakeney, Cator, and Manifold who ran telegraphs. Captains Gordon and Kincaird completed Kitchener's Band of Boys. The Sappers had a world wide reputation for building everything from Cathedrals to cow sheds. It was said of them they were either mad, married or Methodist.

Gerry Girouard inspired such loyalty and affection in his subordinates that his presence alone was sufficient to inspire confidence. He had a keen sense of humour, in contrast to the 'K rule' of Kitchener KCMG - which was 'Kindly Call Me God'.

Kitchener KCMG

The gauge of the line had caused a lot of argument and discussion. Lord Cromer in Cairo had wanted a metre gauge line - or 3 feet 3$\frac{1}{2}$ inches. This was in spite of the fact that the existing lines from Cairo to Luxor ran on the European gauge of 4 feet 8$\frac{1}{2}$ inches. There were also loads of sleepers, rolling stock and even locomotives lying around of that gauge, ready for the new extension from Luxor to Aswan, which could have been used.

Kitchener however, had visions as far-sighted as Rhodes. Although they met on very few occasions, they both planned to link up their bold

*Last spike being
struck*

Last rail being laid

schemes somewhere in the middle of Africa on 3 feet 6 inch Cape gauge lines. Kitchener fought tooth and nail with Cromer and his cronies on this point, and his plan prevailed. Since it was a military operation and he was in overall command, it is to Kitchener that the debt of gratitude should be paid for this enduring legacy of a railway gauge which may one day link the continent from north to south.

Hardly anywhere in the history of warfare has a railway played such a key role in the speedy advance of a fighting force.

Kitchener had wanted it completed in 4 months, Girouard calculated not less than 6 months, and kept his word to the day. At Wadi Halfa a miniature railway town sprang up out of the desert. It was described as a mud village transformed into a miniature Crewe or Chicago. Loco engineers, railway staff, ship builders, store men, all combined to make it a haven of activity. Even Thomas Cook's Nile steamers were struggling to ferry troops and equipment, having been requisitioned by the military. Every rail, every sleeper, every rivet, water tank, pipe, pump, and tool; indeed every ton of coal and and every truck and engine was shipped out from England and transported nearly a thousand miles via Alexandria in Egypt down the Nile to the railhead. Shipped and transhipped... mostly from clumsy sailing boats, and then around the rapids and cataracts on sections of railway, and back again onto the Nile. Rails and sleepers were slung ashore by Cairo donkey boys, conscripts, convicts and murderers, some in ankle chains; for in Egypt under the wise rule of the Khedive murderers could not be hanged except on the evidence of eye-witnesses. The Halfa Province was so disdained that it was often called Half-A-Province. English drivers and firemen were hard to come by. Italian mechanics came into their own, and an Italian Cafe was opened by the military.

Old Wadi Halfa is now no more - swallowed up by the waters of the lake.

Girouard had specially ordered powerful locomotives to draw heavy loads, aware that a large part of each train-load would comprise huge quantities of water for its own engine. In fact he cancelled an order once placed by Kitchener for 6 unsuitable lightweight locomotives - although he usually battled to get any money at all out of the Military Stores. Whilst on a trip to London he confirmed the agreement between Kitchener and Rhodes for the diversion of some invaluable 80 ton engines which were destined for the Cape Railways.

"It is scarcely within the power of words to describe the savage desolation of the regions into which the line and its constructors plunged." Churchill commented.

Water and more water, was sent forward to the surveying, banking and track laying parties from the advancing railhead - a moveable canvas town of some 3000 inhabitants. For the first few miles into the desert no survey was needed. The line ran straight out into the limitless horizon completely devoid of any land fix. Local Arab guides were asked to point the direction. They looked at the sun and peered into the distance. Their line of sight was so accurate that it was found to be only half a degree out.

Two trains ran daily; a material train with 2000 yards of track and five 1500 gallon water tanks, plus 3000 gallons in the locomotive tender. The second daily train was a water train with 500 yards of track.

An alternative scheme of electrically driven locomotives had been proposed to Kitchener. The cost of the generating plant alone would have been more than the entire budget for the whole of Girouard's estimates.

The actual construction was plain sailing, and the monumental supply difficulties were solved by the efficient Railway Battalions, who fought with pick and shovel under the Sappers. Apart from the lack of water the major problem was the shifting sands. The single track stretched over an increasing distance of barren desert. Blown by the wind or raised by the motion of the trains, the sand caused constant break-downs of engines and machines. Yet the lengthy daily run of rails, sleepers and water tanks was steadily maintained. Progress was never less than 2000 yards a day. As distances grew greater and greater, it was feared that if no water was found, by the time the railway rejoined the Nile at Abu Hamed, the engines would be pulling fifteen 3000 gallon tenders just for their own consumption; not to mention the need for watering 3000 men and their Protective Battalions.

At Mile 77 under the splitting sun and red hot sand, the first wells were sunk. Perhaps it was chance; certainly it was fortuitous, or more realistically it was the result of water diviners, that water was struck. At only one other point in the whole journey, at Mile 126, - still known in military parlance as Station No 6, water was struck again. Although many other attempts were made in exactly similar terrain throughout the entire route, from Stations 1 to 10, water was never found again. To this day, Station Number 6 is the only place that sells a proper brew of tea.

On October the 31st. 1897 the rails reached the Nile at Abu Hamed.

On exactly the same day, thousands of miles to the south, with similar hurdles to cross, the Railway had pushed its way through the waterless Kalahari desert to reach Bulawayo. Special trains had already left Cape Town and were trundling up the line for the official opening 4 days later.

Whilst Cecil Rhodes was not at Bulawayo, Kitchener was present at Abu Hamed, planning his advance on Atbara. And because of the industrial strike in Britain, the railway engines that had been earmarked by Rhodes for the Cape had arrived for use on the Sudan Military Railways.

The 3 feet 6 inch Cape Gauge came into its ubiquitous own.

There was a pause at Abu Hamed. Then work recommenced on the 150 miles towards Berber and Atbara. All day at intervals the material trains pulled out with supplies and stores, and puffed off southwards till they were lost in the heat haze. There was no wood for sleepers, so metal 'pea-pods' were brought up with the rails.

After the Battle of Atbara was won, the troops withdrew and remained for four months awaiting the advance of the railway. There was no question of moving further south until the line had reached Berber - to bring up supplies, and until the Nile had risen to make it more navigable for the gun boats. As the troops sat and waited, boredom crept in and enteric fever broke out. General 'Backacher' Gatacre had ordered that the men should not have alcohol. This did not include the daily ration of rum, which was as much a part of army as navy tradition. It was an improvement on Wolseley's mistake during his unsuccessful campaign to relieve Gordon at Khartoum. He had replaced Rum with Jam and Marmalade.

As the line advanced, crucial battles were fought, and reinforcements were rushed through to the 'end of steel'. The rains came, and brought delays. But soon Kitchener's gun boats advanced in parallel to the line.

On the open plains under the Kerreni Hills, 1260 miles from Cairo, the ultimate defeat took place. At the Battle of Omdurman in 1898, 11,000 dervishes were killed, and the savage Mahdi Empire came to an end.

"Fighting the dervishes was primarily a matter of transport. The Khalifa was conquered on the Railway." So wrote the young war correspondent Winston Churchill.

Kitchener hoisted the Union Jack alongside the Egyptian flag over Khartoum, and the Anglo-Egyptian Sudan came into being.

When the Battle of Omdurman was fought, the Colonial Secretary Chamberlain was on the high seas. He had left England for America on the steamer Majestic, to stay with his American wife's parents. The Times reported that on his arrival in New York he learnt of Khartoum's recapture. Turning to one reporter he said: "That settles it for all time. Gordon is avenged. Young man, you will live to see the time when a Railroad will be built through that country to the Great Lakes, the Transvaal and the Cape."

KHARTOUM

"A more miserable and unhealthy spot than Khartoum can hardly be imagined," commented the explorer Baker; "here we find the dregs of the human race."

On a spit of land between where the Blue Nile meets the White Nile, shaped like an elephants trunk (khartoum in Arabic) a notorious slave and ivory centre had grown up in the early 1800's. Its strategic position ensured a constant flow of human misery across equatorial Africa.

Khartoum after 1900

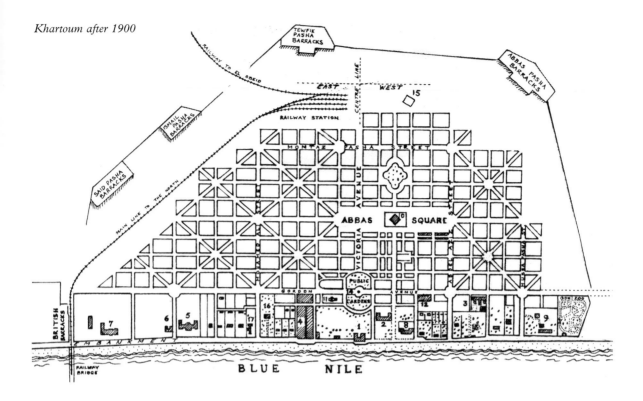

1. The Palace
2. Govt. Offices
3. Madiria & Zaptia
4. Works Dept.
5. Military Hospital
6. Nuzi etc.
7. Gordon College
8. Posts & Telegraphs
9. Grand Hotel
10. Mosque
11. Cathedral
12. Govt. Shops
13. Govt. Market
14. Gordons Statue
15. Christian cemetery
16. Sudan Club
17. R.C. Cathedral.

The Blue Nile is the shortest and strongest of the two tributaries that keep the longest river in the world flowing through the Sudan, the largest country in Africa.

With the arrival of the British, Khartoum was run very much on military lines, largely by those who had arrived with Kitchener's expedition up the Nile. Along the river frontage slumbered all the important government buildings, with behind, a residential area for Europeans and shops of every description.

Smart houses with gardens soon appeared, mostly single storey spacious wooden affairs of the American colonial style, with shutters and wide open verandahs to take advantage of the breezes, and to blow away the dust. The only sealed road was a stretch of about 100 yards in front of the Palace.

Rumours claimed that Kitchener had decreed that the streets of Khartoum were to be laid out in the shape of the Union Jack. In fact he had chosen the Chicago gridiron system simply to minimise distances

The Sudan Club and view of Khartoum. The block of batchelor quarters called Yellow Peril (left), situated on the south side of the Club gardens, was in use from 1912 to 1921. The other block was called Peabody's. (DURHAM UNIV)

View of Khartoum from the air showing the Governors Palace on the river front, with government offices to the right.

across town. This gave rise to the diagonal pattern of many 'Union Jacks' crossing each other as they radiated out from a central point. Very soon, however, the odd wiggly alley-way or house would suddenly appear - cutting across the orderly lines of this patriotic pattern. In contrast, Omdurman across the river where the Sudanese continued to live, had also 'developed' haphazardly into the 'shape' of an Arab crescent, built in concentric circles around the Islamic mosque.

The noise was incessant. Almost everyone seemed to have donkeys in their back yard - either to carry baggage or to commute to work on. Senior administrators were afforded the luxury of either a riding pony or a pony trap. Water for washing and drinking had to be brought daily from the Nile by donkeys carrying skins or canvas bags. Freed slave women, and even young girls from an early age, carried earthenware jars on their heads, precariously balanced upon circular grass rings; and it was this that gave to Sudanese women the beautiful carriage that so distinguished them.

In the Clubs, notably The Sudan and The Khartoum, newly arrived civilians were rather looked down upon by the old military buffer types, kept afloat on waves of drinks, who peered at them over their newspapers from their verandah chairs, often passing such unhelpful comments as: "Who's that blasted civilian, eh?"

There were two daily newspapers, the Sudan Herald and the Sudan

A picnic in the Sudan 1912
(Durham Univ. Sudan Arch.)

Times. Gin was the order of the day. Gin Slings, Pink Gin, Gin Fizz, Gin and 'It' and Gin and Tonic, loaded with Quinine. Tennis and Bridge were the other two main occupations.

Gradually the administration of the country passed from the Military to the Sudan Political Service. Sudan was the most sought after posting in the whole Empire, to which only the best and brightest of the Colonial Service could hope to aspire. An elite corps of some 120 Officers were nominally in charge of one million square miles of territory, an area one half the size of Europe, and one quarter the size of the United States. It was indeed 'a country of Blacks ruled by Blues'.

The facts hid the figures. There were significant numbers of locals and extremely able and reliable Egyptian officials who largely looked after the everyday running. In government offices Syrians and Copts served as clerks, cashiers and accountants. Turks, Albanians, Armenians and other nationalities of the middle East held other posts; as well as Italians and Greeks - who owned most of the stores. The population was the most sparsely spread in the whole of Africa, since the Mahdi had decimated all but a million or two of the inhabitants. These were largely concentrated along the Nile. Distances often belied the areas of responsibility; and in one respect it was a murky question of 'divide and rule', between the Muslin north and the heathen or Christian south, a division which ran almost exactly along the 13th. degree of parallel latitude. Pax Brittanica came into its own.

The officers who followed the euphoric military advance down the Nile had often been prompted by a failed attempt to join the right regiments. So they stayed on in any capacity they could find. It was the hey-day of Empire. In this expanding Edwardian climate more and more bachelors flocked out from India and elsewhere; hunting was an added attraction, since vast quantities of game were to be found.

Adjoining the gardens of the Sudan Club new quarters were built for the increasing number of bachelors. One block was christened Yellow Peril, and the other Peabody's. Nobody really knew what they were all in aid of, since assimilation with local women, although nominally discouraged, was very much a matter-of-fact affair. At that stage of the game few European women were in evidence; in any case new recruits into the Sudan Political Service were forbidden to marry for the first two years of their contracts. Thus 'comfort stations', 'sleeping dictionaries' and 'hidden agendas' were quietly allowed.

Like most equatorial African cities, Khartoum flourished at sundown when the fierce desert heat of the day dropped. A molten pool of golden red light tinted the flamingo coloured waters of the Nile, whilst a cool stillness enveloped everyone and everything. When the wild desert storms whipped up the *haboub*, all living creatures ran from the raging

Visitors and curio sellers on the verandah of the Grand Hotel, Khartoum. (DURHAM UNIVERSITY - SUDAN ARCHIVES)

dust and howling wind than penetrated every nook and cranny with its gritty eeriness.

The first hotel to appear on the river frontage was the Grand. It was owned and run by the Railways Administration, which also started up-country rest houses as well as the Hotel at Juba (opposite Gondokoro), and the Nile Hotel at Wadi Halfa. Other establishments soon sprung up, bearing imperial sounding names like The Royal, The Gordon, The St. James, The Victoria and The Acropole. But the Grand Hotel became an institution in its own right. Originally a double storey wooden edifice facing the river, it had 50 bedrooms, with bathrooms spread conveniently down the corridors, and fans interminably churning the hot air into circulation. On the open verandah, a rich assortment of all manner of traders and dealers plied their wares and bargained with the guests. It was the hub-bub of society outside the Clubs. The locals ebbed and flowed, through the long, cool corridors, carpeted with matting, and out into the adjoining gardens. A representative of Thomas Cook was always in attendance and Nile steamers took off from the wharf at the water's edge.

At Grand Hotel dances most guests arrived on donkeys in full evening dress. Many of the men had to dance together as there were few women, even when the numbers were swelled by the sudden arrival of rare and welcome tourists.

Across the river at Omdurman the desert areas were laid out for recreation. As well as the race course and polo ground there were golf links with ancient Arab ruins serving as hazards. Sand-grouse shooting was a popular pastime especially on Fridays - the Muslin day of rest, when thousands of little birds from inland swept down on to the waters of the Nile.

The city encouraged a hotch-potch of every nationality under the sun, with trade and commerce run by masses of Greeks, Armenians, Italians and every shade of Arab. It became the jumping off ground for big game hunters, and therefore the happy hunting ground for fresh faced English girls.

In 1908 the bridge across the 1700 feet wide Nile was completed. It had 7 spans, carrying the railway, a road and a wide walkway. It was built by the Cleveland Bridge and Engineering Company who had just completed the bridge across the Victoria Falls (1905). Georges Imbault, their Chief Engineer, and the same team from Darlington assembled the construction.

The Khartoum of today stands as a mixture of grand Victorian and later edifices. It is perhaps the most Classic Colonial in all Africa, yet it has reverted to its Arab role. Aid workers are once again almost the only Europeans in evidence. Along El Nil Avenue (originally the Corniche) what was once the Grand Hotel is now the gracious new Grand Holiday Villa. Not far away lies the old Governors Palace, now restored in 'democratic' fashion as the Peoples Palace.

The eccentric little Sudan Club is open to anyone from Europe - and is still run on English Club lines as a last vestige of Empire. The original villa in the centre of town is complete with a swimming pool surrounded

The Grand Hotel front facing the River.

The Grand Holiday Villa today, built on the site of the Grand Hotel.
(Dr. El HUSSEIN)

by lawns and squash courts. Inevitably the restaurant serves English Nursery Food. "The real Sudan lies in the south - moist, undulating and exuberant", said Winston Churchill. South from Khartoum to Gondokoro, near Juba, down the White Nile for about a thousand miles, there was an all year round river service on the Sudan Government Steamers. The last 100 miles to the Ugandan border at Dufile (Nimule) had to be accomplished overland, because of the impossible rapids on the upper stretches of the river, locally known as the Bahr el Jebel.

During the 1850's Gondokoro was the greatest Arab slave-market in the whole of Central Africa, through which all slaves passed on their way to Khartoum. Baker annexed it for his headquarters in his punishing expedition in 1871. Wonderfully positioned on a cliff above the river this squalid collection of bamboo and straw huts and old brick European houses was humid, oppressive and buzzing with mosquitoes. The once great gardens became a wilderness of decay and desolation. Sleeping sickness wiped out all the nearby villages, and Gondokoro was closed down.

The Royal Hotel Khartoum

Across the river, Juba grew up to become the independent capital of the south. The Juba Hotel, once run by the Railways, became a government rest house in fading grandiose style. Greeks settled here and the Greek Club was the centre of night life.

Gordon's score of river-fronted Forts stretched right down from Fashoda almost as far as the Equator. The main ones in the south were Lado, Dufile (opposite Nimule) and Wadelai. The last was Fort Magunga, on the Victoria Nile near Lake Albert and the Murchison Falls. Nearby stands a village called Bugili - echoing to the sound of the ghostly bugle calls from across the river.

Each enclosed fort was at a papyrus-free point on the river with a clear view from both directions. Fronting the river was a landing stage and boat repair yard for all manner of river steamers and other craft. Earth embankments and a ditch fortified the other three sides, with cannons aimed across the open cleared areas outside, in case of attack. The centre of each fort held the administrative and living quarters for the officers, as well as stores, surrounded by the straw huts of the garrison.

Abundant game and Nile perch were always at hand, with an excess of local fruit and vegetables. The only connections with the outside world were

A group of Engineers on the construction of the Blue Nile Bridge. Left to Right: Georges Imbault (Chief Engineer, Clevelands); M.E.Sowerby (Chief Engineer, Sudan Govt Railways); J.S.Hill (Contract Engineer); P.C.Lord (Royal Engineers); R.F.Le Bailly (Contract Engineer) (DURHAM UNIV)

The road and rail bridge across the Nile at Khartoum, built by the Cleveland Bridge and Engineering Company and opened in 1908, three years after they had completed the Victoria Falls Bridge

the visits of the steamers bringing mail and supplies from Khartoum. If the regular service failed, an efficient runner service brought communications from one fort to the next along the river banks. Life was uncompromisingly monotonous, but everyone worked, and it brought such peace and stability that travellers were able to move unmolested from one fort to another.

Twelve miles downstream from Juba, where the Nile becomes a placid lake with an island, lies Rejaf. Founded in 1874 when Gordon's headquarters were moved from Gondokoro, it was taken over from the dervishes in 1897 by a Belgian Congo expedition which re-built the fort. After the Anglo-Belgian agreement of the Lado enclave it came under British rule.

In order to come to terms with the Belgians, the Lado Enclave, bordering the Nile, was leased to the Congo Free State by the Brtitish Government for the life-time of King Leopold. This territorial 'loan' of several thousand square miles was designed to facilitate a way through to the navigable Nile waterway from the land-locked northern regions of the Congo. It was also a Belgium quest to emulate the French by creating a barrier across Africa from the Atlantic to the Indian Ocean. Unlike the French, however, the Belgians were well established with missions and flying columns in outlying areas.

At that time the Congo Government prevented its merchants and officials from returning to Europe by the quick Nile Route. From the Lado Enclave this would have taken about 3 weeks. Instead they had to return

the long and perilous overland route through the Congo to the coast - taking up to 6 months - and then catch a Belgian steamer back to Belgium. Tragedies occurred more than once for the unfortunate officials. A former governor of Lado Enclave, named Renouard, started off on his return home at the end of his period of service. Instead of returning via the Nile route he had to travel through the Congo. On the way down the river the black sailors on his boat mutinied and massacred all on board, with the exception of Governor Renouard and his Engineer, who luckily escaped the fate of their fellows by jumping into the water and swimming to the shore. Once on land they made for the forest, where they hid themselves. The engineer succeeded in climbing into a tree, but the corpulent Renouard was unable to follow suit, and tried to hide under the leaves at the foot of the tree. The mutinous blacks, who were on the track of the fugitives, discovered him and under the eyes of the Engineer, cut him up and ate him alive. For two whole days they remained at the foot of the tree eating the poor Governors body, and only went off when they had

Vankerchoven, a Belgian steamer moored on the White Nile at the headquarters of the Lado Enclave, leased to King Leopold II as part of the Congo Free State until his death in 1910. An expedition was sent through in 1917 with the SS Anka to find the source of potential railway sleepers. (DURHAM UNIVERSITY - SUDAN ARCHIVES)

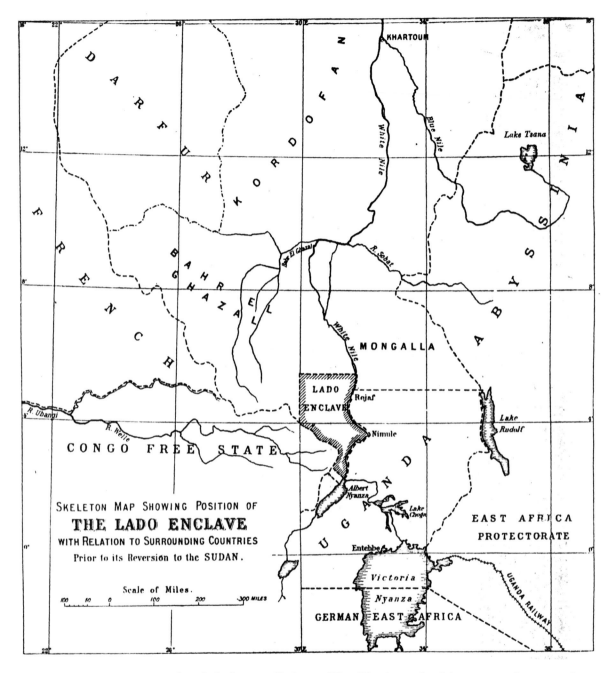

SKELETON MAP SHOWING POSITION OF
THE LADO ENCLAVE
WITH RELATION TO SURROUNDING COUNTRIES
Prior to its Reversion to the SUDAN.

Scale of Miles.

completed their cannibal act. The Engineer had just enough strength to get down from the tree and find the nearest military outpost.

A long forgotten hidden clause in the Lado Agreement allowed the Belgians facilities to construct a railway from the Congo to the Nile waterway in the enclave. One of the last British officers to join the Sudan

Government Railways in a military capacity in 1907 was one of Girouard's close team - Lieutenant Ralph Micklem of the Royal Engineers. Civil engineers were by then filling all the posts. With Lieutenant S.F.Newcombe, Micklem journeyed to the upper Nile to survey and discuss with the Belgians this possible rail link from the Lado Enclave into the Belgian Congo.

Nothing came of it. An interesting sequel to this plan occurred in the summer of 1920. There were rumours that the Belgium Government was willing to lease to Great Britain the eastern part of their Ruanda territory for the construction of an all-red Cape to Cairo rail-route, reviving Cecil Rhodes' original plan. This generous 'reciprocal' offer probably emanated from the long forgotten and by then defunct Lado agreement.

Travelling northwards from Rejaf to Khartoum the 1000 mile journey was by river steamer, passing through the Sudd. Boats were fitted with electric light, fans, hot and cold baths and mosquito netting. Swimming with the current, they sailed past picturesque little stations every 50 miles or so.

Kiro was the principle station of the Belgian Lado Enclave. Mongalla, a neat little garrison town surrounded by forests, was first occupied in 1901 by European and Egyptian government officials. Eighty miles further north was Bor, a dismal, mosquito-ridden place, where the river is less than a hundred yards wide, and the forest comes down close to the Nile. Swamp-lands stretched out, filled with hippos, crocodiles and aquatic birds. It was an inconvenient wooding station and the worst known location for bored colonial service officials. The depressing isolation was repeated at Sambe, 20 miles further north, where the real Sudd began.

The Sudd (meaning block), a massive growth of water plants and papyrus, was only cleared with the greatest difficulty and labour, and constant use of cutters and dredgers, to keep open a narrow waterway. Having battled through to Lake No, the boundary of the Sudd was reached - where the Bahr-el-Ghazal joins the White Nile from the west.★

★The 250 mile long, aptly-named Junglei Canal was built in recent times from Bor northwards to Taufikia near Malakal, to reduce the distance and avoid the worst part of the Sudd.

Arriving by steamer at dusk in some of the remote stations such as Tonga, wooding commenced, and sometimes went on almost all night. Completely naked natives pursued their task to the accompaniment of a monotonous chant, punctuated now and again by fierce shouts and battle cries, and occasionally by a shriek caused by dropping a log on some uncovered foot.

After Sobat, Taufikia - half-way to Khartoum, was an important well-built trade centre chosen by Baker in 1865. Monopolistic Greeks held sway. Nearby Malakal became more important when it took over from Kodok (adjoining Fashoda) lying further north, which was the original seat of government for the district. It was 'a damp hell for men and a heaven for mosquitoes', and the area of demarcation of the Arab-African division of the Sudan from north to south.

THE KOSTI EL OBEID LINE

In 1910 the railway was further extended from Khartoum to Senaar on the Blue Nile, and thence westwards to Kosti on the White Nile. From there it was subsequently extended to El Obeid, and opened by Kitchener. The mineral fields which drew this line southwards were already being developed on the Congo side of the Nile-Congo divide. For a long time it had been the ambition of Robert Williams to explore that region, so convinced was he of the rich discoveries he had made on other watersheds dividing the other great rivers of Southern Africa. It was these discoveries that led the Cape to Cairo Railway to advance step by step into the interior of the continent.

Menu to celebrate the opening of the line from Khartoum to El Obeid by Lord Kitchener in 1912

MENU

EL OBEID, KORDOFAN. Feb. 27th 1912

CAVIAR RUSSE

CONSOMMÉ AUX POINTES D'ASPERGES

SOUFFLÉS DE SAUMON

FOIE GRAS EN ASPIC

COTELETTES DE MOUTON

DINDON FARCI, LÉGUMES

MACÉDOINE DE FRUITS

CRÈME AUX CERISES

SCOTCH WOODCOCK

In 1925, with the help of Major Christy, Williams obtained a prospecting concession over 60,000 square miles from the Sudan Government. He wrote:

"An expedition is now at work in the area and will, it is hoped, discover mineral wealth in such volume as to justify the Sudan in extending their railway system from El Obeid in a southerly direction to connect with the Belgian railway from Stanleyville (Kisangani) to Ponthierville (Ubundu).

If this is effected a complete rail and river route will be established between the Northern and Southern extremities of the African Continent." The line now runs to Wau, only 200 miles from the Congo frontier.

23

CONFRONTING THE FRENCH

MARCHAND'S CONGO-NILE EXPEDITION

"Fashoda is only a symbol.
The great issue is the control of the whole valley of the Nile."
Joseph Chamberlain, Colonial Secretary.

Kitchener's rapid advance up the Nile to the Sudan would not have been possible without the railway. He admitted to Rhodes that if he had not received the 5 locomotives originally destined for the Cape Colony and then diverted to Egypt because of the engineering strike in Britain, the Nile Expedition would have been postponed for at least a year. He had written to Charles Metcalfe expressing the hope that when the lines reached Khartoum the Bechuanaland Railway Company would reclaim its five locomotives.

In this sense the Railway, and also the crucial part played by the Telegraph, thwarted the French occupation of Upper Egypt by Commandant Marchand's Expedition.

Jean Baptiste Marchand (1863 -1934) set out from the mouth of the Congo River on the West coast of Africa literally within days of Kitchener's departure up the Nile from Cairo. For over two years a total of 45,000 porters, mostly conscripted, battled 2000 miles across equatorial Africa with hundreds of tons of supplies and a 60 feet demountable steel boat.

The French 'Grand Design' was to establish outposts all the way across Africa through the vast province of the Bahr-el-Ghazal, and so join up their possessions in the Congo with Abyssinia. The brilliant 40 year old statesman Hanotaux accentuated French interests in West Africa, and for several years he dominated their colonial activity. The utmost expansion of France in Africa was his aim; a great scheme to reach down the continent from the Mediterranean to the Congo, and to transverse it from the Atlantic to the Red Sea. Above all he hoped to constrain Britain's hold over the Nile regions.

Two years after setting out, Marchand's expedition reached its destination of Fashoda on the west bank of the Nile, without a single loss of life through either disease, battle or accident. They had won the race to the upper reaches of the river, since Kitchener had only just re-taken Khartoum, and had not yet ventured further south. But no sooner had the Tricolor been planted on the banks of the river than Marchand was overtaken by events.

The Abyssinian force which he was supposed to join up with failed to turn up. As they settled in at the old slave post of Fashoda - a group of ruined buildings surrounded by a few palm trees, they were attacked by

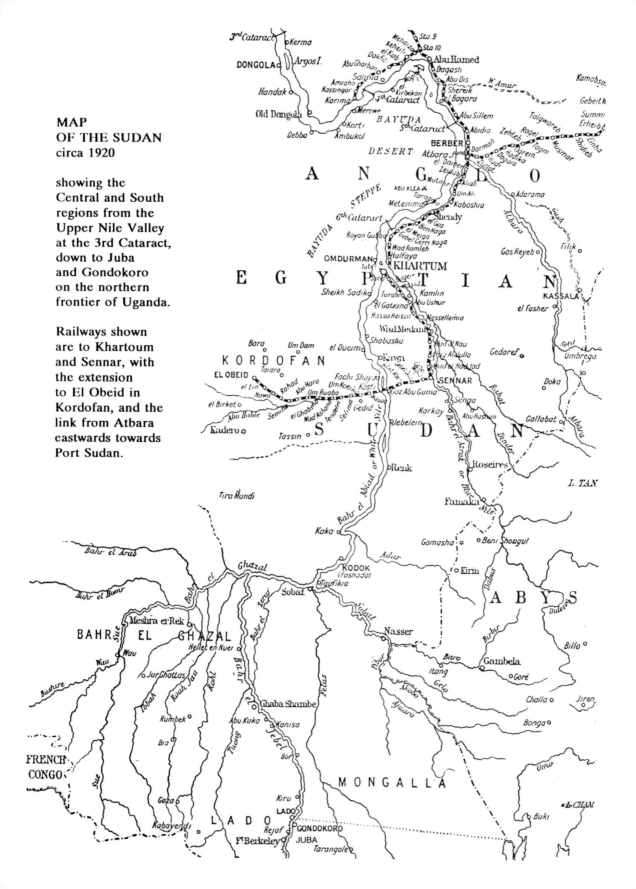

MAP
OF THE SUDAN
circa 1920

showing the
Central and South
regions from the
Upper Nile Valley
at the 3rd Cataract,
down to Juba
and Gondokoro
on the northern
frontier of Uganda.

Railways shown
are to Khartoum
and Sennar, with
the extension
to El Obeid in
Kordofan, and the
link from Atbara
eastwards towards
Port Sudan.

the Mahdi's forces and ran low on ammunition. At the last moment their steel boat arrived down the river with more supplies.

A month later, Kitchener arrived by gunboat with a large force. In the name of Egypt, and not Great Britain, he hoisted two flags in an elaborate ceremony on the river bank, complete with kilted Scottish Highlanders and a 21 gun salute for the Khedive of Egypt.

It was a stand off. In the name of France, Marchand stood firm. That evening the two protagonists dined and wined on copious Champagne brought by the French across Africa. The chivalrous Commandant Marchand retired to await the outcome of British - French government negotiation. But Kitchener had access to one vital aid, which the French were denied. This was the British Telegraph system which ran alongside the railway, and all the way down the Nile to Khartoum. With exaggerated claims, he passed word to the British government, via Cairo, of his paramount position, and the hopeless situation of the French. Meanwhile Marchand was unable to communicate. He was denied the use of the telegraph except from Cairo, which he took weeks to reach; and when he did, it was too late.

For months on end the French hoped that they would be able to extract concessions of territory from the British, retain a right of way across Africa and the use of the outposts which Marchand had left behind him. At the very least they wanted a 'French' open waterway along the Bahr-el-Gazal section of the Nile. But Salisbury and Chamberlain refused. Confrontation was in the air. On both sides of the channel intensive preparations for hostilities went on night and day. It appeared that war was inevitable.

In the end, the French Government - and particularly the French Army - totally distracted and divided by the scandalous Dreyfus affair, backed down, and forced Marchand to withdraw.

As the gallant French pulled out, Kitchener's forces stood on the banks of the Nile. The officers saluted with their swords, and the Sudanese presented arms as the Highlanders band played the Marseillaise. The brave little expedition sailed down the Nile into oblivion - ending forever France's trans-African ambitions.

When Marchand arrived at the French Enclave of Djibouti he was met by the Governor and a Guard of Honour. A special train was laid on, and the small party was escorted the 20 miles from the Port to the Town. Thus they travelled on the last leg of their journey across Africa, along the only section of line ever built by the French as part of their cherished and abandoned Trans-African Railroad.

Marchand never set foot in Africa again, and never spoke of Fashoda. In a gesture of chivalry by the British, the name was erased from maps and replaced by 'Kodok.'

Under the Anglo-French Agreement of 1899, France was given

thousands of extra square miles of barren desert, in return for which she agreed to stay away from the Nile - forever.

A century later Marchands's name is still a bye-word, substituted for the word 'Marchons' in the *Marseillaise* by patriotic Frenchmen of the old school. Chivalrous, expedient, steadfast, and largely successful though his expedition to Fashoda was, it was hugely overrated. Ewart Grogan reckoned that he hardly touched an inch of new territory, but merely carried out an excellent piece of transport organisation with everything in his favour - including unlimited funds for one of the best equipped expeditions ever to set foot in Africa. There was no difficulty in obtaining carriers, by compulsion if necessary. They reached the Nile-Congo divide through hundreds of miles of navigable waterway, and then they simply moved from post to post until they reached the waters of the Nile. The only real difficulty, that of re-occupying the Bahr-el-Ghazil outposts, had been achieved by the Belgians, who the French had then kicked out.

Citizens of Nubia. Berbera Arabs on the Upper Nile c. 1920

The former French Foreign Minister Hanotaux, who 2½ years previously had sent Marchand's expedition on its way, reckoned in hindsight: "It was impossible to foresee at the time, the construction of a Railway which despite the desert and cataracts, would become in the sequel the instrument of Anglo-Egyptian victory over Mahdism."

Few today have heard of either Fashoda or Marchand; victims of betrayal by a perfidious French Government.

Without a shot being fired the entire Nile basin from the Equatorial Lakes to the Mediterranean became in effect part of the British Empire.

24

EGYPT

THE END AND THE BEGINNING

"Drink of Nile water", say the Arabs,
"and you will return to drink it again".

"Drink from the waters of the Nile and you will never drink again;
you will die of enteric fever", said the British

When Napoleon was defeated by Nelson at the Battle of Abu Qir, the French ambled out of Egypt in the early 1800's after an era of debauchery and destruction, having sold their mistresses to the arriving British. Yet they retained a discreet presence, and left an envious legacy of chic French culture, together with a hint of the Levant.

Napoleon's great plan had been to cut off England from her imperial jewel - India. The British had little intention of staying on in Egypt permanently; there was not even a garrison at Alexandria. The prime aim was to forge an overland rail-route to the Indian sub-continent, as well as maintain a Telegraph line via Malta and Alexandria to Bombay, and thence onwards to Singapore and Australia. So the safety of Egypt was the key to the whole eastern Empire.

The desert caravan route was the link between the Mediterranean and the Red Seas. The only alternative was the long ocean journey thousands of miles around the Cape of Good Hope. Napoleon's engineers had already proposed the idea of a water-way to connect the two seas, but they had miscalculated the difference between the levels by as much as 32 feet. The scheme was rejected due to the cost of building enormous locks. As early as 1825 a British Engineer, Alexander Galloway, re-calculated the levels with more modern equipment, and found that a navigable canal was perfectly feasible. James Vetch, a Royal Engineer, later expanded the idea and planned a water-way which was essentially the same as that of Ferdinand de Lessops, the ultimate builder of the great Suez Canal.

The warrior Pasha Mohammed Ali had built himself up as a powerful ruler of Egypt, under the thumb of the Sultan of Turkey.

He had destroyed the rival gangs which had roamed and terrorised the streets of Cairo and Alexandria, and looted the countryside. These included a few left-over deserters from Napoleon's armies who had become independent war-loads. In a 'Night of the Long Knives' in 1811, Mohammed Ali had treacherously invited 500 of them to a banquet. He locked the gates, and all of them - including their retainers and families, were butchered. It was a grand consolidation of power, and the beginning of the next golden age for Egypt.

Mohammed Ali then turned his armies to conquering not just his neighbours, but against the Sultan himself. He even invaded Greece. but was repulsed by an alliance of European Powers. He wrung some concessions from Turkey, and succeeded in retaining the right of succession for his heirs; previously, the Sultan had always appointed the next Pasha in line.

Almost entirely single-handedly, he then energetically set about dragging Egypt into a semblance of civilisation, with everything from schools to hospitals, printing presses and workshops. Ancient canals were re-dug, and thousands of irrigation projects were started with water-wheels and furrows. Docks, shipyards and lighthouse were structured and a regular steamer service ran on the Nile. French agricultural experts imported cotton, and the miraculous climate soon ensured a rich harvest of this valued crop. The Greeks organised the production of olive oil and the Italians the weaving trade, and the Germans installed efficient machinery. For the time being only the British were out of the equation.

Whilst France was pushing the idea of a canal, Britain was vying for Mohammed Ali's attention to build a railway. Neither Power made much headway. He agreed, however, that the French scheme could be decided by an international commission consisting of French, German and British interests. One engineer was despatched from each side to make a site survey of the best route. To the chagrin of the French, the delegation concluded that a canal scheme was totally impractical. The British engineer on the commission turned out to be Robert Stephenson, none other than the son of George Stephenson, the Father of Railways and founder of the steam locomotive.

Britain continued to concentrate on the one field in which she was supreme - railways. In 1834, the same year in which Lieutenant Waghorn had opened his horse-drawn caravan route across the desert, Thomas Galloway had surveyed a railway line from Cairo to Suez. Rival canal interests fought hard to stop it. Materials shipped out to Alexandria were left rotting on the shore whilst the French were busy building the harbour nearby.

The ambitious Mohammed Ali was succeeded by his son, who reigned as Regent for only 2 months, before his demise. He was followed by a 35 year old grandson Abbas, who launched into an maniacal orgy of destruction against nearly everything that his grandfather had built. Hospitals and schools were closed, dams and irrigation schemes pulled to pieces, and the working farmers were driven to begging on the streets. Violently anti-Christian, ruthless, cruel, deceitful and lazy, he hired foreign mercenaries to protect him. French influence wained when he drove out nearly all the distinguished advisers that had surrounded his grandfather.

There was one single trait of this ignorant despot that became a blessing in disguise. Abbas spoke no language except Turkish, which Andrew Murray, the British Consul General was fortunately adept at. The canny Murray badgered him day after day with the idea of a railway, to link Alexandria with Cairo, and then across to Suez on the Red Sea.

As British influence steadily gained ground the Egyptians warmed to the idea of this new-fangled invention. They finally agreed to appoint a Chief Engineer.

Once again, Robert Stephenson appeared on the scene.

In 1851 he concluded a contract that was to make him a handsome profit without so much as paying for anything in the way of materials, labour or rolling stock. As he rubbed his hands with glee, the remaining Frenchmen looked askance, as their golden opportunity seemed to be slipping away in the desert sands.

The first railway line in Africa opened in 1854, from Alexandria to Cairo, with a break across the Nile, amid much pageant and perplexed relief from the 24,000 workers thoughtfully provided by Abbas.

When two years later Abbas was murdered in his sleep, a foretaste of British influence emerged. An attempt to install Abbas' son Ilhami as successor was forestalled by the British Consul General, in favour of his rightful heir and brother, Said - the last son of Mohammed Ali.

Said had been brought up by a French tutor, and introduced from an early age to the whims of international power politics, meeting ambassadors and envoys on an equal level, including the dashing young French diplomat Ferdinand De Lessops, with whom he struck up an enduring and endearing friendship.

It was the beginning of Egypt's *Belle Epoque*, an era of vast extravagance and increased influence of French, British, Italian, German and other European ideas and ideals. The country opened out to the Good, the Bad and the Ugly as more and more profiteers, racketeers and vagabonds arrived from across Europe. Almost all were accommodated by the sympathetic Said. In this climate of heightened generosity and unparalleled opportunity, De Lessops' overtures for a canal were not out of place. He negotiated a contract which was to bring Egypt to its knees, and milk the countryside of one third of the country's labour force, in the course of making a waterway to join Egypt from the 'Med to the Red'

De Lessops, the retired diplomat, knew nothing of engineering, little about business, and had no banking connections. He master-minded the trusting Said, who was naive at almost every aspect of contemporary living except playing soldiers in the sand with his vast army.

It took four years to find the finance before De Lessops' persistence turned to triumph. He had one useful family connection which became sublimely paramount. His pretty little Spanish cousin Eugenie had married Napoleon III - to become Empress of France.

Meanwhile the new British railway from Alexandria covered the 70 miles to the banks of the Nile, though as yet there was no bridge to cross it. On the opposing bank the line reached 50 miles down to Cairo, where a majestic new station of Minaret towers and Moorish arcades greeted the arrival of the stately English carriages on the wide European gauge, built by Robert Stephenson & Co.

Before the bridge was built across the Nile, each railway carriage was transported, one by one, on a flat-bottomed ferry craft. Then a tubular bridge was installed, but as the river was navigable at a low level, the bridge included a middle section which swung aside to allow the river craft to pass.

A 90 mile long rail extension through the desert to Suez was quickly finished, and so, finally, the race to link the Mediterranean with the Red Sea was won by the railroad. Boatloads of British troops arrived off-shore and were hurriedly rushed down the railway line, and then trans-shipped out again to quell the Indian Mutiny. Britain's lifeline for her eastern Empire was at last secured.

The change-over of power quickened. When Said died in 1863, he was succeeded not by his eldest son Ahmed, but by Ismail - a younger son. Ahmed's death in 1858 had been caused by a quirk of railway fate. His father had given a sumptuous party at his Palace in Alexandria. Ismail was unable to attend through illness, but a specially commissioned Khedival train carried his elder brothers, their wives and other potentates on the journey back to Cairo at dusk. Half way across the 400 feet wide river, the English engine driver failed to see that the swing section of the bridge was still open. The onlookers on the banks watched in horror as the engine and carriages crashed down into the turbulent waters. Unable to swim, the heir-apparent Ahmed was swept away.

When Ismail took over as Khedive, Franco-British rivalry was in full swing. In order to profit from the booming Egyptian Cotton trade, caused by the slump in America during the Civil War - the railways were rapidly expanded. Meanwhile France concentrated on the completion of the Suez Canal. Britain continued to oppose it, but realised that a waterway in foreign hands would be disastrous.

During Ismail's era of grand extravagance, which culminated in the country's bankruptcy, Cairo was transformed into the Paris of Africa, with numerous magnificent Palaces and great tree-lined Boulevards. Gas lighting was installed, and a railway was built out into the desert to the Spa and Hotel des Bains at Helwan.

Roads, Railways, Bridges, Canals and Telegraphs were all extended, and the Postal system was run on ultra-efficient lines by the British. But the price was high. In a bid to emulate and surpass all things European, no control had been kept of the Khedival purse strings, and no advice had been forth-coming from the greedy bankers. Ismail was in hock, "lock stock and barrel" to the Banks and money-lenders, from Rothschilds downwards. He only received between a paltry half and three-quarters of the capital advanced after deduction of fees. Almost everyone was corrupt; Turks, Albanians, Egyptians and international peddlers and meddlers. The Army was also corrupt. So a bunch of experienced American soldiers was invited from both sides of the Civil War to run the army on disciplined lines.

Each of his 14 wives was installed in an elaborate palace, but so vociferous was his appetite for women, that he turned to other quarters. One bizarre rumour had it that whilst in the throws of delight with one concubine, another beauty arrived as a gift from the King of Italy. Unable to entertain her, and in order not to offend the donor, he returned her together with two dozen railway locomotives. He was also known as the 'Pimp Pasha', after legalising prostitution and imposing a tax on all 'dancing girls'.

When the momentous construction project he had overseen, the Suez Canal, was finally completed in 1869, the country was bleeding.

Britain, America and Russia absented themselves from the opening ceremonies, but a representative of nearly every crowned head of Europe attended.

The Empress Eugenie, spouse of Napoleon the III, was naturally the prize figurehead and darling of the occasion. She arrived off Alexandria and took the 'English' train to Cairo to be feted at the Station by a Posse of Potentates and a Guard of Honour. Rail travel had 'arrived' in true Imperial style, as Thomas Cook eagerly noted - having been personally invited by de Lessops himself for the opening celebrations.

On the banks of the Nile, the Ghezira Palace had been expanded to house the Empress and her entourage on the grandest scale of all. Weeks of festivities followed. Where East met West, Arabian nights followed Omar Khayan banquets. The unfinished Opera House was awaiting the completion of Verdi's 'Aida'. He failed to finish it in time, and an alternative performance was miraculously substituted.

When the potentates and sovereigns had finally assembled for the grand opening, a great flotilla of over a hundred ships set sail down the new waterway.

Half way through the canal, the procession paused for another Khedival Banquet of unparalleled proportions. Nearly five thousand guests, including numerous gate-crashers, were served an eighteen course meal by an army of 500 cooks and a thousand Italian waiters. After this grand extravagance many guests returned home, rather than continue with this long-winded cruise - but the Empress Eugenie pressed on to the Red Sea. Meanwhile, De Lessops himself spent much of the time asleep in his cabin.

An enormous creation of the French sculptor Bartholdi, representing 'Egypt carrying the light of Asia' had been designed to overlook the Canal at Port Said. The equally huge cost of it forced Ismail to cancel the contract. It ended up as the Statue of Liberty in New York Harbour.

Ismail had little money left except his Suez canal shares. Hearing that the French were on the point of buying them, British Prime Minister Disraeli sped into action. A counter-bid was made and accepted, lasting for only 48 hours. With Parliament in recess, Disraeli turned to Rothschilds to finance the 4 million pound deal with British Government guarantees. Thus the great new water highway to India, which she had originally fought tooth and nail to stop, passed into British hands.

The overall control of Egypt passed out of Ismail's hands, effectively bankrupted. With the connivance of the French, another banker, Evelyn Baring - later Lord Cromer, took charge. Although bought at a huge price, he inherited from Ismail an astonishing legacy of infrastructure. Over a thousand miles of railways had finally been built and the telegraph line reached down to the Sudan. The railway had arrived at Assiut (Asyut) 230 miles south of Cairo, and half way to Aswan.

Ismail had been a skilled, cunning and sometimes cruel scoundrel one minute, but an astute diplomat at the same time. He recognised the need to drag Egypt out of Asia and from the clutches of the old Ottoman empire, into the Western political arena, and make it the leading light of Africa. For this he was as much an imperialist as Cecil Rhodes.

Having acquired control of the largest amount of arable land in the State, he did everything and anything that Rhodes would have done to alter rail routes to suit his ends. Railways were expensive toys, and against the advice of able, but somewhat blinkered surveyors and officials who short-tracked him, he engineered re-alignments to pass through areas of economic importance - like the most prosperous sugar and cotton mills. This is exactly what Lord Cromer suggested to Rhodes for his Cape to Cairo route: "Follow the (mineral) wealth step by step like milestones up Africa".

Cromer became one of the greatest of all Britain's imperial Pro-consuls, reforming virtually every aspect of Egyptian administration between 1883 and 1907. He launched revolutionary ideas to overhaul the country's antiquated irrigation system - to store water behind barriers in times of plenty and to release it slowly in times of drought.

Along the Nile, all the way to the Sudan's borders, water, dam and irrigation engineers - many of them experts from India - were beavering away. In the Nile Delta it was relatively easy, but along the upper river in the troubled Sudan, no facts or figures of the vagaries and quantities of water were available; and no forecast could be made until a railway reached there. For whoever controlled the headwaters of the Nile controlled the whole economy of Egypt and the Sudan. There was even an ambitious idea that the upper reaches could be diverted eastwards to open out vast new areas of irrigable land.

Although Ismail never ventured into the Sudan, his spirited plans to drag Egypt into the European 'way of life' involved regular communications. These included a steamer service on the Nile as far south as Wadi Halfa where the cataracts barred the way, and from where a short-lived railway was started. The Khedive was grandly reported to be "preparing an iron road and a team of iron horses into the heart of Africa, reaching south, to ensure Cairo was in touch with Khartoum 1500 miles by rail and river."

As Railway expansion continued from Cairo, onwards up the Nile, it also opened out the country to tens of thousands of tourists from Britain, for railways were the great levellers.

Whilst Thomas Cook's package-tour Nile Cruises, first started in 1860, were plying the waterways, along the river banks the railways chugged away on the same 4 feet 8$\frac{1}{2}$ inches of Europe. Wide comfortable coaches blazed a trail all the way to Aswan.

Near the quarries where the Pharaohs had obtained their pink granite, The Old Cataract Hotel was built like a Royal palace by Cooks to accommodate their expanding clientele of Egyptologists. It opened in 1899 in time to celebrate the first Aswan dam, one of the great engineering feats of the day, designed by Benjamin Baker - who had also designed the Forth Bridge.

The hotel's pink and white starkness stands in contrast to the perpetual blue sky and waters of the Nile flowing past. It became the haunt of the Aga Khan, and in later years, from its terrace Agatha Christie conjured up

The White Coaches of the wide-gauge Cairo Train at Aswan

View of Aswan c 1920 with the old Cataract Hotel on the far right

her 'Death on the Nile.' Imperial Airways passengers landed in flying boats on the waters nearby. From an overlooking rock setting, Belvedere Terrace guests gazed across at Kitchener Island with its botanical gardens, and at Elephantine Island. Also at Assuan were the Grand and Savoy Hotels.

At Luxor the Old Winter Palace Hotel, renowned as the oldest hotel in Upper Egypt, was similarly built to overlook the Nile from a luxuriant tropical setting.

The Winter Palace Hotel, Luxor c 1920

CAIRO

A mix of three continents under the Egyptian sun, Cairo was where the phantoms of the past mingled with British and French imperial opulence alongside the Nile, twisting like a silver thread on its way from its source in British territory, thousands of miles away in the Mountains of the Moon in Uganda.

Like Cape Town at the other extremity of Africa, Cairo was on the high road to India and Australia - the stopping off point for hordes of officials, Army and Navy men and well-heeled winter visitors.

Boom times came to Cairo from the 1870's onwards. Over one quarter of the city's population were non Egyptians. So scarce and expensive were villas, particularly after the property boom of 1903, that social life revolved around the principal hotels and clubs, each creating societies of their own.

Strolling down the road from the main railway station just inside the old wall of Cairo, the first hotel one came to was Shepheard's, facing the El Ezbekiya gardens. The original building had been a Palace and a harem which became the French headquarters when it was taken over by Napoleon on his entry into Cairo in 1798. It was the beginning of the European influence. The French brought chefs who introduced a new cuisine to local restaurants. When the British followed, a noted pattiseur

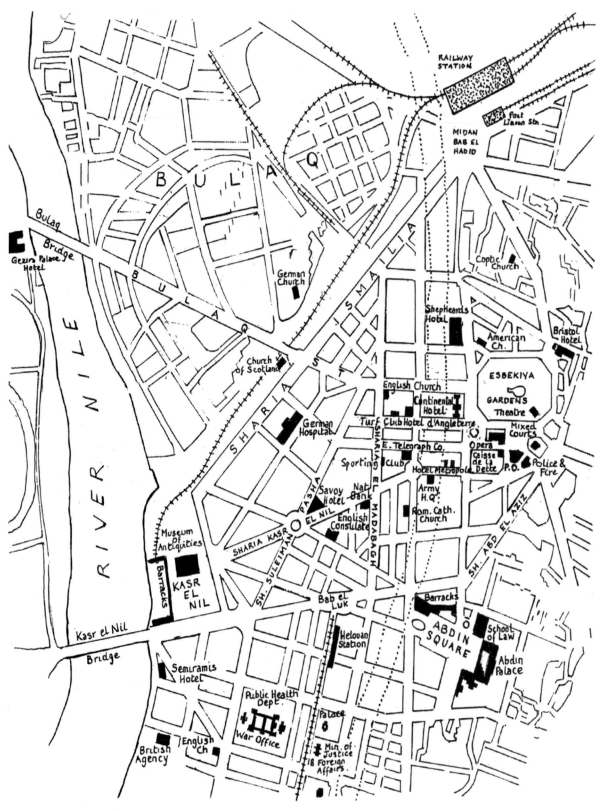

Central CAIRO circa 1900

Samuel Shepheard arrived from Northumberland; he turned the New British Hotel into a hostelry which became renowned as any in the world. It quickly became the lively rendezvous for the English. In 1856 the writer Trollope stayed at Shepheard's whilst negotiating an early contract with the Pasha for the passage of mails through Egypt, en route to India over the newly opened railway lines. Three years later Thomas Cook set up shop in the Hotel foyer offering Nile Cruises, over which he soon acquired an exclusive monopoly. Yet Mark Twain described it as the second worst hotel on earth.

When Shepheard's was completely rebuilt in 1891 not a single stone of the original hotel remained. The gardens and historical associations all vanished along with the time honoured tradition of clapping hands for service. Electric bells, lights and lifts appeared.

One of the first of the other grand hotels was the Bristol, which transported guests from the railway station by omnibus. Founded in 1836 as the Hotel du Nil, it had an oriental feel of wrought iron and graceful arches leading into a tropical garden location of orange and banana trees. On the other side of Esbekiya Gardens was the Opera House, which started life as a hastily erected brick and wood structure for the opening of the Suez Canal. On the next block stood the Grand Continental, and behind was the Turf Club. Once the British Agency occupied by Lord Cromer, it had a reputation for gossip and eccentric English behaviour.

Around the corner, the Khedival Sporting Club was exclusive in its own right and somewhat looked down upon by the British as the haven of

ALEXANDRIA-CAIRO EXPRESS.
EGYPTIAN STATE RAILWAYS.

'Gippos and Foreigners'. Founded in 1870 it included reading rooms and spacious billiard rooms that rivalled any of the London Clubs.

The Savoy Hotel had the reputation of being an old fashioned English establishment with some of the best suites and classic bedrooms, frequented by large numbers of the aristocracy and landed gentry. The Savoy Buffet, the New Bar and the Sphinx boasted American cocktails, Bass and Allsop's Ales.

Facing the Gardens of Esbekiya was the huge Grand Continental Hotel, the French favourite and the largest hotel in Cairo with 300 bedrooms. It also attracted the *jeunesse doré* of Pashadom. At first the rival, it then became the partner of Shepheard's Hotel.

The Esbekiya quarter was indeed famous for its hospitality and all kinds of decadent allures. These ranged from Santi's traditional cafe, which was one of the best restaurants in Cairo, to numerous others like the Eldorado which flashed beautiful Ghawazee dancing girls and the Grand Caffee Egyptien with its Bohemian girls. The Esbekiya Gardens and pleasure grounds contained a kiosque which was used in turn as a Casino, Ball room, Billiard room and Restaurant. Built in Moorish and Spanish style it stood in front of a lake with fountains and an ornamental park with aviaries.

The Seminaris was the only hotel overlooking the Nile. Favoured by the French, it ran one of the finest restaurants and held popular weekly dances.

The Grand Continental Hotel

The Ghezirah Palace Hotel (later called the Omar Khayan) on the

island of Ghezirah was in a class of its own. Built in 1865 as an opulent palace of the Khedive Ismail, it was enlarged for the Empress Eugenie whilst staying for the Canal opening ceremonies. Surrounded by luxuriant gardens and shady avenues, it sat in majestic splendour with views across the Nile. It was acquired by the Compagnie International des Wagons-Lits, along with Shepheard's Hotel, to harmonise their luxurious travel in

The Hotel Seminaris

The verandah of Shepheards Hotel, c 1925

(Thos Cook Archive)

sleeping-cars with equally grand creations at exotic destinations. The connection ended with the outbreak of the First World War.

The neighbouring Ghezirah Sporting Club had extensive croquet lawns, tennis courts, cricket and polo grounds, an 18 hole golf course and the Race course. The Membership was almost exclusively non Egyptian. The huge Park was the fashionable area for promenades and drives - the Rotten Row, or Rue de Roi of Cairo. It was also the mecca for illicit love affairs. Race Meetings became the social events of the Season in which ladies, dressed to kill, mixed with men in straw boaters. Champagne and foie gras picnics were served to the guests in wicker chairs under the jacaranda trees.

A lengthy stay at any of the grand hotels was a passport into Cairo Society. From January to April there was an incessant round of receptions, dinner parties, balls, picnics, gymkhanas, theatricals, tennis parties and other get-togethers. Each hotel in turn gave a weekly ball so that it was possible to dance six nights out of seven throughout the Season.

Everyone wintering in Cairo looked upon it as a right to receive an invitation to the grandest balls of the Season - those of the British Agent and that of the Khedive, the titular sovereign of Egypt. The Khedive once returned the guest list sent to him by the American Consul General with the observation that only those of noble birth were entitled to invitations. The Consul promptly replied: "Every American Citizen considers himself a king in his own right." This brought the bemused Khedive to his bearings, and not only was the list passed, but invitations were also sent to all the guests at Shepheard's Hotel, en masse.

Shepheard's became the favourite of Anglo Indians, Australians and rich Americans. Its central location ensured it was the hub of conviviality and the fulcrum of British life. Sugary Turkish Coffee or syrupy Tea and Scones on the terrace was an institution of Cairo Cafe Society.

Across the verandah and down to the street passed all the famous explorers and personalities - from Speke and Baker to Kitchener. Gordon stayed before his last trip up the Nile to Khartoum. Wearing a pith helmet and long boots, Stanley got cold feet and long stares, every time he ventured outside. After his return from his near-disastrous expedition to rescue the eccentric German explorer, Emin Pasha, he moved out to the discreet Villa Victoria surrounded by a secluded garden. "To avoid the lounging critics that sat in judgement upon me at Shepheard's Hotel" he recalled.

In front of the verandah passed a noisy rabble of entertainers - jugglers, snake charmers, minstrels, jesters, porters, interpreters and itinerant traders of bogus antiques. The dust was kept at bay by the hotel's own water-boy with squirts from his water bag.

In the adjoining streets were a yelling crowd of donkey boys, and a whole range of desert Arabs, bejewelled pashas, and mysterious veiled figures. In the nearby bazaars and native cafes were snake dancers, and girls & boys, steeped in Eastern and Western vice, ostensibly banned by Government decree.

Other sights of Cairo's night life were the howling dervishes. An early guide book found these quasi-religious fanatics decidedly repulsive: "The beginning is comparably sober and restrained. The performers stand in a circle slowly bending their heads to and fro in unison, whilst ejaculating invocations to Allah in a peculiar kind of grunt. Gradually the swaying becomes more violent, the body being bent alternatively backwards and forwards, the shaggy black manes of the dervishes sweeping the floor. The groaning and grunting gets louder, and the pace of the backwards and forwards motions succeed each other so rapidly as to make some spectators giddy. Occasionally some of the more excitable fanatics will fall to the floor in a paraclysm of ecstatic emotion, which has all the appearance of a genuine epileptic fit. At this point ladies, who are usually well represented among the spectators, will be well advised to retire."

The end of April heralded the end of the Season. The Khedive and his entourage moved by train to the Montaza Palace in Alexandria on the coast.

Gazing across at the Pyramids of Cheops, 8 miles from Cairo, the Mena House Hotel was named after the ancient Egyptian Pharaohs. It was originally a hunting lodge of the Khedive Ismail, and was enlarged for the Canal opening celebrations to house European Royalty. Taken over by a

English couple it went through a succession of British proprietors. In stark contrast to the style of Cairo hotels, it was a heady mix of Anglo-Oriental splendour. Log fireplaces and oak carvings contrasted with in-laid furniture and exotic wooden balconies to capture the fresh breezes overlooking the sands surrounding the Pyramids.

Cairo had a London feel, with every conceivable shop and department store. There were English drapers, hosiers and hatters and of course tourist agencies such as the ubiquitous Thomas Cook, whose son had been the first to import such delicacies as York ham and Potted Shrimps. There were trams in Cairo, and, as in Khartoum, numerous donkeys. Even Kitchener rode a donkey to his office.

In 1912 Britain gave sovereignty to Egypt and the Khedive Fouad became King Fouad.

During the First World War, after the disastrous Gallipoli Campaign, thousands of wounded were treated in Cairo's hospitals. Meanwhile two hundred Generals moved into Shepheard's Hotel. In the entrance hall were posted the full range of social events and meetings of the Turf Club, as well as general orders for the military - for it was also an unofficial officers mess like the Mount Nelson in Cape Town.

However, the the first uneasy stirrings of nationalist uprising occurred in 1919 with the murder of British officials.

During World War II the hotel once again became 'lousy with Generals'.

Little more than a thousand miles separated Italian held Libya from the Suez Canal, Britain's lifeline for her Empire. Italians were the largest community in the ever-expanding and diverse range of nationalities. Black shirts were rampant until internment forced many out. The Greek Government in exile under King Paul of the Hellenes established itself in Cairo. French was still the language *de rigeur* of the aspiring classes from Debs to Wheeler-dealers. For the Allies it was a welcome haven. As the War progressed, Cairo was awash with wild rumours. The Great Flap came when everyone expected Rommel to arrive and seize Shepheard's as his headquarters in 1942. The Long Bar was so long and the service so slow that it would have been a serious deterrent to any efficient German takeover. Moreover, the neutral Swiss barman Joe had already concocted a lethal knock-out cocktail.

The German radio of the ultra-efficient Arab Service broadcast from Berlin such wild gems of propaganda that Hitler was a Muslin. The hallowed BBC were out of touch, so to counteract this, hundreds of soothsayers and holy men were roped in from around the mosques. They dispensed equally fantastic rumours, dreamt up by the Arab expert Laurence Graffety Smith's covert and overt propaganda department.

For many it was still 'fun in the sun.' The sound of laughter echoed

Visitors to the Sphinx and Pyramids of Giza c 1925

from the dance parties at Ghezirah, and the Muhamed Ali Club became the grandest place to be seen around.

The bubbly, charismatic Jacqueline Lampson was daughter of the eminent physician Sir Aldo Castellani. He had pioneered tse-tse fly research into sleeping sickness, and had then become Surgeon General of the Italian Forces in Abyssinia. She was the youthful spouse of Sir Miles Lampson, later Lord Killearn. To call him Plenipotentiary would be an underestimation. The extraordinary powers of this Ambassador at large made him, like Cromer before him, an Imperial Proconsul. He took firm control, manipulating King Farouk when nobody knew which way the monarch would jump, nor with whom he would run - the Axis or the Allies.

A keen Golfer and an even better Shot, Killearn combined both activities with diplomatic aplomb. He was once so pestered by the kites that disrupted his rounds at the Ghezira Golf links, that he organised a Shoot. Much to the consternation of the Egyptian hierarchy, he blasted away at these royally protected birds, as they swooped down to grab his golf balls

It was the heyday of Empire at its fatal best. As Killearn stood in the Royal Box at the Racecourse on Ghezira Island, the chords of the National

Anthem resounded over a grandiose English farewell party.*

Most of Cairo's activities continued in the same lively fashion right up to the revolution of 1952 which toppled the Monarchy. When nobody knew which way the winds of change were blowing, Farouk wavered between sacking his government, prevaricating, and playing the fiddle while Cairo was about to burn. Anyway, the Muslin Brethren found it hard to believe that the King was a descendant of the Prophet, since he went on honeymoon with his new wife during Ramadan. They became even more vociferous.

The Canal Zone was the melting pot of the mayhem to come, stirred up by the riff-raff. Strikes and violence set the ball rolling. Radical students and others lost patience with the King and his Ministers. Then the Egyptian government unilaterally and abruptly cancelled the Anglo-Egyptian agreement, and the Sudan agreement of 1899. Too little, too late, the Army moved in against the Muslin Brotherhood, Communists and Socialists.

The police, whose colleagues in the Canal zone had been forced to surrender with 41 casualties, sided with the mobs. Students and police marched shoulder to shoulder. BOAC planes were detained at the airport, and the staff molested.

Then the firebrands moved in. Barrow loads of petrol were wheeled into Cairo. One of the first places to be torched was that hallowed English institution, the Turf Club. The mob broke in and ransacked the place, killing the loyal doorkeeper. Forty Britons were killed inside and tossed on the flames. Ruthless gangs of ruffians cheered on the bystanders, whilst the police stood by and even cut the fire hoses.

More petrol arrived. Anything British was turned to the torch. Thomas Cook, Barclays Bank, BOAC, W.H.Smith, Western cinemas like the Rivoli, all the Jewish Stores, and British institutions like Morris Motors. Almost every Department store, Bar and Wine merchant in the city went up in smoke. Burning was followed by looting.

The only place left was Groppi's Coffee House.

In the afternoon it was the turn of Shepheard's Hotel. Curtains and furniture were piled into the blaze. The domed glass ceiling crashed down. Half dressed and clutching jewellery, the Italian opera girls rushed out. One jumped to her death to escape the flames.

Many cheered as the flames flickered over the last 'Bastions of the British'. But for other Egyptians it was a sad occasion. The aspirations of Mohammed Ali, Said and Ismail to leap into the modern world, and make Egypt the leading light of Africa, evaporated before their eyes. It was the excellence of all things European that went up in smoke - French, Italian, Austrian, German, as well as British.

Cairo was where the Railway started in 1854, and Cairo was where the dream of all Red route through Africa really came to an end.

Footnote: When War ended Lord Killearn turned his back on Africa and was Appointed Commissioner in S.E.Asia. He wasn't sure whether it was "Promotion, Demotion or Commotion".

SUNDOWN

As a man not noted for religious zeal, Cecil Rhodes nevertheless embraced Livingstone's doctrine of Christianity, Commerce and Civilisation. He added a crucial fourth dimensional 'C' for Communication, of which the Cape to Cairo Railway and the Trans- Continental Telegraph were the principal means of advancement through *terra incognita*. In this first golden age of globalisation, he launched the latest communications techniques to speed the advance of his business Empire, to become the unparalleled business leader of the day.

The Colossus of Africa also had great plans for a universal Imperial British family. This Federation would include the United States of America and Germany, to regulate not just Africa but the whole world. In formulating his legacy of Rhodes Scholarships for the helms-men of this Trio of Nations, he urged his trustee Lord Rothschild to emulate the aspirations of the Jesuit Missionary-Explorers. "Take the constitution of the Jesuits if obtainable", he scribbled, "and insert English Empire for Roman Catholic religion".

He admired the principles of their perfectly ordered and regulated society, and he was particularly entranced by the near utopian paradise they had created in their 'Jesuit Republic of Paraguay,' which flourished during the 17th and 18th centuries. This sophisticated South American State, almost the size of Western Europe, embraced not just Paraguay, but the whole of Argentine and Uruguay, parts of Bolivia and a huge slice of Brazil.

The largely Spanish missionaries created not only a new society, but a vigorous state comparable with, and even surpassing that of the Incas. The degree of civilisation reached was certainly higher than anywhere else in the new world at that time. Their towns had paved streets before Buenos Aires and Lima; their churches were comparable in grandeur to the cathedrals of Europe; their musicians astonished visitors. There was no coinage, no capital punishment and no private property. Their tea plantations and cattle ranches were the finest on the continent; and their communications by road and river were more efficient than anything existing there today.

This experiment lasted for 150 years and attained a level of almost unbelievable fulfilment until it came to an abrupt end, when the missionaries were banished by the civil authorities of Europe - namely Spain, Portugal and France - jealous of the success of their stoic stand against colonial exploitation and greed.

In the early nineteenth century, this revolutionary ideal was romantically viewed by the great French philosophers Voltaire and Rousseau as the perfection of a Christian communist community in which everything was held in joint ownership for the equal benefit of all. At the end of the nineteenth century, when Rhodes came on the scene, it was being viewed by the pioneers of the Labour movement as the perfect pattern for British socialism. Robert Cunninghame-Graham, the Radical Parliamentarian, and one of the founders of the British Labour Party, was particularly attracted by what appeared to him the absolute harmony of the ideal socialist state. In 1901 he immortalised it in 'The Vanished Arcadia'.

Rhodes admired the equality among the members of a community in which recent savages were made to work not just for themselves but for the public good. This admiration was certainly well-tempered with a knowledge of the tremendous Jesuit influence in the opening up of Africa. The Portuguese Jesuits had first explored the Zambezi regions, and indeed, one of them is believed to have been the first man ever to have traversed the continent from the Atlantic to the Indian Ocean. These front line missionaries were not just the shock-troops of the Vatican, but the precursors of modern, controlled and benign colonialism; and the doctrine of their constitution was what Rhodes based his own parameters on. He recognised their aims as the nearest that could be achieved in a state in which they were at the same time - founders, law-makers, pontiffs and sovereigns.

A sequel to this was the conclusion reached in the 1930's by the socialist writer J.B.Priestly, later re-kindled by Laurens van der Post, that parts of the British Empire - which included the Anglo-Egyptian Sudan before the First World War, were the nearest that the world has seen to a truly Platonic Society, in which everyone worked for the equal harmony of all.

As described by Phillip Caraman in 'The Lost Paradise' this utopian ideal was also partially apparent until well into the middle of the twentieth century in the country named after its founder - Rhodesia (Zimbabwe). There, a doctrine of 'parallel' development, in contrast to the strict separate development, or *apartheid* system, of South Africa, was evolved. In the self-governing Colony of Southern Rhodesia, the Upper House of Parliament was comprised almost entirely of Chiefs, who were left largely to administer their own territories, in accordance with their own traditions, and in which European settlers were forbidden from trade and exploitation. Yet the neighbouring farmlands, laid out alongside, with identical qualities of land, were to be used as successful examples of good land husbandry by the settlers. This short-lived Federation which was formed with the two neighbouring territories of Northern Rhodesia (Zambia) and Nyasaland (Malawi) to enhance racial partnership in the 1950's, was given no chance of survival. Like the successful Jesuit experiment in South America, the African attempt was doomed by the international Dross.

It was the End of the Era of African Achievement and Advancement. As the countries of northern Europe had reached down for expansion into Africa with its space, silence and sunshine, the roles were reversed. Those from the sunny south reached up for financial aid, as their infrastructures crumbled and their Railways rattled to pieces.

Today, hardly a single scheduled rail passenger service crosses any national frontier in Africa. Apart from the Tanzam Railway, no rail link of any consequence has been completed on the continent since colonial times. The Benguela Railway has been closed for over a quarter of a century, whilst the second longest bridge in the world at Sena, remains impassible to rail traffic.

In financial terms Britain scored immeasurably from her African Empire. In contrast to other countries, most British colonies became almost entirely self-sufficient. They exported vast quantities of minerals and agricultural produce to countries around the world at large, with Imperial preference tariffs granted to sister nations in the Sterling Area. It was Britain's own 'Common Market'. And through the years the British Isles exported far more goods to her colonies than she imported back. This economic success story was the impetus that put the 'Great' into Great Britain.

The main economic goal of most of the world's Colonial Governors was to attain economic self-sufficiency and not rely on the mother country. Few succeeded. Belgium was almost bankrupted by its Congo Free State, in spite of sitting on the richest mineral fields in the world. France was thwarted in her aim of a Trans African Railway and Highway from the Atlantic seaboard to the Red Sea through territory which was largely sterile. Germany, the other great Railway builder in Africa was unfortunate in her ambitious plans and the circumstances of World War One. Africa's oldest (and Europe's smallest) colonial power - tiny, tottering Portugal - struggled to survive to the end of the 1970's. Almost all her African railways were built by the British. Last in the scramble for Africa, Italy's fledgling Empire depended on the mother country for over three-quarters of its budget. Mussolini's idea of copying the Roman Empire included plans to traverse Africa from Libya to Eritrea, engulfing Egypt and the Sudan. These ambitions were expounded by Gabriele d'Annunzio, the Poet, who stated the view of a nation well noted for its rhythmic oratory:
"Africa is the whetstone on which we shall sharpen our swords for a supreme conquest of the unknown future."
It meant everything and said nothing.

The last word should come from the ordinary African; the railwayman on the remote siding at the highest point of the Great Central Plateau - Tara, the Hill of Hope, named after the seat of the ancient Kings of Ireland, where dissident tribes had met at the crossroads of the five main highways.
Amid the chaos and calamities, the famine and hardships, rests the simple and sincere belief than in the end everything will turn out alright:
"When we were together things worked better. Now we don't know what might happen tomorrow. But this is the way we live in Africa."

A Railwayman's family at Tara Halt, Zambia, a remote siding with no communications at the highest point of the great central plateau, 4359 feet above sea level. The Congo Expresses use to cross here, midway between Bulawayo and Broken Hill (Kabwe). When the 'mile-a-day' platelayers passed through in 1908 it was named after the Hill of Tara, seat of the High Kings of Ireland with commanding views across the Emerald Isle, where dissident tribes had met at the crossroads of the five ancient highways. (AUTHOR)

Thus in my corner, I dreamed dreams of yesterday
which, as a man grows old, is common so they say.
The engine whistled, and my train went on its way.

Myles Bourke
The Koppie on a Plain

PERSONNEL

Some of the Personnel engaged on construction of the southern and central sections of the Cape to Cairo Line, including the Beira Railway, the Benguela Railway and the Uganda Railway.

Abbreviations: Bngl = Benguela. Conslt = Consultant. Contr = Contractor. Clvlnd = Cleveland Bridge & Engineering Co.
Eng. = Engineer. N.R.R.= Northern Rhodesia Railways. P & Co = Pauling & Co. Tran Zam = Trans Zambezi Railway.

Anderson, Robert. Chf. Eng. Uganda.
Butler, James. Indep. Contr. Also P & Co.
Beit, (Sir) Alfred. Chm. BMR
Boulton, R. P & Co. Surveyor
Beal, (Col) K. P & Co. Beira Rlwy, Admin
Bissett, J.L. G.M. Bechuanaland Rlwy Co.
Brown, "Long". Benguela Rlwy
Britton, A.C. early Photog. Beira Rlwy
Bremner, (?). Loco Eng. Uganda Rlwy
Bramley. W. Beira Rlwy
Buchan, C.V. P & Co. Beira, & Bngl
Buchan. F.E. (Frank) P & Co. Paymaster
Buchan-Syderf, A. Eng. Uganda Rlwy
Carter, H.C. P & Co.Agt, E. Afr, Congo
Cathcart, d'Arcy. Trnspt. Beira Rlwy
Clayton, J. Eng. Uganda Rlwy
Cooper, A.E. P & Co. Zambez
Corner, C. Chf. Eng. Beira Rlwy & RR
Cleary, Edwin. Assoc. P & Co.
Curtis, J. S. (Ben) Scty. G. Pauling
Creeyer, (?). P & Co. Beira Rlwy
Charlton, G.M. P & Co. Beira Rlwy
Cumberpatch, (?). Engineer N.R.R.
Chapman, James. Benguela Rlwy
Church, Richard. Survey, Uganda Rlwy
Church, Arthur. Survey, Uganda Rlwy
Carpmael. Eng, Uganda Rlwy
Delgardo, Edouardo. Valet G. Pauling
Duthie, R.A. Engineer Benguela Rlwy
Dean, R.B.P & Co. Beira Rlwy
Duncan, (?). P & Co. Survey Umtali
Evans, B. P & Co. Beira Rlwy
Everard, C. P & Co. Surv, V. Falls Rlwy
Elliott, Edwin. Contr, G.W.R. & Ireland
Erlanger, (Baron) Emile. Banker P & Co.
Erlanger, (Baron) Frederik. ditto
Ende, Max Am. Bridge Des Assoc
Eastwood, (?). Chf. Acct. Uganda Rlwy
Freeman, Ralph. Co-Des. Vic. Falls bridge
Firbank, Christopher. Early Ptnr. P & Co.
Fretton, W.H. P & Co Tran Zam Rlwy
Fox, Beresford. Fox & Ptnrs. Cons. Eng
Frame, James P & Co Surv. B.M.R.
Farrar George. P & Co. Agt. Queenstown
Ferguson, Jimmy. Assoc. P & Co.
Francis, Bill. Assoc. P & Co.
Griffiths, (Sir) J. N Contr. Bngl. E. Af.
Grove, Frank. P & Co. Eng. Benguela
Guarracino, H. P & Co. Grce, Trky etc
Geldenhys, (?). Trspt . Kafue. P & Co.
Gibbons, William. P & Co. Constr. Beira

Gailey, (?). Eng. Uganda Rlwy
Hull, P.W. P & Co. Beira Rlwy
Hillnick, R.J. P & Co. Beira Rlwy
Hickes, E.W. P & Co. Kalomo, Magadi
Harris Rutherford. Doctor Cape
Haynes-Lovell, H. Doctor. P & Co. Beira
Hobson, George. Des Vic. Falls Bridge
Homer, E.E. Eng. Benguela Rlwy
Hoy, W.W. G.M. Cape Govt Rlwy
Hyland, J.F. P & Co. Beira Rlwy
Haslam, Capt. Transport, Uganda Rlwy
Imbault, G Eng. Clvlnd. V.F. & K'toum
Jackson (Sir) John. Civil Eng.
Jansen, Johan. P & Co. Agent Cape
Johnstone, Fred. P & Co. Hunter Beira
Keith, John. P & Co. Agent. P.E.
Lee, D.O.E. P & Co. Beira Rlwy
Leane, G.H. Surveyor P & Co.
Lawley, Alfred L. Eng. Partner P & Co.
Lawther, Jimmy. Assnt. Varian, Beira
Lawson, James. Catering Contr. Beira
Larsen (X). Guard turned Hunter Beira
Menaut, Jean. Hotelier & Hunter Beira
Mahoney, Dan. Hunter Beira, and N.R.
Macdonald, (Capt) J. R.E. Surv., Uganda
MacDonald, (?). Platelayer, Beira Rlwy
Murphy, P./Man. P & Co. Congo
Meik, C Cons. Eng. P & Co. London
Mansergh, P. St. G. Surv. P & Co. C. Af
Marsland, E.R. P & Co. Congo & Zam.
McInerry, (?). Eng. P & Co.
Mybergh. H.H. Assnt. H. Pauling, Cape
Machado, J. (Col. Sir) Gov.Moz. & Dir.
Machado, Marianno. Gen. Man. Benguela
Moore, A.M. P & Co. Chief Eng. Beira
Metcalfe, (Sir) C Conslt. Eng. Fox
Micklem, RR.E. Sudan. & N.R.Rlwys
Mayer, J. P & Co Beira Rlwy
Martin, A.H. P & Co. Beira Rlwy
McClaughlan, Trspt. Rider, Zeederburg
McGregor, (?). Masonry - Contr. P & Co.
McColl, F. Drgh't P & Co, Grahamstown
McNab, Ramsey. Hotelier. Assoc. P & Co.
Mostert, Pieter. Stores P & Co. Kimberley
McCullogh, Chief M.O. Uganda Rlwy
Neumeyer. P & Co. Hunter Beira Rlwy
Newman, H.M. P & Co. Beira Rlwy
Nott, G. P & Co. Beira Rlwy
O'Flaherty, Rory. P & Co. Beira & Ug
Ormsby, O.C. P & Co. India and Magadi
Ogilvy, (?). Eng. Uganda Rlwy

Patterson. (Col) J.H. Eng. Uganda Rlwy
Pizzighelli, Richard. Eng. P & Co. E. Line
Paulin (X) P & Co. Hunter Beira Rlwy
Pauling, Henry. Chief Eng. Cape Rlwys
Pauling, George. Snr. Partner P & Co.
Pauling, Harry, Partner P & Co.
Pauling, Harold. P & Co. Chf. Sthn Afr.
Pauling, Percy. Eng. P & Co. Bombay
Pauling, Willie. Doctor/Assoc. P & Co.
Pauling, Richard. Eng. Delhi; Cape
Parry or Percy, E. P & Co Beira Rlwy
Phillips, G.J., P & Co. Surv. Maf - Byo
Penfold, W.F. P & Co. Surv. Maf - Byo
Pooley, Henry. Sec. Pauling. I/C Victuals
Preston, A.H. P & Co. Beira Rlwy
Preston, Ronald. Eng. Uganda Rlwy
Price, T.R. Traffic Man. Cape Govt.
Rudland, Thomas. Eng. P & Co. Beira
Rawling, A.T. P & Co. Beira Rlwy
Robins, E.R. Chf. Res. Eng. Benguela
Rosher, E. P & Co. Surv. Maf - V.Falls
Reynolds, (?). Eng. Uganda Rlwy.
Rawson, Frank. Eng. Uganda Rlwy
Roberts. Assnt Eng. Uganda Rlwy
Ryall, Supt. Police, Uganda Rlwy
Smith, W.F. P & Co. Beira Rlwy
Smith, Bertram.P & Co. Surv. Maf - Byo
Simms, J.C. P & Co Surveyor Maf - Byo
Soley, Alexis. later Chf. Res. Eng. Beira
Southwell, C.H. Eng P & Co. Zambezi
Stephens, F.O. Manager P & Co.
Scott, John. Ptnr. P & Co. London
Sweetman, Walter. P & Co. Magadi Line
Sewell (Maj) Transport Beira widening
Spooner. Eng. Uganda Rlwy
Sandiford. Loco. Supt. Uganda Rlwy
Tucker, A.H. P & Co. Surv. Benguela
Tower, W. Eng. Vryberg, V. Falls, Kalomo
Tristram, C.F. P & Co. Mozbq, Greece
Todd, (?). P & Co. Beira Rlwy
Townsend, S.F. Chf. Res. Eng. Rhod.
Tron, A.C. P & Co. Beira Rlwy
Upsher, Bill. Hunter. Assoc. P & Co
Varian.Harold E.Conslt. Eng. Fox & Ptnrs
Williams, Dr. P & Co. E. Line and Beira
Walker, John. Contrctr. Cape Rlwys
Wibberley, Charles, G.M. Beira Rlwy
Whitehouse, George. Chf. Eng. Uganda
Wilsford, A.G. P & Co. Beira Rlwy

SELECTED BIBLIOGRAPHY

Railway Background

The Railway Navvies. Terry Coleman. Pelican.
The World the Railways made. Nicholas Faith.
Railway Engineers. Anthony Burton.
The Benguela Railway - First 150 kms. Article. African World.
Zanzibar's Bububu Railway. Kevin Prentice. Bahrain.
Railways of Southern Africa. O.S.Nock. A & C Black.
Historical Railway Journeys. Rhind & Walker. M. Walker.
Rhodesia Railways Pamphlet. Cape Colony 1909.
Reminiscences. Baron Emile d'Erlanger
Steam Locos of Rhod. Railways. Hamer. Books of Zimbabwe.
Railways of Rhodesia. A.H.Croxton. 1973.
Railways of Southern Africa. J.R.Day. Arthur Barker.
Railway Comes to Bulawayo. Louis Bolze. Rhodesiana.
Cape to Cairo. Mark Strage. Wolff.
When Life was Rusted Through. O. Letcher. Books of Rhod.

Travel and General

Through Wildest Africa. F.Ratcliffe Holmes. Geoffrey Bles.
Tales from the Dark Continent. Ed. Charles Allen. BBC.
From Cape to Cairo. E.S.Grogan. Nelson.
A.T.T. Article. R. Cherer Smith. Rhodesiana Society 1975.
The Scramble for Africa. Thomas Pakenham. Abacus.
Pax Brittanica. James Morris. Faber.
The Imperial Dream. Ed Grierson. Collins.
Great North Road. Lawrence Green. Howard Timmins.
Under a Sky Like Flame. Lawrence Green. Howard Timmins
When the Journey's Over. Lawrence Green. Howard Timmins.
Africa from Port to Port. M. Mott Smith. Harold Shaylor.
The Lost Paradise. Philip Caraman. Sidgwick and Jackson.
The Vanished Arcadia. R. Cunninghame-Graham.

Biographies

Cecil Rhodes. John Flint. Hutchinson
The Founder. Philip Rotberg. Southern Press
Rhodes. Sarah Millin. Chatto & Windus
Rhodes of Africa. Felix Gross. Cassell.
Brittania's Daughters. Joanna Trollope. Pimlico
Eminent Victorians in South Africa. V.C.Malherbe. Juta
Life of Jameson. Ian Colvin. Edward Arnold.
The Randlords. Geoffrey Wheatcroft. Weidenfeld.
Salisbury, Victorian Titan. Andrew Roberts. Phoenix
Some African Milestones. Harold Varian. George Ronald
Chronicles of a Contractor. George Pauling. Constable.
Autobiog. of an Old Drifter. Percy Clark. Books of Rhodesia.
Old Rhodesian Days. H. Marshall Hole. Macmillan
They were South Africans. John Bond. Oxford University Press.
The Meikle Story. Beverley Whyte. Graham Publishing.
Robert's People, Hutchinson & Martelli.
Rudyard Kipling. Andrew Lycett. Phoenix.

Central and Southern Africa

Out of the Crucible. Hedley Chilvers. Cassell.
The Yellow Man looks on. Hedley Chilvers. Cassell.
In God's White Robed Army. Dominican Sister. Maskew Miller.
Artisan Missionary on Zambezi. MacConnachie. America Tract.
A Scantling of Time. Tony Tanser. 1965. Stuart Manning.
Rhodesian Epic. Baxter & Turner. Howard Timmins.
This is our Land. Frank Clements. 1963.
Old Transport Road. Stanley Portal Hyatt. Books of Rhodesia
90 Glorious Years. John Creewel. Harper Collins.
Tropical Dependency. Lady Lugard. 1905
An African Adventure. Isaac Marcossun. John Lane
1000 miles in a Machilla. Mrs Arthur Colville.
A History of Johannesburg. G.A.Leyds. Nasionale Boekhandle.
The Transvaal from Within. Percy Fitzpatrick. Heinemann.
History of Southern Africa. Eric Walker. Longmans.
History of Southern Rhodesia. L.H.Gann. Humanities Press.
Rhodesian Rhymes. Cullen Gouldsbury. Books of Rhodesia.
To the Banks of the Zambezi. T.V.Bulpin. Books of Africa.
Men, Mines & Animals in SA. R. Churchill. Books of Rhod
History of Zambia. Andrew Roberts. Heinemann.
Africa House. Christina Lamb. Penguin
The Bonds of Africa. Owen Letcher. 1912
South Central Africa. Owen Letcher. Af. Publications.
Zambezi Interlude. Vivien Meik.

East Africa

White Man's Country. Elspeth Huxley.
Nine Faces of Kenya. Elspeth Huxley. Harvill.
Kenya Diary. Richard Meinertzhagen. Eland.
Kenya Pioneers. Errol Trbynski
Happy Valley. Nicholas Best. Secker & Warburg.
White Mischief. James Fox. Penguin.
The Lunatic Express. Charles Miller. Penguin.
Out of Africa. Karen Blixen. Penguin.

Egypt and the Sudan

Egypt's Belle Epoque. Trevor Mostyn. Quartet Books.
Cairo in the War. Artemis Cooper. Hamish Hamilton.
Cairo. James Aldridge.
A King Betrayed. Adel M. Sabat. Quarter Books.
While Shepheards Watched. P.Hughes. Chatto & Windus.
The River War. W.S. Churchill.
Young Winston's Wars. W.S. Churchill. Leo Cooper.
The White Nile. Alan Moorhead. Hamish Hamilton.
Africa the Nile Route. Kim Naylor. Roger Lascelles.
Where God Laughed. The Sudan Today.
With Kitchener to Khartoum.
Royal Engineers in Egypt & Sudan. E.Sandes. Inst. of R.E.

INDEX